MW00906053

RUNNING
YOUR
RACE

Personal Strategies *to*
Help You Stay on Course
and **Reach the Finish Line**

by Stan Willson, Ph. D.

Deep River
B O O K S

Running Your Race

© 2011 Dr. Stan Willson

All rights reserved. This book or any portion thereof may not be reproduced or used in any manner what-soever without the express written permission of the publisher
except for the use of brief quotations in a book review.

Scripture quotations are taken from the *Holy Bible New International Version*, Copyright © 1986 by Holman Bible Publishers, *New International Study Bible*, Copyright © 1985, The Zondervan Corp, Zondervan Bible Publishers, Grand Rapids, MI.

Published by
Deep River Books
Sisters, Oregon
http://www.deepriverbooks.com

ISBN 10: 1-935265-10-5

ISBN 13: 978-1-935265-10-8

Library of Congress: 2011926434

Printed in the USA

Cover design by Contajus Designs

TABLE OF CONTENTS

Module II: Paying Attention to the Holy Spirit's Input 79

Module III: Learning From My Stressors 95

INTRODUCTION

This book started when I was asked by a friend--a local pastor--to give a seminar at his church. What intrigued me about this request was the topic that he asked me to consider and speak on: "God's wisdom for your life: staying on track spiritually in the midst of multiple demands." This was intriguing because I had never formally thought about that topic, although I have, for the last thirty years, been staying on track spiritually while keeping multiple "balls in the air." As I began to unpack my head on this topic, I began to realize that I had developed various strategies for doing this. The information for this seminar just flowed onto the pages. I also began to sense the Spirit's involvement/endorsement of this project, so I accepted this invitation (after all, I know how to manage multiple demands). After the seminar, I began to think that this information might be helpful to fellow jugglers.

Now that it has "materialized," I'd like to thank various people:

- My wife (Verlyn) for the various ways that she has helped to get this in readable form
- My daughter (Liz) for her editing and feedback--our lunches were really an education for me
- My daughter (Becky) for her help in making me more computer literate
- My office assistant (Barb) for the various ways that she has freed up my head and my time--so that I could focus on this project
- The many fellow travelers (especially those that I have worked with in my practice) who have asked the high quality questions, challenged me to provide tools, and road tested the strategies that we have designed together
- The One who continues to help me run my race

WHY I HAVE WRITTEN THIS BOOK.

I have written this book for several reasons:

1. To help sustain my own growth. I grew up in a culture that emphasized hard work but didn't emphasize smart work. It emphasized perseverance but not the skills that would maximize the benefits of that perseverance. It emphasized

survival but not growth. So, when I became aware that such skills existed, I sought them as "pearls of great price" (maybe because I was tired of "keeping my nose to the grindstone"––and losing my nose). As I have incorporated these skills into my life, I have seen my life move from survival mode (where I was treading water) to growth mode (where I was swimming toward my goal). As exciting as that has been, I have come to recognize that there are different levels of skill application. So my journey continues—as I refine my skill applications to better fit me as I (and my circumstances) change. I find this marathon difficult but fascinating; long (certainly longer than my preferences) but empowering; strenuous but energizing; frustrating (at times) but challenging. I commend this journey to you. If my experience is any indication, you will find it transformational.

2. To help the people I work with directly. It is entirely possible (shudder) that I was a psychologist when you were born (and if you are less than thirty years old, that is the case). Consequently, I have worked with thousands of people. Over the years, many clients have expressed appreciation to me for the practical tools that I have helped them work into their lives. (One advantage of growing up on a farm was learning that knowledge is useless unless you apply it in some practical way. That training has given me an eye for tools that can make a real difference.) During these years, I have said to many clients, "These tools will get you from where you are to where you want to be." Such tools are not the only ingredient required for change: they are the "*how to*" change, but they must be mixed with knowledge (which is the *what* and the *why*) and with desire (which is the *want to*). They are, however, a necessary ingredient. I anticipate saying this to many more clients and, now that this book is finished, giving them a portable tool kit.

3. To help the people I work with indirectly. There are times when people feel stuck; they want to change and grow, but they aren't sure how to do that. They may be stuck inside by old, ineffective programs or outside by difficult circumstances. At such times just one tool can start the change process. (Imagine yourself in a locked room with no way out; then imagine that someone comes and slips a key under the door. When you try the key, you find that it unlocks the door. Now you are free to move beyond that place and to feel hope for progress.) This book contains "keys" that will help you to unlock your life so that you can actualize the potentials that you were created with. I invite you to look for those "freeing" keys and to leave the ones

behind that don't fit you or your circumstances. "Freeing" keys will keep you moving toward the finish line.

4. To fulfill a task that, I believe, God asked me to do. Over the years, I have heard that "still small voice" encouraging me to write. For various reasons, I confined myself to writing for myself—to journaling (processing my "stuff" and putting it in His hands) and finishing only first drafts (for use in my practice). With His usual patience, however, He continued to invite me to write "for a wider audience." (He seems to be particularly patient with those of us who are "slow but trainable.") I have felt a little like Gideon (in Judges 6) when the angel of the Lord came to him. At that time, Gideon was threshing wheat in a winepress—hiding it (and himself) from the marauding Midianites. I have been confining what God has shown me over the years to the people that I work with directly. Now, it seems (if I am hearing correctly), God is wanting me to go more public (see Gideon in Judges 6:25–32). Critics could say that I've been suffering from auditory hallucinations and delusions of grandeur. Whether or not I'm delusional, this book was written as an act of obedience (a *long* act of obedience) and with ongoing requests for His help. If I am not delusional, then God has been involved in the writing of this book and—if you have "eyes to see and ears to hear"—you will sense His involvement and (I pray) what His Spirit is emphasizing to you. (By saying this, I am not trying to claim special insight or special authority; I am only suggesting that God involves Himself—upon request—with the most unlikely people [like Gideon] and will work through them to accomplish valuable things. As the old saying goes, "God uses crooked sticks to draw straight lines.") If I am delusional, that should become apparent as you read on. And, even if I am delusional, you could find wheat in the chaff.

WHO THIS BOOK IS WRITTEN FOR

This book is written for anyone who feels stuck or trapped or exhausted or discouraged on his/her journey toward or with God. When what you are doing is not moving you toward your destination, it is time to do something different (not try harder—doing what you already know doesn't work). This book can help you to specify what that "something different" looks like. You could blame yourself for your lack of progress—"I'm too undisciplined... full of self...unloving...lacking in faith..."—but that only compounds the problem (like shooting yourself in the foot as part of your pre-race preparation). Instead, I suggest that you look for a tool that might get you moving again. (If you feel that blame may be helpful, let it come from others; in my experience there will be no lack of such "help.")

HOW TO GET THE MOST OUT OF THIS BOOK

To approach this book in a way that makes it highly nourishing, I'd suggest that you use it in the same way that you use a menu in a restaurant—with each module as a separate meal.

Order the one meal that looks nourishing and begin to eat it. (I don't recommend that you try to eat the whole menu. If you want to have another meal, order it at another time—after you have digested this one.) Each meal has three courses; the first two courses are served together. The "concept" course and the "skill development" course come together. In the concept course, I provide a system or a model to work from; in the skill development course, I provide "tried and proven" strategies to add to your toolkit in the area specified by the module. For dessert, I provide ways of making personal application of the concepts and skills that you have been chewing on.

What I have found nourishing in each meal isn't necessarily what you will find nourishing. (As I have said in each module, "A description of what works for me is not a prescription for you.") So, be on the lookout for any part of the meal that especially fits your palate. Having found it, do the work of chewing and swallowing it, of making it part of you. As Walter De La Mare said:

> It's a very odd thing—
> As odd as can be—
> That whatever Miss T. eats
> Turns into Miss T.

Hopefully, the application strategies that I have provided will help you to add muscle.

- I suggest the following "eating" considerations:
  - You could starve, while debating about or analyzing the food in front of you. These meals were designed to be ingested, not only looked at and understood.
  - Getting what is nourishing for you does not depend on anyone but you. These meals are designed so that the cooperation or permission or agreement of anyone else (for you to be nourished and grow) is not necessary.

MY OVERVIEW OF THIS BOOK

This book consists of four independent modules. In each module are concepts and tools and exercises that help you to understand and apply the content of that module. Each module is self-contained.

Graphically, this book is outlined as follows:

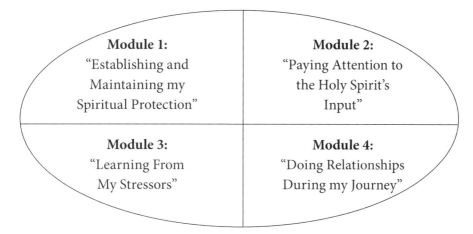

In *module I,* I provide you with my understanding of the spiritual war that we are in. On pages 28–33, I outline the nature of that war. On pages 33–57, I outline what our response to that war needs to include: I talk about what being "strong in the Lord and in His mighty power" involves on pages 34–38; I talk about what "putting on the full armor of God" involves on pages 38–54; I talk about the role of prayer on pages 54–57. On page 57, I outline my protection plan. This prayer system, looked at prayer by prayer and linked to the biblical principles that undergird it, is explored on pages 58–67. The prayer system itself (that I use to prevent spiritual intrusions in my life) is found in appendix B. On page 67, I suggest an application question that you might find helpful to use.

In *module II,* I provide you with what I have learned that promotes an interactive and experiential relationship with the Holy Spirit (whose help is essential to our running/finishing our race). On page 91, I suggest a "next step" (of personal application) that you might find beneficial to take. In appendix A, I outline my morning "race preparation" prayer.

In *module III,* I provide you with my approach to managing stressors. On pages 96–98, I outline my stress management *model.* On pages 98–111, I outline my *beliefs* and *biases* around the issue of stress management. On page 111, I outline the *categories* that I use for doing stressor and stress management. I also include "tried and proven" *strategies* for doing stressor and stress management—in a short-term fashion and in a long-term fashion. (See page 113 for a chart that summarizes these categories and these strategies.) This module also contains nine appendices—from "A" to "I"—so that you can pursue in more depth some of the issues mentioned in the text of the module. At the end of the relevant appendices, I have suggested "next steps" (of application) that you might find beneficial to take.

In *module IV,* I provide you with my approach for doing relationships. On pages 220–221, I outline my *model;* on pages 222–235, I discuss the *"Primary/Vital/Internal" relationships* of life. (On pages 222–224 is my relationship with *God*; on pages 225–235, my relationship with *myself*.) On pages 236–246 I discuss the *"Secondary/Vital/External" relationships* of life. This module also contains five appendices—from "A" to "E"—so that you can pursue in more depth some of the issues mentioned in the text of this module. Appendix A (on pages 247–261) focuses on information and exercises for enhancing my relationship with *God*. (It consists of nine sections, each ending with "next steps" of application that you might find beneficial to take.) Appendix B (on pages 362–386) focuses on information and exercises for enhancing my relationship with *myself*; it ends with "next steps" (of application) that you might find beneficial to take. Appendix C (on pages 387–401) focuses on information and exercises for managing my relationship with *confidants/companions*; it ends with "next steps" (of application) that you might find beneficial to take. Appendix D (on pages 402–408) focuses on information and exercises for managing my relationship with *friends*; it ends with "next steps" (of application) that you might find beneficial to take. Appendix E (on pages 409–411) focuses on information and exercises for managing my relationship with *acquaintances*; it ends with "next steps" (of application) that you might find beneficial to take.

A (POSSIBLY) HELPFUL TOOL FOR APPLYING THE STRATEGIES IN THIS BOOK

As I have already mentioned, the process of internalizing strategies so that they are part of me is a challenge. At a physical level, this involves the establishment of new neural pathways. At a psychological level, this involves "changing my mind"—replacing old (and less useful) plans and procedures with new (and more useful) plans and procedures. At a spiritual level, it involves seeing myself in a new way. At an interpersonal level, it involves relating to the outside world in a way that reflects these (inside) changes. Consequently, this process can involve going two steps forward and then going one (or more) steps back. It can involve finding out what doesn't work before finding out what does work (and, sometimes, the former is a necessary prerequisite to the latter). It can involve change that others are not happy with. ("How dare you upset the status quo!") It can involve effort that I am not happy with. ("Why is this so hard!") For these (and other) reasons it can be difficult to sustain my efforts—especially when my best efforts have not produced any of the results that I had envisioned (and several that I hadn't). At such times, I have found it helpful to use the following tool (to sustain my efforts). It consists of a four step process—applied in the sequence of steps that follows.

I) Forgive Myself

The importance of this step varies greatly from person to person. *Some people* when not getting desired results can adjust and persevere and stay on good terms with themselves. For these people, this step is relatively unimportant (even unnecessary), and they are free to go to the next step. *For other people*, not getting desired results is a more personal issue. They read into this lack of progress messages like, "Something must be wrong with me" or "This is a sign of my incompetence," or "This means that I am not trying hard enough; maybe I am lazy." (Or, if you—like me—have been well trained to react like this, all three). For these people, it is important to forgive themselves for not meeting their own expectations, for not being the kind of people that they believe they should be. It is also important for these people to challenge and change these beliefs, so that they will be free to move on to the next step. *For some other people*, not getting desired results is a critical issue. These people see lack of progress as not only a personal deficiency but also an indication that something is wrong with their relationship with God. Such people say things to themselves like, "I don't have enough faith to access the resources (to be successful) that God has made available to me." Or "God will leave me to my own resources if I can't/won't make use of His resources." It is crucial for these people to forgive themselves—on the basis of God's forgiveness of them—so that they are walking in the truth that "God is for them" (even when they are not performing in ways that they want—or He wants). Otherwise, they will be engaged in an internal conflict that makes moving to the next step an act of futility.

In order to get a sense of what category you fit in, check one of the following:

❑ Not getting the results I want is no big deal. I will adjust and keep at it, until I see progress.

❑ Not getting the results I want calls my ability into question. I begin to wonder if something is wrong with me.

❑ Not getting the results I want not only calls my ability into question, it also calls my relationship with God into question. He wants me to prosper, but what will happen between us if I am not doing my part?

Having found your category, read the (following) section that applies to that category.

If your response to lack of progress doesn't challenge your relationship with God or yourself and if you are able to "do something different" (from what hasn't been working) and to sustain your efforts (to discover if the "something different" will bring progress), you qualify to move on to step two. "Bon voyage."

If your response to lack of progress triggers the playing of old "tapes" of scripts (given by "significant others") that are discouraging and distracting, you will be ready to move to the next step after you:

(a) take the position of being for (not against) yourself, and

(b) rebut those internal messages by replacing them with encouraging and re-focusing internal messages.

Usually, a person takes the position of being against him/herself because that is part of his/her old training. Often, that person has had a personal trainer who subscribed to the "if you can be hard enough on yourself, put yourself in enough pain, (then) you will improve your performance" school of training. Such training sets up an internal conflict, where one part of yourself (a "critic") is sitting in negative evaluation of another part (the "performer"). That conflict is both energy draining and discouraging. There are various ways to change that internal programming, including the following:

- Ask yourself a higher quality question, like, "If I had a good friend who was going through this same struggle, what would I say to him/her?" Since it is unlikely that you would tell a good friend that you think he/she is incompetent or stupid or lazy, pay attention to what you do say. If that feedback is supportive and encouraging, say the same to yourself (since treating yourself the same way that you treat a good friend is a good way to become for—not against—yourself). You will need to give yourself permission to receive that new message to self, even though it won't feel as "right" or familiar as the old internal message. (When you think about it, however, "feeling" that an internal message is right, doesn't make it right—just influential.) There are various ways to help the installation of this new program:
  - Saying it, while looking at yourself in the mirror
  - Writing out a change contract with yourself. (Since I find journaling to be a helpful personal growth tool, I made contracts with myself—including statements of intent with a signature.)
  - Talking with "safe others" about what you are changing and having them agree that this is a constructive change to make
  - Putting the new program on paper or computer or CD so that you can see/hear and affirm it, repeatedly.

Many people use some version of this "good friend" strategy to discover constructive self-talk and use one or more of the above installation strategies to program that self-talk into their life.

However, some of you may have said, "I would say the same (negative) things to a good friend that I say to myself" (showing that you have improvements to make in your skills for developing and maintaining friendships). If that is your response, it will be more effective to use the following "two column" strategy. In the left column, you record the old (self-pressuring and self-discouraging) self-talk; in the right column, you record new (self-supportive and self-encouraging) self-talk. Whenever you catch yourself playing an old tape, you record it (in the left column) and devise and record (in the right column, opposite) a rebuttal that is self-nourishing. When you have externalized (on paper or computer) the primary self-critical scripts (as identified by the frequency that they are repeated), you read and affirm the rebuttal each time you catch the old message playing. By rehearsing the new message, after every playing of the old message, the new message will replace the old message—changing the dynamics of your relationship with yourself. If I am guessing accurately, you are asking "How long will this take?" My best answer is, "That varies from person to person...Give this replacement process all the time it requires, even if it is long and arduous...This investment in yourself will pay such good "dividends" that it is worth whatever time and energy you need to expend." I am living proof that this change can be made and that it is transformational—changing your internal environment from toxic to nourishing.

For those of you who want to pursue this issue more thoroughly, there are sections in this book, entitled "My Relationship with Myself" (on pages 225–234 of module IV) and "Exercises for Enhancing My Relationship with Myself" (on pages 362–366 of module IV) that you can look at.

If your response to lack of progress not only triggers the playing of destructive old training tapes but also calls into question your relationship with God, you will be ready to move on to the next step only after you achieve the following:

(a) Get to the place of being for (not against) yourself. The strategies that we just discussed are relevant.

(b) Get to the place of being on good terms with God.

Within the Christian community, there is training that teaches us to be against ourself. An example of that kind of training is found when some teachers draw specific conclusions from the 1 Corinthians 9:24–29 passage. In that passage, Paul says, "...I beat my body and make it my slave so that after I have preached to others, I myself will not be disqualified for the prize." Some teachers say, "Doesn't that tell us to be hard on ourself—especially if we are not qualifying?" I believe that Paul is telling us that he goes into "strict training" (as athletes do) and that he does whatever it takes to prepare himself for the race. I do not believe that he is specifying the how of that strict training. Paul, and any of us, can hold ourself to high training standards, but do that in a kind and gentle way. There is no New Testament example of Paul beating himself. (There are New Testament examples of others beating him—see the list provided in 2 Corinthians 11:16–33.) Nor is there any New Testament example of Paul beating up on himself internally, by means of self-derogatory self-talk. He certainly would have been tempted, by the "accuser of the brethren," to accuse himself, to be critical of himself, since his personal history included murdering Christians. Instead, he grasped (and hung onto) God's forgiveness of him (1 Tim. 1:12–16) and devoted himself to trusting and obeying the One who had extended grace to him (Phil. 3:12–14). He embodied and lived out the truth that he shared with the Christians in Rome, that God is for us, not against us (Rom. 8:31–39). God is so much for us, in fact, that He even works our failings together for our good. He uses my "mess-ups" to teach me good things. For example, He has used my struggle with (and sometimes giving in to) sin, to teach me—at an experiential level—about His patience and kindness and gentleness toward me. Prior to that experience, I had the false belief that God would "get me" if I sinned.

God has provided the way for us to get on good terms with Him. When I sin, it is fundamental (and wonderful) to know that "If I confess my sins, He is faithful and just and will forgive my sins and purify me from all unrighteousness" (I John 1:9). It is also wonderful to know that, as I learn to treat myself as He treats me, I can forgive myself (and so remain for myself and not against myself). This is not an act of self-indulgence; it is an effective strategy for "not giving the Devil a foothold" (since one of his schemes is to promote self-accusation). I contend that the process of forgiveness is not complete until I have applied it to myself (as much as it is wonderful to have it applied between God and myself). To make this application, I say something like, "Father, on the basis of your forgiveness of me, through Christ, I choose, now, to forgive myself. Thank You that, where my sin has flourished, Your grace flourishes more."

Some people say that forgiving myself doesn't make sense in the same way that solo tennis doesn't make sense. Those critics don't recognize that each person is in a "twenty-four/seven" relationship with him/herself. I am constantly in the roles of participant of my life (where I experience my life) and spectator of my life (where I watch and evaluate what I do). That being the case, all relational dynamics apply to my relationship with myself: I talk to (or ignore) myself, I encourage (or discourage) myself, I face the truth (or lie) to myself, I enjoy (or despise) myself, I blame (or forgive) myself. In relation to this issue (of forgiving myself), Lewis Smedes (one of my mentors in this area) says, "We feel a need to forgive ourselves because the part of us that gets blamed feels split off from the part that does the blaming. One self feels despised and rejected by the other. We are exiled from our own selves, which is no way to live. This is why we need to forgive ourselves and why it makes sense to do it: We are ripped apart inside, and forgiving ourselves is the only way we heal the split."[1]

As I have already mentioned, we have the choice to treat ourself as God treats us or as Satan treats us. God wants us to model His treatment of us—including kindness, patience, gentleness, love, generosity, support, encouragement, forgiveness. As we do this, we further actualize who He created us to be. Satan wants us to model his treatment of us—including unkindness, impatience, harshness, hate, stinginess, undermining, discouragement, unforgiveness. As we do this, we sabotage our God-given potential. Part of our application of the "Good News" is to learn to treat ourself as our heavenly Father treats us. So, we are to apply all the dimensions of forgiveness—from God, to and from our neighbor and to ourself—in order to develop a family (of God) likeness.

It is one thing to commit to forgiving myself; it is another thing to walk in that forgiveness. (In the same way, any of us who have chosen to forgive another person knows that it is "something else" to walk in forgiveness of that person.) So, if I am to walk in self-forgiveness (which means carrying out the choice to forgive myself), I need to know what that involves, what that looks like.

The *internal* dimension of walking in self-forgiveness includes:

(a) Telling myself the truth that when I sin I need to turn toward that sin and acknowledge it rather than turning away from that sin and denying it to myself. I have tried to capture this truth in one of my "mantras": "When I mess up, I need to clean up [the mess] but not beat up [on myself] or cover up [from myself] and, so grow up."

(b) Telling myself the truth that self-forgiveness has to do with what I have done (sins of commission) or have not done (sins of omission); it does not have to do with who I am. In other words, I am not to confuse forgiving myself with accepting myself. I need to affirm to myself that, just because I do bad things, I am not a bad person. I am a person who is unworthy of God's forgiveness of me (in Christ), but I am, in God's economy, a highly valuable creature (one who God sent His only Son to bring back into His family). I am a fallen person (who comes from a fallen race and does wrong things), but I am a redeemable person (who, through Christ's finished and ongoing work in my life, is able to do good things with good motives). So, thanks to God's provision, my worth is established, and my self-forgiveness (rather than being seen as a selfish act) is seen as my response to my Father's instructions of how I should walk.

(c) Telling myself the truth that self-forgiveness does not, finally, depend on anyone other than God and myself. Smedes puts this truth this way:

If I do blame myself for wronging someone, I will still not feel free to forgive myself unless I feel forgiven by the other person. When I am forgiven, I accept the gift of her forgiveness as a license to forgive myself. When I digest her grace inside myself, her permission becomes my power.

But what can a person do if she blames herself, asks to be forgiven, and has the door of rejection slammed in her face? Her only option is an appeal to God. She can admit her guilt to God and seek from him what she could not find in the other. When he forgives her, and she ingests his grace, she actually feels forgiven in her guts, she has both the permission and the power to forgive herself even if the person she wounded does not forgive her.[2]

(d) Giving myself permission to reaffirm my forgiveness of myself as many times as I need to. The need to do this varies from person to person. For someone like myself, I've had to reaffirm my forgiveness of myself (and of others) many times over many months. Again, Smedes puts it well: "Self-forgiveness is not self-induced amnesia. When the memory of the horrid thing we did clicks on, the toxin of guilt spills through and condemns us again. So we need to stand before the mirror, and say it again. Forgiving is seldom done once and for all. It almost always needs repeating. So say it a hundred times if you need to, say it until the meaning begins to filter through your left brain into your soul. Once you get the hang of it, the repeats will get easier and the relief will get faster."[3]

Related to this issue (of reaffirming my forgiveness of myself) is the issue of how I do so. When God forgives me, He "forgets about it." That means, to me, that He treats me (subsequent to my asking for forgiveness/His forgiving me) as if He had forgotten about the offense. (An all-knowing God forgets nothing but, it seems, He chooses to never bring some things up again.) As I apply this truth to self-forgiveness, I must commit myself, when I am retoxified by that memory, to never dwell on that sin or to beat up on myself because of that sin. I am to put it away (under His blood and in His hands) and, so, turn my attention to receiving and experiencing His grace. (God, it seems, puts my sin away so that He can focus on actualizing His good plan for my life.) And what happens when I can't even carry out that commitment consistently? What happens when I catch myself watching reruns on the "past sin" channel and accusing myself for having created that movie in the first place? Then, I remember to treat myself the way my heavenly Father treats me: with encouragement ("I'm glad I caught myself in that old rut; I don't have to stay in it"), with kindness ("Stan, you are not 'stu-pid.' I forgive myself for putting that inaccurate label on myself, and I replace it now with 'work in progress'"), and with support ("That is history. Thank you, Father, that I don't have to carry this with me. I want to be a good steward of my time and energy, so what do you want me to focus on now?")

The *external* dimension of walking in self-forgiveness includes:

(a) Thanking God. Since God really exists and wants me to interact with Him, prayer needs to be an ongoing dialogue in my life. When I begin to walk in His gift of forgiveness, thanksgiving needs to flow to Him. When I respond like the (one) healed leper, who returned to thank Jesus, I acknowledge His good gift to me.

(b) Resisting the temptation to self-retaliate. If I give in to verbal self-retaliation (by saying harsh things to myself, calling myself names, saying untrue things about myself, for instance), then I will clean up that "mess" (by apologizing to myself, delabeling myself, and affirming the truth about myself). If I give in to *physical* self-retaliation (by hitting or cutting myself, by damaging something of mine, by depriving myself of something nourishing, for instance), then I will clean up that "mess" (by bandaging my wounds, replacing my losses, taking the restric-tions or curses off myself). I will acknowledge all feelings that I have toward myself (anger, disappointment, disgust, frustration, for instance) and will let them dissipate (which will happen since self-forgiveness has been done) without acting on any of them toward myself.

(c) Doing something for myself. Since friends give their friends good things, this is an appropriate step to take toward myself. Different people value different things, so I must give to myself in a way that fits me and is truly nourishing. (Otherwise, I could give to myself in a way that doesn't fit me—like giving myself the "gift" of ongoing social involvement because I was told that it would be good for me. Also, I could give to myself in a non-nourishing way—as happens with an addic-tion). For an introvert like myself, a fitting and nourishing gift is that of time and space, to recharge my batteries from the drain of relational interactions. For an extravert like my daughter, Elizabeth, a fitting and nourishing gift is that of more relational interactions, to keep her batteries charged. One way to help clarify (what) and specify (how) to give to ourself, especially for those of us who aren't experienced or skilled at self-giving, is to write a letter to a "good friend" who is going through what we are. This letter needs to contain what we would say to this friend and what we would suggest that he/she do, in order to constructively deal with the circumstances that he/she is facing. Once that letter is completed (and it might be more beneficial to write it in stages, as other suggestions come to mind, rather than at one sitting), we say to ourself, "Since I am working on becoming a friend to myself, I will take and apply my own suggestions."

(d) Moving on. After replacing a flat tire, I get back in my car and get back on the road, with a lessening focus on what has just happened and a growing focus on what will be upcoming. In the same way, when I have done the (internal and external) work of self-forgiveness, I get back into the flow of my day. In this circumstance, that involves getting on to the next step in this (remedial) process.

For those of you who want to pursue this issue more thoroughly, there is a section in this book, entitled "Forgiveness" (on pages 302–325 of module IV) that you can look at.

II) Investigate

Having detoxified my internal environment (of self-condemnation, of regret, of discouragement) by means of self-forgiveness, I am free to start the process of analyzing why my efforts to change have been unsuccessful. I start this process by adopting a constructive attitude toward my situation—that of being curious. To do this, I ask myself high quality questions like:

(a) What happened (or is happening) that contributes to my being stuck?
  • What *external* factors? (who, what, where, when...)
  • What *internal* factors? (what beliefs(s) do I have [or do I buy] that keep me from making progress?)
(b) What old training of mine has contributed to being stuck? (In relation to this issue, my family of origin taught me that...)
(c) What context factors have contributed to my lack of progress? (What happened, in the last three days, that impacted my choice...?)

As I get answers to these questions (and, if you are like me, they will need to be written down), I orient myself toward what happened (rather than not facing what happened). I can only learn from my life experience if I face it. If I turn away from it, I can pretend it didn't happen (self-motivated forgetting) or I can put it in the closet (denial), but I am then burdened by this unprocessed experience.

As I get answers to these questions, I also deepen my knowledge about myself and about how I am operating in my physical, cognitive-emotional, spiritual, and social environments. This knowledge, if correctly applied, can lead to personal and interpersonal growth. This step, like step one, needs to be done in the context of my relationship with God. As I follow the steps of this process, I must resist the temptation to limit it to a human process—where I lean on my own understanding to bring about change. As I invite God's Spirit to lead me into the truth about this situation, I will get deeper insights into myself and into what has contributed to this situation than I would if I was only holding my own mirror up.

The next step in this process is applying what I have learned during this step.

III) Plan

Having established peace with myself (step 1) and having analyzed why I am not making progress (step 2), I have positioned myself to benefit from that analysis.

Again, this step includes asking myself high-quality questions:

  (a) (In light of what I have learned), how would I set up this situation differently next time in order to handle it more successfully?

  (b) What would I do differently? (For example, what would I stay away from? What would I move closer to? What skills do I need to obtain and use? What resource people do I need to involve?)

  (c) What would I say differently to myself? (For example, what new agreement with myself would I make? What new permission with myself would I give? What new boundary with myself would I establish? What truth as it applies to this situation would I rehearse? What lie that I have believed, in relation to this situation would I rebut?)

As I get answers to these questions, an improvement plan will begin to emerge. Since "the opposition" has defeated me in the first half of the game, this is my revised game-plan for defeating them in the second half.

For me, "handling the situation successfully" involves:

  (a) Reaching an achievable and appropriate outcome by a feasible means.
    • Since I live in the real (and fallen) world rather than the ideal world, I need to be sure that the goal I am trying to reach is "doable." (So, a question like, "Is this an achievable goal?" can help me avoid trying to do the impossible).
    • Since I want to direct my energies in ways that fit my values, I also need to ask the question, "Does this goal violate my values in any way?"
    • Since I need "good and sufficient" ways and means to enable me to take the steps required to reach my goal, I also need to ask, "Do I have the knowledge, the skills and the desire necessary to reach this goal?" (And if not, "what do I

need to do in order to obtain them?")

(b) Reaching an outcome (product) by means (process) that stays within my circle
of biblical options. So, the outcome (goal) must be congruent with my values
(which are, hopefully, informed by scriptural principles). Also, the means, which
are always multiple, must be limited to those that are legitimate for me. (In other
words, these means will not be "sin for me" if I use them—see Romans 14:22–23.)
Again, as I invite the Spirit's participation, I will get a sense of where my (process)
limits are. (As vague as this may sound, I find it to be a better option than adopting
someone else's limits. People, all too often, are prepared to make a description of
their limits a prescription for me.) There are times when I have discovered my limit
by stepping over that limit and feeling the discomfort of having done so. (Contrary
to my early training, it is not the "end of the world" to find things out this way. I
have come to believe that God, in His mercy, works even my mistakes together for
good.) So, I step back within my limits, my circle of legitimate options, having discovered and clarified something important concerning myself. So, learning how to
handle a situation better next time—in terms of both process and product—is also
an opportunity for clarifying my understanding of who I am.

Having clarified my improvement plan, I am ready to take my next step: rehearsing
that plan into my life.

IV) Practice

It is one thing to have a plan; it is another thing to use that plan. For some people,
moving from having a plan to using that plan is quick, seamless, and automatic—literally,
a "no-brainer." For others, there is a chasm between theory and application that stops them
cold. Although the ultimate test of how well you go from plan to practice occurs when the
next similar circumstance in the outside world shows up, there are preparations that you
can make, in the inside world, that will help you bridge that chasm. One of these preparations is to visualize yourself, in an (upcoming) similar circumstance, applying the "new
and improved" plan. By doing this rehearsal, you are getting both your mind and your
body ready to respond in a new and improved way when the "outside world" opportunity
presents itself. Some helpful logistics for doing this (adapted from Cameron-Bandler, Gordon, and Lebeau[4]) are as follows:

• Be sure to imagine carrying out the specifics of the new plan, especially noticing the
improvements from the old plan, in the upcoming similar situation.

• This can be effectively done by either

(a) seeing yourself doing the plan, or;

(b) (better yet), visualizing actually doing the steps of the plan. This involves seeing directly what you would be seeing, hearing directly what you would be hearing and feeling the feelings associated with actually doing the plan.

- If you visualize any of the old plan or any undesirable behavior, start over, making sure that your internally generated future is a full representation of you doing the new plan.

- Be as vivid and as thorough as possible, as you see yourself implementing the new plan. If you are not a visualizer, you can rehearse the plan before a mirror or with a friend (to get auditory feedback).

- If, while you are rehearsing the new plan, you experience some "glitch" in that plan, you can incorporate the (resulting) fine-tuning into your next rehearsal.

- Rehearse until you have a smooth, flowing rehearsal sequence of the new and improved plan.

For those of you who have said, "This process is too complicated to use," I would reply that I have talked in detail (to provide a conceptual framework) about a simple plan. In practice, I often have just made one change at each step of the F.I.P.P. plan as follows:

F— I make one prayer to forgive myself.

I— I identify the one biggest/most obvious problem with the procedure that I used (which didn't work).

P— I figure out what I will do differently, next time, as it relates to that (one) problem

P— I visualize implementing that one change into my plan (as my preparation for next time).

With a little practice, you can do this whole plan in a matter of minutes. It is a good investment of time since making one change may be all that is required in order to get a successful/working outcome.

For those of you who have said, "There is no point using this process because I won't face this situation again in the foreseeable future," I would reply that, although that may be true, there is another good reason for using this tool. When you try to handle a situation and your strategy for doing so does not work, you are (and can feel) stuck. When you follow the F.I.P.P. plan, you won't continue to feel stuck (or discouraged) because you will have programmed yourself to get better results (even if you don't have an immediate opportunity to use that program in the outside world). When you upgrade your programming, you change your internal world; when you change your internal world, you change your experience. In this situation, that change of experience is toward hope—that your "new and improved" strategy will provide you with better results.

I have used this plan many times. What follows is an example of how I recently applied this plan. (Again, it looks more complicated on paper than it was in real life.) I have been struggling with how to constructively handle, both internally and externally, situations in which I perceive other (automobile) drivers to be incompetent (and, so, dangerous). The ways in which they have demonstrated their incompetence are legion. My focus here, however, is to demonstrate, by using the F.I.P.P. plan, how I can grow my competence for handling their behavior (and, so, make them helpful trainers in my life).

Step 1: Forgive Myself

Although my reactions have not included behavior directed toward such drivers, it has included verbalizations about such drivers (who they are, what they should do) that I need to confess and move away from. As I do that, I lessen my risk of a driver-directed behavioral reaction. So I start my change process by saying, "God, I'm thankful that your love toward me is unconditional and that your forgiveness includes all my sins—past, present, and future. I just 'messed up' here, when I said 'X' about that driver. Thank You for forgiving me. On the basis of your forgiveness, I forgive myself. Please help me to get this situation to work for me."

Step 2: Investigate

To help me to move from anger to curiosity, I ask myself the following:
    (a) What external events triggered my reactions?
        (i)A driver, driving slow in the fast lane, blocking me from getting past him or around him
    (b) What internal self-talk or beliefs gave me permission to react in a destructive way?
        (i)"Drivers should obey the traffic rule/sign that slower traffic use right lane."
        (ii)"Drivers should be competent."
        (iii) "He must be drunk!"
        (iv) "He is going to cause an accident!"
    (c) What rebuttals to this anger-escalating self-talk would help me to "rev down"?
        (i) "In an ideal world, drivers would obey the rules. In this real world, they won't, so I need to reset my expectations accordingly. (Personal insight: at times, I confuse the "ideal" with the "real.")

(ii) "For some drivers, competence is not a priority. They have a right to set whatever competence priorities they want. (Personal insight: at times, I would like to impose my priorities, one of which is "driving competence" on others.)

(iii) "He may not be drunk; he may be in pain...or tired...or reeling from a recent crisis—maybe he just lost his job." (Personal insight: if I can think of another explanation for his driving, that is just as feasible as my original assumption but more out of his control, I can begin to access my ability to be patient.)

(iv) "He may contribute to an accident. Right now, all I have to do is make sure that it isn't an accident that I'm in." (Personal insight: if I can go from certainty to being tentative, I can begin to rev down.)

(d) What old training of mine set me up for this reaction?

(i) "This is the same feeling that I used to have when I drove a taxi and was under time pressure. Now I can relax—I don't have to get anyone to a plane."

(e) What context factors set me up for this reaction?

(i) "I'm tired—I want to get home to start 'life after work.' I guess I can start having 'life after work,' right here, right now."

Step 3: Plan

To help me to know and do better next time, I need to ask myself the following:

(a) How would *I set up this situation differently* next time, in order to handle it more constructively?

    I will be better prepared to just ease through this situation through the following:

• Having a CD ready, to listen to and enjoy, if the traffic slows down.

• Reminding myself that "revving down" is a better option (in heavy traffic) than "revving up." I will do this by deep breathing and listening to music.

• Reminding myself that there is no precise time (deadline) at which I have to arrive home. (And if there was, I would call on my cell and change it.)

(b) What would I *do* differently?

• Listen to music

• Deep breathe

• Focus on my game-plan for *easing* through this situation. (Not focus on how

someone else is driving, except to figure out how to get around him/her.)
- Take a bottle of water with me

(c) What would I *say to myself*, differently?
- "Driving home can be an opportunity to relax and start 'life after work.'"
- "Any obstacle on the drive home will only be a '*brief inconvenience*,' nothing to spend reaction energy on."
- "Driving home can be an opportunity to practice my deep breathing skills."
- "I don't have to focus on how someone else is driving; I've done enough analysis for the day...and I don't get paid for this (overtime) analysis."

Step 4: Practice

To help me rehearse my "new and improved" plan, I will, just before leaving for home, do the following:
- Read my (new) game-plan.
- Gather what I need to take (for example, a bottle of water).
- See myself following the plan, if the traffic begins to slow down, and saying to myself, "This is the competent way to handle this situation." I will "pre-feel" the satisfaction of handling this stressor in an effective way and will say to myself "I'm glad that I've become a 'hard target' for that stressor."
- Pray, "Holy Spirit, please help me to make this plan happen. Please show me anything else that You want me to know or do. I'll do my best to learn from whatever You show me."

This process is parallel to the Japanese concept of Kai Zen (constant and ongoing improvement by means of small steps). In the same way that this concept revolutionized the Japanese economy, these steps can revolutionize my (and your) personal economy.

ENDNOTES
[1] Smedes, L., *The Art of Forgiving*, New York: Random House, Inc., 1996, p. 96.
[2] Smedes, p. 101.
[3] Smedes, p. 102.
[4] Cameron-Bandler, L. Gordon, D. and Lebeau, M. *Know How*, San Rafael, Cal.: Future Pace Inc., 1985.

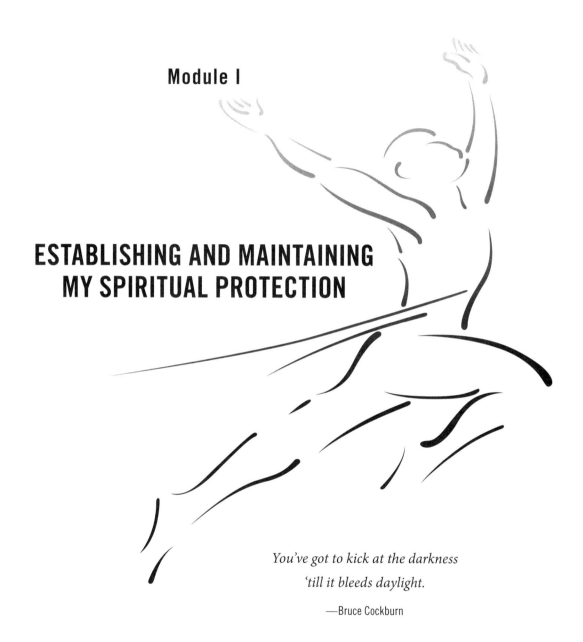

Module I

ESTABLISHING AND MAINTAINING MY SPIRITUAL PROTECTION

You've got to kick at the darkness
'till it bleeds daylight.

—Bruce Cockburn

INTRODUCTION

When I became a believer, the world got much bigger. Now, there was more than matter in motion. I was faced with an environment that contained a Being—who pre-dated matter—and who interacted with the material universe. During one of His interactions, He had actually taken on materiality. As if that wasn't enough to adjust to, I found out that the unseen (and non-material) world was at war. I had no doubt that the seen world was at war—I experienced it every day in the culture I grew up in and I saw it on the news—but to discover that there was a another war (ongoing and interactive with the seen conflicts and involving me) was, to say the least, frightening. I began my search for the spiritual equivalent of Switzerland, only to find that neutrality was not an option. God was at war. My world was at war. And I was at war—whether I liked it or not. Growing up on a farm had taught me that, if there was a problem, I had better face it (since there was no one else to pass the problem on to). So, I ran to find out what my (newly found) God was saying about this war. I'm not sure of all my motivations for taking that course of action, but I know that my primary motivation was to avoid becoming a casualty. Some people who keep statistics on war equate "casualty" with "kill." In this war, however, "casualty" means "noncombatant." This is a global war—everyone is a combatant—so if anything occurs that results in someone stopping fighting, that person has become a casualty (although he/she still has a heartbeat). Given this definition, there can be many strategies for producing casualties. My experience confirms the use of many such schemes.

In this module, I have outlined the basic understandings that God has shared with us about that war. I have taken these understandings, primarily, from the central New Testament passage on this subject—Ephesians 6:10–18. Also from this passage, I have outlined what our responses in this war need to include. My consideration of this passage provides the context for my protection game-plan, for what I do to keep from becoming a casualty. In this module, I look at my game-plan, step by step, to establish that it is rooted in biblical principles. The plan itself—in the form of a prayer system—is found in appendix B of this module. In response to questions that I have received about this prayer system, I have written a "commentary" on the system. If you are interested in that information, I have made it available (free of charge) on my website; at the end of this module, I give you the address for accessing it. I have also—at the end of this module—provided you with an application question, for the purpose of enhancing your "take away" from this module.

THE NATURE OF THE WAR

What kind of a war are we in? The following propositions sketch the answer.

Our war is not, primarily, against other humans. This is another way of saying "… our struggle is not against flesh and blood" (Eph. 6:12a). Our war involves human enemies—as any soldier would attest to—but this war contains deeper levels. So, if all our human enemies were made casualties—through death, imprisonment, exile, truce, or whatever means—the war would not be over.

Our war is, primarily, against enemies that operate in the spiritual realm of existence. This is another way of saying, "… [our struggle is] against the rulers, against the authorities, against the powers of this dark world and against the spiritual forces of evil in the heavenly realms" (Eph. 6:12b). This verse gives us a glimpse into history that predates the existence of the human race. Before the creation of humankind, there was an attempted coup in the spiritual realm. Satan—a high ranking angel—rebelled against God's rule and tried to overthrow Him. He was thrown out of heaven (God's dwelling place in the spiritual realm), a fact that Jesus spoke about to his disciples (Luke 10:18). Satan took one third of the angels with him (Rev. 12:4, 9) and came to earth to set up his kingdom in opposition to God's kingdom. (Satan, like any finite being who wants to be King, can only do so by setting up a kingdom and proclaiming himself to be king.) He became "the god of this [evil] age" (2 Corinthians 4:4), having the whole world under his control (1 John 5:19). Satan set up his kingdom in a hierarchy of power, with himself at the top—an organizational structure that he pirated from God's kingdom. Tom White clarifies that structure as follows:

Satan	*Satanis*	"strong man"	Mark 3:27
		"prince"	John 14:30
		"ruler"	Eph. 2:2
Rulers/	*Archai*		Col. 1:16
Principalities		Dan. 10:13, 20	

These beings, as depicted in Daniel, seem comparable to the archangels. They are the "generals" assigned to implement and oversee major aspects of Satan's counter kingdom. It is also apparent they have authority over certain geographical areas.

| **Authorities** | *Exousia* | Eph. 1:21 |

In Paul's understanding, the "authorities" were both natural and super-natural. The fallen powers seek to promote and maximize their deception of humanity through the corruption of human institutions, e.g., governments, organizational structures, crime syndicates, etc.

| **Powers** | *Dunamis* | Eph. 6:12 |

Evidence from clinical encounters seems to document that the "powers" are satanic forces set over certain regions, i.e., cities, geographical areas, people groups, etc.

| **Spiritual Forces** | | |
| **Of-Evil** | *Kosmokratoras* | Eph. 6:12 |

These spiritual "forces" are the variety of evil spirits that operate in the lower atmosphere and on earth to afflict and deceive. It is these spirit beings that are characteristically confronted and cast out in most deliverance encounters.

Demons	Mark 3:15
Evil Spirits	Matt. 12:43
Deceiving	I Tim. 4:1
Divining	Acts 16:17
Antichrist	I John 4:3
Unclean	Mark 1:23; 6:7
Rebellion	Eph. 2:2
Fear	2 Tim. 1:7
Infirmity	Luke 13:12[1]

These are the "spiritual forces of evil in the heavenly realms" (Eph. 6:12b) that Christians wrestle against.

The clash of kingdoms is the context for the earliest days of the human race. Satan deceived our earliest ancestors into breaking their (original) harmonious relationship with God and into putting themselves in Satan's hands. God the Father sent His son, Jesus Christ, to make a new harmony with humankind possible and to invite them back into His kingdom. Jesus' coming dealt a fatal blow to Satan's aspirations of having humankind as permanent slaves in his kingdom. Jesus' coming was the beginning of the end of Satan's domination over humankind (as D-day was the beginning of the end of Nazi rule over Europe in the 1940's). Presently, the clash of kingdoms continues (as was the case, to continue with the World War II analogy, after D-day). This clash will continue until Jesus comes to earth again—bringing V-day. Our world is—during this time between D-day and V-day—a war zone. In this present age, we experience different kinds of conflict—we conflict with ourself, we conflict with other people, we conflict with our environments, and we conflict with God. And, as a driving force behind these conflicts, the kingdom of darkness is the (usually) unseen kingdom that is in opposition to God's kingdom. This context helps to make sense of Paul's text when he says: "For though we live in the world, we do not wage war as the world does. The weapons we fight with are not the weapons of the world. On the contrary, they have divine power to demolish strongholds. We demolish arguments and every pretension that sets itself up against the knowledge of God, and we take captive every thought …" (2 Corinthians 10:3–5).

In this text, Paul sheds light on our war. In this war, we use different weapons (than those used in human-on-human wars). An example of such a (different) weapon is prayer—a weapon we use in order to get "tuned in" to this war (2 Kings 6:8–23) and to receive our marching orders (Isa. 30:21). Another difference between the "weapons of the world" and the weapons we use is the source that empowers the weapon. A weapon of this world is empowered by the human who wields it. The weapons we use are empowered by God (who, as in all aspects of our lives as believers, wants us to cooperate with Him). We wield these (divinely empowered) weapons against strongholds that the kingdom of darkness has set up. The concept of a stronghold, of course, is familiar to all warriors. Throughout the history of this fallen world strongholds have been used—from walls around a city to castles to aircraft carriers. What is unique to the strongholds of the kingdom of darkness is their location (inside a person's head) and their composition (feeling-thoughts or thought-feelings). This kingdom sets up "head nests" of lies—, of thought-feelings that either pervert or suppress truth (especially about God – who is Truth). The exact means by which our weapons impact these strongholds is not spelled out here, but the outcome is demolition.

My response to the kingdom of darkness's use of strongholds was, "what a sneaky way to attack people!" Such tactics are characteristic of this enemy.

Our war involves taking our stand against the Devil's schemes (Eph. 6:11b). (A "scheme" is a carefully arranged and systematic program of action, an underhanded plan or plot.) The Devil uses different schemes for different people and different situations: he comes to us as a tempter (1 Thess. 3:5), enticing people to turn away from God and away from the marching orders that God has provided to soldiers in His kingdom. Temptation is often his strategy when his targets are under pressure and persecution—as the believers at Thessalonica were. It's easy to imagine him saying something like, "Would God, if He really loved you, let you go through all this pain? … Let me show you an easier way." He also comes as an accuser (Rev. 12:10), trying to sow disunity between the people in God's kingdom and God Himself (as well as disunity between members of God's kingdom and within members of God's kingdom). By this tactic, Satan promotes a "you against me" paradigm (with its attendant power struggles and manipulation dynamics) in contrast to the "you with me" paradigm that God advocates. This scheme is often used when his targets are ambitious and competitive. This contrast of paradigms is evident in Paul's letter to the believers in Galatia:

> So I say, live by the Spirit, and you will not gratify the desires of the sinful nature. For the sinful nature desires what is contrary to the Spirit, and the Spirit what is contrary to the sinful nature. They are in conflict with each other, so that you do not do what you want. But if you are led by the Spirit, you are not under law. The acts of the sinful nature are obvious: sexual immorality, impurity and debauchery; idolatry and witchcraft; hatred, discord, jealousy, fits of rage, selfish ambition, dissensions, factions and envy; drunkenness, orgies, and the like. I warn you, as I did before, that those who live like this will not inherit the kingdom of God. But the fruit of the Spirit is love, joy, peace, patience, kindness, goodness, faithfulness, gentleness and self-control. Against such things there is no law. Those who belong to Christ Jesus have crucified the sinful nature with its passions and desires. Since we live by the Spirit, let us keep in step with the Spirit. Let us not become conceited, provoking and envying each other (5:16–26).

This passage contrasts the "fruit" produced when we gratify the desires of our sinful nature with that produced when we keep in step with the leading of the Holy Spirit. The understanding that Satan entices us to act on the desires of our sinful nature is made clear from this passage in James: "When tempted, no one should say, 'God is tempting me.' For God cannot be tempted by evil, nor does he tempt anyone; but each one is tempted when, by his own evil desire, he is dragged away and enticed. Then, after desire has conceived, it gives birth to sin; and sin, when it is full-grown, gives birth to death" (1:13–15). He also comes as a roaring lion (1 Pet. 5:8), trying to intimidate and overwhelm his quarry. When people are suffering and are prone to fear, Satan will execute a frontal attack—after roaring his intentions—in order to devour them. At other times, however, he comes as "an angel of light" (2 Cor. 11:14), masquerading as a messenger from God and carrying a message destructive to God's people and God's kingdom. This strategy works well when his targets are not familiar with God's written word or sensitive to the voice of His Spirit. This approach illustrates Satan's skill as a deceiver (2 Cor. 11:3), who has been using lies to trick human beings from the beginning of the human race.

Our war involves getting prepared so that we can endure when "the day of evil comes" (Eph. 6:13). There will be days when we are under attack—complete with "the flaming arrows of the evil one" (v. 16)—and we won't be able to stand against that attack unless we have made specific preparations. As any soldier would tell us, if we do not prepare for our battle, we lose. And our preparation must be "good and sufficient"—just any old preparation will *not* do. I have never fought in a human to human war, but I have played football (a sport with several similarities). Not only was there preparation at a personal level (so I would have the strength to play my position and the stamina to play the whole game and hopefully do both better than my counterpart on the opposing team), but there was also preparation at a team level (so we would have a game-plan for choosing our plays/strategies and for defending ourself from the opposition's plays/strategies). If both kinds of preparation were not accomplished in ways that equipped both me and us for the specific opponent who was arriving on game day, we would get beat (a painful experience that I am quite familiar with). God has graciously provided us with a game-plan for fighting in the cosmic war. If we make our preparations using that game-plan we will not get defeated (an experience that we endeavor to remain unfamiliar with). This next section outlines His game-plan.

OUR RESPONSE IN THE WAR

Although unstated in the Ephesians 6 passage, Paul is instructing us to respond to this war by becoming soldiers (people who not only survive the conflict but also are useful in God's service). There is no doubt, however, that Paul—in this passage—is implying that instruction (after all, who but soldiers should be learning to put on the armor that God supplies). Also implied here is our partnership with God: We have a significant role (of learning to be soldiers); God supplies the armor but we must put it on and use it. In other passages, Paul is clearly calling followers of Jesus to become soldiers. For example, in his second letter to Timothy (who he called "my true son in the faith"), he said, "Endure hardship with us like a good soldier of Jesus Christ. No one serving as a soldier gets involved with civilian affairs—he wants to please his commanding officer" (2 Tim. 2:3–4). He also said, in his first letter to Timothy: "Timothy, my son, I give you this instruction in keeping with the prophecies once made about you, so that by following them you may fight the good fight, holding on to faith and a good conscience" (1 Tim. 1:18–19). And Paul—the old warrior who had mentored and loved this timid young man—said to Timothy about himself (in possibly his last letter before his death): "For I am already being poured out like a drink offering, and the time has come for my departure. I have fought the good fight, I have finished the race, I have kept the faith" (2 Tim. 4:6–7). The following propositions outline what we as soldiers are to do.

We are to be "strong in the Lord and in His mighty power" (Eph. 6:10). From this instruction, it is clear that we are to draw on and use the power of our Commander in Chief (rather than depending on our own). But what, specifically, does that involve?—at least, the following:

– Inviting the Lord into my place in the battle.

As Paul sees it, our battle is ongoing, so (inevitably) I will be attacked. I am not to rely on my own strength or skill or cunning, but I must invite God to come and supply me with His resources. When I invite Him, I am claiming one of His promises to me—that He is an ever-present help in a time of trouble (Ps. 46:1). I am also showing the seen and the unseen world that I have a relationship with Him and that I trust Him. When He shows up, the "spiritual forces of evil in the heavenly realms" take notice, since they have eyes to see Him. (Have you noticed that when our Lord was on earth there were times when only the demons recognized who He was?) As He comes, I ask His spirit to give me eyes to see what He is doing and ears to hear His marching orders for me. These orders will differ from situation to situation: He may command me to attack (Acts 13:6–12), to retreat (Ps. 9:9–10) or—as is emphasized here—to stand my ground (Eph. 6:13b). To obey these orders, with all the strength that He gives me, is my responsibility. (And, if I am not sure what His orders are, I will do what the situation seems to call for, trusting that He will confirm or disconfirm that course of action.)

– Using resources that He has given me.

His orders may include my directed use of His provisions which, used for warfare purposes, could be called weapons. Such "weapons" include the following:

Angels. In Hebrews 1:14 we are told that angels are "ministering spirits sent to serve those who will inherit salvation." Although I don't direct their service directly, I can ask God to deploy them as He sees fit.

Authority. In Luke 10:19 we are informed that Jesus has given us authority to "overcome all the power of the enemy." As with any weapon, we can misuse it (by, for instance, trying to take authority over people, places or things that God has not led us to do), but—if we invite His Spirit to 'aim' that authority—we can 'pull the trigger' with effective results.

Discernment. In 1 Corinthians 2:6–16 Paul talks about discernment. When God's Spirit reveals information to us concerning the battle we are in, we become formidable warriors.

There is a fascinating account in 2 Kings 6:8–23 that illustrates the use of such resources by a warrior of God, the prophet Elisha. This account begins with the sentence, "Now the king of Aram was at war with Israel." Within that context, we read that the king of Aram, wanting to ambush the Israelite army, would set up his camp at a certain place, but that repeatedly Elisha would send word to the king of Israel, informing him of that location (so that he could avoid that place). I can hardly think of a more practical use of discernment in the context of war. The account goes on to say,

> This enraged the king of Aram. He summoned his officers and demanded of them, "Will you not tell me which of us is on the side of the king of Israel?" "None of us, my lord the king," said one of his officers, "but Elisha, the prophet who is in Israel, tells the king of Israel the very words you speak in your bedroom." "Go, find out where he is," the king ordered, "so I can send men and capture him." The report came back: "He is in Dothan." Then he sent horses and chariots and a strong force there. They went by night and surrounded the city. When the servant of the man of God got up and went out early the next morning, an army with horses and chariots had surrounded the city. "Oh, my lord, what shall we do?" the servant asked.

If you are like I am, it is fairly easy to put yourself in the shoes of that servant. I can easily envision myself uttering the same words that he did, when he looked at the seen world on that morning. I can also envision myself saying other things—like, "did you have magic mushrooms for dessert last night?" when the prophet replied, "Don't be afraid. Those who are with us are more than those who are with them."

Then Elisha asked God to enable his servant to see what he had already seen (through his God-given gift of discernment). And Elisha prayed, "O Lord, open his eyes so he may see." Then the Lord opened the servant's eyes, and he looked and saw the hills full of horses and chariots of fire all around Elisha.

This account does not directly address the question of whether Elisha had asked for that heavenly army to be there, but I certainly know it would have been on my prayer list. And why had God deployed such an army? Maybe for the encouragement of His warriors, since the Israelite army wasn't experienced in seeing God's intervention (in a "seen world" battle). As the enemy came down toward him, Elisha prayed to the Lord, "Strike these people with blindness." So he struck them with blindness, as Elisha had asked.

Here we see God giving Elisha authority over the Aramean army. This use of resources rendered that army helpless. "Elisha told them, 'This is not the road and this is not the city. Follow me, and I will lead you to the man you are looking for.' And he led them to Samaria. After they entered the city, Elisha said, 'Lord, open the eyes of these men so they can see.' Then the Lord opened their eyes and they looked, and there they were, inside Samaria. When the king of Israel saw them, he asked Elisha, 'Shall I kill them, my father? Shall I kill them?'"

I may be reading too much between the lines here, but I think I detect an eagerness in the king's question (and who wouldn't want to get rid of enemies once and for all?). "'Do not kill them,' he answered. 'Would you kill men you have captured with your own sword or bow? Set food and water before them so that they may eat and drink and then go back to their master.' So he prepared a great feast for them, and after they had finished eating and drinking, he sent them away, and they returned to their master. So the bands from Aram stopped raiding Israel's territory."

Elisha's response here demonstrates (again) a wisdom and a groundedness that provides evidence of the fact that he was "plugged in" to God and was following His directions. These "counter-reasonable" instructions for the treatment of prisoners of war not only avoided an escalation in that war but also (as the last sentence confirms) led to a time of peace. The king of Israel was wise to listen to Elisha; we would also be wise to pray for eyes to see and ears to hear what our Commander in Chief is saying to us—about the specific battle we are fighting—and for hearts to obey Him. Although our orders may often be counter to "the wisdom of this world," we will, sooner or later, be beneficiaries of our obedience.

In Acts 19:13–16 there is a historical account of what happened to warriors who were in the battle but who were not strong in the Lord. These Jewish exorcists knew about Jesus but they did not know Him—in the sense of having a personal relationship with Him. There-fore, they could not draw on His power and protection when faced by a powerful demon.

In James 4:7 we are shown the two sides of the coin of being strong in the Lord. The first side—that of loving well as a good soldier—is clarified by the instruction, "submit yourselves … to God." The second side—that of hating well as a good soldier—is clari-fied by the instruction, "Resist the Devil, and he will flee from you." If, like me, you have been taught that "it is good to love but bad to hate," then you (like me) will have been unable to become a first-class soldier. Until I understood that there are constructive and destructive ways to love as well as constructive and destructive ways to hate—and that I must do *both* constructively—I remained a liability as a soldier. (In the terms I used at the beginning of this module, I was a casualty—trying to love Satan made me one.) As many of us learned while growing up in dysfunctional families, there are destructive ways to be loved. For example, we may have been loved by someone who taught us that we were obligated by that love, that we had to accept that love and show appreciation for that love in ways that "giver" specified. When a lover does so on his/her own terms, that process is more like a hostage-taking, than a nourishing gift. If we were to model that training and apply it to our relationship with God, we would be carrying ongoing expectations of God Who should be giving us what we want in light of our giving to Him and we should have ongoing disappointment toward Him for the times that He did not meet our expecta-tions. (Sound familiar?) God, who loves us constructively (including no guilt-trips like, "How could you do that after all I have done for you!?"), also shows and teaches us how to constructively love Him—by submitting to Him. Submission is defined as "yielding to the power and control of another" and "deferring to the judgment or decision of another." So God, my Commander in Chief, says to me (in effect), "If you want to love me effectively as a soldier, do what I tell you to do—nothing more or less, situation by situation—and keep on doing it until I say, 'We're done, for now.'" Any soldier who is not operating in that way is a liability to the army of the kingdom of light, even if he/she thinks otherwise. Loving God constructively, as a soldier, involves sustained action toward the goal of obeying His marching orders.

As many of us also learned while growing up in dysfunctional families, there are de-structive ways to be hated. For example, we may have been hated by someone who equated us with our behavior and so, while trying to get rid of behavior which was unacceptable to him/her, also "blew up" our relationship. People who hate constructively make a distinc-tion between the person and his/her behavior, going "soft" on the person (treating the per-son with respect and love) but going "hard" on the behavior (using the energy of their hate to address and change the unacceptable behavior). This is the human-to-human version of the truth that "God loves the sinner but hates the sin." When it comes to relating to other people, I must hate in a way that solves problems, rather than creating problems. When it comes to relating to the kingdom of darkness, I must hate by resisting. I must use the energy of my hate to move myself away from the object of my hatred, away from Satan and his followers and what they do (since they chose to fight God). Resisting means moving away from any attachment with what I hate as well as "withstanding, opposing, fending off, standing firm against." So God, my Commander in Chief, says to me (in effect) "If you want to serve me effectively—as a soldier against my enemy—(then) resist Satan. Hate him constructively, not with a large show of emotion (which will wane) but with a settled attitude that continually distances yourself. Non-participation is the ultimate hatred." When I am loving constructively and hating constructively, I will be an asset to the army of the kingdom of light.

A former pastor of mine has developed a prayer that powerfully personalizes and applies the truths of James 4:7.[2] He uses it daily to remain strong in the Lord. I have included that prayer in appendix A for your consideration and use.

We are to "put on the full armor of God" (Eph. 6:11, 13). In this central passage, on what is involved in becoming a good soldier, Paul repeats this instruction twice. In verse 11, the reason to put on the whole armor of God is to be able to "take your stand against the Devil's schemes." In verse 13, the reason is "… so that when the day of evil comes, you may be able to stand your ground, and after you have done everything, to stand." We put on the armor so that we can *stand* against the (inevitable and varied) attacks that we will experience. There are several implications in the word "stand," including the following:

- If we are going to stand, we need to put on *all* of the armor (not just some of it). God supplies each piece of armor for a reason. Even if we don't know what that reason is, as a good (obedient) soldier, we will still put it on. We do not pick and choose what pieces we put on.
- If we are going to stand, we must prepare. In addition to putting on the armor, we must not ask ourselves low-quality questions, like "why me?" (Why not you? The Scripture makes it clear that believers can expect such conflict—as our Commander in Chief did), but we must ask ourselves high-quality questions like, "What else do I need to do, in order to complete my preparations?"
- If we are going to stand, we must face the enemy. So, all our cognitive focus needs to be on how to stand, not how to retreat. (Do not develop an exit plan; develop a plan for holding on.) Your armor will protect you if you are facing

the enemy; it will only slow you down if you are running away. (This principle applies if I understand this armor to have a literal, physical dimension of
application or if I understand this armor to have a symbolic, spiritual dimension of application.) So, our attitude is "I plan to win (as the Lord empowers
and directs me). I refuse to lose. Resisting the enemy until he flees from me is
a win. (Although he will withdraw from me only until another opportunity
to attack arrives, when he will usually employ a different scheme. See Luke 4:13.)
I will never retreat unless my Commander in Chief tells me to." Although
such simple and constructive "stubbornness" will not help us in every dimension of our life, it will serve us well when we fight.

– If we are going to stand, we must give one hundred percent to that endeavor. In the same way that we are to "love the Lord our God with all
our heart and with all our soul and with all our mind and with all our
strength" (Mark 12:30), we are to fight for him with all our heart … soul
… mind … strength. If we are half-hearted or unfocused or unplanned or
unmotivated, we are setting ourselves up for a fall—and one that may have
far-reaching ripple effects.

– If we are going to stand, we must put this battle within a bigger picture. We
fight – and stand – to honor Jesus (who fought and was killed and was raised
again, for us). My father was a veteran of World War II. He carried the scars
of that war to his deathbed, but he also carried a sense that he had participated and done his part in a great and good fight. He was proud of having
done that for Canada's freedom. His model has helped me to look for a big
picture purpose that will sustain me in my fight. I have found that purpose in
the words of my Lord, "Well done, good and faithful servant! You have been
faithful … come and share your master's happiness!" (Matt. 25:21). These
words were spoken to a servant who had received gifts from the master, long
before, and who had made good use of those gifts (in extending the master's
kingdom). When the master returned and saw the tangible faithfulness of his
servant, he uttered these (preceding) words. I "eagerly desire" to hear these
words from my Lord and (so) have committed myself to constructively using
what He has given me in order to extend His kingdom. This means my "long
obedience in the same direction." This also means, becoming a good soldier
– who will stand when the day of evil comes.

Now, let's look at each piece of the armor, what it is and how to put it on.

THE BELT OF TRUTH

When Paul wrote this letter to the Christians in Ephesus he was in jail in Rome. One Roman practice for keeping prisoners was to chain them to Roman soldiers (and passages like Philippians 1:12–14 indicate that Paul experienced that practice first hand). Consequently, he was well acquainted with the pieces of armor that the soldiers used and with the order in which they put those pieces on their body. For the Roman soldier, the belt was put on first because it held his clothing in place and because other pieces of his armor, like his breastplate, were hooked to it. For the Christian soldier, the belt of truth is to be put on first because it (too) holds everything else in place. It is the framework that gives meaning and coherence to all our practices as Christ followers. This "belt of truth" refers to the Christian worldview as a whole, not to specific Christian truths or principles (which will be looked at when we come to "the sword of the Spirit, which is the word of God"). The Christian worldview is the glasses through which believers see and make sense of the world. That worldview provides Christians with unique perspectives—that we are created and valued beings (not just an accident of matter in motion), that our existence on this planet is for the purpose of establishing and growing relationships (not just acquiring things and power), that the world we live in has fallen away from its original harmony and is at war (as we are focusing on here), and that my life goes beyond death (*where* it goes being dependent on the choices that I make during this life). Such perspectives inform my values, my priorities, my lifestyle; they are the road signs that guide my moment-by-moment choices (which specify how I will spend this life). The truths of this worldview were lived in front of us and clarified for us when God's only Son arrived to live among us. He—who is the Truth—demonstrated these truths in time and space. In John 8—in the middle of a heated debate that Jesus was having with His Jewish kinsmen—he told them: "If you hold to my teaching, you are really my disciples. Then you will know the truth, and the truth will set you free" (v. 31–32).

The truth that He is talking about here (the sum of His teaching, not any specific teaching) is the "belt of truth" that we are considering. And, if we hold on to that teaching, what are we set free from? The text tells us that it is slavery to sin that we are freed from (see verses 33–36). It is also the case that—if we know and do Jesus' teachings—we will be able to identify the lies that Satan is perpetrating and (so) be able to reject them, thus freeing ourselves from them. And how does that happen today, since Jesus is not here to show us or to teach us, as He did His disciples—both by the writings of His forerunners (2 Pet. 1:21) and His students (2 Tim. 3:16). In both cases, that writing was guided by the Holy Spirit. In our individual and personal situations, we also have the promise that He will guide us into the (freeing) truth (John 16:5–15). When we hold on to our Lord's teachings, something special happens—they hold on to us. They give us eyes to see the landmines that we must navigate around, they bring us to green pastures and still waters, they give us perspectives that transcend our circumstances, they transform our suffering (making it work *for* us), and they provide us with a banquet—even in the presence of our enemies. They envelop us in joy (that no one can take away), they nourish us—so that we can produce fruit in our life and can withstand drought, and they root us in hope.

In light of these considerations, let me ask: "Who is the primary beneficiary (in the ongoing, difficult task of 'holding on …')?" The (Good News) answer is, "us."

Our instructional text puts it this way, "Stand firm then, with the belt of truth buckled around your waist …" As clear as that instruction may be, it does not address the issue of whose responsibility it is to do the buckling—it is ours (not God's). So, there would be no twisting of the intent of the text if it was to read, "Stand firm then, having buckled the belt of truth around your waist …." And how do we do that buckling? In (at least) the following ways:

By asking the Holy Spirit to lead you into the truth—of your origins, your life on this planet, your destiny—so you can glimpse the grand design of the Grand Designer and begin to orient yourself accordingly.

By studying the Scriptures, with "big picture" glasses on. When I want to capture a vista with my camera, I put on the wide angle lens. When I want to understand Christianity's answers to the big questions, I have to ask them:
– Where did I come from?
– Who am I?
– What am I to do with this life?
– Where am I going?

And having discovered those answers, I need to integrate them into my life in ways that satisfy my thinking, feeling, and choosing. (The journey of discovery and the journey of application will continue throughout our lives, if we are committed to life-long learning. What an adventure!)

Look at the Christian worldview and how it compares and contrasts with other worldviews. Books such as these do both:
– *The Universe Next Door*—James Sire[3]
– *Christian Faith and Other Faiths*—Stephen Neill[4]

Take a course on the comparative study of religion.

THE BREASTPLATE OF RIGHTEOUSNESS

For the Roman soldier, the breastplate (put on after the belt) covered his body from the base of his neck to the upper part of his thighs—protecting his vital organs. For the Christian soldier, this piece of God-given armor is provided in order to protect vital parts of us—our heart (seen in Paul's day as the seat of emotions), our conscience (evaluating in those days as it does today), and our desires (which energize us)—from the schemes of the Devil. As related to our heart/feelings, a demonic scheme would be to get us to use our feelings to assess our connection with God. If we do that, we will feel close to God one day, distant from Him the next and not even in His family the next (not a good experiential context for fighting and holding our ground). As related to our consciences, Satan reminds us of our sins—sometimes with high definition visuals and surround sound auditory input. This makes for intense experiential impact. If we believe his accompanying commentary, " … And you think that an all-righteous God will have anything to do with a "super-sinner" like you …!?," we will be divided (from our Commander in Chief) and conquered. As related to our desires, Satan will intensify some of these desires ("inflaming them," as Paul says in Romans 1:27). This imagery—of attack and being set on fire—is in keeping with the "flaming arrows of the evil one" imagery found in Ephesians 6:13. Although desires—in and of themselves—are not wrong, if they are intensified until they are managing us (rather than us managing them), we will be led into all kinds of wrongs.

Against such attacks on these vital functions, God provides us with a breastplate of righteousness. In Philippians 3, Paul talks about righteousness—contrasting his attempt to be righteous by keeping the law (in verses 4–8) with righteousness that comes from God to him (in verse 9). He concludes, in his quest to become righteous, by saying: " … that I may gain Christ and be found in Him, not having a righteousness of my own that comes from the law, but that which is through faith in Christ—the righteousness that comes from God and is by faith." (v. 9).

Christ's purpose for coming into this world, which "lays in the grip of the evil one" (1 John 5:19), was to make a way for us—who are unrighteous beings—to get back to having peace with God (who is a righteous Being and who does not connect with unrighteousness). Jesus did that by paying the debt of unrighteousness that the human race had accumulated when it believed Satan and turned away from God. When a human being receives that gift from God—by faith, by believing that Jesus is God's Son and that He did what He claimed to do for humanity—that person is clothed with the righteousness of Christ. That person is also made righteous (1 John 3:9), so that his/her relationship with

God is restored. As we are clothed with and indwelt by the righteousness of Christ, we are wearing the breastplate of righteousness.

How does this breastplate protect our heart, our conscience and our desires from the accusations of the Devil? When Satan tells us that real Christians feel close to God—no matter what the circumstances—and, since we don't always feel close to Him, we are not really connected to Him, we can reply that our way of knowing that we are connected to Him is whether or not we have received God's gift of relationship with Him (which we access through faith in Jesus). Our relationship with God has everything to do with receiving what God has done for us; it has nothing to do with how we feel at any moment of our lives. When Satan reminds us that we have sinned and quotes the Scriptures to us that "our sins separate us from God," we can reply that Jesus died to make a re-connection with God possible and since "we have confessed our sins [Jesus] is faithful and just and will forgive us our sins and purify us from all unrighteousness" (1 John 1:9). We can affirm that our conscience is not the infallible guide to our standing before God (see 1 Corinthians 4:3–4); the infallible guide is what God has done for us, and God is greater than our conscience (1 John 3:20). When Satan intensifies our desires, for the purpose of getting them out of our control (and, so, using them to push us toward sin), we can ask God to use this piece of armor to reduce the intensity of that experience. Having done that, we are better able to receive from God's Spirit—and apply to our lives—His gifts of "power, love, and self-control" (2 Tim. 1:7). As we respond to Satan's accusations in these ways (by trusting in God, not our feelings; by receiving and resting in God's provision for my sins; by receiving God's protection from overwhelming experience— see 1 Corinthians 10:13), we are using the breastplate of (His) righteousness.

We put on His breastplate when we exercise our faith. When we receive, by faith, God's free gift to us—of ongoing connection with Him, based on Jesus' work—we have access to His provisions for us. As we ask for this provision (of His breastplate)—trusting Him, as the "Giver of all good gifts"—we will receive what we need for our protection. If we need confirmation that we have become connected to Him (and, so, His provisions), we can ask for an experience of His love toward us. (When we receive His gift, we become members of His family; when that happens, His anger toward us—as unrighteous beings—is replaced by love.) In Romans 5, it says: " … God has poured out His love into our hearts by the Holy Spirit, whom He has given us" (v. 5). Experiencing such love confirms our relationship with Him; it also transforms us.

FOOTWEAR

The text says, " … with your feet fitted with the readiness that comes from the gospel of peace" (v. 15b). The word "readiness" means "equipment," so the text is indicating that the gospel of peace should equip or prepare or make ready the armor we put on our feet. How does the gospel ("good news") of peace equip us for war? When the Father sent Jesus into this world, it was to reverse the effects of the fall: in restoring peace with us, He makes it clear whose side we are on. Paul puts this aspect of the gospel of peace clearly when he says, "Therefore being justified by faith, we have peace with God through our Lord Jesus Christ; by Whom also we have access by faith into this grace wherein we stand" (Rom. 5:1–2). This good news also restores my peace with myself, setting me free from my own conflicts so that I can be a useful soldier. This good news also restores my peace with other recipients of God's grace, enabling me to fight the real enemy (rather than other soldiers in His army).

When Paul looked at the feet of a Roman soldier, what did he see? Roman soldiers wore sandals, consisting of a tough sole and of straps for securing it to his foot. On the bottom of the sole were studs or nails to keep the sandal from slipping. In addition to traction, this footwear protected the soldier from traps in the ground. (In those days, they didn't have landmines, but they did have sharpened stakes, which were hidden in the ground in order to puncture the foot of whoever stepped on them). Also, this footwear helped the Roman soldier to be mobile, to be able to move far and fast when a battle called for that strategy. Paul made a spiritual application of each of these characteristics of the Roman soldier's sandal. First, in the same way that the nails in the sandals kept the soldier grounded, the Christian soldier was to "put on" what enables him to stay grounded (no slipping or falling) when in battle. D. M. Lloyd-Jones talks about what this means, practically, when he says:

> This means that you must be resolute; that you have to resolve to be "a good soldier of Jesus Christ," come what may. You have to resolve to adhere to this Gospel, no matter what hosts of foes may be arrayed against you. You have to take a firm grip of yourself. You must not come into the Christian life and continue in it half-heartedly, half in and half out, desiring benefits but objecting to duties, wanting privileges but rejecting responsibilities. You have to start by being firm and solid and resolute and assured. Paul's mention of the sandals carries that notion.[5]

It also means understanding and "holding on to" (adhering to) the gospel that comes from God (in and through Jesus Christ) rather than falling for another gospel (see Galatians 1:6–12). When we do personal applications of those beliefs, we will "no longer be infants, tossed back and forth by the waves, and blown here and there by every wind of teaching and by the cunning and craftiness of men in their deceitful scheming" (Eph. 4:14).

Second, in the same way that the tough sole of the sandal kept the soldier from receiving a disabling injury from hidden traps (set by the enemy), the Christian soldier should "put on" what enables him/her to avoid "the snares of the Devil." To Paul that involved alertness, an ongoing watchfulness for the spikes, hidden by the enemy, that will make us a casualty if we aren't careful. In Ephesians 5:15, Paul's exhortation has been translated into the (archaic English) phrase "walk circumspectly"—meaning that we should be careful where we put our feet. Paul knew—from his own experience—the power, the relentlessness, the subtlety and the flexibility of Satan's attacks. Our enemy is a being for whom the ends justify the means; he will do whatever is in his power to get what he wants. Consequently, we need to "be on our guard (against Satan's varied temptations to sin); stand firm in the faith; be men of courage; be strong" (1 Cor. 16:13).

Third, in the same way that the (light but hobnailed) footwear of the Roman soldier enabled him to be mobile, the Christian soldier should put on what enables him to move quickly and precisely and flexibly, as the Spirit of God leads him. In his consideration of this issue, Lloyd-Jones says:

> The Church today too much resembles David in Saul's armor. Goliath challenges Israel with his armor and his spear and sword; and Israel quakes and trembles, and does not know what to do. All are frightened of this man, who has killed so many. Then David, the stripling, a mere shepherd, arrives in the Israelite camp, and, moved by the Spirit of God, shows himself to respond to Goliath's challenge. Saul and his company, thinking in the old [categories of warfare] instead of spiritually, say, "He seems convinced that he can do it; let us fetch Saul's armor and put it on him." They believed that the only way in which anyone could fight Goliath was in Saul's armor. So they put it on him. But David realized at once that if he went in that armor he would be killed. He could scarcely move, the armor was too heavy for him, and too big for him. So he got rid of it. He said, "I cannot fight in Saul's armor; I must use my own method of fighting, and in the name of the living God I am going to do so." . . He wanted to be mobile, and to be able to move quickly and respond and react to every move of Goliath.[6]

When our Commander in Chief speaks to us (as He did to David—see 1 Samuel 17:34–38), we must keep ourselves free in order to be able to respond in obedience. Such obedience also involves freeing ourselves from the destructive reactions of people in our own army. Eliab, David's oldest brother, attacked David verbally when David began to inquire about what the Israelite army was going to do about Goliath (see 1 Samuel 17:28). David did not debate with Eliab, he just turned away and kept on with his inquiry—freeing himself to do what God was leading him to do.

Since it is our job to put on the armor that God has provided, the question of how to put each piece on is always relevant. Putting on His footwear involves (at least) the following:

My *grounding* develops as I resolve to be a good soldier. Included in that resolution is deciding to make this goal a top priority, a "centerpiece" of my life (around which other goals in my life adjust). My lifestyle must reflect this priority (as would the lifestyle of a person who prioritizes music or athletics or academics). Also included in that resolution is a commitment to become a "better" soldier, a soldier who keeps improving his character and his skills as time passes.

My *grounding* develops as I deepen my understanding of God's revelation to me (through the Scriptures, the person of Christ, the work of the Holy Spirit). God's word to me (delivered to me in various ways) must come to inform my beliefs and my actions in every dimension of my life. About this process, Peter says

"… make every effort to add to your faith goodness; and to goodness, knowledge; and to knowledge, self-control; and to self-control, perseverance; and to perseverance, godliness; and to godliness, brotherly kindness; and to brotherly kindness, love. For it you possess these qualities in increasing measure, they will keep you from being ineffective and unproductive in your knowledge of our Lord Jesus Christ. … if you do these things, you will never fall…" (2 Pet. 1:5–8, 10b).

My *watchfulness* develops as I use the principles for living correctly (that God has given) like a pair of glasses through which to view and to evaluate my lifestyle. An ongoing question to apply that evaluation is "Is this action within the circle of biblical options?"

My *watchfulness* develops as I become familiar with what the Scriptures say about Satan's strategies.

My *watchfulness* develops as I study warfare.

– God at War[7] by Gregory Boyd gives an overview of how warfare is part of the biblical worldview.
– Praying With Power,[8] Warfare Prayer,[9] Prayer Shield,[10] Breaking Strongholds in Your City[11] and Confronting the Powers,[12] are all books in C. Peter Wagner's prayer warrior series. These books draw on the experiences of people who are on the frontline of the spiritual war.

– The Art of War[13] by Sun Tzu offers fascinating insights into the strategies of war.

My *mobility* develops as I learn to hear (and accurately identify) God's voice. When I have "ears to hear" (and am ongoingly listening), I will be walking in His moment-by-moment leading, I will be "keeping in step with the Spirit" (Gal. 5:25).

At this place in the text, Paul changes verbs—from "having" to "taking." In his discussion of the first three pieces of armor, he talks about "having put on," fastening them to your body so that they will stay in place. Now, for the next three pieces of armor, he talks about "taking up," picking them up and using them as the situation requires. As a soldier on duty, you will have the first three pieces on, even when you are resting (implying that the benefits to us are ongoing). As a soldier on duty, you will pick up and use the next three pieces only as the need arises (implying that the benefits to us are greater at certain times).

THE SHIELD OF FAITH

The text says, "In addition to [what is already put in place], take up the shield of faith, with which you can extinguish all the flaming arrows of the evil one" (v. 16). One tactic of warfare in Paul's day was to shoot flaming missiles at the enemy—to "soften them up" before hand to hand combat. (This tactic is still used today, using artillery or guided missiles.) Anyone who has seen the movie "Gladiator" will remember—in the opening scenes—the Roman army's devastating use of fiery missiles and of their use of shields to protect themselves. The shield used by the Roman solder was large. One and a half meters long and almost a meter wide. It was covered with leather (which was soaked in water, in order to extinguish any flaming arrows that hit it). A soldier could hide behind such a shield and when shields were arranged side-by-side (as soldiers were taught to do), they were protected from almost anything that their enemies could throw at them.

When Paul made spiritual application of this piece of armor, what did he have in mind? He was warning us to be prepared for the Satanic "flaming arrows" that will be shot at us (and, since Satan tailor makes his attacks to fit the weaknesses he sees in us, they will test the defenses of each of us, specifically). The purpose of these missiles is to "soften us up"—to distract us, frighten us, discourage us. The missiles he uses are primarily thoughts, intrusive thoughts that hit our inside life and seek to disrupt our stand. They may take the form of doubts ("If God's love seems too good to be true, it probably is") or blasphemy ("The virgin birth was just a cover-up for sexual intercourse outside of marriage") or fears ("I will be fired if I say anything about that …"). To stop such thoughts from disabling us, Paul tells us to take up and use the shield of faith. In this context, faith means (to quote Lloyd-Jones) "the ability to apply quickly what we believe so as to repel everything the Devil does or attempts to do to us."[14] Since many of Satan's flaming thoughts are designed to challenge what we believe, faith also means applying to our life and situation what God tells us to know and do (rather than what Satan is telling us to know and do). As seen in this definition, faith involves belief and action; it means doing (or using) the beliefs that we have been given. Do we believe and act on who God says He is or do we believe and act on who Satan says God is? God says that He loves us (and has shown us that love primarily by sending Jesus). Satan says that God doesn't love us (and points to things that have happened to us—or are happening to us—saying, "if God loved you, He wouldn't have let that happen to you"). God says that He is all-powerful (and points to creation, to His interventions in the lives of His people and to the life, death, and resurrection of Jesus as evidence). Satan says that He is not all-powerful (and points to the events of this world—in the past and in the present—saying "if God was all-powerful, would He have let these atrocities occur?") God says that He is trustworthy, that He keeps His promises (and points to how He has done so in the lives of people—like Abraham—who have had a relationship with Him). Satan says that God is not to be trusted (and points to requests that we have made to God that were not answered, saying "God said that He would keep His promises to you. You asked Him for … You didn't get …, so how can you trust Him?") When Satan challenges what God has said to us, we—as creatures with the freedom to choose—decide who we will believe. If we choose to believe God, we will respond with "God says...I believe …, so I will do …"; that is holding up the shield of faith. For example, when Satan challenges what God says about loving us, we respond by saying, "God showed me His love for me by sending Jesus … He also tells me that "Nothing will separate me from His love," so whatever the reason is for God allowing this in my life, it isn't because He doesn't love me. I ask God for the strength to deal with this and for the ability to learn from and grow from this …" That is what holding up the shield of faith looks like.

Doing the following will help us to hold up the shield of faith.

When thoughts come that don't agree with what the Scriptures tell us. (In other words, the text is wrong or the context is wrong. The context can be wrong in terms of how the Scripture is interpreted and/or in terms of how the Scripture is applied.)

We *don't buy* the thought. Instead, we say to ourself things like, "This thought came to me; I didn't develop it or generate it, so I will not own it or take responsibility for it or get distressed because I have had it. I know that Satan sends thoughts like that, so I will talk to God, saying to Him that I do not receive or accept this thought, I just let it go by and focus on something else …"

We *don't believe* the thought. Instead, we say to ourself things like, "What does the Scripture say about this issue?" When we discover what the Scripture says, say, "God, I accept and receive what You tell me about this issue and [if/as needed] I will act on what You say to me."

We *don't dwell on* the thought. Instead, we say to ourself things like, "Any sustained reaction to this thought keeps me engaged with it, and not focusing on something more constructive. What could I focus on now that would be nourishing?"

Many people—myself included—have wished to avoid having such thoughts. Obviously, the Scriptures are clear that—in this fallen world—such thoughts will come (so we can't prevent them, but we can effectively handle them). The Scriptures encourage us, for instance, to "Take every thought captive" (2 Cor. 10:5); in order to do that, we must have the thought. Our focus, therefore, needs to be on how to effectively handle them (along the lines of what I have suggested above). For many of us, that is not good news since such thoughts can be highly disruptive. There is good news, however, in knowing that—in the next world (where we will be walking by sight rather than faith and where we will be separated from the presence of evil)—such thoughts will be no more.

Discover the promises that God makes to His family members. When we know these promises, we can apply them (by our faith) against incoming flaming thoughts, in order to extinguish them. In a fallen world, we will be faced by difficult situations and people. Sometimes, Satan is involved in "heating up" these circumstances so that they get too hot for us to handle constructively. Such circumstances—called "trials" in the Scriptures—can be interpreted by us as evidence that God doesn't care about us (especially when these circumstances are prolonged and unrelenting). Obviously, this is an interpretation that Satan is wanting us to buy, believe, and dwell on (and he is very willing to help us, in that regard). The Scriptures, however, promote another interpretation—that trials can produce personal growth (if we respond to them correctly). So we read, in James 1:

"Consider it pure joy, my brothers, whenever you face trials of many kinds, because you know that the testing of your faith develops perseverance. Perseverance must finish its work so that you may be mature and complete, not lacking in anything. If any of you lacks wisdom [as to how to deal with these trials], he should ask God, who gives generously to all without finding fault, and it will be given to him" (v. 2–5).

"But," Satan may say to us, "this situation is too big, scary, personal, nasty, ongoing, embarrassing … for it to develop good things in you." To this we can reply (if we know

God's promises), "God said that in all trials He works for the good of those who love Him … (Romans 8:28). "But," Satan may say to us, "This situation is too much for you; can't you already feel that!?" To which we can reply (if we know God's promises), "God said that He will not let me be tested beyond what I can bear but, when I am tested ("tempted" from Satan's perspective), He will provide a way out so that I can stand up under it" (I Cor 10:13). When our response to Satan's "spin" on these circumstances is to quote God's word and to stand on that truth by the exercise of our faith, we are holding up the shield of faith.

In the account where Satan was tempting our Lord, and He was countering these temptations by quoting the Scriptures (see Matthew 4:1–11), the result was that the battle was over quickly. Since that is not always the case (at least, not in my experience), we may need to—for a period time—resist what is being shot at us. So, while we are countering what Satan is saying to us with what God has said to us, we must also trust God with the duration of the battle (knowing that He won't let us be overwhelmed). If we demand of God that He end the battle when we want, we have just put Him to the test—a practice that good soldiers avoid (see Hebrews 3:7–19—especially verses 9–11).

There are various resources that have been designed to help us know and use God's promises. If becoming more familiar with His promises is a valuable next step to take—to improve your ability to hold up the shield of faith—the following resources will be helpful. (God has revealed His promises to us, our job is to know them, to *interpret* them correctly, and to *apply* them correctly. When we have done our part, His promises will enable us to stand.)

> *Bible Promises For the Healing Journey*—Lana Bateman[15]
> *God's Promises For You*—Max Lucado[16]
> *God's Inspirational Promise Book*—Max Lucado[17]
> *Promises To Live By: The Pocket Promise Book*—David Wilkerson[18]

THE HELMET OF SALVATION

The helmet that the Roman soldier wore was a leather cap, with strips and plates of metal fastened to it. On the top of the helmet there was a crest or plume, primarily for ornamentation. The application that Paul made to the Christian soldier emphasizes our need to protect our head, our thinking—as it relates to our faith. We have already looked at particular temptations that get directed at us; this piece of armor is to protect our faith life as a whole (using military terms, our focus now is on the whole campaign rather than a particular battle). Paul is telling us that one scheme of the enemy is to push us into giving up entirely our life of faith. We should not "be ignorant" of such an attack and we should know how to protect ourself from it. When Paul wrote to the believers in Galatia, he was writing to people who were being attacked about the legitimacy of their faith. He told them, "Let us not become weary in doing good, for at the proper time we will reap a harvest if we do not give up." (6:9) He was asking them to not over-focus on the present struggles (and, as a result, give up), but to remember that if they sow what pleases God—and keep sowing—good results will arrive, sooner or later. (6:7–8). In other words, he is asking them to put on the helmet of *salvation*. The word "salvation" is a comprehensive word, involving a past tense (encompassed by the theological word "justification"), a present tense (encompassed by the theological word "sanctification") and a future tense (encompassed by the theological word "glorification"). So, as believers, we have been saved, are being saved and will be saved. Paul is asking the believers in Galatia (and us) to remember and focus on the future dimension of our salvation—when the present struggles that we are experiencing will be replaced by the harvest of good things that God has for us. This is exactly what Paul is getting at when he says to the believers in Thessalonica, " … put on … the hope of salvation as a helmet" (I Thess. 5:8). As we remember and act on the truth that (again to quote Paul), "our light and momentary troubles are achieving for us an eternal glory that far outweighs them all" (2 Cor. 4:17), we are putting on hope (which is the antidote to the poison of believing that the battles of today will continue forever).

Since we have already been looking at how to put on the helmet of salvation (as well as what it is), I'll just suggest some strategies that I have found helpful for putting on/keeping on this piece of armor.

- I remind myself of what my Lord said in Luke 18. The principle that His parable (found in verses 2–8) was illustrating is found in verse 1,

" … that [His disciples, us included] should always pray and not give up."

So when we have battles, we are to involve God—that is what prayer does. For me, knowing that God is there, that He cares for me, that He listens to me, and that He will respond to my prayer, is very comforting. It helps me to keep fighting, not to give up. He may not answer how I'd like or when I'd like, but, since that is His business, I leave it in His hands. In my hands is the issue of how to keep fighting.

- I've been asked the question (and I've asked myself the question), "How long should I keep fighting?" The short (and vague) answer is, "For as long as it takes." When I played football, the timeframe was clear—until the end of the game (and, since football and spiritual warfare are both wars of attrition, they will usually be won in the fourth quarter by the people who will "hang in there" and "keep fighting"). In my training as a Christian soldier, I have learned to fight until the following:

(a) The enemy backs off

(b) We reach a stalemate (for whatever reasons)

(c) I retreat and get to a safe place

I have committed myself to be a soldier (and, so, fight) until the following:

(a) I die

(b) The Lord returns

In life, that is the end of the game (and, in this fallen world, it is failure to set my expectations differently).

– When the Scripture gives glimpses of the future dimension of my salvation—when the Lord returns, the marriage supper of the Lamb, getting to the place that is being prepared for me—I enter into that dimension (as well as I can) by visualization with prayer requests and by asking the Holy Spirit to lead me into that truth. I have not been taken to the third heaven (as Paul was, see 2 Corinthians 12:1–10), but I trust that He will give me all I need in order to go through this dirty present and get to my glorious future. And, when Satan says to me, "That is just a 'guiding fiction' for you, a false comfort, pie in the sky …," I respond by saying, "I put my hope in God and live my life accordingly … I bet my life on Him."

THE SWORD OF THE SPIRIT

The text says, "Take up the sword of the Spirit, which is the word of God." In contrast to the belt of truth, which refers to the Christian worldview, this piece of armor refers to a detailed knowledge of the Scriptures. With this knowledge, we counter the lies that Satan thrusts at us, and we drive him back with the truth that God has revealed to us in His word. (Of all the pieces of armor that Paul mentions, this is the only one that can be used offensively as well as defensively; this is how we "resist the Devil" so that "he will flee from us.") Our responsibility is to learn the Scriptures. When we are attacked, God's Spirit will bring to our minds the specific truth that is relevant to the attack (so that the "logos"—written word—becomes the "rhema"—living word—to and for us). Then, our responsibility is to use that word internally (by affirming it to ourself and receiving the consequent benefits—like peace) and externally (by speaking the truth into the circumstance that we are facing and receiving the consequent benefits—like the enemy backing off).

The sword that the Roman soldier carried was straight, sharp on both sides and coming to a sharpened point—so it could be used for both cutting and thrusting. It was contained in a sheath or scabbard that hung from the soldier's belt. (It was seventy-four to eighty centimeters long, five centimeters wide, with a blade length of sixty-four to seventy centimeters.) Soldiers were called "men who draw the swords."

The primary New Testament example of the Word of God being used to combat the Devil (and cause him to retreat) is found in Matthew 4:1–11—where the account of Satan tempting our Lord is found. In addition to the primary theme of this passage—Jesus using His detailed knowledge of the Scriptures to repel Satan's temptations—there are also (the following) insights into spiritual warfare:

(1) God the Father, at Jesus' baptism, had just declared "This is my Son, whom I love; with Him I am well pleased" (3:17). The Spirit of God had just come down and settled on Jesus (3:16). Then, the first place that the Spirit led Jesus was "into the desert to be tempted by the Devil" (4:1). So, sometimes at the high point of our spiritual life, God will lead us into a battle (sometimes upending our expectation that the Spirit will always lead us to "green pastures and still waters").

(2) Satan tailor makes his temptations to our present circumstances. Jesus had been fasting (4:2) and was hungry. Consequently, Satan crafted his first temptation to the reality that our Lord was hungry. Our Lord countered that temptation by quoting Deuteronomy 8:3. Scriptural truth, personalized by the work of God's Spirit, is the guide for my actions (not my personal needs).

(3) Satan can incorporate Scripture into his temptations. In his second temptation of our Lord, Satan quotes Psalm 91:11–12. Our Lord countered this temptation by quoting Deuteronomy 6:16. Not every voice that quotes the Scriptures has the growth of God's kingdom at heart. We must learn to recognize the voice of God's Spirit, who personalizes God's Word to us—the right principle at the right time in right context.

(4) Satan's goal is getting power over human beings—our Lord included. He is a powerful being who has control over the kingdoms of this world (which he offers Jesus, in exchange for His worship—see 4:8–9). Our Lord countered this temptation by quoting Deuteronomy 6:13. We are to worship and serve God only; we are to follow the example of Jesus who—at His highest point of worship and service—said to His Father, "Your will, not mine, be done."

(5) Satan will retreat—but he will be back. In the Matthew account, it says, "Then [after the temptations] the Devil left him [Jesus]" (4:11a). In Luke's account there is an addition, " … until an opportune time" (4:13). So, Satan was looking for an opportune time to attack Jesus again (and we see those attacks throughout Jesus' ministry— through Peter [see Matthew 16:21–23] and through Judas [see Luke 22:1–6]—people close to our Lord). In this world, we will have times of combat, until our Lord comes again or until we go to be with Him.

(6) We will be given help before, during and after Satan's attacks. The last phrase in Matthew's account says, " … and angels came and attended him" (4:11b). When Jesus was in this world, and going through battles, He was given help that originated in the spiritual dimension of reality. In this account, He was strengthened by the Holy Spirit before and during this encounter (Matt. 3:16–17; 4:1) and strengthened by angels after this encounter (Matt. 4:11b). God, who is "a very present help in a time of trouble" will strengthen us also (by these and other means) if we ask Him.

In light of what has already been said, there is no mystery about what is involved in taking up the sword of the Spirit. Anything that leads us to attaining a detailed and working knowledge of the s is involved. As with many other aspects of "doing faith," however, the best way(s) for us to acquire that knowledge varies from person to person. In this culture, at this time, there are many options available: study Bibles, Bible studies, commentaries, sermons (live or in auditory and/or visual format), on-line study programs, study guides, and spiritual mentors, to name a few. While some of these options will fit us better than others, we are all responsible to hear, distinguish and follow that voice which makes the Scriptures live and grow (and produce fruit) in our lives.

Paul has now finished his instruction on the armor of God—yet he hasn't. All the pieces of armor have been discussed but his text, itself, clarifies that he has something else to mention. Here is the relevant text: " … And pray in the Spirit on all occasions with all kinds of prayers and requests. With this in mind, be alert and always keep on praying for all the saints. Pray also for me, that whenever I open my mouth, words may be given me so that I will fearlessly make known the mystery of the gospel, for which I am an ambassador in chains" (6:18–20).

The issue that he has yet to discuss is PRAYER; the text connects it to the previous verses (where he is talking about armor) with the word "and." Some people have held the view that prayer is the seventh piece of armor, but Paul doesn't hook this activity to any piece of Roman equipment, as he has in each of the six previous activities (that Christian soldiers should "put on" or "take up"). So, why does he link prayer to his discussion of the armor and what, exactly, is the linkage? I think Paul links prayer with armor because prayer is the context for the appropriate use of the armor. When Paul said, " ... be strong in the Lord ...," that wasn't accomplished by simply putting the armor on; "putting on" and "taking up" had to be done in the context of a living relationship with God—and prayer is how that "living" occurs. When we pray we contact God: we invite Him into our life process, we ask for His strength, we receive His provisions—against our common enemy. So, prayer—both speaking to God and listening to Him—is our dialogue with Him. It is a dialogue that informs our use of the armor.

In his instructions on prayer (as it relates to warfare), Paul makes several practical points. These instructions help us to be good soldiers:

We are to pray *in the Spirit*. Since we have a living relationship with God (and the Spirit of God lives in us), we are to pray in agreement with the Spirit, as His Spirit directs us. We are not to "lean on our own understanding" when we pray (whether or not that is related to warfare); we are to learn to sense His leading and His emphasis and pray in line with that input. In Romans 8:26, Paul says, " ... the Spirit helps us in our weakness. We do not know what we ought to pray for, but the Spirit Himself intercedes for us ..."

He does that *for* us, and He also does that *with* us—helping us to tune in on what the will of God is, in each situation. As we learn to do this, we are "keeping in step with the Spirit" (Gal. 5:25).

When I was a new believer, I had no sense of the Spirit's leading so I prayed "what was right in my own eyes." I had been told to make a list of the things/people/events that I should pray for—which I dutifully did. Over the course of the next couple years, that list grew and grew. Every time that I considered taking something off that list (now having become "lists"), I would say to myself, "What if this is something that God wants me to keep praying for?" And so the lists (and my sense of being overwhelmed) grew. Finally, as an act of desperation, I said to God, "If You are as bored with these lists as I am, You'll be asleep ..." My relief was dramatic and tangible as I sensed that the Spirit was not grieved by my impertinence and that He would help me to edit what I should/should not pray for. Thus began my journey away from "vain repetitions" and toward Spirit-directed prayer (where my role is to settle myself, let Him know that I will obey Him as well as I can and, then, listen to His voice). That journey has included instruction on what I need to do/not do when the kingdom of darkness has me in its cross-hairs. With His help, I have become a "hard target" and am still standing.

We are to pray *on all occasions*. This means that we are to pray in every circumstance of our life. All aspects of our life are to involve God via prayer; if our life is like a house, He is to be invited into every room. At one time, I struggled with what it meant to "pray without ceasing." I've concluded that, for me, it means that my default setting is dialogue mode. So, no matter what is happening in my life, sooner or later God—like any good friend—hears about it. As soon as I am not engaged in some activity or interaction, I talk to Him about it—sometimes with questions (like, "What is he doing!?" or "What should I do?"), sometimes with exclamations (like, "O Lord!"), and sometimes with something a little more articulate (like, "Lord, I put him in Your hands; please involve Yourself with him"). When we apply this instruction to the context of warfare, what Paul said to the believers at Philippi is very relevant: "Do not be anxious about anything, but in everything, by prayer and petition, with thanksgiving, present your requests to God. And the peace of God, which transcends all understanding, will guard your hearts and your minds in Christ Jesus" (4:6–7).

Warfare will generate anxiety. We can fret about it or we can pray about every aspect of our concern—with the promise of receiving His peace (which makes no sense, given the situation we are in).

We are to pray *with all kinds of prayers and requests.* To pray with all kinds of prayers is to think and pray inclusively. In other words, there is no "right" way to pray: we can pray privately and publicly; we can pray walking and standing; we can pray kneeling and prostrate; we can pray externally and internally; we can speak our prayers and write our prayers; we can pray in languages that we know and (if appropriately gifted) in languages we don't know; we can pray with interpretation of those prayers and without interpretation of those prayers; and we can pray in planned, articulate ways and in spontaneous, inarticulate ways. Prayer is communication with God; do it in any way that works for you (and don't be held hostage by anyone who may tell you that their way is the right way).

To pray with all kinds of requests is (again) to think and pray inclusively. In other words, there is no wrong way to make requests: we can pray for ourself and for others, we can pray for people and events in the seen world and for people and events in the unseen world, we can pray for any aspect of who we are as humans (physical, cognitive, emotional, spiritual, emotional), and we can pray for our pets. Anything that concerns us also concerns God—because He loves us. If we recognize that we might be requesting something that is not good for us or for others, we can request that God edit our prayers according to His will. (And "yes," "no," "wait" and silence are *all* answers to our prayers.) Maybe an analogy to food would be helpful: some people have scheduled meals, some people "graze" throughout the day, some people follow an eating plan, some people wouldn't know an eating plan if it followed them, some people create a meal from fresh and raw ingredients, and some people consider fast food to be too slow. *How* you get food is a lifestyle choice that each of us makes; *that* you get food is the survival issue. In the same way, *how* you pray is a result of personal choice (and many options are legitimate); *that* you pray is what is crucial—especially in a time of war.

We are to *be alert* and *always keep on praying for all the saints.* The issue of being alert has already been looked at (in the "footwear" section of "putting on the armor"). Now, we look at it in connection with intercessory prayer. Obviously, the instruction to "always keep on praying for all the believers" isn't without boundary conditions (if we were always praying for them, we could get nothing else done. Also, we usually don't know all the believers—even in our church, let alone our community). Consequently, I am suggesting that we translate this instruction as follows: be alert (to input from God's Spirit) when He brings to mind any believer (and it will usually be someone that you know), keep on praying for that person until you sense/hear/see otherwise. So, the boundary condition is the leading (into intercessory prayer and out of that prayer) of God's Spirit. Without such a boundary, we are left to lean on our own understanding (which, in my case, lead to feeling overwhelmed by the enormity of the task, as I perceived it). One job of soldiers is to support other soldiers—this is how to carry out that job.

We are to pray for leaders we know, who are carrying out God's calling. In Paul's final paragraph of his teaching on prayer, he starts by saying, *"Pray also for me …."* He personalizes his teaching and asks believers who know him to support him in prayer. He is specific about what he wants support for—to carry out the calling that he received from God shortly after he "saw the light" on the road to Damascus. When we see people who are serious about doing what God wants them to do (people who are walking the talk, not just talking the talk), we know that they will be under spiritual attack—as Paul was (see 2 Corinthians 11:16–33). In all likelihood, as we listen for the Spirit's confirmation of such a request, He will endorse it—and, so, use us to help that fellow warrior "fight the good fight."

MY PROTECTION PLAN

As my knowledge of the war grew, I began to realize that I needed a way to make use of that knowledge. As a psychologist, I have worked with people who gained a lot of knowledge about a struggle they were encountering but who didn't find a way to apply that knowledge to their life and circumstances—so the struggle continued. I want to be a "doer—not a hearer only—of the Word." My prayer system, found in appendix B, is my attempt to apply (in a proactive way) the principles that God has given us for doing war.

What follows is my prayer system, looked at prayer by prayer, and linked with the biblical principles that undergird it.

PRAYER STEP

A1 Define what is "yours" (i.e. your property, pos-sessions, people under your spiritual protection, your areas of spiritual authority).
Lord Jesus Christ, I put the following (that You have given me) under Your jurisdiction, now...
a. My house and property
b. My office
c. My family [each person named specifically] and myself
d. My vehicle
e. My profession
f. My ministries
g. My pets
A2 Commit all on the list to God.
Lord Jesus, I commit everything on this list to You. I give it into your care, now.

BIBLICAL PRINCIPLE

Psalm 91:1–6
He who dwells in the shelter of the Most High will rest in the shadow of the Almighty. I will say of the Lord, "He is my refuge and my fortress, my God, in whom I trust." Surely he will save you from the fowler's snare and from the deadly pestilence. He will cover you with his feathers, and under his wings you will find refuge; his faithfulness will be your shield and rampart. You will not fear the terror of night, nor the arrow that flies by day, nor the pestilence that stalks in the darkness, nor the plague that destroys at midday.

Here, we are putting ourself (and what God has given us) "in the shelter of the Most High." This is the first step in protecting ourself and in looking after what He has put under our care. The kingdom of darkness uses many destructive tactics (as noted in verses 3, 5 and 6) but we—as we trust in God—will be safe.

A3 Ask God for angels to protect everything on the list from the kingdom of darkness.
Lord Jesus, please send angels, now, to protect every-thing under your jurisdiction. I ask that You would send angels up to and including the principality and power levels (and beyond if necessary) to be around both these environments and people. I ask that You would commission and deploy and cover and reinforce and equip these angels so that nothing from the kingdom of darkness can intrude on us. Please enable these angels to remove any beings—individuals or groups—that are or will be astral traveling around us.

Hebrews 1:14
Are not all angels ministering spirits sent to serve those who will inherit salvation?

Continued

Lord Jesus, if any reinforcements for the angels involved here are needed, please send them now; if any have been hurt, please have them taken care of.

Lord Jesus, please provide a container—if needed—that will suck all beings from the kingdom of darkness into it (and hold them until removal), should their numbers quickly increase.

Lord Jesus, thank You for this provision.

This verse makes it clear that God sends angels to help us; we can (and need to) ask for that help.

Psalm 91:9–13

If you make the Most High your dwelling—even the Lord, who is my refuge—then no harm will befall you, no disaster will come near your tent. For he will command his angels concerning you to guard you in all your ways; they will lift you up in their hands, so that you will not strike your foot against a stone. You will tread upon the lion and the cobra; you will trample the great lion and the serpent.

These verses confirm God's use of angels to "guard us in all our ways."

A4 Ask for God's provisions.

Lord Jesus,

Thank You for supplying me with Your armor. Please help me to put it on and use it; I receive these gifts by faith. Please guide my applications of Your armor so that I am protected today in a way that is good and sufficient.

Ephesians 6:10–18

Finally, be strong in the Lord and in his mighty power. Put on the full armor of God so that you can take your stand against the Devil's schemes. For our struggle is not against flesh and blood, but against the rulers, against the authorities, against the powers of this dark world and against the spiritual forces of evil in the heavenly realms. Therefore put on the full armor of God, so that when the day of evil comes, you may be able to stand your ground, and after you have done everything, to stand. Stand firm then, with the belt of truth buckled around your waist, with the breastplate of righteousness in place, and with your feet fitted with the gospel of peace. In addition to all this, take up the shield of faith, with which you can extinguish all the flaming arrows of the evil one. Take the helmet of salvation and the sword of the Spirit, which is the word of God. And pray in the Spirit on all occasions with all kinds of prayers and requests. With this in mind, be alert and always keep on praying for all the saints.

The previous section of this chapter looked at God's provision of armor and how we are to use it.

Holy Spirit,
Please quicken my mind so that I can be sensitive to what You want me to know or do today. I want to be in harmony with Your will for my life, today. Please enable me to hear Your voice clearly and in distinction to my own voice or those from the world or from the kingdom of darkness— so I can know your agenda for today (in order to do it).

John 14:15–17
If you love me, you will obey what I command. And I will ask the Father, and he will give you another Counselor to be with you forever—the Spirit of truth. The world cannot accept him, because it neither sees him nor knows him. But you know him, for he lives with you and will be in you.
John 16:5–7, 12–15
Now I am going to him who sent me, yet none of you asks me, "Where are you going?" Because I have said these things, you are filled with grief. But I tell you the truth: It is for your good that I am going away. Unless I go away, the Counselor will not come to you; but if I go, I will send him to you.
I have much more to say to you, more than you can now bear. But when he, the Spirit of truth, comes, he will guide you into all truth. He will not speak on his own; he will speak only what he hears, and he will tell you what is yet to come. He will bring glory to me by taking from what is mine and making it known to you. All that belongs to the Father is mine. That is why I said the Spirit will take from what is mine and make it known to you.

These verses record Jesus telling his disciples (and us) that He will send the Holy Spirit—"to guide us into all truth." So, it is appropriate to ask His Spirit to guide us in the war that we are caught up in.

A6 Ask the Lord to turn evil strategies to good purposes. *Lord Jesus Christ, Please make all interactions between anything from the kingdom of darkness and those of us under Your jurisdiction to work together to further Your kingdom.*	Matthew 6:13 And lead us not into temptation, but deliver us from the evil one.

This step—which puts all interactions (between the kingdom of darkness and us) in God's hands, so that He can work them together for good—is our request to "not let temptation overwhelm us" and to "deliver us from the evil one."

A7 Command that everything from the kingdom of darkness be bound. *I command, in the power and authority of the Lord Jesus Christ, that anything from the kingdom of darkness wanting any form of involvement with me/mine today, be (a) stripped of all your armor, now, and (b) able to carry out only the functions that God allows you to have to further His purposes.*	Luke 10:17–20 The seventy-two returned with joy and said, "Lord, even the demons submit to us in your name." He replied, "I saw Satan fall like lightning from heaven. I have given you authority to trample on snakes and scorpions and to overcome all the power of the enemy; nothing will harm you. However, do not rejoice that the spirits submit to you, but rejoice that your names are written in heaven."

In these verses, our Lord makes it clear that He saw Satan's original defeat and that He has given us authority to stop the schemes of the kingdom of darkness. This is the first of several commands in this system where we use that authority.

A8 Ask for a hedge of light and fire. Establishing this hedge of light and fire can be done as follows: a. Via prayer *Lord Jesus, I ask that You would place, now, a hedge of light and fire around and over and under [whatever places you specify] so that these environments become holy ground*	Zechariah 2:5 And I myself will be a wall of fire around it, declares the Lord, and I will be its glory within.

Continued

and those of us in these environments become encased in Your presence and holiness. I also ask that this hedge make a barrier that would keep everything from the kingdom of darkness outside and unable to come in or to see in or to hear in. I also ask that this hedge would trap everything from the kingdom of darkness that is already here inside—until they are dealt with by You. Lord Jesus, whether You provide this hedge or are this hedge, I thank You for that provision.

b. Via command (if you have equipment for wielding spiritual authority).

Lord Jesus, I take that sceptre of power and authority that You have given me, and by that means I draw a hedge of light and fire over, under, and around [whatever places you specify] so that these environments become holy ground and those of us in these environment (including the angels You want inside) become encased in Your presence and holiness. I also command that this hedge make a barrier that will keep everything from the kingdom of darkness outside and unable to come in or to see in or to hear in. I also command that this hedge trap everything from the kingdom of darkness that is already here inside—until they are dealt with by You. Lord Jesus, whether You provide this hedge or are this hedge, I thank You for that provision.

In Step A7 , we saw that all soldiers have been given authority by the Commander in Chief. Here, we see that that authority can be wielded in different ways.

A9 Optional prayers/commands (for when guests come into our secured environments).

Lord Jesus Christ, as these people come into my territory, I ask that you would do what is necessary to have them experience the good things that we experience in Your presence and protection. I also ask that they come under Your jurisdiction and—while here as my/our guest(s)—come under Your protection.

To that end, I use Your power and authority to establish the following:

a. Anything on them from the kingdom of darkness—as they come—be taken and kept outside the hedge of protection that surrounds this property, for as long as they are here

b. Anything in them from the kingdom of darkness be bound and stood aside from all functions, for as long as they are here

Lord Jesus, please send angels (and/or whatever else is needed) now to carry out these tasks.

This is an extension of Step A1

A10 Optional prayers/commands (for when you choose to "stand in the gap" for someone).
Lord Jesus Christ,
a. I thank You that You protect us.
b. I choose, starting now, to stand in the gap for [person's name], until [time/day]. Until that time, I ask that Your protection (of angels, armor, force fields, invisibility or whatever You want) be around and on both of us.
For [person's name], I ask, Lord Jesus, that nothing from the kingdom of darkness be able to touch [person]—physically, mentally, spiritually, emotionally—between now and then.
For myself, I command—in the power and authority of the Lord Jesus Christ—that anything from the kingdom of darkness trying to touch [person's name] in any way, discover that they must come through me to do so.

This step defines my understanding of "standing in the gap" and demonstrates another application of the authority that we have been given.

B1 Confession.
Ask for the Holy Spirit to reveal any sins or errors that would give the enemy a place to attack.
Holy Spirit, please reveal any sins or errors that I have made today, that I need to put under Jesus' blood.
[Briefly listen to what He says to you …]
Follow these steps to deal with anything that He brings to mind:
a. Lord Jesus, I confess to you …
b. I renounce and turn away from … now.
c. On the basis of Your promise to me (in 1 John 1:9), I receive Your forgiveness and cleansing … now.
d. Thank you, Jesus, that Your blood covers this sin.
e. (If necessary) I will take these steps … to promote reconciliation and/or restitution …

1 John 1:9
If we confess our sins, he is faithful and just and will forgive us our sins and purify us from all unrighteousness.

Sin in our life that isn't dealt with gives our enemy a target for his attack; confessing/renouncing/receiving is how we remove that target. And, if we walk in the light of God's forgiveness, "we will have fellowship with one another, and the blood of Jesus will keep on cleansing us …"

C₁ Revelations of evil.

1. Ask the Lord to reveal and deal with any curses, pacts, oaths, covenants, incantations, hexes, or vexes that have been placed upon me/mine and that need to be dealt with.

Lord Jesus, if there have been (or are) any curses or pacts or oaths or covenants or incantations or hexes or vexes put upon me/mine today,

a. I command in Your name and authority that they be made null and void—now.

b. I ask, Lord, that You would send angels (and/or whatever else is needed) to deal with them as You see fit. I put all such beings and/or strategies and/or structures in your hands to be dealt with now as You see fit.

c. I ask, Lord, that if I need to specify the source in order to make the enemy's strategy null and void, You would reveal that to me, now. [Briefly listen to what He says to you …]

1 John 2:20
But you have an anointing from the Holy One, and all of you know the truth.

This step has the following parts:

(a) command (based on the biblical principle discussed in Step A7) to nullify all kingdom of darkness strategies

(b) prayer (based on the biblical principle discussed in Step A1) to put all kingdom of darkness strategies in God's hands

(c) prayer (based on 1 John 2:20—which has resulted from our Lord sending His Spirit, as discussed in Step A5) to have God reveal whatever I need to know in order to do my part. This part isn't always required; follow it only if God's Spirit gives you information.

D₁ Command against intrusions.

I command, in the power and authority of the Lord Jesus Christ, that all opposing spiritual enemies and forces that try to intrude upon anyone or anything under His jurisdiction, be

(a) covered with the blood of the risen Lord Jesus Christ and

(b) surrounded by the light and fire of His holiness—now!

This step (based on the biblical principle discussed in Step A7) is designed to make my environment very repulsive to the forces of the kingdom of darkness.

D2 Ask for God's blessing.

Lord Jesus Christ, I thank You for all the blessings of salvation that You have made available to me/mine. I ask that all blessings that You want us to receive or claim today be applied to us, now. I also ask that Your blessings be upon everything from the kingdom of darkness that comes in contact with what has been put under Your jurisdiction (i.e. me/mine) so that those blessings will keep on canceling out all curses that may be coming from the kingdom of darkness today.

See Ephesians 1:3–14 for a list of these blessings.

Luke 6:28a:

"Bless those who curse you."

Romans 12:21:

"Do not be overcome by evil, but overcome evil with good."

The principle of "blessing those who curse us" makes sense at a psychological level (so that we don't get into a process of escalating negativity, of moving toward revenge. As we apply this principle, we are preventing a root of bitterness from growing in our life. Consequently, we are free to focus on "whatever is true … noble … right … pure … lovely … excellent …" and, so, experience joy and peace). I believe that it also makes sense at a spiritual level (where actual directed negative power is neutralized by actual directed positive power).

To those of you who may be saying to yourself, "I thought that curses were already nullified in Step C1, so why are we going through this, again?," I would mention that there are different kinds of curses. Some curses are like arrows (coming at one time; able to be stopped at one time). Other curses are like rivers (continuing to flow toward us, needing to be ongoingly continuously stopped). Step C1 is effective for dealing with "arrows"; this step is effective for dealing with "rivers."

D3 Command for isolation.

I command, in the power and authority of the Lord Jesus Christ, that anything from the kingdom of darkness trying to have any involvement with me/mine (a) be put into confusion, now, and (b) be separated now from all communication or connection you have with anything else from the kingdom of darkness—including all links, paths or channels on all levels in the kingdom of darkness hierarchy.

D4 Command for surrender.

I command, in the power and authority of the Lord Jesus Christ, that anything from the kingdom of darkness trying to have any involvement with me/mine

(a) surrender, now, to God's holy angels,

(b) be stripped, now, of all spiritual armor and unclean spirits,

(c) be stood aside from all functions, now, and

(d) be in submission to the binding of God's holy angels for God's specified time (starting now, if it is His will).

These steps (based on the biblical principle discussed in A7) have been separated because they serve two different purposes (isolating and surrendering). They can, however, be commanded as one step.

Requests of God.
E1 For Final clean up.
Lord Jesus, I ask that you would gather (or have gathered) all remaining enemies—individuals, groups, spirit hybrids, or whatever—and (a) strip them of all their armor, (b) bind them and stand them aside from all their functions, (c) deal with them, for today, as You see fit.

This step (based on the biblical principles discussed in A3, A6, and A7) includes steps that we learned while doing spiritual warfare. The final destination of our spiritual enemies is God's hands—to be dealt with as *He* sees fit.

In the context of our Lord washing His disciple's feet at their last supper together, Jesus and Peter interact around the issue of getting clean/staying clean. Although they are talking about the actual cleaning of body parts, there is another level of meaning being hinted at—which the disciples would understand later (v. 7). What they would come to understand was Jesus' teaching about cleansing from personal sin: that cleansing could only occur as a person received what Jesus was providing (v. 8); that once Jesus has cleansed a person, that person only needs to clean off (via confession to Jesus) the dirt/sin from his/her daily journey (v. 9–10). This step (in the system I use) is my attempt to extend the cleansing and restoration that our Lord offers to everyone and everything that I have put under His jurisdiction.

When I pray that "everyone that I've put under Your jurisdiction be filled with Your Spirit… and [receive] cleansing or healing …," I realize that, as a result of the choices of those people, that prayer may not be fulfilled. If that is the situation, I see that prayer as one that goes into the bowls in heaven (Rev. 5:8), where God collects them until the time is right for them to be poured out on/for those people.

E3 For revelation.
Lord Jesus Christ, as I wait upon you now (and throughout this day) and do my best to listen to your voice, please reveal any information that I need right now (or throughout this day) or any strategies that I need

right now (or throughout this day) that will enable me/mine to walk in your complete protection and in Your directed will.

[Briefly listen to what He says to you …]

This step (based on the biblical principle discussed in A5) is designed to focus my listening into the future (for the remainder of this day).

F1 Final Command
I establish, in the power and authority of the Lord Jesus Christ, that all prayers and commands given here and now, remain in effect until they are completely and totally obeyed and until everything from the kingdom of darkness is subjugated to the Lordship and direction of God the Father, the Son, and the Holy Spirit for this day.

This step (based on the biblical principle discussed in A7, is my attempt to "put the period at the end" of the prayer system.

In an attempt to answer questions that I have been asked about my prayer system, I have written a "commentary" on that system. If you are interested in getting a copy of that document, go to my website **www.drstanwillson.com** and download it. (There is no cost for obtaining that document.)

APPLICATION QUESTION

In light of what I have learned in this module, what would I add to my present spiritual protection game-plan? List those additions below:

a. _____

b. _____

c. _____

d. _____

e. _____

Appendix A

PASTOR DEL MCKENZIE'S APPLICATION PRAYER FROM JAMES 4:7

Father God, today I submit my will to You.
I offer my body to You as a living sacrifice.
I offer each part of my body to You to be used as an instrument of righteousness.
I submit to everything that comes from
Your Word, *Your* ways, *Your* will, *Your* wisdom, *Your* works,
And Your character.
I submit to Your holiness, *Your* purity, *and Your* righteousness.
I submit to everything that comes from You no matter how
Hard, unnatural, unnecessary, *or* unexplainable *it may be.*
I do this by faith in Jesus Christ.
Lord, remind me throughout this day that
Everything that You permit to come my way is because
You are more concerned about Your kingdom *and* my character,
Than about my comfort.
I set my will against and resist Satan *and*
Everything that he and his demons would bring against me today.
I resist sin, carnality, worldliness, demons, error, false teachers, death,
And all those who would seek to harm me in word or in deed.
Lord, I know that I am easily deceived and that
I am not smart enough *to always know what is* from You
And what is not from You *or* not of You.
I ask You, Jesus, to be my wisdom *so that* I can know
What is from You *and what is* not from You *or* not of You.
Lord, I know that I am not always strong enough *to* resist
What is not of You *and to* receive *what is* from You.

I ask You, Jesus, for Your strength to resist the devil *and everything that is* not of You,
And for Your grace to receive everything that is from You.
Holy Spirit, take away any desire for anything
That is not of You *and* is of me,
Because I want more of You and less of me.
Empty me of myself and fill me with You in all of Your fullness.
I ask these things in Your name, Jesus, believing that
You are who You say You are
And I am who You say I am
And I can do what You say I can do
Through the power of the Holy Spirit
Living within me.

Appendix B

MY PRAYER SYSTEM FOR PERSONAL PROTECTION

ESTABLISHING YOUR PROTECTION IN RELATION TO THE SPIRITUAL REALM

Introduction:

1. This is a prayer system—a sequence of prayer steps that leads to more comprehensive protection. It is important to be taking the *correct steps* in the *correct sequence* (like a telephone number).

2. This is to be done daily. The mercies of the Lord are renewed daily; the schemes of the evil one are renewed daily; our protection needs to be renewed daily… (Matt 6:13). (Everything in our Lord's prayer—including "Don't let temptation overwhelm us" and "Deliver us from the evil one"—is to be seen as a *daily* request.)

3. For some of you this may be familiar; for some of you this may be new. Look at this material to see if there is anything in it that would improve your protection game-plan. (Use this as a supplement to what you are already doing, if you like.)

4. This is the system I use. You'll notice that it involves both prayers (where we ask our Lord to supply us with His help) and commands (where we use the authority He gives us as believers to bind or loose things). Prayers can be done inside or outside your head; commands are best done out loud (but quietly) e.g. under your breath.

5. There is a bigger need to use this kind of system if you are in leadership or doing frontline ministry.

6. This system works as we appropriate it by faith. We don't, however, have faith in this "system"—but in the One who has promised to protect us if we do our part.

7. This is necessary preparation for doing listening prayer—since shutting down intrusion from the kingdom of darkness is a prerequisite to hearing from God. Protection is sometimes an end in itself; often it is a means to help us draw close to the Lord (James 4:7–8).

8. There appear to be redundancies in this prayer system. This system (which looks redundant) was developed from my experience of praying and commanding against the kingdom of darkness. I have learned that the impact of my prayers/commands is not instantaneous in the kingdom of darkness, so it is effective to give a command and (then) pray/command related details before going to the next step. By doing it this way, I am giving time for each command to fully impact opposing forces. As a consequence, the system seems repetitious.

Last Updated October, 2008

A. Establish spiritual boundaries that protect self/family/property.

1. Define what is "yours" (i.e. your property, possessions, people under your spiritual protection, your areas of spiritual authority).

    Lord Jesus Christ, I put the following (that You have given me) under Your jurisdiction, now...

    a. *My house and property*
    b. *My office*
    c. *My family [each person named specifically] and myself*
    d. *My vehicle*
    e. *My profession*
    f. *My ministries*
    g. *My pets*

    [Commentary: be clear about who and what you can take spiritual authority over and who and what you can't...]

2. Commit all on the list to God.

    Lord Jesus, I commit everything on this list to You. I give it into your care, now.

3. Ask God for angels to protect everything on the list from the kingdom of darkness.

    Lord Jesus, please send angels, now, to protect everything under your jurisdiction. I ask that You would send angels up to and including the principality and power levels (and beyond if necessary) to be around both these environments and people. I ask that You would commission and deploy and cover and reinforce and equip these angels so that nothing from the kingdom of darkness can intrude on us. Please enable these angels to remove any beings—individuals or groups—that are or will be astral traveling around us.

    Lord Jesus, if any reinforcements for the angels involved here are needed, please send them now; if any have been hurt, please have them taken care of.

    Lord Jesus, please provide a container—if needed—that will suck all beings from the kingdom of darkness into it (and hold them until removal), should their numbers quickly increase.

    Lord Jesus, thank You for this provision.

4. Ask for God's provisions.

    Lord Jesus, thank You for supplying me with Your armor. Please help me to put it on and use it; I receive these gifts by faith. Please guide my applications of Your armor so that I am protected today in a way that is good and sufficient.

5. Ask for sensitivity to the Holy Spirit.

   Holy Spirit, please quicken my mind so that I can be sensitive to what You want me to know or do today. I want to be in harmony with Your will for my life, today. Please enable me to hear Your voice clearly and in distinction to my own voice or those from the world or from the kingdom of darkness—so I can know your agenda for today (in order to do it).

6. Ask the Lord to turn evil strategies to good purposes.

   Lord Jesus Christ, please make all interactions between anything from the kingdom of darkness and those of us under Your jurisdiction to work together to further Your kingdom.

7. Command that everything from the kingdom of darkness be bound.

   I command, in the power and authority of the Lord Jesus Christ, that anything from the kingdom of darkness wanting any form of involvement with me/mine today

       a. You be stripped of all your armor, now

       b. You be able to carry out only the functions that God allows you to have to further His purposes.

8. Ask for a hedge of light and fire. Establishing this hedge of light and fire can be done as follows:

   a. Via prayer

   Lord Jesus, I ask that You would place, now, a hedge of light and fire around and over and under [whatever places you specify] so that these environments become holy ground and those of us in these environments become encased in Your presence and holiness. I also ask that this hedge make a barrier that would keep everything from the kingdom of darkness outside and unable to come in or to see in or to hear in. I also ask that this hedge would trap everything from the kingdom of darkness that is already here inside—until they are dealt with by You. Lord Jesus, whether You provide this hedge or are this hedge, I thank You for that provision.

   b. Via command (if you have equipment for wielding spiritual authority)

   Lord Jesus, I take that sceptre of power and authority that You have given me, and by that means I draw a hedge of light and fire over, under, and around [whatever places you specify] so that these environments become holy ground and those of us in these environments (including the angels You want inside) become encased in Your presence and holiness. I also command that this hedge make a barrier that will keep everything from the kingdom of darkness outside and unable to come in or to see in or to hear in. I also command that this hedge trap everything from the kingdom of darkness that is already here inside—until they are dealt with by You. Lord Jesus, whether You provide this hedge or are this hedge, I thank You for that provision.

9. Optional prayers/commands (for when guests come into our secured environments).

> *Lord Jesus Christ, as these people come into my territory, I ask that you would do what is necessary for the following:*
>
> > *a. To have them experience the good things that we experience in Your presence and protection*
> >
> > *b. To have them come under Your jurisdiction and—while here as my/our guest(s)—come under Your protection*
>
> *To that end, I use Your power and authority to establish the following:*
>
> > *a. Anything on them from the kingdom of darkness—as they come—be taken and kept outside the hedge of protection that surrounds this property, for as long as they are here*
> >
> > *b. Anything in them from the kingdom of darkness be bound and stood aside from all functions, for as long as they are here.*
>
> *Lord Jesus, please send angels (and/or whatever else is needed) now to carry out these tasks.*

10. Optional prayers/commands (for when you choose to "stand in the gap" for someone).

> *Lord Jesus Christ,*
>
> > *a. I thank You that You protect us…*
> >
> > *b. I choose, starting now, to stand in the gap for [person's name], until [time/day]. Until that time, I ask that Your protection (of angels, armor, force fields, invisibility or whatever You want) be around and on both of us.*
>
> *For [person's name], I ask, Lord Jesus, that nothing from the kingdom of darkness be able to touch [person]—physically, mentally, spiritually, emotionally—between now and then.*
>
> *For myself, I command—in the power and authority of the Lord Jesus Christ—that anything from the kingdom of darkness trying to touch [person's name] in any way, discover that they must come through me to do so.*

B. Confession.

1. Ask for the Holy Spirit to reveal any sins or errors that would give the enemy a place to attack.

> *Holy Spirit, please reveal any sins or errors that I have made today, that I need to put under Jesus' blood.*

[Briefly listen to what He says to you …]

Follow these steps to deal with anything that He brings to mind:

   a. Lord Jesus, I confess to you …

   b. I renounce and turn away from … now.

   c. On the basis of Your promise to me (in I John 1:9), I receive Your forgiveness and cleansing … now.

   d. Thank you, Jesus, that Your blood covers this sin.

   e. (if necessary) I will take these steps … to promote reconciliation and/or restitution …

C. Revelations of evil.

   1. Ask the Lord to reveal and deal with any curses, pacts, oaths, covenants, incantations, hexes, or vexes that have been placed upon me/mine and that need to be dealt with.

      Lord Jesus, if there have been (or are) any curses or pacts or oaths or covenants or incantations or hexes or vexes put upon me/mine today,

      a. I command in Your name and authority that they be made null and void—now.

      b. I ask, Lord, that You would send angels (and/or whatever else is needed) to deal with them as You see fit. I put all such beings and/or strategies and/or structures in Your hands to be dealt with now as You see fit.

      c. I ask, Lord, that if I need to specify the source in order to make the enemy's strategy null and void, You would reveal that to me, now.

   [Briefly listen to what He says to you …]

D. Clean up.

   1. Command against intrusions.

      I command, in the power and authority of the Lord Jesus Christ, that all opposing spiritual enemies and forces that try to intrude upon anyone or anything under Your jurisdiction:

      a. (You) be covered with the blood of the risen Lord Jesus Christ and

      b. (You) be surrounded by the light and fire of His holiness now!

   2. Ask for God's blessing.

      Lord Jesus Christ, I thank You for all the blessings of salvation that You have made available to me/mine. I ask that all blessings that You want us to receive or claim today be applied to us, now. I also ask that Your blessings be upon everything from the kingdom of darkness that comes in contact with what has been put

under Your jurisdiction (i.e. me/mine) so that those blessings will keep on cancel-
ing out all curses that may be coming from the kingdom of darkness today.

3. Command for isolation.

I command, in the power and authority of the Lord Jesus Christ, that anything
from the kingdom of darkness trying to have any involvement with me/mine:

   a. *(You) be put into confusion, now.*

   b. *(You) be separated now from all communication or connection you*
   have with anything else from the kingdom of darkness—including all
   links, lines, paths, or channels on all levels in the kingdom of darkness
   hierarchy.

4. Command for surrender.

I command, in the power and authority of the Lord Jesus Christ, that anything
from the kingdom of darkness trying to have any involvement with me/mine:

   a. *(You) surrender, now, to God's holy angels.*

   b. *(You) be stripped, now, of all spiritual armor and unclean spirits.*

   c. *(You) be stood aside from all functions, now.*

   d. *(You) be in submission to the binding of God's holy angels for God's speci-*
   fied time (starting now, if it is His will).

E. Requests of God.

1. For final clean up.

Lord Jesus, I ask that you would gather (or have gathered) all remaining en-
emies—individuals, groups, spirit hybrids, or whatever.

   a. *Please strip them of all their armor.*

   b. *Please bind them and stand them aside from all their functions.*

   c. *Please deal with them, for today, as You see fit.*

2. For reclaiming.

Lord Jesus, I ask that You would reclaim, clean, and fill everything under Your
jurisdiction with Your Holy Spirit and with the structures of the kingdom of light.
I ask that everyone I've put under Your jurisdiction be filled with Your Spirit and,
if any cleansing or healing needs to be done, You would do that. I ask that all con-
nections between those of us under Your jurisdiction be established by Your struc-
tures and strategies and that these structures be clean and filled with Your light.
I ask that if any damage has been done to Your structures or Your property, You
would repair and protect them. I ask that such restoration be done now—unless
Your timing is different.

3. For revelation.

>   *Lord Jesus Christ, as I wait upon You now (and throughout this day) and do my best to listen to Your voice, please reveal any information that I need right now (or throughout this day) or any strategies that I need right now (or throughout this day) that will enable me/mine to walk in Your complete protection and in Your directed will.*

[Briefly listen to what He says to you …]

F. Final command.

>   *I command, in the power and authority of the Lord Jesus Christ, that all prayers and commands given here and now remain in effect until they are completely and totally obeyed and until everything from the kingdom of darkness is subjugated to the Lordship and direction of God the Father, the Son, and the Holy Spirit for this day.*

ENDNOTES

1 White, Thomas, B., *Spiritual Warfare Bootcamp: Basic Training.*

2 McKenzie, Del, "Handout from a sermon given in 2006."

3 Sire, James, W., *The Universe Next Door*, Downers Grove, Illinois: Inter-Varsity Press, 1976.

4 Neill, Stephen, *Christian Faith and Other Faiths*, Downers Grove, Illinois: Inter-Varsity Press, 1984.

5 Lloyd-Johnes, D. M., *The Christian Soldier*, Grand Rapids, Michigan: Baker Book House, 1977, p. 275.

6 Lloyd-Jones, D. M., *The Christian Soldier*, Grand Rapids, Michigan: Baker Book House, 1977, p. 287.

7 Boyd, G. A., *God at War*, Downers Grove, Illinois: Inter-Varsity Press, 1997.

8 Wagner, C. Peter, *Praying With Power*, Ventura, California: Regal Books, 1997.

9 Wagner, C. Peter, *Warfare Prayer*, Ventura, California: Regal Books, 1992.

10 Wagner, C. Peter, *Prayer Shield*, Ventura, California: Regal Books, 1992.

11 Wagner, C. Peter, *Breaking Strongholds in Your City*, Ventura, California: Regal Books, 1993.

12 Wagner, C. Peter, *Confronting the Powers*, Ventura, California: Regal Books, 1991.

13 Tzu, Sun, *The Art of War*, Boston, Massachusetts: Shambhala Publications, 1988.

14 Lloyd-Jones, D. M., *The Christian Soldier*, Grand Rapids, Michigan: Baker Book House, 1977, p. 305.

15 Bateman, Lana, *Bible Promises for the Healing Journey*, Westwood, New Jersey: Barbour Books, 1991.

16 Max Lucado, *God's Promises for You: Scripture Sections*, Nashville, Tennessee: Thomas Nelson, 2006.

17 Max Lucado, *God's Inspirational Promise Book*, Waco, Texas: Word Books, 1996.

18 David Wilkerson, *Promises to Live By: The Pocket Promise Book*, New York: Gospel Light Publications, 1999

Module II

PAYING ATTENTION TO THE HOLY SPIRIT'S INPUT

[When] I go, I will send the Counselor [the Holy Spirit]
to you … when He, the Spirit of truth, comes, He will guide you
into all truth [about how to run your race].

—my adaptation of John 16:7, 13

INTRODUCTION

As we run our marathon, the Holy Spirit (who is Emmanuel to us, now) will lead us, strengthen us, and comfort us in this race. Is this orthodox theology? Many of you reading that first sentence are able to give the scriptural support for each assertion. Is this your daily experience? Since this question can be answered in the negative, we are facing a crucial distinction—between cognitive knowledge and experiential knowledge. Cognitive knowledge is necessary for progress to be made in any endeavor. But experiential knowledge (where truth is *done*, not just known) is necessary *and* sufficient. A believer's spiritual life involves knowing certain things (for example, Jesus Christ, God's only Son, died for our sins …, and has sent His Holy Spirit to have a relationship with us), but, if that person's spiritual life is alive, it will also involve experiential knowledge (for example, the Spirit Himself testifying with our spirit that we are God's children). Since Jesus came to make a way for us to have a relationship with Him, we will be experiencing that relationship (if it is alive). As with any relationship, our knowledge must include the experiential or we will only know *about* the other person rather than knowing him/her. If our spiritual life doesn't involve the experiential, it is deficient (if not dead). As in any relationship, it is the responsibility of both parties to promote life and growth; by ourself, we can't make life and growth happen, but it is essential that we do our part. ("A relationship is like an airplane— it takes two wings for it to fly ….")

The rest of this module outlines what I have learned about promoting a living relationship with the Holy Spirit. This is how I do my part. (This is what I actually do, not what I should do; this is what I really do, not what I "ideally" do). I talk about my part as it relates to (1) what I do in the morning, (2) what I do as I study the Scriptures, (3) what I do as I pray/listen/journal, (4) what I do as I interact with people throughout the day, and (5) what I do when I get tired. As I do my part, God—in His ongoing kindness and initiative to me— supplies me with direction and power and encouragement for the "race that is set before me" (Heb. 12:1). The apostle Paul said, about the race that had been set before him, "I have fought the good fight, I have finished the race, I have kept the faith" (2 Tim. 4:7). One factor that enabled him to accomplish that victory was his personal application of what he said to the Galatians, "Since we live by the Spirit, let us keep in step with the Spirit" (Gal. 5:25).

As you read and evaluate what I do to keep in step with the Spirit, I'd suggest that you ask the Holy Spirit to show you what your next step(s) need to be (including any application of something that I am doing).

The *first activity in my day* that begins to orient me toward paying attention to the Holy Spirit's input is the prayer I make as I am driving to work in the morning. Now, I can imagine readers of this page saying, "What! Are you saying that you haven't done your morning devotions?!" So before I lose all spiritual credibility, let me say, "Yes, that is what I am saying—but with this explanation." In order to design—into our lives—programs that we will be able to maintain (and, in this application, will keep us open to the Spirit's input), such programs need to fit us. For example, if you were going to run a marathon, you would want your shoes to fit you. Since I am a person who can't both walk and chew gum in the morning, I have designed my programs to help ease me into the day. I do my spiritual disciplines at times during the day when I am more functional. (Yes, there are people who— as a result of inherited biorhythm patterns—fall into the categories of "lark" and "owl"). However, I came into God's family in an era when family members were asking converts to "fit the programs" rather than helping those converts to find the programs that fit them. Here is instruction (from that era) that prescribes when I should pray:

> In the first chapter of Mark, verse 35, we read, "And *in the morning*, rising up *a great while before the day*, he went out, and departed into a solitary place, and there prayed."
> *Jesus chose the early morning hour for prayer.* Many of the mightiest men of God have followed the Lord's example in this. In the morning hour the mind is fresh and at its very best. It is free from distraction, and that absolute concentration upon God which is essential to the most effective prayer is most easily possible in the early morning hours … More can be accomplished in prayer in the first hours of the day than at any other time during the day. Every child of God who would make the most out of his life for Christ should set apart the first part of the day to meeting God in the study of His Word and in prayer. The first thing we do each day should be to go alone with God and face the duties, the temptations, and the service of that day, and get strength from God for all. We should get victory before the hour of trial, temptation, or service comes.[1]

Such instruction (and many like it) has provided me with wonderful opportunities to discover what doesn't work for me (and to discover how to handle my experience of guilt when my best efforts were unsuccessful). It also provided me with years of practice at re-programming my applications of the basic spiritual disciplines. If you want to avoid that "journey" ("dead end" may be a better term), I'd suggest that you discover and implement spiritual discipline applications that meet the criterion of "what works for you." As you may remember, the Pharisees had confused whether the Sabbath was made for mankind or whether mankind was made for the Sabbath (Mark 2:23–28). I'd suggest that you not live with the same confusion (of thinking that you must fit someone else's applications of the spiritual disciplines rather than designing applications that fit you).

Now, if you are a reader who hadn't asked the (above) question about my spiritual credibility, and so have skipped the (above) explanation, here is where you pick up on my "driving to work" activity. It takes me twenty minutes to drive to work. I consider that a "gift of time" and an opportunity to invite—into this new day—the involvement of God's Spirit. To those of you who may have the suspicion that God has Alzheimer's disease (in other words, He keeps forgetting what He should be doing and needs our daily reminders), I'd respond by saying that the mercies of the Lord are renewed every day. The schemes of the evil one are renewed daily; the categories of the prayer that our Lord taught his disciples (us included) are to be requested daily (see Matthew 6:5–12). My invitation for Him to draw close to me (which is contained in my morning prayer) is to be done daily. Otherwise, I may forget that the Christian life is (essentially) about developing a living and growing relationship with God and that this pursuit requires me to do my part—daily. Therefore, much of my prayer is addressed to the Holy Spirit, who is God with me. (The content of this prayer is found in appendix A). Foundational to that prayer is the request, "Holy Spirit, please come and fill me now; I invite you to do so now." Am I afraid that He may have drained out overnight? No, this asking is my attempt to obey a command that enables me to keep in step with the Spirit. The command I am referring to is found in Ephesians 5:18—"Be filled with the Spirit." An expanded rendering (from the Greek) of this command (to all believers) is "… Keep on letting yourself be filled (with the Spirit)." Implied here is that we cannot fill ourselves (so we ask Him and give Him permission to fill us) and that His filling is to be ongoing, not once and for all time (so we ask daily…). About this command, John Stott says,

> " … Ephesians 5:18 contains the well known command to all Christian people to be filled, that is, to go on being filled (a continuous present imperative) with the Spirit.[2]

Since I am a cognitively oriented person who has been trained in the naturalism, rationalism, and materialism of North American culture, I must take a number of antidotes daily in order to avoid succumbing to the poison of "leaning on my own understanding." This is particularly important when I interact with Scripture. So, when I *read and study Scripture* (at some time during the day when I am alert), I take steps to pay attention to the Holy Spirit's voice.

Most people reading this probably agree that Bible study is an obvious time to hear from Him. (He wrote the Scriptures through humans … He lives in us … He wants to communicate with us … He wants to develop a "family-likeness" in us … He wants to use "His word to us" to promote that—you know the theology.) Most readers probably also know that the Pharisees, who were the "doctors of theology" in Jesus' day (and who knew the Scriptures better than anyone of that time), didn't recognize the Messiah when He did walk through their soup. So, a person can know the Scriptures without that knowledge helping to grow his/her relationship with God. So, in order to make my study of Scripture a personal (not impersonal) event, I do the following:

- I invite the Holy Spirit to speak to me. I do this by claiming a promise, found in Revelation 3:20, where He says to me, "Here I am! I stand at the door and knock. If anyone hears my voice and opens the door, I will come in and eat with him and he with me." In response, I say "Spirit of Jesus, please come into this time (of study) and make Your written word a living word to me. Please give me ears to hear and eyes to see what You want to say to me and to show me, now." This *prayer* is the context within which I approach the text.

- Having invited Him to come, I anticipate and look for His coming. I do this by noticing—as I read the text—what begins to "stand out" to me or to "grab my interest." To me, that signals His arrival; it also signals what I should pay attention to. In other words, I should get interested where He is directing my attention.

- Sometimes, to help me get in focus what He wants to show me, I read the text over—repeatedly and carefully. As I do this, I notice a "dropping down" to a deeper level of connection with the text: I notice details in the text that I didn't notice before; I notice connections within the text that I didn't notice before; I notice implications from the text that are new to me. To me, these are indications of His involvement with me and of His leading me into His truth for me. Now, Scripture study is a living and interactive event.

- Sometimes it is helpful to put myself into the text: to visualize the situation, to listen between the lines, to feel the impact of the words. As I move from "spectator of the text" to "participant with the text," the Holy Spirit meets me and underlines what He wants me to know and do.

Since I have made a commitment to not be a "studier" only, but also a "doer" of His word, I work to capture and apply what I have been given. An essential capturing tool for me is *journaling*. Since Scripture reading and study is an interactive event for me, I use journaling (the writing down of these interactions) in various ways:

- I write down what I have learned or have been directed to do, as a result of my study.

- I write down my prayers of response to what I have been given. ("Thanks!" … "I'm sorry; please forgive me …," "You are amazing!" … "I never saw that before," "From now on, I commit myself to …," "Please work this into my life …," "I claim this gift …," "Would You please take this initiative …"). Today, as I was studying Psalm 106 (I try to digest—along with my lunch—a Psalm), I noticed that it was a catalogue of the ways that "we have sinned, even as our fathers did" (v. 6). Now, I am recording the ways that the children of Israel sinned in Egypt, while leaving Egypt, while in the desert and after getting into the promised land. Soon, I will journal a prayer in relation to each kind of sin, asking the Lord to help me avoid it. Already, I am gaining a deeper understanding of and appreciation of His great patience and love for me (v. 45).

- I write down what He says to me as I *listen* to Him. When I entered God's family, I was told that "God speaks to you through the Scriptures, you speak to God through prayer …." I've come to learn that God speaks to me in many ways (if I have ears to hear), some of which are as immediate and personal as what He says to me *about* the Scriptures. When Jesus talked about His sheep hearing (and knowing) His voice (John 10:1–21), that is to be our experience. Consequently, I have been learning to listen to Him and to distinguish His voice from others (including my "teachers," my own, and those from the kingdom of darkness). When I hear from Him, I find it crucial to write that input down—so that I can clarify it, assess it, and apply it. (Gordon MacDonald was a knowledgeable tour guide during my trip to Journal-land; his book, *Ordering Your Private World* contains a detailed roadmap.[3])

Here is how I set up—both my environment and myself—to listen to Him:

- I do my part to protect my environment from intrusion by the kingdom of darkness. Learning to listen, for me, has involved learning how to eliminate (as much as possible) all input sources that compete with the Holy Spirit to be heard inside me. Since I know that one of the "schemes of the evil one" (Eph. 6:11) is to deceive me by masquerading as "an angel of light" (2 Cor. 11:14), I know that scheme will include talking like an angel of light. Such talk is the "good cop" complement to the "bad cop" intrusion that Scripture calls "the flaming arrows of the evil one" (Eph. 6:16). I "gate out" such talk by ensuring that the environment around me— as I listen—is protected from demonic input. (Ensuring that my *internal* environment is also clean is another important issue, but one beyond the scope of this book). The prayers/commands that I use to protect my environment are found in appendix B of module I.

- (As I did in the context of Bible study), I invite Jesus to come and speak to me. I find it encouraging to remember that He is standing at my door and knocking (taking an initiative toward me). Apparently He is also talking—and expecting me to hear Him—since He says, "If anyone *hears my voice* and opens the door …." When I open the door and invite Him into this situation ("… please come in"), I can also expect to be spoken to—since He continues " … I will come in and eat with him …" (which is the context for dialogue). In this context, I expect God's input to me to be auditory—like thought impressions. I have also experienced His messages visually (where a picture is given to my mind's eye) and/or kinesthetically (where He gives me a sense of His message). *How* we experience His input to us will differ from person to person and from situation to situation. My part in this dialogue is to remain open to whatever way(s) He uses to relate and to ask for eyes to see, ears to hear, and a heart to do whatever He reveals to me. Since my lead input system is visual, I often receive His messages in picture form (sometimes "still" pictures, sometimes "movies"). In order to distinguish between images that I generate (*my* input to me) and those images that I receive from Him (*His* input to me), I need to distinguish between generative visualization and receptive visualization. When I *generate* a visual image—as I just did, of a green elephant in my waiting room—there is an active and intentional and directed quality to that process. When I *receive* a visual image—as I sometimes do when listening to God—there is an unbidden and (often) a surprising quality to that experience. What I see "comes to me" and isn't what I would have expected to see. When we can make such distinctions, we are less likely to be confused about the source of that input (and, so, have a better sense of what is from Him).
- I ask high-quality questions, to help me tune in to His input. These questions are asked for "product" reasons (the responses I get) *and* for "process" reasons (the way the responses come). Such questions orient me toward and tune me in to His response (like a scanner on a radio orients it to the message from the station). My initial question is:
    - "Lord Jesus Christ, will you speak to me about … , now?"

      If the answer is "no," I ask if His answer has anything to do with me. (For example, I ask, "Lord, is there anything that you want me to do before You speak to me?" If there is, I obey His instructions; if there isn't, I take that issue [for now] off the discussion table.) If His answer is "yes," I say something like, "Thank you for speaking to me … Your servant is listening—as well as I can …"

- Next, I ask "Lord, what do you want to say to me about … now?" Then, as He speaks, I journal what I am seeing/hearing/sensing.
- If I get "off station" or hear something that concerns me or see something that doesn't "feel" right, I ask Jesus, "Lord, is what I just received from You?"
  If the answer is "no," I disregard what I have heard while "off station"; then I go back to the first question. If the answer is "yes," I carry on with the journaling.

(These are the mechanics of "living by faith.")

Consequently, I have a written record of what I have heard Him say to me. In order to increase the accuracy of that record, I (1) listen within a protected environment (in order to gate out input from the kingdom of darkness); (2) put myself in receiving mode, confess any sin I am aware of, and state my willingness to obey what I receive (in order to gate out input from myself); and (3) subject everything I hear/see/sense to the authority of biblical truth—as both my reason and the Holy Spirit informs me (in order to gate out input from my "teachers": my family of origin, my culture, and my education). As a result of such steps, do I claim infallibility? As fallen beings in a fallen world, it is utopian to believe that infallibility during this process is attainable. Communication between any two beings (except within the members of the Godhead) will be less than perfect—but it can be substantially accurate. The rationale for these "gating out" procedures is the same as the rationale for "active listening" and "perception checking" procedures—to increase the accuracy of understanding in person-to-person communication. Although God communicates perfectly to me, I may not hear Him accurately (I do not have the immaculate perception). I may not interpret His message accurately (my own biases may skew the data), and I may not apply—even if I have heard and interpreted correctly—that message accurately. (I may use that data to build my own kingdom, not His.) Having said this, I (and anyone else with perfectionistic tendencies) must resist the temptation to throw up my hands and say, "If I can't have certainty about what God is saying to me, it is too risky to hear from Him at all." (If you took that position with your family members, how many of those relationships would you be able to sustain?) Instead, I need to say, "I will do all I know how to do in order to increase my ability to hear Him accurately and I will trust that He—who ongoingly takes relational initiatives toward me—will confirm what I have heard accurately and will correct what I have not heard accurately." The just shall communicate by faith. The confidence I have that I am keeping in step with Him is not rooted in the certainty that I have heard/interpreted/applied His input to me accurately. It is rooted in my certainty that He will hold my hand—as I commit myself to walk with Him—and will say to me, "This is the way, walk in it (Isaiah 30:21) … This is not the way, don't walk in it." (This modus ope-randi is in stark contrast to that of the Pharisees and teachers of the law, who asked Jesus to provide them with a miraculous sign that would make them believe—no faith required). As any of us know, who have walked (or stumbled or crawled) with Him for awhile, He shares His way with us in various ways: by speaking to us, by dreams, by intuitive experi-ence, by scriptural content, by fellow travelers (and opponents), by open (and closed) doors of circumstance, by trials, by visions, by angels. He is big and creative; He has unique and tailor-made means of communicating with each of us—no matter how blind or deaf or in-sensitive we may be.

On my journey of relationship growth with Him, doing my part includes fine-tuning my listening skills (but not, finally, relying on them) and learning to "come near to God (so) He will come near to me" (James 4:8a). This developing walk requires ongoing talk—as in any relationship. If I am walking close to Him, then I cannot run ahead of Him—in presumption—assuming that every voice I hear is from Him (and so no confirmation or disconfirmation of those voices is required). Nor can I lag behind Him—in unbelief—sub-jecting every voice to proof requirements that call into question the validity of any voice.

In my profession (as a psychologist) it is crucial that I pay attention to the Holy Spirit's input *as I interact with people throughout the day.* Many of my clients want more than a con-structive relationship ("therapeutic alliance") and competence in my approaches to helping them change, they also want to get a sense of direction in their journey toward Him. When, many years ago, I read Brother Lawrence talking about how he was able to practice the presence of God in the middle of multiple (kitchen) demands, it was simply impossible for me to apply that concept. Looking back, however, I believe that my reading planted a seed in me and, although it didn't germinate for many years, it is now (thanks to the One who brings about the increase) growing. (A valuable prayer for spiritual marathoners to make is that, when the time is right, God will germinate in us the seeds that will equip us to be sensitive servants in His kingdom and that we—as part of our spiritual act of worship—will water them.) The essence of how I pay attention during my work with clients is found in the concept of "participant-spectator." As *I participate* with them (actively listening, noticing non-verbals, perception checking, sensing feelings, clarifying goals, suggesting strategies and using other tools of my trade), I also listen with my "third ear" for movements in "the Force." By this, I mean that I am also a *spectator* in this process, noticing what comes from Him during the flow of the therapeutic conversation. As I have mentioned, there are times to directly talk to Him and listen to Him, but this is not one of them. This is a time to let Him take the initiative toward me: to give a pivotal impression or idea, to give a sense of rightness to a conversational direction, to give a sense of confirmation to what was just said, to reveal—by a reaction from the kingdom of darkness—a stronghold that will need to be dealt with, to indicate—by a sense of His arriving Presence—that the time for a next step has come. I have asked for eyes to see and ears to hear what He is doing; now, my part is to get in step with His initiative (message to self: get with the program). For some therapists this will be evidence of my pathology; for me, this is evidence that God rewards those who earnestly seek Him and who invite Him into their lives.

There are days, as I run the multi-demand marathon, when *I run out of gas*, when the demands (some scheduled, some by surprise) exceed my resources. At these times, like a boat that has been overloaded, I experience a "sinking" feeling. I used to interpret that feeling as an indication that I wasn't trusting God to the place where I could draw on His strength. In those days, any time for personal recuperation included feelings of embarrassment and a turning away from God (whom I thought was less than pleased with me). As my relationship with Him has matured, and I have come to understand that He is "for me and not against me" (Romans 8:31), in contrast to some people, I have come to take my "time outs" *with* Him, rather than *from* Him. I have come to trust Him—who said, "Come unto me, all you who are weary and burdened, and I will give you rest" (Matthew 11:28)—enough to come to Him. As in most circumstances of my life, I follow a game-plan. Here is my game-plan for entering into His rest, for finding Him who is an oasis in the desert of demands.

- I make sure that I am in a protected environment. (Usually, this is accomplished by going through the prayer sequence found in appendix B of module I.) If I am needing to rest in an environment where I do not have authority, my first step is to establish authority (by including—in A1 of that prayer system—the part of that environment that surrounds me). Then, in order to establish protection, I pray A2 and A3 of that system. An example of this kind of circumstance is when I stay in a hotel; I establish authority (then protection) over the room I rented, but not over the entire building. Sometimes I need to rest in an environment where I have no positional authority—like in a university where I have no office. In that circumstance, I ask God to supply me with an angelic bodyguard so that, while there, I have that kind of protection. As you might infer, I don't rest until I am in a safe place.
- I relax. Years ago, I learned a relaxation training procedure that equipped me to relax on demand. Because I have practiced this skill for many years, I can reach a state of deep physical relaxation within a few seconds. As I "drop down" to that place of relaxation, it also helps to center me and to shift my focus from the external world to the internal world.

- I invite the Lord Jesus Christ to come. This is always a crucial step because it demonstrates that I—who can choose—am choosing to make contact with Him. For me, the first indication of His Presence is warmth—I feel warmth (like a gentle heat source) on the part of my face which is toward Him. When He comes into my presence, He will operate differently: sometimes He stands at the door, sometimes He sits in a chair, sometimes He comes close in front of me, and sometimes He comes close behind me. As was the case when He appeared to the disciples, He is not confined to space and time the way I am. It is possible that the Lord—in his generosity to me—has come in these different ways so that I could learn to pay attention to Him. When I am able to feel where He is, I am able to orient myself toward Him and to focus on what He wants me to "know, do, experience or receive." (My prayer, at this time, is "Lord, help me to hear/see/sense and obey what You want me to know, do, experience, or receive.")

- I also talk to Him—about what I am thinking or feeling, about what I need, about what I am struggling with. The content of my sharing is similar to what I hear from my clients—who come to me for clarification or comfort or information or planning. Sometimes, after my sessions with these people, I simply put them in His hands, since their burdens feel like loads that I can't carry alone. He is the Counselor that I go to. I remember one time (years ago, now) when I came to Him— I was weary to the point of exhaustion, discouraged about what I had been hearing and how I had been responding, concerned about not having my "ducks in order" as I came to Him and worried about what He might say to me or ask of me …

- I listen for His response. On that (years ago) occasion, I had come to Him with trepidation because—at that time—I did not have substantial experience in coming to Him personally. I felt vulnerable to Him, knowing that He could ask me to sacrifice what was most precious to me and that He had every right to ask for such sacrifice. I was not at all sure that I could (or would) obey His request. What had intensified my fear was my experience with the church (the "powers that be" within that community. In my experience, this church had been as harsh taskmasters—as were the Egyptians when the children of Israel were slaves in Egypt. Both had demanded "more bricks … with less straw"). Consequently, I was anxious—I knew that another task could be required of me. I also knew that I had nothing left to give. As I sensed Him coming closer—in response to my sharing with Him of my weariness and discouragement and frustration and fear—all I remember were His words to me: "just rest." (I may never hear sweeter words on this side of heaven). That time of "stepping into the Jordan," as risky as it felt, was what took me out of the desert of demands and into the promised land of His Presence and His provision.

As is obvious by now, I consider paying attention to the Holy Spirit's input to be crucial in my running (and finishing) the multi-demand marathon. Now, I am asking myself, "what can I say that you might find helpful, if you are—or are interested in becoming—a fellow runner?" Well, I can refer you to the experienced runners who helped me. Richard Foster's books are profound; a delightful introduction to this skill set is outlined in his booklet *Meditative Prayer.*[4] Dallas Willard wrote a book—now entitled *Hearing God*[5]— that gave me a mental feast. When he shared how he listened to God, he also gave me courage to put knowing into doing. Another coach was Joyce Huggett, who shared her listening instruction in *The Joy of Listening to God.*[6] I can also refer you to the one who said, "Since we live by the Spirit, let us keep in step with the Spirit" (Galatians 5:25). Paul was a world-class listener and "marathoner"—maybe the best there has ever been. (And, if you doubt that he had multiple demands to contend with, read 2 Corinthians 11:16-33.) In 2 Corinthians 12 (where he was "boasting" to the immature believers in Corinth so that they would not see him as inferior to the "super-apostles" who had been discrediting Him), we get a look at Paul listening and (so) keeping in step with the Spirit. This chapter begins with Paul recounting visions and revelations that he had received from the Lord. (To me, such experience demonstrates that the Spirit can and does interact with us; He is there to be talked—and walked—with.) He had been taken up to the third heaven and had heard things that convinced him of the reality of that world. As a consequence of that visit, a nasty experience started and continued—a demonic entity began to harass Paul physically ("a thorn in the flesh"). When I was in Bible college, I was told that his "thorn" was related to his eyesight. Although I am not sure if a result of the attack had impacted his eyes, I do know that the source of that attack was spiritual ("a messenger from Satan") and that it was painful ("to torment me"). Paul already knew that keeping in step with the Spirit could lead to painful experiences, but he—like many of us—didn't think that such experiences should happen—especially since he was close to God. (After all, hadn't he just been to the third heaven?) Since Paul assumed that his pain was to be avoided, he did what people who are in a relationship do—communicate. He prayed to his Lord intensely (" … I plead") and repeatedly (" … three times") to have this harassment taken away. And God's response (as so often has been the case in my experience) upends Paul's expectations. Instead of granting Paul's prayers, God gave him a new perspective on the experience (saying in effect, "I won't take this experience away, but I will empower you to live with it") and a reason to endure the experience (saying in effect, "You need this experience in order to prevent you from becoming conceited—because of the revelations that I gave you; I want others to see a strength in you that is supernatural when you are facing hardships like this one). When Paul received this revelation, he immediately changed his game-plan from pleading to have the "thorn removed" to "boasting … gladly about my weaknesses so that Christ's power may rest on me." So, keeping in step with the Spirit involves communication (even if what we are asking for is not what God wants) and sustained communication until a response comes (which, obviously in this situation, was not immediate). When God's response does come, it also means getting with His program for us (rather than trying to get Him to rubberstamp our program) and—as was so characteristic of Paul—coming to delight in doing God's will. ("That is why, for Christ's sake, I delight in weaknesses, in insults, in hardships, in persecutions, in difficulties.")

May God give us eyes to see and ears to hear what He is doing and a heart to do His will. Without those gifts, we could be keeping pharisaism (a form of religiosity that does not keep in step with Him but which exploits His reality) alive and well in this generation.

NEXT STEP

Earlier, I suggested that you ask the Holy Spirit to show you a "next step" on your journey of deepening your sensitivity to Him. Now, I'd suggest that you prepare for and take that next step—by selecting an activity or a skill development exercise and writing out your application game-plan (including when, where, and how you will apply that step). Also include who (live, on paper, or on-line) you will recruit to help you make that application.

Appendix A

MY MORNING PRAYER

Thank You God, that You love me and care for me.

Thank You that Your love and care takes practical form so that I can ask again today for Your protection over me and mine, according to Your love and mercy, power and will.

Thank You as well, Lord Jesus, that You have sent Your Spirit. *Holy Spirit, please come and fill me now; I invite You to do so now.* With Your fullness, may I also know Your wisdom and direction, Your discernment and strength today.

Holy Spirit, I don't want to quench or grieve or resist You today, but I do want to keep in step with You. As I do that, I pray that I will abide and be fruitful. I pray that You will lead me into the truth. I pray that I will get to know You better and get to know how You input to me so that I will have rapport with You today.

Holy Spirit, I pray for Your pure, gentle wisdom––Your wisdom, which will enable me to deal with whatever circumstances that I face today. Enable me to deal with them in a way that is biblical, efficient, effective, and loving—whether these circumstances pertain to the kingdom of light or the kingdom of darkness, to Yourself, God, or to myself, to family or friends, or to clients or colleagues.

Holy Spirit, I don't want to just be surviving circumstances today but also to be thriving. I want to be growing and changing my internal programming so that I am becoming the kind of person that You created me to be (and want me to be) and the kind of person that I want to be.

Holy Spirit, as I both survive and thrive today, I ask for your help—at both a mind and a heart level. In my mind, I ask for Your insights: I ask for Your leading and guidance. I ask for Your encouragement. At a heart level, I ask for Your compassion and passion. I ask for these gifts so that I am better equipped to both know and do Your will. Please help me—as I survive and thrive—to do both in cooperation and coordination with You, and to consort with You (and, by so doing, please You).

Holy Spirit, I also pray for Your intuitive/implicit/unconscious leading, as well as Your explicit/cognitive/conscious leading in my life today. Consequently, I will know Your leading—both outside and inside consciousness. May I end up being where You want me to be, doing what You want me to do.

I pray that your direction *in* my life today will produce meaning and purpose, challenge and growth, focus and adventure. I pray that Your direction *through* my life today will produce relationships that are characterized by rapport, grace, growth, and encouragement.

I pray that Your discernment in my life today will produce a deepening of our I-Thou relationship. I pray that Your discernment *through* my life today will produce edification for all involved—myself included.

Holy Spirit, I pray for Your empowerment. I pray that Your strength, stamina, energy, endurance, and enthusiasm will be my experience today so that the quality and quantity of what I do today will be high and will be pleasing to You.

Lord Jesus, I pledge allegiance to You, now. May my life today—both outside and inside—reflect that allegiance.

ENDNOTES

[1] Torrey, R.A., *How to Pray*, Chicago: Moody Press, p. 89–90.

[2] Stott, John R.W., *Baptism and Fullness*, London: Inter-Varsity Press, 1964, p. 50.

[3] MacDonald, G., *Ordering Your Private World*, Nashville: Oliver-Nelson, 1985.

[4] Foster, R., *Meditative Prayer*, Downers Grove, Illinois: Inter-Varsity Press, 1983.

[5] Willard, D., *Hearing God*, Madison, Wisconsin: Inter-Varsity Press, 1999.

[6] Hugget, J., *The Joy of Listening to God*, Downers Grove, Illinois: Inter-Varsity Press, 1990.

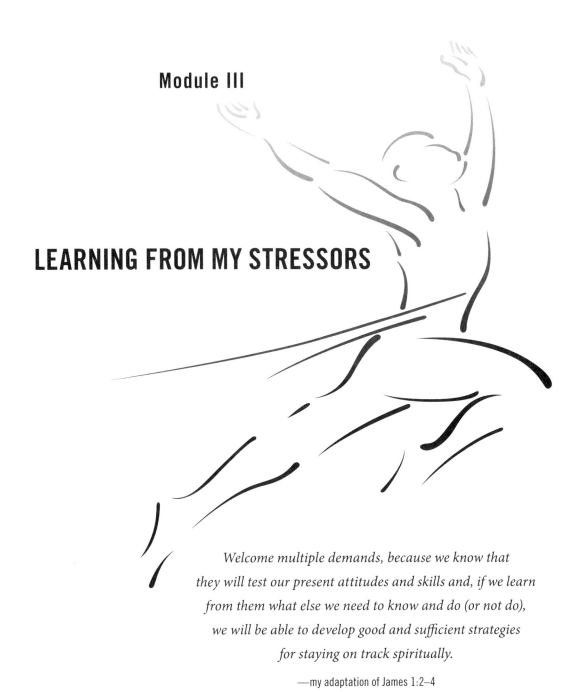

Module III

LEARNING FROM MY STRESSORS

*Welcome multiple demands, because we know that
they will test our present attitudes and skills and, if we learn
from them what else we need to know and do (or not do),
we will be able to develop good and sufficient strategies
for staying on track spiritually.*

—my adaptation of James 1:2–4

INTRODUCTION

Since the race we are in is a marathon (not a 100 yard dash), we need to learn how to sustain ourselves during that race. If we run this race like it was a dash (all out, all the way), we have set ourselves up to not finish. When Paul tells Timothy that he has " … fought the good fight … finished the race … kept the faith …" (2 Tim. 4:7), he was talking about a marathon. In his marathon, he had been " … in danger from rivers, in danger from bandits, in danger from my own countrymen, in danger from gentiles; in danger in the city, in danger in the country, in danger at sea; and in danger from false brothers" (2 Cor. 11:26). During that race, Paul had learned how to sustain himself: "I have learned to be self-sufficient whatever the circumstances" (Phil.4:11). (The word "self-sufficient" here means "independent of circumstances or conditions or surroundings"—something more active and skill based than the English translation "content," found in many translations.) Paul had learned that "I can do everything through him who gives me strength" (Phil. 4:11-13).

In the context of the multi-demand marathon, it is not feasible to stop and take a course on stress management (after all, finishing a race implies that you keep moving). We are already carrying enough of a load; we don't need it increased by the "solution" of extended stress management training. (And, as we all know, some approaches to finding a solution actually strengthen the problem.) I am not saying that I am against extended stress management training (when I used to teach a course on stress management, it was a nine week course). What I am saying is that, while we are running, we need strategies that fit the context and actually lighten our load. Have you seen a marathoner take in water? As they continue to run, they grab a bottle or cup of water from helpers who extend those containers out over the course. The runner then quickly gulps the water, splashes some over his/her head, and drops the container, while never breaking stride. In this chapter, I will emphasize such "pit stop" and "on the course" strategies, so you will not have to break stride in your quest for the finish line.

In this chapter, I will outline the model I use for doing stress management. I will clarify my beliefs and biases about doing stress management, so my emphases become clear. I will outline "tried and proven" strategies for doing stress management. (Since stress management involves dealing with both our outside and inside environments, I will focus on both the behavioral and the cognitive dimensions of "de-stressing.") Finally, I will supply more in-depth information (in the appendices) to help you further design your tailor-made stress management game-plan. As the verbs here imply, this is all about "doing" stress management.

STRESS MANAGEMENT MODEL

In the model I use for doing stress management, it is important to make the distinction between "a stressor" and "stress" or "stress reaction." A stressor is a pressure (on a person) which results in a stress response (from that person). Stress or a stress reaction is a fairly predictable arousal of psycho-physiological (mind-body) systems (of that person). So, stress is a person's reaction to a stressor. It is also important to know that the stress reaction (of any person) has three components—physiological, cognitive, and behavioral. Let me illustrate these concepts in the following way: suppose you are walking in the woods in the fall of the year, and you see a bear. Under normal circumstances, seeing a bear would be a stressor that would produce a stress reaction within yourself. That reaction would include a physiological component (increased respiration rate, increased heart rate, increased muscle tension, increased perspiration rate, pupil dilation, to name a few), a psychological component (experience of fear and some cognition approximating "bear = danger," to name a couple) and a behavioral component (freezing or running, to name a couple). Such a reaction is designed to mobilize you so that you can respond to a danger—by "fight" or "flight" or "freeze." Such a (self-preserving) reaction only becomes destructive to you if the reaction is too intense (for example, causing a heart attack) or too prolonged (for example, you keep visualizing the bear and, so, keep your stress reaction going, long after the bear has gone). If your reaction is too intense or too prolonged, it will fatigue and damage your physiological systems.

Again, let's suppose that you are walking in the woods, in the fall of the year, and you see a bear—but this time you are a researcher of bears. Again, the bear would be a stressor and you would have a similar physiological reaction. However, in this context, your psychological component would be different—your arousal would be interpreted (by yourself) as excitement rather than fear and you would be saying to yourself some version of "bear = subject to be observed." On the basis of that different interpretation, your behavior would be different—not including running and (possibly) including pulling out your camera. When a stressor is positively perceived, your reaction will also be experienced positively (this is called "eustress").When the same stressor is negatively perceived, your reaction will also be experienced negatively (this is called "distress"). So, whether or not you enjoy the experience of your reaction to a stressor depends on how you perceive/interpret that stressor. If someone could positively perceive every life event, that person would not need many other stress management skills. There are circumstances, however, that we perceive as negative and which produce too intense and too prolonged a mind-body reaction (for example, a tyrannical boss). For such circumstances, we need distress management skills. The purpose of such skills is not to eliminate such distress (that will only occur when we get to heaven) but to enable us to constructively manage ourselves in the face of such circumstances. These circumstances will then begin to work for us, not against us (as they will if they remain negatively perceived and if they continue to trigger too intense or too prolonged a reaction in us). If we do not learn stress management skills that are "good and sufficient," for constructively handling our circumstances, our circumstances will end up handling us—and providing us with many negative consequences. Such consequences include declining health (for example, recurring headaches, indigestion, fatigue, higher blood pressure, and infections); declining well-being (for example, disruption in sleep pattern, muscle tensions, anxiety, worrisome thoughts, irritability with others, times of feeling "down," and difficulty concentrating); increasing consumption of "pain-killers" and "mood changers" (for example, food, alcohol, prescription medication, and non-prescription medication—like Tums); and "burnout," which is a syndrome created by unrelieved stress and characterized by emotional exhaustion, (where the person feels drained, used up, and out of energy); depersonalization (where the person experiences "compassion fatigue" and begins to disconnect from other people); and reduced personal accomplishment (where the person gets less done and sees themselves as having failed). If you are interested in a more developed discussion concerning the "stressor/ stress/consequences/interventions" process, for the purpose of deepening your understanding of these interrelated concepts, you will find such a discussion in appendix A.

If you are interested in discovering how much impact stressors are having on you, take the "Stress Self-Assessment" Inventory contained in appendix B. (This inventory is adapted from James Mills' book *Coping With Stress*.)

BELIEFS AND BIASES

My beliefs and biases about doing stress management in a successful way are as follows:

Stress is *inevitable*. Having stressors and experiencing distress is an unavoidable part of this life; it comes with the territory and no one is exempt. If we overlook this fact, however, and assume that everything in our life should go smoothly, we will be unprepared for the bumps. About this issue, Mills says: "Do you own a car? Something will go wrong with it. Do you have children? They will not always do what they are told. Do you go shopping? Stores will sometimes be crowded, and merchandise will sometimes be defective. Are you employed? Your co-workers will sometimes be unreliable."

There is one easy way to increase stress in your life: ignore the last paragraph and expect everything to go your way. Strangely enough many of us do just that without realizing it.

We do not anticipate difficulties. We make detailed schedules without allowing for the possibility that events may not happen as planned. We are caught by surprise when the unexpected happens.

How do we react under such circumstances? We get angry and upset and act as though life was especially unfair to us. We kick the tire that goes flat, implying that such things should never happen to us. We become angry when our boss, teacher, or family member does something we don't like, forgetting that people aren't always going to do what we want. It's easy to think, "How terrible! This shouldn't happen to me!"[1]

If we don't overlook the fact that there will be bumps (stressors) on the road of life, we will be able to give ourself an "expectation adjustment" so that we can come to accept stressors as natural and inevitable and expect, anticipate and handle them more effectively. Mills talks about it this way: "…We can reduce stress if we cultivate the attitude of accepting realities in life. *Accepting* realities means recognizing their existence without undue upset, anger, or resentment. It means taking life as it comes and responding to it as it is without demanding that it be otherwise. Acceptance allows us to stop saying, "This should not happen to me," and to say instead, "I'll take what happens and work with it. I can live with this right now."[2]

Once we learn to recognize stressors as an inevitable part of life, we can often adopt a problem-solving attitude toward them. We can learn to view stressors as problems to be solved rather than injustices to be reacted to. When we stop resenting the demands and frustrations (stressors) in our life and start accepting their reality and approaching them as problems to be solved, we can significantly decrease the distress we experience.

A problem-solving attitude includes asking yourself high-quality questions that get you into problem solving mode:
- Is there something in my reaction to this stressor that shows me a "growing edge" (i.e. an area where I need better skills)?
- Is there something, related to this situation/stressor, that I need to learn to accept?
- Is there any resource I need to help deal with this stressor?

Don't ask yourself low-quality questions such as the following:
- Why is this happening to me?
- Why don't he/she/they change?
- How could they treat me this way?
- Why are they making me feel so awful?

(After getting in problem-solving mode) ask yourself further high-quality questions that help you to develop your action plan:

• What is a solution-focused, low reaction way of dealing with this stressor?

• If I was going to ease through this stressor (rather than react), what would I do?

• What is my first step, in handling this stressor effectively?

• What specific action can I take to make things better?

Don't ask yourself low-quality questions:

• I hate this; why are they doing that to me?

• Why won't he/she/they do what I ask them to do?

• What am I supposed to do about this?

• Why are they so mean/uncaring/selfish/inconsiderate?

• How will I ever get through this …?

Stress management is a *process*, not an event; doing stress management means working toward lifestyle change, not a "quick-fix." Stress management strategies and skills are habits that we build into our lives to stabilize and protect the rest of our lives, not changes we make on a weekend, lasting for a week. To re-apply one of Dr. Phil's life principles: stress is managed, not cured. Some strategies we may learn quickly, others slowly, but in both cases they need to be applied into our lives until they have their effects ongoingly. There was a time (many years ago, now) when driving a vehicle was, for me, a conscious and deliberate process of applying (driving) skills into my life. Today, I drove to my office without giving one thought to these skills but, since they have been practiced into my life, they automatically operate to keep me safe and get me where I want to go. The same process has occurred with my stress management skills. Therefore, I am recommending that you adopt the perspective that you will practice the stress management skills that work for you until they will keep you safe ongoingly (without a lot of conscious effort on your part; then you know that you have mastered those skills).

Stress management is a process that is *unique to you*. You are a unique human being. The stress management strategies that are a best fit for you, as well as how you will use those strategies, will also be unique to you. In other words, what works for me (and how I make it work) will be different from what (and how) works for you. Beware of Greeks (and authors) bearing a stress management "gift" that, they say, will fit all cases, places, and races.

Stress management is not about knowing more information but *doing a few significant things differently*. We all know that water will quench our thirst. If we want to apply that truth to our life, we need not learn more about the nature of water or about the conditions under which it will change to a solid or a gas (as interesting as that information may be), but we have to pick up the water container and swallow the (liquid) contents. Stress management is about picking up the right strategies and ingesting them into our life.

The good news about stress management is that doing just two or three things differently will reduce our experience of distress significantly (and, sometimes, quickly too). In this chapter, I will be supplying you with a half dozen "tried and proven" strategies. That number is more than enough to change your life, making it possible for you to get your stressors to work for you. The bad news is that you may need to use the "trail and error" method in order to discover which strategies/tools are significant for you (as a unique person) to use. Sometimes I am a slow learner, so there were numerous trials and not a few errors before I (experientially) learned that regular exercise is a functional necessity, not just a luxury option, for me. Growing up on a farm, I gave no consideration to exercise—it came daily and found me (in the form of "chores"). When I left home to go to university, I took my work ethic with me but not my lifestyle, so any thought of exercise got left at the library doors. Similarly, when I started my career (and my wife and I started a family), I saw exercise as an option for after the work and family responsibilities got completed. As the years of work and responsibilities piled up, I began to get "feedback" that I was a few skills short of a wellness lifestyle: my body began to complain more frequently and intensely. A stress assessment shocked me, since my scores were off the top of the scale. A loss precipitated an illness that put me in the hospital. The persistence I had learned on the farm, however, enabled me to "keep my nose to the grindstone" and to gate out any feedback that would suggest a lifestyle change. It began to dawn on me, however, that if I were to continue to keep my nose to the grindstone, the result would be no nose. So, slowly and painfully, I've come to give myself permission to pursue a life after work—including exercise. I have realigned my priorities, protected myself from well-meaning people who had an (ill-fitting) plan for my life. I have designed a tailor-made way of exercising and practiced it into my life until I am getting positive feedback from my body, my mind, and my physician. Hopefully, you will be a better learner: more sensitive to feedback, more willing and quick to adjust to new realities, more able to balance your life—but even if you aren't, learning slowly is good enough. Even slow learning can get you to a place of adding years to your life and life to your years.

My wife, on the other hand, would consider exercise (at least the way I do it) to be her definition of a stressor, so what has come to work for me would work against her. Each person must look for and discover what relaxes your body, refreshes your mind, and tunes you in to your spirit. Using those discoveries is crucial in becoming a good steward of this life you have been given.

Stress management includes an *internal* dimension—involving how we relate to the environment we are immersed in and how we relate to ourself. Whether we are fully conscious of it or not, we are in constant internal dialogue with ourselves. What we say to ourselves is a product of our personal history, including family of origin training and (broader) cultural training, in interaction with our decisions (as it relates to that training). That dialogue can be destructive or constructive, pressure increasing or pressure decreasing, disempowering or empowering. In other words, that dialogue can be a stressor (triggering a stress reaction) or it can be a de-stressor (buffering us from too intense and too prolonged stress reactions). As an illustration of how our selftalk can work against us or for us, let's look at different attitudes we can take toward an important topic: stress management.

STRESS PRODUCING SELFTALK	STRESS REDUCING SELFTALK
(a) My stress reactions are caused by external events and other people, so they are outside my control.	(a) My stress reactions are not only caused by external events and other people but also by my response choices, so I can modify these reactions.
(b) My stress reaction is an automatic response that can't be changed.	(b) My stress reaction is a learned response; anything that I have learned, I can change.
(c) If I don't put myself under a lot of pressure, I won't achieve to the max.	(c) If I reduce the pressure I am under—to a more manageable level—I will free up energy that I can direct toward achieving.
(d) I hate pressure … I can't stand pressure … I always fall apart under pressure …	(d) I welcome some pressure, since it will energize me to get at what I need to do … pressure empowers me to focus on the task at hand …

Here's what Dr. Phil says about our relationship with ourselves:

> Throughout your day, you're engaged in dialogues with many other people, but your most active and consistent dialogue is the conversation you have with yourself. You may be with ten different people throughout any given day, but you're with yourself day in and day out, and you talk to yourself more than everybody else in your life combined.
>
> Your selftalk is the real-time mental conversation, the flow of thoughts, that you have with yourself about everything that is going on in your life. It is what you are saying to yourself, about yourself, about the world, about what happens to you, right now, all the time.[3]

Consequently, it is crucial to be on good terms with yourself, so that you will (ongoingly) be seeing yourself positively and treating yourself constructively. Again, notice how what you say to yourself—about yourself—can work against you or for you:

TOXIC SELFTALK	NOURISHING SELFTALK AND ...	RELATED BIBLICAL PRINCIPLES
(a) I will never be able to make these changes ... I always give up too soon ... I'm a failure ...	(a) If I work at making these changes a day at a time, I'll make progress; if I "slip up," I'll learn from that mistake so that I can do better next time. I only fail if I give up or if I don't learn something from my mistakes.	Let us not become weary in doing good, for at the proper time we will reap a harvest if we do not give up(Gal. 6:9).
(b) I've never been able to do this before, so what makes me think that I can do this now ...	(b) The past does not equal the future. Even one new idea or skill or understanding can be the key that gets me out of the place that I am now confined to ...	Then Jesus told his disciples a parable to show them that they should always pray and not give up(Luke 18:1).
(c) I've had a bad background ... my parents did X ... they messed up my life ...	(c) I can't change my background, but I can get past it by learning better ways to live. Blaming and a dollar will get me coffee ... I'm not responsible for my background, but I am responsible for my present ... what is one thing I can do, right now, to transcend my past ...?	When the angel of the Lord appeared to Gideon, he said, "The Lord is with you, mighty warrior." "But sir," Gideon replied, "if the Lord is with us, why has all this happened to us? Where are all his wonders that our fathers told us about when they said, 'Did not the Lord bring us up out of Egypt?' But now the Lord has abandoned us and put us into the hand of Midian." The Lord turned to him and said, "Go in the strength you have and save Israel out of Midian's hand. Am I not sending you?" "But Lord," Gideon asked, "how can I save Israel? My clan is the weakest in Manasseh, and I am the least in my family." The Lord answered, "I will be with you, and you will strike down all the Midianites together." Gideon replied, "If now I have found favor in your eyes, give me a sign that it is really you talking to me. Please do not go away until I come back and bring my offering and set it before you" (Judg. 6 especially v. 12–18)

(d) Why me? Why do I have to struggle so much? Why do I have to make these changes; If only they would change ... it isn't fair ...	(d) Where did I get the fantasy that life would be easy and fair? I need to take that idea out and kill it—and replace it with the belief that life is a battle (that I need to get equipped to fight) and that this struggle is really a disguised skill development opportunity.	Endure hardship as discipline; God is treating you as sons. For what son is not disciplined by his father? If you are not disciplined (and everyone undergoes discipline), then you are illegitimate children and not true sons. Moreover, we have all had human fathers who disciplined us and we respected them for it. How much more should we submit to the Father of our spirits and live! Our fathers disciplined us for a little while as they thought best; but God disciplines us for our good, that we may share in his holiness. No discipline seems pleasant at the time, but painful. Later on, however, it produces a harvest of righteousness and peace for those who have been trained by it. (Heb. 12:1–12).
(e) I feel all alone ... I don't feel capable of dealing with this issue ... I feel overwhelmed ...	(e) I may feel all alone—but really I am not, since God is with me, and I am with me. If I need more support for handling this situation, I'll find it ... I may not feel capable but I can become capable, since I am capable of learning ... I will feel less overwhelmed if I focus on what next step I can take ...	The Lord is my light and my salvation—whom shall I fear? The Lord is the stronghold of my life—of whom shall I be afraid? When evil men advance against me to devour my flesh, when my enemies and my foes attack me, they will stumble and fall. Though an army besiege me, my heart will not fear; though war break out against me, even then will I be confident. I am still confident of this: I will see the goodness of the Lord in the land of the living. Wait for the Lord; be strong and take heart and wait for the Lord. (Psalm 27 especially v. 1–3, 13–14).

The effective stress manager always puts him/herself in supportive company, by cultivating constructive and growing relationships with him/herself and with God.

Stress management includes an *external* dimension—involving skill development. Skills are the tools we use to improve our responses to situations that are pressuring us;

they get us from where we are (being pressured and experiencing distress) to where we want to be (handling pressure and experiencing calm). Finding and using the appropriate tool (for you) is the essence of this dimension. It is crucial that, while you are looking at the skills outlined in this module, you look for the key skill(s) that will make a practical change for you. Some people recognize that key tool (either a cognitive tool or a behavioral tool) by sensing that it is a fit for them (like when you see the piece of clothing that is a fit for you). Others (as I have mentioned) discover what fits by "trials and errors"—finding out what works by trying it on and evaluating the results. The effective stress manager, like the effective house builder, has various useable tools in his/her tool kit.

Implied in the concept that stress management involves skill development is the understanding that stress management is a personal growth opportunity. The Chinese symbol for crisis has two characters: one means danger, the other means opportunity. The same is true of a stressor: it is an event or situation that presents danger but also offers an opportunity. Whether this stressor turns out to be more of a danger or more of an opportunity depends on how we respond to it. If we see every stressor/stressful situation as a personal trainer that will show us where our skill gaps are and where our growing edges are located, as well as where we are succeeding, we will be better able to constructively orient ourselves to that situation and learn from it. (For me, asking high-quality questions and getting curious about what I could learn shows me that I am on the "opportunity" track). Of course, there is no requirement that I like this situation, just that I will do what it takes to make it work for me (in other words, take a "bad" situation and relate to it in a way that brings about a "good" result).

A time in the hospital (brought about by overwork, vulnerability to the demands of others, perfectionistic expectations of myself, and trusting others when the hard data didn't warrant such trust) precipitated a crisis in my life. It put me face to face with my skill gaps as well as what would happen to me if I didn't do something different. One of the different things I did was to get serious about learning/doing stress management. What I have learned and applied (as a result) has not only enabled me to be around to enjoy the process of my daughters' growing up (which was in doubt at the time of my hospitalization) but it has also qualified me to write about it—hopefully in a way that will benefit you, too.

Stress management involves *giving ourselves permission to change*. Change, by definition, is disruptive. Some people find it easier to welcome and embrace change; some people find it easier to resist and avoid change. There is a time to resist change, but this isn't one of them, so you need to open your heart and your mind to this disruption—seeing it, for instance, as a growth opportunity.

Having done that, we also need to understand and apply principles related to the "how" of change:

(a) Label "change" positively. Choosing to perceive change as inevitable ("life is flux") and as an important reality to learn to cope with or as "an adventure" or as "a way out of my present struggle" promotes getting at (and sustaining) the journey of adjustment. Choosing to perceive change as "a burden on my already heavy load" or as "a scary unknown" or as "something that I have to do" does not promote getting at (and sustaining) that journey.

(b) Work on making only one or two changes at a time. If you try to change too many things too quickly, you can overload (and stall) yourself. If you work on only one or two things, you can more easily sustain your focus and energy (until the change is implemented). Some people have found it helpful to see a resource, like this book, as a restaurant menu—where you choose from it just one or two nourishing items to chew on and digest.

(c) Pray about the change. When we pray, we invite the God "who stands at the door and knocks" into this aspect of our life. Being invited, He will "come in and interact with us" about this process (especially if we don't tell Him how to get involved or what we "must" see happen). His involvement will make a qualitative difference that is often noticeable. If we ask Him to give us "eyes to see and ears to hear" what He is doing, if we adopt an attitude of curiosity, if we begin to look for (and write down) the insights and lessons that He is providing, we will be doing our part to facilitate the change process.

(d) Never give up. Always keep adjusting (until you experience progress). This is a profitable attitude to adopt once you are in the change process. Your adjusting is in response to the feedback that you are getting from your initial efforts (to bring about change). The (two) rules of thumb are as follows:

i)   If what you are doing is working for you (producing progress), do more of it.
ii) If what you are doing is not working for you (not producing progress), do something different.

When changing, treat yourself in a constructive way:

• With patience (For instance, don't put yourself under pressure by putting deadlines on yourself.)
• With kindness (For instance, do not say anything negative or critical to yourself.)
• With forgiveness (For instance, do not hold any mistake or "failure" against yourself.)

Do not treat yourself destructively. For instance, if you treat yourself harshly, such treatment will distract you from putting your best effort (of focus, time, energy) into making change happen—and we all know that "half-baked" efforts will produce "raw" results.

Stress management involves the issue of *power*. Whenever two (or more) people co-exist, there will be interactional dynamics; those dynamics always involve the issue of power. Interactional dynamics have to do with coming to specify the rules (for any relationship) and the roles (for each participant). These dynamics also involve the issue of who makes these rules and roles—and this (inevitably) has to do with power. Some people (because of training and personality) have a relational style that focuses their efforts on gaining power; some people (because of training and personality) have a relational style that focuses their efforts on giving away power. The former gravitate toward setting the rules and carrying out leadership roles; the latter gravitate toward letting the rules be set and carrying out followership roles. Generally speaking, the more you have a say in the rules and the roles you are living out, the less stressful it will be (since, if a rule or a role is stressful, you can change it). The less you have a say in these rules and roles, the more stressful it will be (since, if a rule or role is stressful, you have no voice or power with which to change it). For people who have learned to give (their) power away, they also need to learn how to get it back or they will remain the nail rather than the hammer. People have learned to give their power away in various ways.

One of the common ways is by taking on the role of victim. People who take on this (disempowering) role give in to and go along with outside input (including others who have a plan for his/her life). Victim selftalk includes "I must agree/go along with what X wants, and I can't do Y—I need someone to look after me." Victim behavior is characterized by compliance, passivity, and diminishing joy and energy.

Another common way is by taking on the role of blamer. At first glance, this role may not look disempowering, but people in this role don't use their anger for self-mobilization but for complaining. Whether the blame is directed toward others or toward self, it is a distraction because it focuses the person on "sitting in judgment" rather than taking personal responsibility. Blamer selftalk includes "how dare X do (not do) Y …" and "I am in X because he/she did Y …" Blamer behavior is characterized by anger, arrogance and self-justification.

Another way is by taking on the role of escaper. People in this role try to disappear—whether or not they stay in the environment with other participants. Escaper selftalk includes "I can't stand it here—I need (a pain-killer)" and "I'll focus on X, while they involve themselves with Y." Escaper behavior is characterized by low energy in the situation, more energy outside the situation and addictions.

A final way is by taking on the role of over-giver. People who take on this role move giving from being a slice of their pie to being the whole pie. Like the car that is being used so much that no time is taken for maintenance or gas, over-givers provide so much that no time is taken for self-nourishment or recovery. In both cases, they will end up (sooner or later) stranded on the road. Over-giver selftalk includes, "I must give to whoever asks whatever they need or want, and I must never disappoint him/her/them." Over-giver behavior is characterized by a frantic pace, frustration, or discouragement of plans that don't go well and some form of collapse when in a safe environment (for instance, when he/she is alone).

Recovering your power does not mean getting power over the people/situations who have had power over you. It does mean developing the skills that enable you to have power/control over yourself while in the presence of those people and situations (so that they will not be able to dictate your responses). As it relates to the disempowering styles just listed, taking back power involves these changes:

For the victim, giving him/herself permission to have his/her own thoughts and voice, developing assertiveness skills and developing "adult-to-adult" relationships (not parent-to-child relationships) are steps toward taking back power.

For the blamer, downloading his/her expectations of others, taking personal responsibility for his/her choices, and developing an action-plan that helps him/her to carry out those choices are steps for taking back power.

For the escaper, giving him/herself permission to "show up" in a relationship, developing communication skills, and using these skills to talk from the "I" perspective are steps for taking back power.

For the over-giver, giving him/herself permission to disappoint others at times, learning to establish boundaries and learning to include him/herself in his/her giving are steps for taking power back.

Stress management involves *applying faith*. Faith is a powerful stress management tool. Routinely, for people who exercise faith, their life is enhanced. For me, the question of "faith in what?" is answered by my commitment to Christianity or, more precisely, to Jesus Christ. My belief is that Jesus came to earth to show and tell us that God loves us and wants to establish (and grow) a relationship with us. When we do our part to establish that relationship with Him (which is to accept and receive—by faith—what God has done to enable that relationship to happen), we have access to life enhancing resources. Being in a living relationship with God provides us with help for dealing with life's challenges—from the philosophical to the mundane. The following examples (of the stress management benefits of having a relationship with God) are some of those that I have worked into my life as I studied Paul's letter to the people at Philippi. In my estimation, this letter is a treasure house of stress management principles.

For me, entering into a relationship with God involved discovering (finally) that I wasn't alone in the universe. In my first year of university, as part of a drama class, I had seen Samuel Beckett's play *Waiting For Godot.* Although I, at that time, knew little about existentialism (a worldview stating that we are alone in the universe and that our life is meaningless except for the meaning we create by our choices), I got the message. When, later that year, I first heard about Jesus in a meaningful way and entered into a relationship with Him, it was like entering a warm house from a cold and windy winter day. And not only was God there, but He also loved me, and so (as I wrapped myself in that truth), I discovered that I would never have to go back into the cold (of an impersonal and uncaring universe) again. As I stayed in this "green house," new growth sprouted in my life and joy (a powerful stress antidote) blossomed.

> In Philippians 3, Paul describes his coming in from the cold (albeit from Judaism rather than paganism). He talks about that paradigm shift by saying "I consider everything a loss compared to the surpassing greatness of knowing Christ Jesus my Lord" (v. 8).

When I entered God's family, my life took on meaning and purpose. I found it highly stressful to have to create my own meaning and purpose; life became an adventure as I embarked on discovering and experiencing God's purpose for me.

> As Paul puts it (again, in Philippians 3): " … I press on to take hold of that which Christ Jesus took hold of me.… , I do not consider myself yet to have taken hold of it. But one thing I do: Forgetting what is behind and straining toward what is ahead, I press on toward the goal to win the prize for which God has called me heavenward in Christ Jesus" (v. 12-14).

When I entered into a relationship with God, I was given provisions to sustain me on my journey through this (fallen) world. Scripture became my "north star," for navigation toward what would actualize my life and away from what would diminish or destroy it. I no longer had to be a finite god, making life and death decisions without any point of reference. Among my provisions are these assurances (in Paul's words):

> "He (God) who began a good work in you will carry it on to completion until the day of Jesus Christ" (Phil 1:6).
>
> "God will meet all your needs according to his glorious riches in Christ Jesus" (Phil. 4:19).

When I connected with God, I was warned that my journey through this world would be difficult. Jesus' life (and those of his disciples) provided clear illustrations of this truth. This enabled me to adjust my expectations from "idealistic" to "realistic" (a powerful stress management strategy) and to avoid asking low-quality (and stressful) questions like "why me?" when difficulties arrived at my door. Paul, in his letter to the people at Philippi, talks about what God taught him to do, so that he could get through (not out of) such difficulties. These are insights that I have been/am/will be continuing to discover and to work into my life. As I do that, I am doing my part to get these difficulties to work for me—by having them promote my skill development.

> Paul says, " … I have learned the secret of being content in any and every situation, whether well-fed or hungry, whether living in plenty or in want. I can do everything through him who gives me strength" (Phil. 4:12-13).

Paul has *learned* to deal with "any and every situation." The word "content" in this text is better translated as "able to handle myself." Lloyd-Jones says about this word, "It really means that he is self-sufficient, independent of circumstances or conditions or surroundings, having sufficiency in oneself."[4] That does not mean being in control of the circumstances; it does mean being in control in the circumstances. Paul also makes it clear that he learned this sufficiency as God strengthened him. It was a process that depended upon partnership. So, as I ask God to strengthen me (so that I can learn what I need to, for coping with life's circumstances), I will experience that help. By myself, I would not be sufficient to deal with life's circumstances; with Him (as I access His strength by faith) I will be sufficient.

> Paul says, "Do not be anxious about anything, but in everything, by prayer and petition, with thanksgiving, present your requests to God. And the peace of God, which transcends all understanding, will guard your hearts and your minds in Christ Jesus" (Phil. 4:6-7).

When I am faced with difficulties, I tend to get anxious: "Will I be able to handle this?" "Will I be able to do what pleases God?" "Will X do Y to me, again?" Paul instructs me to make a paradigm shift: from an unfruitful monologue with myself (with the only fruit being sustained anxiety) to a fruitful dialogue, via prayer, with God about my concern (with the fruit being His peace, experienced in both my emotions and my thoughts). This peace, in the midst of my difficulties, will not be understood by me since difficulties are not usually the context within which peace comes. If this isn't a gift from God for stressor management, I don't know what could be!

When I entered into relationship with God, I discovered that life does not end at death. Before that time I had agreed with Bertrand Russell who, in succinct fashion, had concluded that "when I die, I rot."[5]

I had also been coming to conclude that, if death was the end of existence, life was rearranging the deck chairs on the Titanic. Jesus' resurrection, however, challenged those conclusions and, as I read Paul's writings, I encountered a follower of Jesus who had integrated that truth into his life. From what the New Testament told me, Paul's post-conversion life had not been a picnic and, when he wrote his letter to the believers at Philippi, he was in jail (in Rome) with the sword of Nero (not Demacles) hanging over his head. (According to church history, it fell on him shortly after this letter was written.) So, it is remarkable to hear Paul say:

> Yes, and I will continue to rejoice, for I know that through your prayers and the help given by the Spirit of Jesus Christ, what has happened to me will turn out for my deliverance. I eagerly expect and hope that I will in no way be ashamed, but will have sufficient courage so that now as always Christ will be exalted in my body, whether by life or by death. For to me, to live is Christ and to die is gain. If I am to go on living in the body, this will mean fruitful labor for me. Yet what shall I choose? I do not know! I am torn between the two: I desire to depart and to be with Christ, which is better by far; but it is more necessary for you that I remain in the body (Phil. 1:19-24).

What Paul is referring to when he says, " … what has happened to me" is his imprisonment. It is clear that he was seeing staying alive as one kind of deliverance and dying as another kind of deliverance. He saw both deliverances as containing positive outcomes—"fruitful labor" if he stays alive, being with the risen Christ if he dies. So we get a glimpse of how he could rejoice in the midst of such circumstances: he knew that God would help him in this world and would be with him, "face to face," in the next.

Paul was capable of the mental gymnastics required to "think positively" (after all, he had been a Pharisee), but it was his relationship with Jesus that enabled him to be sufficient in these (toughest of) circumstances. He remained fruitful to the end of his life (including the writing of Philippians) and saw his Lord walking with him *through* the valley of the shadow of death.

As we appropriate, by faith, the resources available to us through our relationship with God, our journey through this world will not cause us to "lose heart."

STRESS AND STRESSOR MANAGEMENT CATEGORIES

The categories that I am using to distinguish the strategies for doing stress and stressor management are as follows:

1. Changing my environment or changing my relationship to my environment in order to reduce pressure is stressor management.

2. Changing my reaction to a given environment or pressure so that situation is experienced as less pressurizing is stress management. I can change my reaction at a

physical level, at a cognitive level, and at a spiritual level, so each level will be considered separately.

3. Building up my general health enables my mind and body to handle stress
   more effectively.

4. Building up my support system produces additional resources for handling
   stress effectively.

Within each of these categories, I have included "tried and proven" stress and stressor
management strategies that are short-term or "on the course" (they are included in the
text) and long-term or "in the gym" (they are included in the appendices). These strategies
are "tried and proven" in the sense that many people (including myself) have applied them
and found them to be helpful—but that doesn't mean that you will. So, pick and choose
among these strategies and find (through your experience of applying them) which ones
work for you; that is how you design your stressor/stress management game-plan. As you
go through this material, you will notice that some strategies could be put in a different
category (or in more than one category). If, like me, you have been trained in analysis and
critique, you could distract yourself (or amuse yourself) by re-categorizing these strategies. If re-arranging strategies will help you to apply them (so that they can practically help
you), please do so. If this is your way of "fiddling while your body burns down," I'd suggest
that you do something useful, instead.

Graphically, the outline of these strategies is shown on the following table. This
outline organizes the rest of this module.

1.   Changing Your Environment or Changing Your Relationship to Your Environment.

Although there are times when you can change the environment that you are in (for
example, quitting a job), more frequently it is feasible to reduce stress by changing your
relationship to the environment. A widely used *(short-term) strategy*, that I have used for
many years, is sometimes called "breaking away," sometimes called "taking time out."
This strategy consists of getting out of the situation (or taking a break *in* the situation) and
using that time to physically and mentally regroup. I started using this strategy when I
worked in a job (as a teacher) where I was "on deck" throughout the day (and various evenings). In those days, I knew little about stress management and was not designing my lifestyle to enhance my preservation. Growing up on a farm, I was (implicitly) taught that you
must handle (directly and personally) whatever happens. That is a good belief when you
have some control over what you do and how fast you do it; it is not a good belief when you
are working in an organization that has your welfare as its seventy-ninth priority. More

CATEGORIES	SHORT-TERM STRATEGIES	LONG-TERM STRATEGIES
1. Change your environment or change your relationship to your environment.	Taking time out	Strategies for changing my relationship to my demands (appendix C)
2. Change your reaction to your environment.		
a) Physically	Single breath relaxation (appendix D)	Progressive relaxation (appendix E) Identifying, challenging, and revising
b) Cognitively	Daily record of distress-producing thoughts (appendix F)	stress—including selftalk (appendix G)
c) Spiritually	Relaxing into Jesus' presence (page 22) Prayer (page 22) Claiming God's promises (page 23) Remembering what God has already done for us (page 23–24)	Growing our understanding of who God is and how He operates (page 24–25) Modifying (toxic) expectations (page 25–26) Ongoing refinement of what we believe (page 26–27)
3. Build up your general health.	Stress related "first aid kit" (page 27–28) Scheduling for a life after stressors (page 28)	Strategies for building up your general health (appendix H)
4. Build up your support system.	Prayer (page 29) Intentionally choosing "uptime" or "downtime" (page 29–30)	Strategies for building up your support system (appendix I)

out of desperation than design, I began to go to the public bathroom to get a break from the students and the telephone. In the stall, I found that I could breathe easier, relax tense muscles and strategize for my re-entry. I began to ask myself some version of this high-quality question: "What is my next step for handling what I am now facing?" Like a boxer who is reeling from his opponent's flurry of punches and finds the time between rounds to be crucial for getting his feet under him again and for getting new instructions, I found the time in the bathroom.

In appendix C, you will find a collection of strategies that I have gathered for changing your relationship to your environment. (Some of these ideas are adapted from *Coping With Stress* by James Mills[6] and from *Burnout: The Cost of Caring* by Christina Maslach.) Although implementation time for some of these strategies may be longer than the strategy I have just talked about, you may find one (or more) of them to be a worthwhile investment in your game-plan.

2.   Changing Your Reaction to Your Environment.

Changing my reaction to a stressor is an option that I always have available to me, even if I can do little to change the stressor. At a physical level, research has demonstrated that, if I can manage my breathing, I can manage my level of stress. When under pressure, people tend to breath more rapidly and in a more shallow fashion. If I (deliberately) breath more slowly and deeply, my body tends to stay more relaxed and my mind tends to stay more calm. (This is not surprising since my body and my mind always work as a unit.) Since breathing continues whether I manage it or not, it is a good investment to learn to manage it. When I do so, I can modify my stress level immediately and ongoingly and privately (even when I am in public). In my own experience, I have noticed that deep breathing (or breathing that involves my diaphragm) keeps my thoughts from racing, enabling me to stay focused on the task at hand. In appendix D, I have included a handout—from Neidhardt, et.al's book *Quieting*[7]—on "Single Breath Relaxation" which shows you how to do it.

If you are interested in learning a more comprehensive form of relaxation, which teaches you to deliberately relax the muscles in each muscle group of your body, you can look at the handout called "Progressive Relaxation"—in appendix E—from Davis et.al's. book *The Relaxation and Stress Reduction Workbook*.[8] I did not learn this skill from this source but, over the years, this skill has enabled me to break the buildup of pressure during the day and to get a half-hour's rest in five minutes.

There are various "on the job" ways to modify my *cognitive* reaction to a stressor. Shakespeare said (and many have paraphrased him since)"There is nothing either good or bad, but thinking makes it so …"[9]

This statement implies that what you say to yourself about a stressor can *decrease or increase* the pressure you experience. It is crucial that you become proficient at talking to yourself (and others) in ways that decrease your pressure. One short-term method is the "Daily Record of Distress-Producing Thoughts" (Graphically outlined below; found in appendix F—in reproducible size—for your applications.)

Date	(2) Situation	(1) Emotions	(3) Automatic Thought(s)	(4) Rational Response	(5) Outcome	(6) If I was to act upon my rational responses … I would do the following (1) (2)

This strategy (developed by Aaron Beck and adapted by David Burns) is excellent for identifying and replacing pressure-increasing selftalk. The numbers above the columns show you the order in which you fill in the columns.

1.   In this column, you *label the emotion* you are experiencing and—on a scale from 1 to 100—rate the intensity of that feeling. Do this as soon as possible after experiencing an intense and negative emotion. (The more intense the experience, the higher the number: for example, 50 = somewhat intense, 75 = quite intense, 90 = very intense.)

2.   In this column, you *identify the external event* or *the internal event*—experienced as a thought (auditory mode) or as a picture (visual mode) or as a sensing (kinesthetic mode)—that led to the unpleasant emotion.

3.   In this column, you *identify any "automatic" thought* (any thought that is presently engrained in your thinking because it is part of your learning history) that preceded the emotion. You also rate this thought—on a scale from 1 to 100—in relation to how much you believe it (how impactful it is for you, now).

4.   In this column, you write down a *rational (pressure-reducing) response* to the automatic (and pressure-increasing) thought. You also rate this thought—on a scale from 1 to 100—in relation to how much you believe it (how impactful it is for you, now). Have at least one stress-reducing response for every stress-increasing piece of self talk.

5.   In this column, you *re-rate* how much you believe the automatic thought and how much you believe the rational response, after completing columns (3) and (4). Typically, identifying and replacing this old stress-increasing thought will have the effect of reducing its impact on you; typically, identifying and rehearsing the new stress-reducing thought(s) will have the effect of increasing its (calming) impact on you.

6. In this column, you identify and write out how you would *behave* if you were to act on your stress-reducing beliefs/self talk, as they apply to the situation you are facing. As you follow this process, you will constructively change your reaction and response to the stressor at hand. Here is an example of my application of this strategy, from the time when I was preparing to teach the course on stressor/stress management.

DAILY RECORD OF DISTRESS-PRODUCING THOUGHTS

	(2)	(1)	(3)	(4)	(5)	(6)
Date	Situation Describe: 1. Actual event leading to unpleasant emotion or 2. Stream of thoughts, daydream, or recollection leading to unpleasant emotion	Emotions 1. Specify: sad, anxious, angry, etc. 2. Rate degree of emotion 1– 100% (1 = trace, 100 = most intense possible)	Automatic Thought(s) 1. Write automatic thought(s) that pre- ceded emotion(s) 2. Rate belief in automatic thought(s) 0–100%	Rational Response 1. Write rational response to automatic thought(s) 2. Rate belief in rational response 0–100%	Outcome 1. Re-rate belief in automatic thought(s) 0–100% 2. Re-rate belief in rational thought(s) 0–100%	If I was to Act upon my rational response (to my automatic stress-increasing thoughts) I would do the following (in relation to the situation): 1. 2. 3. 4.

MY EXAMPLE

| Event: beginning to prepare for group session... | Anxiety/ tension in stomach 80% | 1. "I must do this right (i.e. perfectly)" ...70% | 1a. "Nobody does this kind of work perfectly ..."
1b. "I'll just do the best I can ..."
1c. "I'm setting myself up for failure if I expect this of myself ..." 70% | AT 1:30%
RR 1:70% | 1. Relax and prepare thoroughly

Continued |

		2. "I must not make a blunder while presenting this material ..." 70%	2a. "This is not a realistic expectation of myself; giving them my best, is ..." 2b. "Making a mistake is not the end of the world; I'll just correct myself (relax) use humor and go on ..." 80%	AT 2:20% RR 2:80%	2. Affirm myself: I do well at this ... I have experience ... They'll probably benefit from this since, I have ... I'll use humor if I blow it ...
		3. "I must give everyone what they want (i.e. please them) ..." 70%	3a. "I can't please everyone all the time ..." 3b. "I will relax and let them assume responsibility for how they use this material—I'm not responsible for them, just to them ..." 70%	AT 3: 20% RR 3: 80%	3. Say to myself: "Don't get into 'It's my fault if you don't like it' posture—that's over-responsibility". Calmly and positively give the best I have. Calmly and rationally handle criticism—stay on the side of the critic. (Remember that this will help me to improve the course.)
		4. I must not fail ... or be perceived to have failed ..." 90%	4a. "If they don't like it, that's not the end of the world—I'll just learn from their feedback and do better next time. Their not liking it doesn't mean that I've failed. I only fail if I give up or don't learn something ..." 80%	AT 4: 10% RR 4: 80%	4. Say to myself: "Let my anxiety over failing push me to prepare thoroughly ..." "I'll be kind and gentle with myself if I don't get the results I want ..." "If I don't get the results I want, I'll turn that into a learning opportunity ..." "I only fail if I give up or if I don't learn something ..." "If I don't get the results I want, that doesn't diminish my worth as a person ..." (i.e. separate self-worth and self-esteem from performance.)

In Mill's book *Coping With Stress*, he outlines a useful procedure for identifying, challenging, and revising the beliefs and rules (that people have learned and accepted) and which puts pressure on them. In appendix G, I have included my adaptation of that material for you to use (if you have discovered that changing your cognitive reaction is vital to your stress management plan).

There are many "on the course" strategies that, at a *spiritual* level, will modify my reaction to a stressor. In one sense, this is a version of changing my cognitive reaction to stressors. In other ways, it is distinct (for instance, the content of this level is different and the dynamics of this level are different). One such strategy is relaxing into Jesus' presence or (to borrow the language of brother Lawrence) "practicing the presence of God." For me, this process starts with physical relaxation (discussed previously) but doesn't end there. As I am physically relaxing (which happens quickly for me, in light of years of practice), I am also inviting Jesus to come and be with me in a way that allows me to experience His presence. You are probably familiar with Jesus' teaching where He says to His followers (us), "Here I am! I stand at the door and knock. If anyone hears my voice and opens the door, I will go in and eat with him, and he with me" (Rev. 3:20). He wants a relationship with us, but He will not impose it on us. He waits to be invited before coming and interacting with us. So my invitation is something like, "Thank You, Lord, for being willing to come into my situation and to come close to me now. You are invited now—please interact with me." Then, as I continue to relax, I also pay attention. I typically feel Him, initially, as a heat source—sometimes enveloping me, sometimes coming close to me, sometimes sitting at some place in the room. Once I have "located" Him kinesthetically, I respond to His coming: "Thank You, Lord, for being near me; I feel safe now. Is there anything You want to say to me?" or "Thank You for coming close, Lord, is there anything that You want me to know or do?" or "Thank You for coming, Lord, is there anything in my life that is keeping You (over) there? Is there somewhere that You want to lead me?" After asking those questions, I (again) pay attention to what He shows me, says to me, leads me into. At various times, He has said to me, "Just rest" … "I want you to X" … "I want to show you Y …" There are many ways to interpret such experiences: auditory/visual/kinesthetic hallucinations, creating God in my imagination, wish fulfillment. Seen through the eyes of faith, I believe this is actual contact with the One who has created me "in His image" (so that I could have a relationship with Him). As it relates to such experiences, I'm not sure of many things, but I am sure of one thing—it is stress reducing (and I suggest that you "taste and see" that the Lord's presence is calming).

As you probably noticed, the strategy I've just discussed (of inviting God to be part of my journey) is foundational: foundational to relationship growth and foundational to

other strategies. Inviting Him naturally leads to talking to Him (as already indicated)—
which is what prayer is. (Two-way communication is to a relationship what blood is to a
body.) Prayer serves many purposes:

- downloading my concerns to Him ("casting my cares upon Him"[10] to use King
  James English)
- asking for His help (I know that You are a very present help in time of stress[11])
- asking for His guidance (You have promised to say to me, "This is the way, walk
  in it"[12])
- thanking Him for being a good friend (Lord, when You were here, You said to
  Your followers, "I no longer call you servants, but friend's"; I'm glad to be in that
  category too[13])
- putting another prayer in the bowl (Lord, here is another prayer about X; when
  the time and circumstances are right, please "pour them out" on the situation to
  bring about change)[14].

I have not mentioned that some believers use prayer as a means to get what they want
from God (as if He was a cosmic candy dispenser and prayer was the coinage for getting
their "goodies"). These are the people who, when God does not answer their prayers immediately and in the way they want, get angry at Him or discouraged at Him or turn away
from Him—as if to say, "How dare You not give me what I put my money in for!" It is a
necessary paradigm shift, if you want to grow in your relationship with Him, to accept His
answer. You certainly don't have to like or agree with or understand that answer – just adjust accordingly. You can also talk to Him about your preferences, your feelings, and your
questions. By making that shift, you are doing your part to develop trust in Him, rather
than trying to use Him.

Another immediate strategy (at a spiritual level) that we can use for de-stressing is (that
of) remembering and claiming promises that God has made to His people. Also, we can remember (if we have a history with Him) what He has done in *our* past to help us get through
stressful times. In times of pressure, I have found it helpful to remember the following:

- God is *for* us not against us (Rom. 8:31–32).
- … In all things (including stressors) God works for the good of those who love
  Him, who have been called according to his purpose (Rom. 8:28).
- …Who shall separate me from the love of Christ? Shall trouble or hardship
  or famine or nakedness or danger or sword?…[Listed is an excellent list of
  stressors.]…As it is written: For your sake we face death all the day long; We
  are considered as sheep to be slaughtered. No, in all these things we are more

than conquerors through him who loved us. For I am convinced that neither death nor life, neither angels or demons, neither the present nor the future, nor any powers, neither height nor depth, nor anything else in all creation, will be able to separate us from the love of God that is in Christ Jesus our Lord" (Rom. 8:35–39).

So, we will never be alone—even when we feel alone.

- …No temptation (stressor) has seized me except what is common to humankind. (In other words, other people have faced—and survived—these "things" before.) And God is faithful; he will not let me be tempted (stressed) beyond what I can bear. But when I am tempted, he will also provide a way out so that I can stand up under it (I Cor. 10:13).

What a good reason for inviting Him into my circumstances …!

- Consider it pure joy, my brothers (and sisters), whenever we face trials of many kinds (stressors—a subset of trials—also come in all shapes and sizes) because we know that the testing of our faith develops perseverance (James 1:2–3). Stressors produce skill and character development, if we face them in the right way. According to Hebrews 12, three attitudes we must avoid (in order to get stressors to work for us) are as follows:

  (1) Ignoring the stressors (v. 5). Instead, we must face them, learn from them, adjust to them.

  (2) "Losing heart" or giving in to the stressors (v. 5). Instead, we must see them as growth opportunities.

  (3) Letting a root of bitterness grow in us—as a response to the stressor (v. 15). Instead, we must adjust our beliefs and our expectations so that curiosity and prayerfulness and gratitude grow.

    Perseverance must finish its work so that you may be mature and complete, not lacking anything. If any of you lacks wisdom (for dealing with these stressors), he should ask God, who gives generously to all without finding fault, and it will be given to him (James 1:4-5).

    For those of us who are familiar with these truths, a danger we face is that we will affirm the truths (and, maybe, memorize them) without—by faith—receiving them in a way that makes an experiential difference for us. God is more than a concept, and His promises more than affirmations; He is a living Being, and His promises make real differences in our life (as would the help of any other friend).

When the children of Israel were in trouble, they would often rehearse what God had already done for them (see Psalm 105). We, on an individual level, can do the same. Whether we just remember what God has done for us or whether we write our own psalm, it is comforting (and stress reducing) to remember that God has already entered our experience and is planning to use all of our life experience to deepen His connection with us.

There are also various *long-term strategies at a spiritual level* that have proven valuable as stress reducers. One such strategy is growing our understanding of who God is and how He operates. Doing this, so that we can get in line with His agendas for our treatment of nature, other people, ourselves, and Him, is foundational to our being in harmony with all that is around us. In this (life-long) endeavor we must believe two things: that He exists and that He rewards those who earnestly seek Him. A primary method for discovering his agendas is studying Scripture. There, we get a window into how God related to those who were seeking Him (and some who were not). Scripture states that such history was recorded for our benefit. It is by study that we discover and (as God's Spirit leads us) make personal application of those benefits. (In Psalm 119—a psalm that emphasizes adherence to God's agendas—Scripture is stated as being "a lamp to my feet and a light for my path." To walk in the light is a stress reducing experience.) There are many good methods for studying the Scriptures; my only suggestion is that you find one that makes such study a means (to knowing God and His ways better), rather than an end in and of itself. To make study an end is to study for a reason that doesn't grow your relationship with Him. Consequently, you may know more about Him without knowing Him.

As we begin to get to know God and His ways better, we begin to build up expectations of what He will do and when and how He will do it. And, if we aren't careful, we begin to put Him (and ourselves) in a box. Maybe you have heard some of these expectations:

• "God loves me, so He won't let me suffer…"
• "I'm sure that God is calling me to do X, so it will be a successful venture…"
• "I feel very drawn to this person, so I'm sure that God will endorse this relationship…"
• "God related to me like this before, so I know that He will do that again…"
• "God blessed this work before, so He is obligated to bless it again."

• "I've done this for God; since He is no man's debtor, He is obligated to give back to me."

It is not our job to get God to rubber-stamp our agenda. It is our job to adjust our agendas to fit His will. (The prototype for all prayer is … "Your will, not mine, be done.") This means an ongoing revision, in light of His ongoing input to us, of our thoughts and actions (which, for people like me, feels like an ongoing disruption). This disruption is proof that I am not yet at the place where I can comfortably flow with His agendas. One tool that is helpful for evaluating and revising personal expectations that will (otherwise) produce distress is the two-column strategy:

EXPECTATION	UNDERSTANDING
(Write out here the expectation that is causing struggle/tension/conflict between what you believe and what your experience is telling you.)	(Write out here the understanding(s) that will help you to modify that expectation.
For example: "God loves me, so He won't let me suffer … but I am experiencing suffering …"	That isn't what the apostle Paul said about his life as a believer … suffering can produce great things—if I cooperate with it …There is a promise that God will not let me be overwhelmed by suffering; that implies that I will suffer … (I give myself permission to receive suffering and to learn from it, whatever its lessons are … I do this, knowing that whatever comes to me comes through God's directed or permitted will …)

Another long-term (and ongoing) strategy that promotes stress management and sustained personal growth flows from the biblical principle (and permission) to "Evaluate everything; Hold on to the good" (I Thess. 5:21). This implies that everything that we consider true and (so) hold on to has been personally chosen. We are not to have unconsidered loyalty to any person or organization (in part because no person or organization has the immaculate perception of truth). This also applies to the study of Scripture which, although "God-breathed," comes to us through the glasses of translations and theologies and organizations which are not God-breathed. So, as believers, we are to submit to God's word and—at the same time—ask His Spirit (who wrote it through men) to enable us to understand, interpret and apply His word in an increasingly pure and accurate and personally relevant way. This refinement (which includes evaluation and holding on/letting go) will certainly involve other people and organizations, but in a collegial way. Unconditional loyalty is reserved for God and His Spirit alone (otherwise we are into idolatry). As we carry on with this refinement process, we are developing a way of doing faith that fits us. Such a fit is stress reducing (as it would be to wear glasses that are designed for our eyes, rather than someone else's eyes).

In Philippians, Paul—after stating that he has not yet arrived at the goals "for which Christ Jesus took hold of me"—says that he continues to strive toward those goals (Phil. 3:12-14). Of all people who could say he had arrived—in light of what he had seen/heard/done—it would be Paul. His focus, however, is on ongoing growth and refinement. He goes on to state:

- "All of us who are mature should take such 'an ongoing growth on life's journey' view of things" (Phil. 3:15).
- "And if on some point you think differently, that too, God will make clear to you" (Phil. 3:15). (God's Spirit is the One who will lead us into the truth.)
- "Only let us live up to what we have already attained" (Phil. 3:16). (Growth has to do with walk as well as understanding.)

And, in the inevitable challenges that life supplies, we continue to practice and hone our skills. So, growth is developmental. My prayer of response (to such growth-promoting challenges) is "Lord, may the challenges that You send or allow into my life have the same effect as the grain of sand in the oyster's life—producing disruption but, ultimately, a thing of beauty."

(3) Building Up Your General Health

In the category of building up my general health, all *short-term strategies* are present applications of principles that, as they are consistently applied over time, are my long-term strategies. Even so, it is crucial to have strategies at my fingertips that will (at least) preserve my health—starting at this moment. Again, I'll illustrate from my experience; hopefully the process will be helpful for you, even if you have to change the content. Having given myself permission to pay attention to the feedback that my body is giving me to indicate pressure (neck tension, stomach discomfort, experience of fatigue, sweating …), I ask myself the question (when having these experiences), "What do I need to do right now to reduce this pressure?" I use that question to access my stress-related "first aid kit" (which is my list of "here and now" de-stressing and replenishing activities). Here is my list:

- Go to the bathroom.
    - Rub neck muscles, to restore circulation…

- Say (to self), "I have nothing to do, now, but put some 'gas in my tank'...
  what, right now, does that need to include?"
- Go and get coffee.
  - Breathe deeply as I go down the stairs from my office...
  - Play the song—on my vehicle's CD player—that I put in, for this time.
  - Say (to self), "When I get back with coffee, I'll read X."(I always have an in-
    teresting book with me. Nothing takes my head away from present pressures
    more quickly.)
  - Say (to self), "When I get back...I'll also journal X—that is valuable to
    remember."
- Pray (Nehemiah-like prayers), for example:
  - "Lord, I put this situation in Your hands."
  - "Lord, please help X to follow through on what we agreed on ..."
  - "Lord, please make 'my five loaves and two fish' into a banquet (for him/her/
    them).
- Give myself permissions, for example:
  - "No taking or giving (telephone) calls until 1:00."
  - "Write it down" (whenever I catch myself trying to remember anything by
    beginning to rehearse it in my mind).
  - "I'll relax for ten minutes."
  - "What do I have lined up tonight, that I can look forward to...?"
  - "No rehearsal now of that session (that didn't go well); I'll do that when I
    write up that session..."
  - "What else do I need to do now – that will help to re-energize me?"
  - "What am I experiencing right now that I need to acknowledge/learn from/
    deal with?"

In my economy, nothing is as freeing as a good schedule, so another tried and proven
(immediate) strategy is that of scheduling for "life after stressors." I am writing this material on a Friday afternoon, with clients yet to see, but in my portable memory (my daily
planner) I have written—for 7:00 p.m. this evening—"family movie night." So, I know that
at 7:00 p.m. this evening (barring some cataclysmic event) I will have my feet up, popcorn
in hand, watching a movie with people who (also) like movies and who I am at ease with.
For those of us who run our lives like a military operation, we have a (near) guarantee that
we will experience a de-stressor when we schedule that de-stressor. That upcoming event
gives us something to look forward to, making present stressors less overwhelming. So, if

my remaining sessions today become a mess, I already know that they will not become a sustained mess (because I will not take them to the movie tonight). Research has discovered that it is sustained stress that damages us. If we schedule so that the stress will not be sustained, we preserve our health.

Long-term strategies for building up your general health are found in appendix H (some of which are adapted from Mills book; some of which are adapted from Stephen Covey's work).

(4) Building Up Your Support System

In the category of building up my support system, it is also the case (as it was in the category of building up my general health) that short-term strategies are just different applications of long-term strategies. In this category, however, the context for these strategies is relationships. Building up a support system has to do with developing and maintaining a constructive community in and around my life (and, conversely, downloading the impact of any destructive community in and around my life). *In* my life, these dynamics (of "building up" and "downloading") apply to two relationships: my relationship with God and my relationship with myself (both 24/7 relationships). *Around* my life, these dynamics apply to relationships with other people. These people can be put in the categories of "confidant" (those closest to me), "friend" (those with whom I have some significant connection), and "acquaintance" (those with whom I have some less than significant connection). See pages 220–246 in module IV for a more developed discussion of these different kinds of relationships. We were built to be in community ("It is not good for man to be alone" (Gen. 2:18-24). When we have constructive community, we have a powerful stress buffer.

Among the many *short-term strategies* that promote a constructive support system, I'll mention two of the tried and proven ones. As it applies to my relationship with God, one of my favorite prayers is "Help!," followed closely by Nehemiah-like prayers—such as the one found in the book of Nehemiah 1:11–2:5:

> …I was cupbearer to the king. In the month of Nisan in the twentieth year of King Artaxerxes, when wine was brought for him, I took the wine and gave it to the king. I had not been sad in his presence before; so the king asked me, "Why does your face look so sad when you are not ill? This can be nothing but sadness of heart." I was very much afraid but I said to the king, "May the king live forever! Why should my face not look sad when the city where my fathers were buried lies in ruins, and the gates have been destroyed by fire?" The king said to me, "What is it you want?" Then I prayed to the God of heaven, and answered the king, "If it pleases the king and if your

servant has found favor in his sight, let him send me to the city in Judah where my fathers are buried so that I can rebuild it."

Nehemiah was a man who, while taking action, was fervently praying (inside). Since prayer is a way of inviting God into our (stressful) circumstances, we will receive the comfort of His presence and help when we do. Notice how both presence and help are promised in this biblical instruction: "Therefore since we have a great high priest who has gone through the heavens, Jesus the Son of God, let us hold firmly to the faith we profess. For we do not have a high priest who is unable to sympathize with our weaknesses, but we have one who has been tempted in every way, just as we are—yet was without sin. Let us then approach the throne of grace with confidence, so that we may receive mercy and find grace to help us in our time of need" (Heb. 4:14–16).

I reduce the impact of destructive community (at a spiritual level) by plugging into kingdom of light resources and unplugging from kingdom of darkness involvements. Since (to quote Paul), "Satan himself masquerades as a angel of light" (2 Cor. 11:14), I need to choose my spiritual community carefully.

See module I for more on this issue.

Short-term strategies that foster a nourishing relationship with myself are those that move me toward treating myself like a confidant or good friend. One such strategy, for me, comes from a permission that I have given myself—to separate "uptime" and "downtime." Uptime is the label for time that I am in "participant" mode. In that mode, I am focused on incoming data (on all channels), connecting with that data, being unself-conscious and gathering data. Downtime is the label for time that I am in "spectator" mode. In that mode, I am focused on evaluating incoming data and my responses to that data, disconnecting from the flow of data, being self-conscious, and selecting data. We all shift back and forth between these modes; it is helpful to do that intentionally (and to know when to utilize each mode). In my pre-skill life, I would shift between these modes when it wasn't in my best interest to do so. For example, I would be taking notes in a class (a classroom was a dominant environment of mine for about the first 30 years of my life), the teacher would say something interesting, so I would step back—into spectator mode—to think about/ evaluate that information and (so) would miss the next (and maybe more interesting) piece of information. For another example, I would say something in class, then step back—into spectator mode—to evaluate my performance, thereby stepping out of the flow of conversation and (so) not handling well any rebuttal or feedback given to me. In those days, I was especially good at "sitting in judgment" on myself (being negatively critical of most of what

I was saying or doing). My permission, to separate these modes in time, has had self-nourishing results. Let me illustrate some of these results using the above examples. Now, when taking in information, I stay in uptime—thereby gathering data on all channels (seeing/hearing/feeling the data) and immersing myself in the data (getting "into" the data; getting in touch with the significant concepts and the connections between them). In that way, I "take in" the data in a more comprehensive way, maximizing my in-session understandings and connections. Then, *after* the session, I go into downtime—thereby evaluating and interacting with that data so as to prioritize and apply it toward my goals for that data. For me, this represents a more effective (two-step) learning style. Now, when participating in dialogues, I also stay in uptime—thereby focusing on what is happening "out there" (*in* the other person/people and *between* him/her/them and me) and staying with the interactional flow. Then, *after* the dialogue is over, I move into downtime—thereby drawing my conclusions/applications for improvements. For me, this bypasses my tendency to sit in judgment on myself, because there are no intrusive evaluations in uptime. When I move into downtime, I do that evaluation (if I didn't get what I perceived to be "good" results) in the constructive F.I.P.P. format (elaborated on in the introduction, pages 12–26). Now that I am in the role of coach/friend (rather than critic) toward myself, I feel better (since I am creating a positive internal environment) and function better (since I am not being distracted from performing by the pain caused by self-criticism).

Strategies that foster a toxic relationship with myself are those that move me toward treating myself like an opponent or enemy. I reduce the impact of this toxic approach by committing myself to treat myself like a confidant. So, when my (unacceptable-to-me) performance tempts me to get into the role of critic, I say some version of the following prepared message to myself: "I've messed up (not handled that well, not responded well). I don't yet know what I am going to do to clean that up, but I do know what I am not going to do. I am *not* going to get against myself. (I refuse to lose that way.) I'll get this cleaned up, and I'll do it in a way that includes being kind and gentle to myself."

See module IV (pages 225–234 and 362–386), for more on this issue.

When it comes to building my support system with the people around me, how effectively I do that depends on how well I dialogue (have two-way communication) with those people. (Notice that the other person in this dialogue is equally responsible for the quality of the interaction—it does not only depend on me. I might be very willing and able to do my part to communicate well, but if the other person isn't willing and able to do the same, the dialogue won't go well. It takes two people to make it work, only one person to stop it from working.) Many books have outlined the rules for constructive communication.

My purpose here is not to review these rules but to touch on some of the considerations involved when relating to confidants, friends, and acquaintances.

If I have confidant(s) in my life, it is because I have had constructive dialogues with that person/those people for a period of time. These successful conversations will have produced the necessary (and unique) features of this kind of relationship: trust over a period of time, mutual acceptance (in spite of risky revelations), mutuality (both people giving *and* receiving in the relationship), and mutual permission and encouragement to grow and change. To have developed a relationship where these dynamics are present is no small accomplishment—and worth all the effort that such development requires. These are the relationships which broaden and deepen our life, so we should grow one at least. (There are various ways to do this: by deepening a friendship, by getting a dog—who is great for trust and acceptance but less great for growth encouragement, or by purchasing one in therapy.) For a biblical example of a relationship with these dynamics, look at that of David and Jonathan. Since having a confidant implies that the relationship has already been established, I'll mention how to constructively utilize this relationship when you are stressed. A confidant is *for* you: "Jonathan became one in spirit with David, and he loved him as himself" (I Samuel 18:1). However, he/she may not have the understandings or skills to be helpful, so it is valuable to let him/her know what you need. (When a confidant knows what you need, he/she will do everything in his/her power to supply what you need.) If you aren't sure what you need, asking your confidant to listen as you sort out what you need will be a valuable first step. (The probability is high that a confidant, who has your best interests at heart, will not try to push you or break confidentiality.) Generally speaking, these are the people that you explore most deeply with and listen most closely to when they give you feedback. They are also the people who can hurt you the deepest if they choose to betray your trust. If such betrayal happens (and there are no guarantees in relationships—as one person quipped to me, "If you want a guarantee, buy a washing machine!"), the only way to download the impact of this betrayal is to draw on other relationships (especially your 24/7 relationships) to help you through the grieving and recovery processes. To live in a fallen world is to risk and relationships are risky business indeed. Whether or not reconciliation should be pursued after such a betrayal is a matter of debate. I believe that forgiving the offender for such a betrayal is required (whether or not you tell him/her) but that reconciliation is optional (depending on what the offender is prepared to do, on whether you are willing to risk with that person again, and on other factors). So, that decision is made on a "case-by-case" basis. (For a more detailed look at this issue, see module IV, appendix A, number 6.)

When considering the development of my support system with friends (people with whom I share some significant connection), I have to do some risk assessment. It may be risky to share deeply with such people about my stresses. If I do, I could gain a confidant (if they handle that disclosure in a constructive way) or I could lose a friend and gain an acquaintance (if they handle that disclosure in a destructive way). Implied in this last sentence is the understanding that relationships (like all living things) can develop or diminish. Acquaintances can develop into friends; (a few) friends can develop into confidants; confidants can diminish into friends; friends can diminish into acquaintances. Such migrations occur as a result of the decisions made (consciously or unconsciously) in light of the interactions between the people involved. When we have the intention and the skills to use our personal power constructively (for example, to build up another person), we promote the migration of development (and its attendant joys). When we have the intention and the skills to use our personal power destructively (for example, to manipulate or control another person), we promote the migration of diminishment (and its attendant sorrows). If we take the risk of sharing with a friend about our stresses and they respond with constructive support, we have gained a confidant and have strengthened our support system (our new confidant will also have gained from his/her giving. As relations are deepened, it is always a win-win deal.) However, if he/she responds in a destructive way, we have lost a friend (or, at least, strained the friendship) and have created another stressor. The safety net to fall into, if we fall off the high wire of this friendship, is that of an increased reliance on our more intimate relationships (especially our 24/7 relationships) and of pre-planning our game-plan for handling loss. One principle that will help to download the impact of destructive responses—as we move along the high wire of doing relationships—is to let the data speak to us (rather than listening to our expectations), when it comes to deciding what to do in a particular relationship. I'll illustrate this principle from my relationship journey. At various times in my life I have met someone and, in the course of getting to know him/her, have discovered that he/she was a believer in God. With that discovery, I would immediately (and subconsciously) import a set of expectations for that person regarding his/her values, priorities, and lifestyle. Such expectations can be helpful if seen as only "baseline data," modifiable by subsequent "interactive data." However, such expectations are not helpful if they become the glasses through which I see—*and keep seeing*—that person. In some instances, because I was continuing to hold on to my expectations of how he/she should/would behave (rather than noticing how they were actually behaving), I have been negatively impacted. This might be when they wouldn't pay me for services I provided (while I continued to say to myself, "He/she is a believer; he/she will be honest with me; Christians are people of integrity"). The fact is that *some* Christians are people of integrity; some are not. We discover which are which by gathering data from his/her interactions with us. On the basis of that data, we decide to trust him/her more (or less), to let him/her draw closer to us (or not let them), to move closer to him/her (or away from them). We do not, except to our detriment, assume that we can infer behavior from labels that we have given (although sometimes it would be safe to do so). It is totally appropriate to say (possibly) to a recent acquaintance and (certainly) to say to ourself, "You may very well be a person who lives the label, but I don't have enough data yet to know that …."

When considering the development of my support system with acquaintances, "people with whom I share a less than significant connection," I again need to do risk assessment. Without risking, acquaintances don't become friends but, since I don't have much data by which to assess such strangers, I usually (if time allows) risk incrementally. By that, I mean risking in small steps over a period of time so that I can gather data about their trustworthiness. If time doesn't allow (for incremental risking), I need to decide whether—like the turtle—I will stay in my shell (where I am protected) or stick my neck out (since turtles only get somewhere by sticking their neck out). At this level of relationship, one principle that will help to mitigate the impact of a destructive response is that of not expecting too much too soon from such relationships (unless, of course, you are in a relationship where the "contract" is that you share deeply from the outset—as in therapy).

Long-term strategies for building up your support system are found in appendix I. (Some of these strategies are adapted from Mills' book.)

NEXT STEP

Anyone who wants to get anywhere is into "next steps"—whether it is the first step of a thousand mile journey, the next (refining) step of a meandering journey you have (long) been on, or the next step on a road to mastery. So, now is your opportunity to do a next step:

- Prayerfully select a stress management strategy that you know will make a positive and practical difference for you.
- Write out your application game-plan (in other words, how you will implement that strategy into your life). Most of the following appendices, that have been referred to in this module, have exercises at the end of them to help you develop your application game-plan.
- Include all helpful logistics (including who could give you a hand, when and where you will make this application, and for how long you will make this

application a conscious priority). Again, the exercises at the end of the following appendices may be helpful.

• After doing this game-plan, select (if needed) another strategy. Follow (again) the application steps, until you have implemented "good and sufficient" stress management strategies for constructively handling the stressors currently in your life.

Appendix A

STRESS CYCLE AND INTERVENTIONS

The following is a diagram of the way we conceptualize stressors, stress, and the effects of stress.

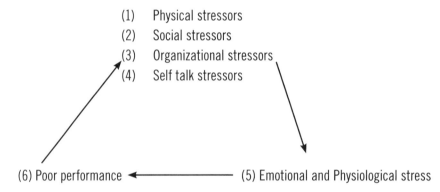

(1)   Physical stressors
(2)   Social stressors
(3)   Organizational stressors
(4)   Self talk stressors

(6) Poor performance   (5) Emotional and Physiological stress

As you can see, there is a cyclical manner in which stress develops, manifests itself physiologically, and ultimately results in poor performance on the job, at school, or in personal situations.

Some stressors come from our physical environment. These include such things as a small working space; no windows in a working area; a hot, sticky room or a room that is too cold; and traffic jams and slow elevators when you are in a hurry. These types of examples are labeled *"physical-environmental stressors."*

There are other factors, *"social stressors,"* that can also begin a stress cycle. Examples of stressful social situations are angry or aggressive people, having to give or receive negative feedback (such as a performance evaluation, or criticizing a colleague), and dealing with people who have difficulty expressing themselves or stating their needs. For those of you working in service industries, examples might include very ill people or ungrateful clients.

Another category of stressors are *"organizational stressors."* Examples of such stressors are a lack of clear priorities in work objectives, conflict between units or departments, or time pressure from work deadlines. All organizational stressors are not in the workplace.

Families are themselves organizations, and various family roles may cause conflict. Educational institutions represent another group of organizations with role-related stressors.

In addition to external factors, and probably our most common contributor to stress, is *"self talk."* This refers to the self-imposed demands we place on ourselves in the form of "shoulds," "musts," "ought to's," and our own professional and personal "myths" or performance expectations. For example, many women suffer from the myth of the "perfect wife" or "perfect mother," while at the same time expecting to be the "perfect employee." Men suffer from the myth of the "macho man" (who will make things happen), while at the same time expecting—and being expected to be—the sensitive and caring supporter.

Actually, expecting to be the "perfect" anything can only lead to chronic dissatisfaction with one's performance, generating such self talk as: "I'll never be able to please them," "I really should be pleasant to everyone," "I should do a better job," and so on. These "verbal scripts" or self-dialogues are personal stressors, that, either by themselves or in combination with physical-environmental stressors, social stressors, or organizational stressors, can lead to physiological and emotional stress—which is the next step in the stress cycle.

Stress is our mind-body response to stressors. Cognitive-emotional responses include racing thoughts and experiences of worry, anxiety, impatience and frustration. Physiological responses include fatigue, sweating, tensions in the body (for example, in the back of the neck or shoulders), an upset stomach, and headaches.

When these responses are perceived negatively, are of higher intensity, and are of longer duration, they will impact our performance. Therefore, as we move along the cycle, the cognitive-emotional and physiological stress reactions cause poor performance on the job and/or at home. This poor performance can be manifested by losing our tempers, blaming others, taking it out on our families, or by simply not doing something as well as we usually do. "Burnout" (a syndrome characterized by emotional exhaustion, depersonalization, and reduced personal effectiveness) is a result of unrelieved stress.

If we are not doing what we expect of ourselves, more negative self talk results—which again can be a stressor for us. The cycle continues as we become a stressor to ourselves and/or to someone else (which may begin the cycle for them). Unless we do something to intervene in the cycle, it can snowball, fester, and lower our effectiveness on an ongoing basis.

There are various ways to intervene in the stress cycle. Often, physical-environmental stressors cannot be avoided—you're stuck in a traffic jam and that's that. But you can use a breathing exercise to alleviate the full brunt of the stressful situation. You can also have an "emergency stress aid kit" available for use—including a relaxing CD, water, and a list of pressure reducing self talk (for example, "I just need to ease through this …").

Assertiveness training has been found to be highly effective for social stressors, particularly in reducing stress from angry or aggressive people or in dealing with difficult interpersonal situations. Also, active listening, rather than reacting, can help to deal more effectively with other people who are themselves under pressure. Active listening is the communication strategy in which you feed back to the other person what you heard him/her say. An example is, "What I heard you say was that you weren't comfortable with my proposal. Is that accurate?" The format of this strategy includes a beginning ("What I heard you say was …"), a middle [where you feedback what you heard], and an ending ("Is that accurate?"). Active listening can help you stay out of someone else's stress cycle.

Negative self talk can be handled by "cognitive restructuring"—changing your myths and belief system to be more rational and more realistic (and thus easier on yourself). If you always expect perfection from yourself and do not always achieve it, you need to learn a new way to talk to yourself.

Organizational stressors may require intervention at many different levels, including the interpersonal communication level, where changes can be made in relationships. None of us has enough power to change everything that bothers us about an organization (even when it is our own family). Thus, stress management with regard to organizational stressors may be utilized to either effectively change some of those stressors or to better cope with them if they cannot be changed.

If all, or any, of these stressors lead to physiological stress, relaxation exercises can help to minimize the effects of the physiological (and the emotional) reaction. You cannot be relaxed and stressed at the same time.

If the cycle progresses to the place of poor performance, you may need to re-evaluate where the stressors exist for you and what intervention is appropriate. Any stress management strategy could be a part of a complete stress management program. All strategies, combined or singly, can be effective in reducing and handling stress. The key is to know which strategy is appropriate for you at various points in your stress cycle, and how to "plug in" the intervention effectively.

Appendix B

STRESS SELF-ASSESSMENT INVENTORY

We can deal with stress more effectively when we are aware of it. Of course, it seems obvious that we are at least partly aware of our stress already, or we wouldn't be trying to manage it. However, even when we are aware that we are stressed, there is much about our stress that we don't know; consequently, taking an inventory of our stress can be an enlightening experience.

Stop for a minute and think about your life. Ask yourself some questions: What is happening to me? What conflicts am I experiencing? What pressures? What frustrations? What changes? What is it that makes me feel guilty? Ashamed? Depressed? Afraid? Anxious? Tense? Jealous? What do I do or feel that makes me upset with myself and down on myself? What parts of myself am I trying to hide—even from close friends? As you answer these questions, see what you can learn about yourself. You will gain a better perspective on the stress in your life—and maybe a surprising one. The exercises at the end of this appendix have been developed to enable you to complete this inventory systematically.

Taking inventory is very important. We cannot develop effective strategies for dealing with our stress until we know the pattern of stress we are experiencing. Once we have an understanding of the different kinds and sources of distress in our lives, we can examine them and identify key areas and key stressors. Frequently, people find that most of the stress they experience comes from one or two sources. Once those sources have been identified, effective action can be taken. Taking inventory is not simple: it takes time, effort, and patience. My experience with those who have completed the exercises in this inventory indicates that the results are well worth the effort. Take your time and complete the exercises thoughtfully. You need not try to complete all of them—or even one of them—in one sitting. Taking inventory is a continuous process, and you will want to do it periodically while utilizing other methods in this module.

Once you have completed the inventory, you will find that there are many ways to organize what you have learned about your stressors. You may organize it around sources and occasions for distress: Does most of it come from your job or your family? Does most of it come from outside yourself (demands, pressures) or from within (personal expectations)?

Do you find yourself stressed at certain times during the day or week? Does your stress consist of only a few disturbing emotions, like anger or jealousy? Does your stress center around external tasks and situations or around people and your interactions with them?

You will need to take some time to think about situations that are stressful for you—and to ask, "Why does this situation upset me? What is it about this situation that makes me anxious or guilty or angry?" Get at the reasons *behind* your stress reaction. When you ask yourself why you respond as you do, don't settle for the obvious but think carefully about the situation until you have considered it thoroughly. Get behind the obvious, to the thoughts and wishes that are so much a part of you that you don't think about them and take them for granted so that you aren't even aware of them. Maybe, for example, you're upset with your supervisor. For some people, this shows a problem with authority; for others, it might reflect fears about one's own inadequacy. Worry over money could reflect worry over providing for one's family or an unrecognized need for absolute certainty ("I must know that I will have enough money for tomorrow's needs.") Getting at the reasons behind the stress reaction is essential. You may find that most of your distress centers around a few fears, needs, or problem areas and discover that you can start to deal with these stressors more effectively.

In addition to thinking each situation through carefully, you might try talking about it. Find a friend that you trust who is willing to take time to listen to you. Ask that friend to attempt to understand what you are feeling without approving or disapproving of your reactions in any way. As he/she listens, whenever he/she is not certain about how you feel or why you feel as you do, have an agreement that he/she will question you to get further information. At this point in your stress management process, you are not seeking advice but are only talking about your stressful situations to help understand them and yourself better. This procedure will not only help you complete your inventory but will also help you feel better, since talking with a friend constitutes seeking support—a very effective method of dealing with stress.

You can also ask your friend to role play a stressful situation with you. Imagine that you are having difficulty in working things out with your father. Ask that friend to pretend to be your father and to talk with you as your father would about the situation. Your friend should take your father's point of view and act as much as he can like your father. Even if your friend does not know your father, you can brief him/her about the essentials of the problem. While role play is not a substitute for actually trying to work things out with your father, it will help you to understand your feelings and the reasons behind your reactions more clearly.

Another interesting use of role playing consists of asking your friend to play "a part of" yourself. For example, suppose you are having a problem with procrastination and that is causing you considerable distress. Ask your friend to role play with you the procrastinator. The procrastinator's task is to defend himself, tell you why procrastinating is not as bad as you think, argue with you about trying to eliminate him from your life, and otherwise represent the thoughts and feelings within you which lead you to procrastinate. I have seen this device result in considerable insight on the part of the participants. The friend who role plays with you need not be an excellent actor nor need he understand your situation fully. The interaction itself will enable you to learn about your stressor.

In addition to talking it over with someone and role playing, you can gain some insight into your stressful situations when working by yourself. If you are upset with someone, for example, you might pretend that he or she is in a chair near you. Talk to that person as if she were present. Say all the things you want to say, particularly the things you are reluctant to say when the person is actually with you. Don't organize or censor your thoughts—just let them come. You may be surprised at what you learn. If there is a part of you that upsets you, put yourself, or that part of yourself, in a chair and talk to it. Thus, you might speak angrily for a few moments to the "procrastinator you." If you do, you will learn more about why procrastination bothers you so much. This suggestion may seem a bit strange. We aren't used to talking to empty chairs! It will feel awkward at first. But a deeper understanding of your stress is essential, and this exercise could help. So try it—if it feels silly, it's okay. In time, the silliness will wear off, and you will gain the benefits of the exercise.

Still another way to gain insight into the reasons behind your distress is to utilize the *awareness exercise*. This important exercise will not only add to your understanding of your own distress but will also help you deal with it. The best way to use the exercise is to read the directions (see pages 142–144) and become familiar enough with them so that you can do the exercises without referring to them.

Awareness is accomplished by listing the sources of distress in your life, organizing that material, asking yourself why each situation results in stress, talking out some of the situations with yourself and/or another person, and utilizing the awareness exercise.

EXERCISES

1. In the left-hand column below, list the major sources of distress in your life. Note the source briefly, using any terms that make sense to you. You might name specific people, indicate particular responsibilities, note certain

situations, and so on. In the right-hand column, list why that person, responsibility, situation is stressful to you. Use the awareness exercise to help you.

(Note: After completing this exercise, you may want to keep a notebook with you for a week and jot down additional sources of distress as they occur to you. You may not think of all sources of distress in one sitting.)

SOURCE OF DISTRESS	REASON WHY THIS IS STRESSFUL

1. Stress has been defined as the experiencing of unpleasant or uncomfortable feelings. In brief, we experience stress by feeling bad. Below are listed a number of unpleasant/uncomfortable feelings. After each one, list a situation or situations that evoke that particular feeling in you, and indicate why you react as you do.

    Anger, rage: _____

    _____

    _____

    _____

    Anxiety, fear: _____

    _____

    _____

    _____

    _____

    Guilt, shame, humiliation: _____

    _____

    _____

    _____

Frustration: _____
_____
_____
_____

Panic: _____
_____
_____
_____

Jealousy: _____
_____
_____
_____

Insecurity: _____
_____
_____
_____

Hopelessness: _____
_____
_____
_____

Helplessness: _____
_____
_____
_____

Worry: _____
_____
_____
_____

Distress: _____
_____
_____
_____

Embarrassment: _____
_____
_____

1. The Stressful Emotion Chart (page 145) lists a variety of unpleasant/uncomfortable emotions in the left-hand column. Record in the next column to the right, under the word *Extent*, a number indicating how much, in general, you experience each emotion. Use the following rating scale:

    1 = I rarely (less than once a month) experience this emotion.

    2 = I sometimes (more than once a month) experience this emotion.

    3 = I often (once a week) experience this emotion.

    4 = I quite frequently (several times a week) experience this emotion.

    5 = I almost always (daily) experience this emotion.

When you have completed the column entitled "Extent," note that the next column is entitled "Self." In this column you record the extent to which you experience each emotion in reaction to something in yourself, (thoughts you have, things you do or don't do, or habits you have). Here you are recording how often you are angry at yourself, ashamed of yourself, or worried about yourself. Use the system described above for your ratings. Thus, if you are angry at yourself almost every day, you would put a five in the row labeled "Anger," in the column headed "Self." (In this part of the exercise and those that follow, there may be some emotions that won't apply. In those instances, you may record a zero or leave the space blank.)

When you have completed the Self Column, list—in the place for headings for the next several columns—those people who are important in your life and with whom you have frequent or important contact. Then, under the name of each person, put a number from one to five by each emotion (using the following system) to indicate how often your contacts with that person result in your experiencing that emotion. The system for these numbers is as follows:

    1 = I rarely (5% of the time) experience this emotion in my relationship with this person.

    2 = I sometimes (6–35% of the time) experience this emotion in my relationship with this person.

    3 = I often (35–70% of the time) experience this emotion in my relationship with this person.

    4 = I quite frequently (71–90% of the time) experience this emotion in my relationship with this person.

    5 = I almost always (91–100% of the time) experience this emotion in my relationship with this person.

For example, if you are angry with your brother about seventy-five percent of the time you have dealings with him, you would place a four in the row to the right of Anger, in the column headed by the name of your brother.

When you have completed all the columns of significant people, list, in the next set of columns—situations which you encounter frequently in your life. This could include specific situations at work (report writing, interruptions, etc.), dealing with the phone company or electric company, shopping, housework, dating, managing money—any situation which is an important part of your life. Then, using the same system as you used in describing your relationships with people, put a number under each situation—indicating how much of the time being in that situation results in your experiencing each emotion. For example, if you are angry every time you are interrupted at work, then you would put a five in the row to the right of Anger under the heading Interruptions. (You need not use the situations listed here. They are only suggestions and a means to help you list those situations which are important to you.)

In the last row, labeled "Total," insert the sum of the numbers in each column. Look at these totals and the chart in general to see what patterns emerge. Note where and with whom most of your distress occurs.

1.   Our body and our behavior also help us discover our stressors and how we "do" stress. To determine whether you are experiencing stress related disorders, rate yourself on each item of the following checklist, with reference to the past month. Use the following scale:

      1—Never
      2—Occasionally
      3—Frequently
      4—Constantly

In the last month I have had or experienced:

    1. Tension headaches. 1   2   3   4
    2. Difficulty in falling or staying asleep 1   2   3   4
    3. Fatigue. 1   2   3   4
    4. Overeating 1   2   3   4
    5. Constipation. 1   2   3   4
    6. Lower back pain. 1   2   3   4
    7. Allergy problems. 1   2   3   4
    8. Nightmares. 1   2   3   4
    9. High blood pressure 1   2   3   4
  10. Hives 1   2   3   4
  11. Alcohol/non-prescription drug consumption. 1   2   3   4
  12. Minor infections 1   2   3   4

13. Stomach indigestion 1   2   3   4
14. Hyperventilation (rapid breathing) 1   2   3   4
15. Dermatitis (skin rashes) 1   2   3   4
16. Menstrual distress. 1   2   3   4
17. Nausea or vomiting. 1   2   3   4
18. Irritability with others 1   2   3   4
19. Migraine headaches 1   2   3   4
20. Early morning awakening 1   2   3   4
21. Loss of appetite 1   2   3   4
22. Diarrhea 1   2   3   4
23. Aching neck and shoulder muscles 1   2   3   4
24. Asthma attack 1   2   3   4
25. Colitis attack 1   2   3   4
26. Arthritis 1   2   3   4
27. Common flu or cold 1   2   3   4
28. Minor accidents. 1   2   3   4
29. Prescription drug use 1   2   3   4
30. Peptic ulcer. 1   2   3   4
31. Cold hands or feet 1   2   3   4
32. Heart palpitations 1   2   3   4
33. Sexual problems. 1   2   3   4
34. Difficulties in communicating with others 1   2   3   4
35. Inability to concentrate 1   2   3   4
36. Difficulty in making decisions 1   2   3   4

                    Total Score   _____

Research has shown that high levels of distress are associated with greater numbers of health problems.

Look at the items that you circled "3" or "4." The more frequently you circled "3" or "4," the more likely it is that you are being impacted by stressors and that your body/mind is reacting. Use this chapter to identify concepts and strategies that will de-stress you.

5. *Awareness exercise*: Seat yourself in a relatively comfortable chair. Take a minute or two to let yourself settle down and relax. You know your mental set when you sit at a desk and are about to engage in some serious work, and you know your mental set

when you lie on the beach with the idea of doing nothing. Pretend that you are settling back for a long period of rest. This mental set is important because it enables you to let go and permits thoughts to come to you. Think of this exercise not as one in which you are going to figure something out but as one in which you are going to sit back and let answers come to you. This *receptive attitude* is essential. As you get settled in the chair, close your eyes and keep them closed for the duration of the exercise. For a minute or two, try very hard to hear every sound around you. Strain to hear everything that is going on. Even when you are alone in a quiet place there will be some noises. Listen carefully and strain to be sure that you don't miss a single one. After a minute or so of doing this, change your attitude. Stop trying to hear all the sounds around you, and instead, let the sounds come to you. Don't reach out to hear them—let them come to you. Think, "If those sounds want to be heard, they will have to come to me." Sit back and let them come. Then, return to the earlier attitude of straining to hear the sounds. After a minute or so, return again to the attitude of letting the sounds come. After doing this for a few minutes—first straining to hear the sounds and then settling back and letting them come to you—you will feel the difference between these two attitudes. You will notice that it is more comfortable to let sounds come to you. When you are able to notice the difference in these two attitudes, proceed to the next step.

Now, let yourself be aware of your body as well as the sounds around you. Let different sensations from your body make themselves known to you, just as you have learned to let the sounds in the room come to you. Then, let whatever thoughts or feelings you have within you come to you. That is, you are not going to try to think about anything at all, but you are just going to relax and *be aware*— letting thoughts, feelings, and sensations come to you. We'll call this experience *being aware.*

After you have done this a few times, you will get the feel of it. You can then use this skill in two different ways. (1) Sometime when you are stressed (when you feel anger or uneasy or tense), sit down and just *be aware*. That is, practice the awareness exercise. Don't try to figure out why you feel as you do, just let your thoughts and feelings come. Soon you will learn more about why you feel as you do. (2) Even when you are not currently concerned about a given situation but want to know more about it, you can use your skill to deepen your understanding of that situation. With your eyes closed, remind yourself of a situation which concerns you and, instead of thinking about it or analyzing it, just imagine it happening again. Then, after working it through in your imagination for awhile, just *be aware*. You will discover more about why you feel as you do.

Reactions to this exercise:_____

_____

_____

_____

_____

_____

_____

_____

_____

_____

_____

_____

_____

_____

_____

_____

_____

_____

_____

_____

_____

_____

_____

STRESSFUL EMOTION CHART

EXTENT	SELF	PEOPLE							SITUATIONS						
Anger															
Shame, Guilt															
Fear, Anxiety															
Depression															
Frustration															
Panic															
Jealousy															
Insecurity															
Helplessness															
Worry															
Distress															
Embarrassment															
Total															

Appendix C

STRATEGIES FOR CHANGING MY RELATIONSHIP TO MY DEMANDS

When most people are asked about their stress, they talk about the pressures that they are under. Our typical image of the stressed person is that of someone with a great deal to do, rushing from activity to activity, feeling hassled and frantic, trying to complete work in the time available. Sometimes the stressed individual is seen as one who shoulders considerable responsibility and who must make important decisions. This way of looking at stress emphasizes the external component of stress: the demands placed on us. When stress results from too many demands or from having particular types of demands, we can reduce stress by changing our relationship to these demands.

This does not mean that there is a direct relationship between the amount of demand on us and the degree of stress experienced. Since stress results from our internal reaction to external demand, we may feel little stress even when we face many demands, as long as our reaction to those demands is not one of anxiety or worry. People differ in their response to external demands—some seem to thrive on having a great deal of work to do. Those who work with enthusiasm, engage in many family activities, and involve themselves in community affairs, often enjoy this level of activity and would not describe these demands as stressful at all. In fact, they would find the elimination of these activities as stressful. Others, however, do find that excessive demand or limited time in which to complete their work is stressful. Further, we frequently discover that a particular task or responsibility, while not excessive, may be very stressful for us.

Review the stress in your own life as noted in your Stress Self-Assessment Inventory (appendix B). How much of it comes from demands placed on you? In addition to altering your response to those demands by using some of the methods discussed in the text of this module, you can also change your relationship to these demands.

Reducing demand is not always easy or even possible. Some demands come with our job, for example, and we are obligated to meet them. But others are self-imposed and so much a part of our way of living that we are reluctant to give them up. Often when we say that we can't stop any of the things we are doing, we mean that we won't stop anything we are doing. A careful review of the demands to which we are responding shows that some of those demands can be reduced. As you complete your review, ask yourself if you are trying to do too much. Must you do everything that you are trying to do? Are there self-imposed demands which might be reduced? An honest attempt to answer such questions helps you find where demand can be reduced.

ESTABLISH PRIORITIES

One way to change my relationship to my stressors so as to reduce pressure is to set clear priorities. That process, however, can be difficult. Sometimes we want to do everything and find the prospect of eliminating any activity to be unpleasant. We can help ourselves in this effort by establishing priorities. We must think through all that we are trying to accomplish and decide what things are more important than others. If we do this thoughtfully, we can more easily give up activities of lower priority.

Women who entered the work force after being married and bearing children find it difficult to keep up with the demands of both work and family. The pressure (and guilt) they feel in such situations can be painful. Experience has shown that women who managed this new situation best are those who did not try to be the complete career woman and the complete homemaker at the same time. That is too much to ask. Instead, successful women select their career or homemaking as their number one priority. They fulfilled the demands of the number one priority as much as possible and responded to the demands of their second priority as time allowed. This does not mean that women who chose a career as number one priority neglected or ceased to care for their families. It means that they accepted the fact that they would not be as complete homemakers as they would like. They even established priorities within the various responsibilities of homemaking—for example, deciding to spend their time with the children and let entertaining and housekeeping take less of their time. If they had to entertain less or keep a less-than-perfect house, that was okay—because they were sticking to their clear priorities. Men, as well, get caught between those two important roles and (so) need to prioritize. When both members of a couple are in both roles, it is valuable for them to have negotiated win-win agreements with each other so that their expectations of each other are appropriately set. This enables them to take coordinated action toward solutions (which often involves bringing others in—for child care, housekeeping, or house/yard maintenance) to help download demands and allow both partners to stay on priority track.

None of us can do all that we want. Consequently, we have to decide what is most important for us and concentrate on that. First, we must learn to sort out important from unimportant demands. When we find that we cannot do all we would like to do in a given period of time, we can decide what demands are important and what can be left unmet. You may decide that taking your child to the zoo is clearly more important than finishing the housework, and since you cannot do both, the housework is set aside. Second, we can help ourselves if we learn to separate major tasks from details. We can address ourselves, for example, to the task of keeping up on the news without worrying about each detail of every story.

Some priorities are lifelong or nearly so––for example, our commitment to family or career. We should also make our physical and mental health a lifelong priority. From time to time, our short-term priorities change. When we're physically exhausted and run-down, rest takes priority over work or recreation; at other times these priorities are reversed.

Once we have established our priorities, we can set out to work on our tasks one at a time. Start with the first priority, then the next, and so on. In fact, even without going through all the work of establishing priorities, we help reduce stress by making a list of tasks needing completion and working on that list, one item at a time. If we find ourself unable to give up items of low priority, perhaps we are living by the unspoken rule: "I must complete every task." If this is the case, then we want to learn to replace that rule with a more reasonable one.

ELIMINATE SOME ACTIVITIES

We can eliminate some of the demands we face even without being concerned with overall priorities. Whenever we can eliminate some activity in an overloaded schedule, we are decreasing demand and thereby reducing a source of stress. Many people, for example, work very hard at their jobs and then try to crowd a complicated social life into evenings and weekends. A simpler social life might be of advantage for a while. Other people have many different projects going at one time; they might better confine their efforts to a few. In any circumstance, ask if you must do everything you are trying to do or if you might eliminate some of your activities. You may find that while you have assumed that every-thing you are doing is essential, in reality you can abandon some of those activities with-out any problem.

MAKE SOME ACTIVITIES LESS COMPLEX

When we are about to begin a very large project, the prospect of having to complete a great deal of work may be stressful in itself. Often we worry about particularly complex assignments. We can make these assignments less complex if we break them into parts and work at each part individually. A person making a long-range plan for a corporation, for example, might find the task easier to approach by outlining its component parts: gathering data, interviewing people, establishing goals, ordering the goals, setting timetables for achieving goals, and so on. Planning a meal for several guests might appear less difficult if we think about each course or type of food to be served separately as well as by concentrating on the various parts of this task: selecting the menu, making the shopping list, shopping, cleaning house, preparing some food the day before the meal, and so on. If we can learn to look at the various parts of our task without, of course, losing sight of the entire picture, we can then focus on one task at a time. Instead of being distressed by the complex task in front of us, we can say, "Now what is the next step and what is the one thing I must do today?"

SCHEDULE DEMANDS

There are times when we want to reduce the number of demands but cannot eliminate many of them completely. We may be able to schedule those demands so that we don't have to deal with too many of them at any given time. The person who does the Christmas shopping early is applying this principle in a very practical way. The student who keeps up with a study schedule and completes term papers before the crush of finals week is scheduling demands so that they do not all come at once. People experiencing intense grief may want to postpone major decisions until a later time. The decision to schedule demands means we must fight the temptation to postpone every task until we absolutely have to do it. When we do that, we have no choice but to take work as it comes. If we keep up with our demands, we can gain some control over them and schedule them to make our lives more comfortable.

REFUSE DEMANDS THAT ARE UNREASONABLE TO YOU

Considerable stress results from our tendency to meet demands, often unreasonable ones, that are imposed on us by other people—sometimes without their being aware of it. Melvin Gurtov once stated, "Looking back, I see that for most of my life I lived and worked in accordance with other people's dreams and expectations. Now I claim my time."[15] Most people associated with us have some idea of how we should behave or what we should think. They let us know, in both obvious and subtle ways, just what they expect of us. We run into difficulty when we unthinkingly accept those demands and attempt to meet the expectations of others. Frequently we spend an enormous amount of time and energy trying to be what someone else wants us to be. When others do not accept us as we are but instead insist that we be different, we run the risk of denying our needs in an attempt to meet their vision of who we should be.

Interestingly, the demands others place on us are often unreasonable and sometimes impossible to meet. Few students, for example, are perfect, and those who try frantically to live up to their teacher's expectations of perfection have a hard time. The same is true of children, parents, supervisors, and employees. The person of influence may not openly say, "You must be this or that" and, in fact, may even deny that they are making a demand, but we know the demand is there. Often the demands of different people contradict and compete with one another, and we find ourselves caught between them. Teenagers often find that they can't be the son or daughter their parents want and be the type of person their friends want, at the same time. The more they try to please everybody, the less they please anyone.

Even worse is the situation where one person gives us contradictory demands. Sometimes young adults have received contradictory messages from a parent:

1.   Go out and get married.
2.   Stay home and take care of me.

Or

1.   Succeed.
2.   Don't do better than me.

These are "no win" situations: no matter what you do, the other person won't think you've done the right thing. If, when you elect Susan to chair a committee, she complains you are giving her too much work to do and when you do not she feels you don't like her— you can't win! You can reduce stress considerably at these times by refusing this unreasonable demand by saying to yourself, "I will not let people put me in such predicaments; I will not attempt to do the impossible. If there is no way I can win, I'll just focus on how best to stay in this situation. However, if the expectations of staying in this situation are too pressurizing (and I can't find a way to download them), I'll start my exit plan."

Sometimes refusing a demand is as simple as not accepting a task which is unreasonable or impossible. I was once asked to give a twenty-minute talk on how to reduce stress. I refused, saying that such a large topic could not possibly be covered in twenty minutes. Instead, I talked about one specific way to reduce stress. Instead of agreeing to requests that put us in impossible situations, we can learn not to accept such demands in the first place.

None of this means that we aren't concerned about requests that others make of us or that we should be indifferent to the expectations that others have of us. Responding to expectations of parents, teachers, and supervisors can be a way to learn and grow. Of course, we want to be sensitive to the wishes of significant people in our lives. The difficulty comes when we strive so much to live up to other's expectations that we neglect our own needs and wishes—or when we try to meet the expectations of others when they are so unreasonable and contradictory that they cannot be met.

REDUCE SELF-IMPOSED DEMANDS

The expectations of other people are not the only source of unreasonable demands. We frequently impose such high demands on ourselves that we experience excessive stress. Sometimes we do this while believing that the demand comes from others, not realizing that we are the unreasonable taskmasters.

Take, for example, the perfectionist. This person demands (of him/herself) to do everything in absolutely the best possible way. If the supervisor of this person asks for a written report, the perfectionist will fret and struggle because he/she believes that he/she must write the best and most complete report ever written. Well-done is not enough. Ambitious and hard-working people are to be commended, but those who push themselves to try to meet impossible standards are not working efficiently or effectively.

For some people, it's not perfectionism but some other internal demand that causes the pressure. For example, a person who demands of him/herself that he/she never waste any time, experiences frustration and regret—even guilt—on every occasion when some time is wasted. If he/she could reduce this demand and attempt to be as efficient as possible while realizing that everyone wastes some time once in a while, then he/she could better manage those inevitable moments when he/she is not working at full efficiency.

One self-imposed demand that frequently gets people into distress is the demand to please everyone. A person who resolves never to disappoint anyone, never to be different from what others wish him/her to be, and never to get anyone angry is in for a stressful time. Not everyone you know will like you. You will not win everyone's approval. The attempt to please everyone increases distress. Earlier we discussed the demands that others place on us; now we can see that a complementary problem is to demand of ourselves that we meet those other demands. We need not.

Another type of self-imposed demand that causes people considerable unhappiness is the (often unspoken) self-demand that we do for others what only they can and must do for themselves. Suppose you have a friend or relative who has a pain in her mouth but won't go to a dentist. You offer reasons why good dental care is needed and why postponing the inevitable is foolish. She still doesn't go. You argue some more; you beg and plead—but she won't go. If you do all that you can reasonably do and then accept the fact that she won't seek dental help, you are in a manageable situation. If, on the other hand, you decide that you must make her go, you are putting yourself in an impossible situation. Only she can decide to go to the dentist. You can do your part as any friend would, but you must leave to her what only she can do.

Sometimes a friend feels depressed, and we decide to help him feel better. That commendable effort will turn to an unreasonable self-imposed demand if we believe that we must make him feel better. If we judge our efforts by how hard we tried (process evaluation), then we can feel good about what we have done. But, if we judge our efforts by whether or not the other person responds (product evaluation), we will feel that we have failed.

This is not to say that we should not attempt to help other people. In fact, helping others helps us as well as them. The danger to avoid is doing for (or trying to do) for others what they must do for themselves. We can offer our help and assist in anyway possible—and then respect the other person's right to choose how they will do their life (whether or not we like or agree with his/her choice).

Another self-imposed demand is that we be someone other than who we really are. Many people have an image of who they feel they should be, and they reject the person that they are. We're not talking here about the desire to grow and improve who we are but about the rejection that comes from a lack of self-acceptance.

This discussion illustrates how our inner demands interact with external demands; frequently, they are difficult to separate.

CHOOSE BATTLES CAREFULLY

As we relate to others and make our way in the world, we will frequently encounter difficulties and frustrations. Often circumstances will not be as we wish: people will be unresponsive; people will block our goals. We must decide when to accept things as they are and when to fight to change them. That decision is a difficult one, each person needing to decide, in each situation, which path to take. We will be helped if we remember that struggles take considerable time and effort; they are stressful, so we do well to choose our battles carefully.

Some situations can't be changed very much. If I choose to protest every time the government did something I didn't like, I'd write to some level of government at least once a day. I save that energy by taking the government as it is and writing only on matters that are of particular importance to me. When people around us have habits that we find annoying, we can talk to them about possible options, but we are wasteful to make every concern a major issue. When we make molehills into mountains, we end up doing a lot of climbing. We are wise to save our energy for struggles which are important. Many people invite distress by confusing the unimportant with the important and continually fighting battles which could be left alone.

Think of the areas in your life where you are working to get someone or something changed—particularly those that demand considerable energy and effort on your part. These are your battles. Ask yourself, "Is it possible to give up some of these battles?" Select the important ones and decide to let the others go. It is prudent to focus your energy on the few battles that will make a genuine difference for you and give up those that are less significant. Perhaps your spouse has an annoying habit that you can decide to live with rather than criticize. Maybe your supervisor has a way of giving instructions that you don't like but can learn to tolerate. Consider carefully those battles which are important enough to take your time and energy, and consciously say to yourself, "I need not fight the insignificant battles any longer."

DEPERSONALIZE DEMANDS

When we lose perspective on demands—seeing them, for instance, as personal insults or evidence of unfair treatment, standing back and looking at the situation in more abstract and intellectual ways can lessen the pressure caused by emotional entanglement.

One way to get a better perspective on demands (and to gather valuable data for deciding what you will do in relation to those demands) is to keep a Daily Stress and Tension Log. Such a log contains the following categories:

DAILY STRESS AND TENSION LOG

Description of physical signs of stress	Time of day	Where? Doing what? With whom?	What thoughts or feelings did I have?	What did I do in response to the stress?
1.				
2.				
3.				
4.				
5.				

This log should be kept on a daily basis for the *entire* day. For example:

1. Headache, tight neck muscles, fatigue	2:30 p.m.	At work, doing intake with new clients	Frustration, anger	Took a coffee break
2. Tension, insomnia	11:00 p.m.	At home, trying to fall asleep	Thinking about mistakes I made, worrying about tomorrow	Watched TV, took a tranquilizer

Record this information for a week or two, and then examine it for patterns of emotional response, possible causes, and styles of coping. For example, you may find that feelings of anxiety arise whenever you are dealing with older people or authority figures. Or perhaps irritability seems to peak in the late morning, regardless of the situation. Armed with this information, you can begin to explore possible answers to these questions: Why am I feeling this way? What could I do about it that would be better than what I am now doing? For instance, knowing that certain times of day are problematic, you could schedule more low-key tasks for those times (and do the more emotionally stressful work at another time). Other options include scheduling a break at that time (instead of earlier or later) or doing different activities during that break (such as leaving the building and taking a short walk instead of staying at your desk and drinking coffee). Choose coping techniques that are tailored to fit your personal needs within a particular situation. Your informed choices can only be based on an informed understanding of yourself.

TAKE "TIME OUT" FROM DEMANDS

One way to break the pressure buildup of demands is to take a break from them. There are various ways to do that: (1) taking a break while remaining (physically) in the (pressurizing) environment, (2) taking a break by leaving that environment in a way that leaves the demands behind, and (3) staying out of the demanding environment.

Taking a break while staying in the pressurizing environment can serve as an emotional breather—allowing you to relax and get some psychological distance from a particular demand. Maslach (in her book, *Burnout: The Cost of Caring*) says about such breaks:

> One type of break is a short pause that is built in to your contact with people. Although brief, this is a "pause that refreshes" because you have enough time to slow down, regain calm, stop a situation that is getting out of hand, and start all over again. Sometimes the pause is explicitly stated as such. For example, one therapist reported that if the therapy hour was not going well, he would say to the client, "Wait

a minute—let me think about what you've just said." Then he would take a minute or two to sit silently, eyes closed or covered by his hand, while he tried to relax and figure out what to say to get the discussion back on the track (p. 154).

Taking a break in a way that leaves the demands behind can happen in the middle of the demand time or at the end of the demand time. Maslach contrasts (in her same book) ineffective and effective ways to get a break in the middle of a demand time, when she says the following:

> Official breaks from work, such as coffee breaks and the lunch hour, are standard procedure in most organizations. These can be ideal opportunities for emotional recharging, but unfortunately they are sometimes misused in ways that aggravate burnout. Most commonly, people continue to work during their breaks, catching up on paperwork, making telephone calls, or doing some other chores. To go back to our automobile analogy, although these people are keeping their foot on the accelerator only lightly, they should be putting it on the brake. Whatever gains come from working around the clock are usually outweighed by the loss of energy and patience and by the increase in errors or poor judgments toward the end of the workday. It is far better to take advantage of these breaks and really get away from the pressures and demands of the helping role. When the lunch hour comes, leave the office and go for a walk, read a book, get together with friends, play cards, jog, listen to music, plan a sumptuous dinner, visit a local art gallery—indulge yourself (p. 154–155).

Taking a break in a way that leaves the demands behind, at the end of the demand time, is crucial in order to protect the quality of your life after demands. Authors, like Maslach, talk about the value of designing a time of transition between demand time (usually related to work) and life after demands (usually related to life after work). About understanding and designing this transition time, she says the following:

> The tension and emotional strain of work are not easily left behind and can be bad for relationships with family and friends. To cope with this problem, you should think of work and home as two very different environments and recognize that a special transition is needed to get from one to the other … People working in an environment of high emotional pressure need to *decompress*—to get completely out of that high-pressure environment before moving into the "normal pressure" of their private life.

But just what is decompression for a provider? … As I have defined it, *decompression* refers to some activity that: (a) occurs between one's working and nonworking times, and (b) allows one to unwind, relax, and leave the job behind before getting fully involved with family and friends. The activity is often in sharp contrast to the typical work routine. Since the emphasis in care giving occupations is usually on problem solving and intellectual skills, many decompression activities avoid mental exertion. Little or no original thinking is necessary, and thinking about the job is brought to a halt. On the other hand, since many of these jobs involve minimal physical exertion, exercise is often a key element in decompression (p. 169–170).

If we look at the issue of decompression through the glasses provided by the Myers-Briggs Type Indicator, we discover criteria for helping us find activities that "fit" us.

If our personal preference is *Introversion* (so we need to spend time alone to recharge our energy batteries), solitary decompression activities will probably fit us best. Those activities include reading (what you choose); an individual hobby (like developing pictures in a dark room); window shopping; resting or napping; listening to music (especially when the music is in the middle of your head); learning something (for example, language instruction from an ipod); physical exercise (like walking, cycling, gardening, running, working out in a gym, dancing, swimming, yoga—to name a few); soaking in a hot bath; sitting in a sauna; or getting a massage. Just driving or commuting home provides an opportunity to decompress in solitary ways. To maximize the (decompression) benefits of these activities, we need to give ourself permission to do and enjoy them (so, no messages to self like "this is too expensive" or "this is too time consuming," or "why hasn't this worked already"). Also, the benefits are greater if the decompression activity is very different from what we were doing during the workday—so that our body and our mind are getting a real change. So, if we are confined to a desk during the day, an activity that gives us movement after the work day is particularly beneficial. Maslach gives a good example:

The experience of Ronald S., a vocational rehabilitation counsellor specializing in psychiatric disabilities, provides testimony for the power of physical activity as a way to decompress: I think a large part of my ability to cope with burnout is that for years I have been a competing AAU weight lifter. The hobby is excellent diversion from the very complex, abstract, tension-producing work of vocationally rehabilitating chronic mental patients. The three-hour workout sessions allow me a chance to become totally concrete, physical, and at times even primitive. The opportunity to ventilate physically and actually concretely "build" myself has a tremendous prophylactic effect against burnout (p. 172–173).

Some people (usually extraverts) express a concern that solitary decompression practices will cause an isolation from loved ones. Actually, if introverts get these times (and, so, get their batteries recharged), they will be more available to/for loved ones.

If our personal preference is *extroversion* (so that we need time with other people to recharge our energy batteries), group decompression activities will probably fit us best. Many of the activities mentioned above can be done with others. (Learning can be a corporate venture, as can walking or running or dancing or yoga. And less strenuous activities—like soaking in a hot tub or sitting in a sauna—can be done with a friend.) Some decompression activities however, are necessarily social—like team sports, socializing with friends after work, talking things over with your partner, and consulting with a co-worker.

Knowing your preference for introversion or extraversion can help your search for the best-fitting decompression/re-energizing activities, but nothing beats trying the activities on and discovering how they feel.

Maslach also points us to another category of decompression activity: "Whether done alone or with company, a favorite hobby or interest is an ideal candidate for a decompression activity. Many people read, some play music, and still others engage in some artistic activity (painting, photography, pottery). Carpentry, stamp collecting, gourmet cooking—these and many other leisure activities can be used as the vehicle for transition from work to home" (p. 172).

There are times when staying out of the demanding environment is the best way to take a time out from demands. This option is most helpful when demands are particularly difficult or frustrating. Since the feasibility of this strategy varies widely across people (more feasible for people working their own hours; less feasible for people not working their own hours), it is helpful for each person to pre-plan such an exit in the way that best fits his/her demand context. Some people have cancelled appointments to shorten the day; others have stretched out the lunch hour; others have taken a day of sick leave or a mental health day. For some people, planning what they will do during their "exit time" will maximize the benefit. For others, keeping the "exit time" unplanned will maximize its nourishment to them. Each person must discover and apply what works best for him/her.

DESIGN A LIFE AFTER DEMANDS

About this issue, Maslach says the following:

> What do you do when you are not at work? What are you besides your job title? If you have a lot of answers to these questions, then you have an effective strategy for handling demands. There is more to your life than your work, and that "more" can off-set the emotional strain of that work and help you "recharge your batteries." However, it is a sign of trouble if your nonworking hours are just that—an *absence* of work or recovery from work rather than a *presence* of something else. When your whole world is your work and little else, then your whole world is more likely to fall apart when problems arise on the job. Your sense of competence, your self-esteem, and your personal identity are all based on what you do in life, and they will be far more shaky and insecure if that base is a narrow one. The lesson to be learned here is the importance of a rich and varied private life to complement the public one. Or, to rephrase Irving Berlin, do not put all of your eggs in one basket.
>
> The *first step* in strengthening your private life is to protect it from encroachments by your work. Setting up clear boundaries between job and home means that when you leave the job, you really *leave* it—psychologically as well as physically (p. 174–175).

It is easier said then done, however, to keep your job out of your home life. Your job can be like a river in the spring that floods home territory. The following activities are signs of flooding; I will identify four of them and discuss possible ways of shoring up your boundaries.

(1) Rehashing the work day problems at home. There are ways to manage this tendency constructively; otherwise, you could drag the problems home and use up (precious) time and energy reviewing them. (One thing I have said to myself is "I am not prepared to give my job these free hours of overtime.") This does not mean that all conversations—about work—in home time and space is off-limits (although that is the deal that fits some couples). Some couples bring home amusing stories or information or ideas that make for enjoyable and profitable personal conversations. It is the rehashing of *problems* that creates a toxic flood.

However, some people say, "I need to talk about my day—the good, the bad, and the ugly—before I can go on with anything else. Otherwise, I will be fighting with intrusive thoughts and feelings for the whole evening." (As one person graphically said to me, "I need to mentally and emotionally vomit!") For such people, there is a (tried and proven) strategy for getting (constructively) through his/her experience *and* preserving home life. This strategy consists of arranging for "download" time (a time when work's unfinished emotional business can get processed and put away). For some people, such downloading works best when another person is involved. For example, many people have arranged with their partner for a download time shortly after getting home (usually started by the partner saying something like "how was your day?") What makes this different from a "rant" is the prearranged agreement that there is a time limit on the response. (The time limit can vary but usually is set between fifteen minutes and half an hour.) During this time, the sender downloads his/her experience and the receiver listens for understanding (not solutions). When the time is up, as indicated by a timer going off or a watch beeping, they switch roles, if agreed upon. Sometimes, there is an explicit transition; for example, "That sounds X … I'm sure that you will find a way to Y … I'm glad that you can file that now, so you can get on with Z …" Sometimes, there is an implicit transition so that, when the download time is up, the couple just moves to planning the rest of their day together or doing life after work. If the sender, while talking, has "connected the dots" so that he/she recognizes a possible solution or an important task to schedule for tomorrow (or whatever), putting that "next step" on paper/in computer can be the transition activity. For some people, downloading works best when that person is alone (and for some people downloading privately and individually is a necessity). For example, many people download via "journaling" where, on paper or tape or hard-drive, they process (within a specified time period) whatever issue(s) would otherwise pursue them into their life after work. Often, this journaling informs their game-plan for the next day.

Sometimes, the problems of the day don't require such direct processing. More *indirect* (and less labor-intensive) strategies include a "cooling-off" time (where, after getting home, the "problem carrier" follows the rule of "nothing negative"). He/she might do something alone—like nap, walk the dog, play an internet game, do household chores. He/she might do something with others—like have tea, watch T.V., go for a couple walk, play with the children. Whatever he/she does, following the "nothing negative" rule allows the problems to lose steam. Another indirect strategy is prayer, where the "problem carrier"—alone or with someone else—puts the problem in God's hands, who invites us to "cast all [our] anxiety on Him, because He cares for [us]" (1 Peter 5:7).

Whether it takes one or a combination of these strategies to protect your life after work, it is a worthwhile investment.

(2) Taking work—from your job—home to complete in the evening or on the weekend. There are times when taking work home is inevitable—at "pressure-points" of the

work year, in light of an emergency, when it is necessary to cover for a co-worker. During these (exceptional) times, home life can temporarily flex with no damage done. There are, however, employers (and personal goals) that can make this practice part of a lifestyle— then damage will be done. Saying "no" to this lifestyle before it swamps family relationships is crucial. (Couple life and family life has many special and one-time events—like all the "firsts" of your child's life—that will either be participated in or missed with no second chance.) In my experience, one effective way to insure that career work doesn't take over home life is to schedule couple and family events and to (then) prioritize that schedule so that nothing but an emergency could interrupt it. And, during those times when homework needs to be done, it is helpful to compartmentalize it and to schedule it around "fixed" family activities, like family supper or couple coffee time or children's bedtime.

(3) Working overtime. (This circumstance differs from the one just discussed in that this extra job work is done away from the family home.) Again, this may be a required part of your job, but saying "no" to requests that go beyond your share of overtime (so that it isn't "over [all-the] time") is crucial. Also, having ways to flex overtime (like having a deal with a co-worker so that you can trade overtimes) can keep you available for crucial family activities.

(4) Being "on call." This situation (again, a possible requirement of your job) automatically prioritizes work demands above home life. As previously discussed, a key to constructive management is having a say about *how much* you are on call ("I'll arrange to be on call only three nights a week") and *when* you are on call, so that you can plan family activities accordingly.

Work related demands tend to increase (leaking into your home life), especially if you are doing a good job. Among the cognitive tools that will help to plug that leak is the understanding that you have two equal and competing priorities in your life that you must work to keep in (dynamic) balance. So, your strategy is different than prioritizing home over work or work over home which, if acted on, will create an imbalance—and consequent stressors. Your role is to do both, remaining vigilant so that—if one priority needs more of your time and energy for a short time—you will arrange for the other priority to have a similar time of ascendance. Maintaining *both* wings of the airplane makes for a better flight.

Having set aside some private time, the *second step* is to do something with it. Leisure activities of any kind are a great help in handling stress. Not only are these "mini-vacations" a diversion from job tensions, they can also provide positive experiences with other people and can give an important boost to your sense of competence and self-esteem. They replenish and rejuvenate you, offsetting the exhaustion and emptiness of unrelenting demands. By giving *to* yourself you will feel more able to give *of* yourself to others.

Again, let me quote Maslach:

> Leisure activities can take many forms. Hobbies, sports, art, music, and literature are all valuable pursuits during your private time, as are entertainment and travel. Choose whatever is most fun and rewarding for you, but be sure to translate those choices into *action*. Good intentions are not good ways to cope.
>
> In some cases, a leisure activity may become an avocation or even a second job. Moonlighting is often done to earn extra income or develop new job skills, but it is also an effective coping technique. If moonlighting brings you into contact with individuals under pleasant and rewarding circumstances, then it can offset the negative reaction toward people that is so characteristic of stress.
>
> Although privacy and solitude are a part of one's private life, many "off hours" are spent in the company of others. These other people—whether they be family, friends, or acquaintances—are important allies in your battle against demands. They are a source of aid and comfort, of recognition and rewards, of good feelings and pleasurable experiences .… Personal strength often comes from strong social supports. Research shows that people who are part of a solid social support network are better able to cope with physical ills and psychological problems (p. 177-178).

EXERCISES

The following exercises are to help you make application of the strategies that have been outlined in this appendix. Some exercises may apply to more than one strategy (and that will be stated). Some strategies don't have a related exercise (because of my lack of ingenuity). For instance, the strategy "Schedule Demands" has no related exercise because I couldn't think of one apart from knowing the content of your schedule. Hopefully, you can make applications of this strategy without the benefit of an application exercise. (By the way, if you want to design exercises that improve on the one's I've included, be my guest; you are also invited to share those improvements with me through e-mail. My e-mail address is drstanwillson@shaw.ca).

Exercise A

1. This exercise is designed to help clarify and specify your applications of the strategies of "Establish Priorities," "Eliminate Some Activities" and "Make Some

Activities Less Complex."

In column I below, list seven activities which take a significant portion of your time. Avoid overly large categories (work, school, family, etc.) and list specific activities in each category. In column II, estimate how many hours you devote to each task each week. In column III, put a number from one to five which indicates how willing you are to spend less time on that activity—or even to eliminate it altogether. The number one means "not willing at all," three means "moderately willing," and five means "very willing."

I. ACTIVITY	II. TIME SPENT	III. WILLINGNESS

Now take seven three by five cards and label them from A to G. Record each activity on a separate card. Take these cards two at a time and ask yourself, "Which of these is more important to me than the other?" When you decide, record a mark in the Count Column beside the letter of the most important activity. (To insure that you compare all possible combinations, compare the following pairs: A-C, A-B, A-D, A-E, A-F, A-G, B-C B-D, B-E, B-F, B-G, C-D, C-E, C-F, C-G, D-E, D-F, D-G, E-F, E-G, F-G.) When you have finished, list the activities on the priority list, putting the activity with the most marks in position one, the activity with the second highest number of marks in position two, and so on. This constitutes your list of priorities.

COUNT COLUMN	PRIORITY LIST
A.	1.
B.	2.
C.	3.
D.	4.
E.	5.
F.	6.
G.	7.

2. Prepare a plan for reducing demand. Beginning with the activity lowest on your list of priorities, ask yourself these questions:

– How can I spend less time on this activity?

– Do I need to spend as much time on this activity as I currently do?

– Is it as important as I have been assuming?

– Although I would prefer to spend more time on this activity, do I need to?

– Would there be disastrous consequences if I did not?

Decide how you will spend less time on that activity—and on every activity as you move up your list of priorities. Record your plans below.

Plan for Reducing Demand:

Ways to reduce demand no. 7 on priority list: _____

_____

_____

_____

Ways to reduce demand no. 6 on priority list: _____

_____

_____

_____

Ways to reduce demand no. 5 on priority list: _____

_____

_____

_____

Ways to reduce demand no. 4 on priority list: _____

_____

_____

Ways to reduce demand no. 3 on priority list: _____

_____

_____

_____

Ways to reduce demand no. 2 on priority list: _____

_____

_____

_____

Ways to reduce demand no. 1 on priority list: _____

_____

_____

_____

Exercise B

This exercise is designed to help clarify and specify your applications of the strategy "Refuse Demands That Are Unreasonable to You."

Select at least three situations involving your relationships with other people that are stressful for you. Describe each one in a few sentences. Think through each situation carefully to see if there is some demand that the other person is placing on you—some way that the other person wants you to be. Record that demand. Then ask yourself if you want to fulfill that demand; if not, consciously and deliberately decide to refuse it.

Design your refusal plan (in other words, how you will refuse that demand). If you fail to plan, you plan to fail.

Situation 1: _____

_____

_____

_____

Demand: _____

_____

_____

_____

My plan (for refusing this demand) is as follows: _____

_____

_____

_____

_____

_____

_____

Situation 2: _____

_____

_____

_____

Demand: _____

_____

_____

_____

My plan (for refusing this demand) is as follows: _____

_____

_____

_____

_____

_____

Situation 3: _____

_____

_____

_____

_____

Demand: _____

_____

_____

_____

My plan (for refusing this demand) is as follows: _____

_____

_____

_____

_____

_____

_____

Exercise C

This exercise is designed to help clarify and specify your applications of the strategy "Reduce Self-Imposed Demands."

Select at least three situations which are stressful for you (particularly situations in which you feel badly about yourself). Select situations in which you are angry at yourself, upset with yourself, ashamed, guilty, or concerned about your faults, limitations, or failures. Describe each one in a few sentences. Think through each one carefully to see if there is some demand that you are making on yourself, some internal expectation that you are expecting yourself to meet. Record that demand. Then ask yourself if you must fulfill that demand: Is it reasonable? Is it absolutely necessary? Would it be disastrous if you didn't fulfill it? When appropriate, consciously and deliberately decide to refuse that demand. (Again, it is crucial to design *how* you will refuse that self-demand. Make sure that your plan includes a rebuttal of each self-demand you are making.)

Situation 1: _____

_____

_____

_____

Demand: _____

_____

_____

_____

_____

My plan (for refusing this self-demand) is as follows: _____

_____

_____

_____

_____

_____

Situation 2: _____

_____

_____

_____

Demand: _____

_____

_____

_____
_____
_____

My plan (for refusing this self-demand) is as follows: _____

_____
_____
_____
_____
_____

Situation 3: _____

_____
_____
_____

Demand: _____

_____
_____
_____
_____

My plan (for refusing this self-demand) is as follows: _____

_____
_____
_____
_____
_____
_____

Exercise D

This exercise is designed to help clarify and specify your applications of the strategy "Reduce Self-Imposed Demands."

Seat yourself comfortably in a chair, close your eyes, and see yourself in one of the situations selected in exercise C. Visualize that situation for a few minutes, experiencing the situation as vividly as you can. Then repeat to yourself the following statements:

• I am a human being and therefore imperfect.
• While I strive to improve myself, I also accept myself as I am; I will hold myself to a high standard but in a gentle way.

- I may feel badly about my human faults and weaknesses, but I will forgive myself for having these faults and weaknesses. I will strive to deal with these faults and weaknesses.
- The best thing I can do for myself right now is to accept myself as I am; having done that, I can focus my energies on refusing unreasonable self-imposed demands and working on reasonable self-imposed demands.
- Repeat this procedure for each situation in exercise C and record your reactions below.

Reactions to this exercise: _____

_____

_____

_____

Exercise E

This exercise is designed to help clarify and specify your applications of the strategy "Choose Battles Carefully."

Make a list of battles that you are currently fighting. People you are quarrelling with, situations you are protesting, arguments you are having. Put an X beside each battle which is genuinely important and worth the time, energy, and aggravation it costs you. Draw a line through all the others; consciously and deliberately decide not to fight them anymore.

CURRENT BATTLES	THIS BATTLE IS IMPORTANT

For every battle that you drew a line through, make a list of the things that you will need to do, so that you won't get pulled or provoked back into that battle. (In other words, develop your "exit and staying exited" plan.)

Develop that plan below:

Battle I will not fight: _____

My "exit and staying exited" plan: _____

_____

_____

_____

_____

Battle I will not fight: _____

_____

My "exit and staying exited" plan: _____

_____

_____

_____

_____

Battle I will not fight: _____

My "exit and staying exited" plan: _____

_____

_____

_____

_____

Exercise F

This exercise is designed to help clarify and specify your applications of the strategy "Depersonalize Demands."

Having examined your Daily Stress and Tension Log (see section 8 in text—on "Depersonalizing Demands") for patterns of emotional response, possible causes, and your styles of coping. It is time to develop an action plan that will lead (in light of that information) to higher quality coping strategies.

WHAT I HAVE DISCOVERED FROM \ MY DAILY STRESS AND TENSION LOG	WHAT I WILL DO TO HANDLE THAT DISCOVERY IN AN EFFECTIVE WAY
(1)	
(2)	
(3)	

- Fill in your discoveries in the left-hand column.
- Fill in *at least one* thing you will do that will help you to benefit from that discovery, in the right-hand column.
- Do that one thing for at least a week, noticing what difference that makes for you.
- If that one thing is making a positive difference, you may only need to keep doing that in order to keep benefiting from that change.
- If that one thing is not making a positive difference (or enough of a positive difference), select a different thing that could be beneficial for you to do. (Notice that this choice is based on more relevant data than was your first action plan, because you now know more about what doesn't work. This is why doing something that doesn't work is still valuable.)

Exercise G

This exercise is designed to help clarify and specify your applications of the strategy "Take Time Out From Demands."

1. There are various ways (in addition to the examples provided by the Maslach quote) to take a break, while staying in the pressurizing environment. Among the ways that I use are the following: opening mail, making a cup of tea, going to the bathroom, making a phone call, reading something—either professional or recreational, doing a five-minute relaxation routine, having a snack, planning what I will do (after work), listening to a song.

    - Taking into account your circumstances, your preferences, and your demands, select at least three (personally appropriate) ways to do a "pause that refreshes." Write them down.

On-site break options:

(1) _____

(2) _____

(3) _____

- If any of them require preparation (e.g. bringing an Ipod), complete that preparation.
- Do those on-site activities over the next week (as needed).
- Notice, as you are doing them, which one seems to make the most difference in your experience. Also, notice which one makes the least difference.
- After a week, replace the activity that makes the least difference with another activity (that you think has greater "help" potential).

2. Since taking a break that leaves the demands behind is actually a "larger pause that refreshes," the following exercise will focus on the time of transition between "demand time" and "your life after demands."

- Read (again) what Maslach says about decompression activities.
- Taking into account your circumstances, preferences and demands, design your decompression game-plan. Write it down.

    My Decompression Game-Plan(including what, when, where, how long and with whom [if relevant]):

    _____

    _____

    _____

    _____

    _____

Exercise H

This exercise is designed to help clarify and specify your applications of the strategy "Design a Life After Demands."

It is crucial that your "life after demands" be tailor-made to you. As such, it will not be your ideal "life after demands" or the "life after demands" that someone else thinks you should have or the "life after demands" that your culture advocates. Your design of that life will take time and adjustment. It will include "experiments" (trying new and different things) and "errors" (learning what doesn't work). You are looking for those activities that actually (not theoretically) "nourish" you: excite you, engage you, develop other aspects of you, make you more whole.

Below, write the first draft of what your "life after demands" needs to include. (Read the following considerations before writing your first draft. These considerations will help you to shape that draft.)

My Life After Demands (Today's Version):

_____

_____

_____

_____

_____

_____

- A high-quality "life after demands" will include activities that nourish the various dimensions of who you are:
    – Physical dimension (for example, some form of exercise)
    – Cognitive dimension (for example, learning something new)
    – Emotional dimension (for example, becoming self supportive)
    – Spiritual dimension (for example, doing something that deepens your connection with God)
    – Relational dimension (for example, developing a deeper relationship with another person)
- If you have an introverted personality style, you will find nourishment in individual and private activities (where you will get your battery recharged). If you have an extraverted personality style, you will find nourishment in corporate and public activities (where you will get energy from those interactions).
- "Nourishment comes from our roots." If there are activities from your background which you previously enjoyed (or still are enjoying), they are prime candidates for present nourishment.
- Talk to your "significant others." The significant people in your life can give you feedback on what nourishes you, can support your goal for life after work, can participate with you in that life after work, and can help hold you accountable to your commitments. Involving such people is an important asset.

Appendix D

SINGLE BREATH RELAXATION

SINGLE BREATH RELAXATION

As correct breathing is the basis of this technique, breathing must first be described. This is followed by a description of the "single breath relaxation."

Breathing:

Breathing involves different groups of muscles of the trunk. Some are located in the chest wall; a few even extend from the shoulders up into the neck. A large muscle devoted primarily to breathing is the diaphragm, located between the chest cavity and the abdomen. Relaxed breathing is done primarily by the diaphragm.

The lungs are shaped something like this:

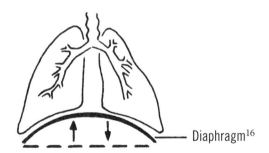

Diaphragm[16]

As you can see, the greatest volume is in the lower part of the lung next to the diaphragm. Using the diaphragm, therefore, moves a large volume of air, and allows for slow rhythmical breathing. At rest, a rate of six to ten breaths per minute is usually adequate. Most of us, however, do not breathe primarily with the diaphragm, but primarily with the chest. We wrongly try to keep "our tummies tucked in" and immobile. This chest breathing causes us to take in smaller amounts of air with each breath and the breathing rate is closer to ten to sixteen per minute at rest.

Breathing in a slow easy manner with the diaphragm will help induce relaxation. Our heart rate slows as a response to relaxed diaphragmatic breathing.

To practice relaxed breathing, start by breathing in as if you were filling your abdomen. Then let the chest become full as you continue to breathe in. When you are close to a maximum breath in, relax and let the air flow out gently and evenly.

As you can see—the stomach has to go out as the diaphragm comes down.[17]

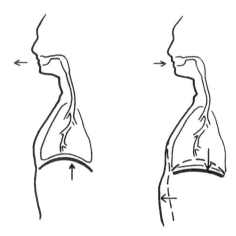

Contrary to popular ideas on posture, we should have an abdominal wall which protrudes gently as we breathe in.

If you have difficulty doing this breathing, practice by putting your hand on your abdomen. Your hand should move out as you breathe in. After you are good at getting the abdomen to move, then try to get both the abdomen and the chest moving. By starting with the abdomen, the chest will fill out naturally as you continue breathing in. Practice in front of a mirror after a shower or bath.

Some people habitually chest breathe and may require repeated practice sessions before being able to breathe properly with their diaphragms. You are encouraged to practice until you can do it evenly and spontaneously.

The Single Breath Relaxation:

Take a full breath in, as described above, and then as you breathe out say to yourself, "I am calm and quiet." Practice this repeatedly and in different situations until it becomes spontaneous. Don't be discouraged if you don't obtain a relaxed feeling the first few times. Keep practicing—it will become increasingly more noticeable with time.

Appendix E

PROGRESSIVE RELAXATION

PROGRESSIVE RELAXATION

You cannot have the feeling of warm well-being in your body and at the same time experience psychological stress. Progressive relaxation of your muscles reduces pulse rate and blood pressure as well as decreasing perspiration and respiration rates. Deep muscle relaxation, when successfully mastered, can be used like an anti-anxiety pill.

Edmond Jacobson, a Chicago physician, published the book *Progressive Relaxation* in 1929. In this book he described his deep muscle relaxation technique, which he asserted required no imagination, willpower, or suggestion. His technique is based on the premise that the body responds to anxiety-provoking thoughts and events with muscle tension. This physiological tension, in turn, increases the subjective experience of anxiety. Deep muscle relaxation reduces physiological tension and is incompatible with anxiety: the habit of responding with one, blocks the habit of responding with the other.

Symptom Effectiveness:

Excellent results (after this technique is mastered and used as needed) have been found in the treatment of muscular tension, anxiety, insomnia, depression, fatigue, irritable bowel, muscle spasms, neck and back pain, high blood pressure, mild phobias, and stuttering.

Time for Mastery:

One to two weeks. Two fifteen minute sessions per day.

Instructions:

Most people do not realize which of their muscles are chronically tense. Progressive relaxation provides a way of identifying particular muscles and muscle groups and distinguishing between sensations of tension and deep relaxation. Four major muscle groups will be covered:

1. Hands, forearms, and biceps.
2. Head, face, throat, and shoulders, including concentration on forehead, cheeks, nose, eyes, jaws, lips, tongue, and neck. Considerable attention is devoted to your head, because from the emotional point of view, the most important muscles in your body are situated in and around this region.
3. Chest, stomach, and lower back.
4. Thighs, buttocks, calves, and feet.

Progressive relaxation can be practiced lying down or in a chair with your head supported. Each muscle or muscle grouping is tensed from five to seven seconds and then relaxed for twenty to thirty seconds. This procedure is repeated at least once. If an area remains tense, you can practice up to five times. You may also find it useful to use the following relaxing expressions when untensing:

- "Let go of the tension."
- "Throw away the tension—I am feeling calm and rested."
- "Relax and smooth out the muscles."
- "Let the tension dissolve away."

Once the procedure is familiar enough to be remembered, keep your eyes closed and focus attention on just one muscle group at a time. The instructions for progressive relaxation are divided into two sections. The first part, which you may wish to tape and replay when practicing, will familiarize you with the muscles in your body which are most commonly tense. The second section shortens the procedure by simultaneously tensing and relaxing many muscles at one time so that deep muscle relaxation can be achieved in a very brief period.

Basic Procedure:

Get in a comfortable position and relax. Now clench your right fist, tighter and tighter, studying the tension as you do so. Keep it clenched and notice the tension in your fist, hand, and forearm. Now relax. Feel the looseness in your right hand, and notice the contrast with the tension. Repeat this procedure with your right fist again, always noticing as you relax that this is the opposite of tension—relax and feel the difference. Repeat the entire procedure with your left fist, then both fists at once.

Now bend your elbows and tense your biceps. Tense them as hard as you can and observe the feeling of tautness. Relax, straighten out your arms. Let the relaxation develop and feel that difference. Repeat this, and all succeeding procedures at least once.

Turning attention to your head, wrinkle your forehead as tight as you can. Now relax and smooth it out. Let yourself imagine your entire forehead and scalp becoming smooth and at rest. Now frown and notice the strain spreading throughout your forehead. Let go. Allow your brow to become smooth again. Close your eyes now, squint them tighter. Look for the tension. Relax your eyes. Let them remain closed gently and comfortably. Now clench your jaw, bite hard, notice the tension throughout your jaw. Relax your jaw. When the jaw is relaxed, your lips will be slightly parted. Let yourself really appreciate the contrast between tension and relaxation. Now press your tongue against the roof of your mouth. Feel the ache in the back of your mouth. Relax. Press your lips now, purse them into an "O." Relax your lips. Notice that your forehead, scalp, eyes, jaw, tongue, and lips are all relaxed.

Press your head back as far as it can comfortably go, and observe the tension in your neck. Roll it to the right, feel the changing locus of stress, and roll it to the left. Straighten your head, bring it forward, and press your chin against your chest. Feel the tension in your throat and the back of your neck. Relax, allowing your head to return to a comfortable position. Let the relaxation deepen. Now shrug your shoulders. Keep the tension as you hunch your head down between your shoulders. Relax your shoulders. Drop them back, and feel the relaxation spreading through your neck, throat, and shoulders—pure relaxation, deeper and deeper.

Give your entire body a chance to relax. Feel the comfort and the heaviness. Now breathe in, and fill your lungs completely. Hold your breath. Notice the tension. Now exhale, let your chest become loose, and let the air hiss out. Continue relaxing, letting your breath come freely and gently. Repeat this several times, noticing the tension draining from your body as you exhale. Next, tighten your stomach and hold. Note the tension; then relax. Now place your hand on your stomach. Breathe deeply into your stomach, pushing your hand up. Hold, and relax. Feel the contrast of relaxation as the air rushes out. Now arch your back, without straining. Keep the rest of your body as relaxed as possible. Focus on the tension in your lower back. Now relax, deeper and deeper.

Tighten your buttocks and thighs. Flex your thighs by pressing down your heels as hard as you can. Relax and feel the difference. Now curl your toes downward, making your calves tense. Study the tension. Relax. Now bend your toes toward your face, creating tension in your shins. Relax again.

Feel the heaviness throughout your lower body as the relaxation deepens. Relax your feet, ankles, calves, shins, knees, thighs, and buttocks. Now let the relaxation spread to your stomach, lower back, and chest. Let go more and more. Experience the relaxation deepening in your shoulders, arms, and hands, deeper and deeper. Notice the feeling of looseness and relaxation in your neck, jaws, and all your facial muscles.

Shorthand Procedure:

The following is a procedure for achieving deep muscle relaxation quickly. Whole muscle groups are simultaneously tensed and then relaxed. As before, repeat each procedure at least once, tensing each muscle group from five to seven seconds and then relaxing from twenty to thirty seconds. Remember to notice the contrast between the sensations of tension and relaxation.

1. Curl both fists, tightening biceps and forearms (Charles Atlas pose). Relax.
2. Wrinkle up forehead. At the same time, press your head as far back as possible, roll it clockwise in a complete circle, and reverse. Now wrinkle up the muscles of your face like a walnut: frowning, eyes squinted, lips pursed, tongue pressing the roof of the mouth, and shoulders hunched. Relax.
3. Arch back as you take a deep breath into the chest. Hold. Relax. Take a deep breath, pressing out the stomach. Hold. Relax.
4. Pull feet and toes back toward face, tightening shins. Hold. Relax. Curl toes, simultaneously tightening calves, thighs and buttocks. Relax.

Special Considerations:

1. If you make a tape of the basic procedure to facilitate your relaxation program, remember to space each procedure so that time is allowed to experience the tension and relaxation before going on to the next muscle or muscle group.
2. Most people have somewhat limited success when they begin deep muscle relaxation, but it is only a matter of practice. Whereas twenty minutes of work might initially bring only partial relaxation, it will eventually be possible to relax your whole body in a few moments.
3. Sometimes in the beginning, it may seem to you as though relaxation is complete. But although the muscle or muscle group may well be partially relaxed, a certain number of muscle fibers will still be contracted. It is the act of relaxing these additional fibers that will bring about the emotional effects you want. It is helpful to say to yourself during the relaxation phase, "Let go more and more."
4. Caution should be taken in tensing the neck and back. Excessive tightening can result in muscle or spinal damage. It is also commonly observed that over tightening the toes or feet results in muscle cramping.

Appendix F

DAILY RECORD OF
DISTRESS-PRODUCING THOUGHTS

DAILY RECORD OF DISTRESS-PRODUCTING THOUGHTS

DATE	(2) SITUATION	(1) EMOTIONS	(3) AUTOMATIC THOUGHT (2)	(4) RATIONAL RESPONSE	(5) OUTCOME	(6) If I was to act upon my RATIONAL RESPONSE (to my automatic stress-increasing thoughts), I WOULD DO THE FOLLOWING
	Describe: 1. Actual event leading to unpleasant emotion or 2. Stream of thoughts, daydream, or recollection leading to unpleasant emotion	1. Specify: sad, anxious, angry, etc. 2. Rate degree of emotion 1–100% (1 = trace 100 = most intense possible)	1. Write automatic thought(s) that preceded emotion(s) 2. Rate belief in automatic thought(s) 0–100%	1. Write rational response to automatic thought(s) 2. Rate belief in rational response 0–100%	1. Re-rate belief in automatic thought(s) 0–100% 2. Re-rate belief in rational thought(s) 0–100%	1. 2. 3. 4.

Appendix G

IDENTIFYING, CHALLENGING, AND REVISING STRESS-INDUCING SELF TALK

Have you ever thought about how many rules we obey every day? Almost every minute of every day is bound up by rules, customs, and mores. Sometimes we are aware of the rules that we are obeying. This morning I put on a coat and tie to go to work; I am obeying the rule about dressing professionally. The job seeker knows about the rule that one should not be late for appointments with a prospective employer. Most of us know and respect the rule not to break promises made to children, to keep the speed limit, or to not "jump the cue" when in line to get lunch.

On the other hand, there are other rules that we aren't aware of. We take these rules for granted; they don't seem like rules at all, but seem like the right or only way to behave. For instance, until we stop and think about it, eating three meals a day may seem like the natural and only way to obtain nourishment. In fact, this is a custom not adhered to in many parts of the world. Anyone who has studied life in different cultures knows that many ideas that we accept as representing "the way to do things" is just *our* way of doing things—our rules. Many of these rules are so unnoticed that they are rarely spoken aloud; they are the unspoken rules—conditions we live by (without questioning them). Some of these unspoken rules are shared by almost everyone in our society, but others may be unique to a particular person.

These unspoken rules are a powerful influence in our lives; trying to live up to them is a major cause of pressure. The disappointment, frustration, anger, anxiety, and guilt that results from violating these (unspoken) rules often triggers our body to respond with a stress reaction. Becoming aware of these unspoken rules, challenging them, and revising them is an effective way of managing that stress reaction. Experts in human behavior have long understood the importance of these unspoken rules. Shakespeare said, "Nothing is either good nor bad, but thinking makes it so." Recently, pioneers like Albert Ellis and Aaron Beck and David Burns, have written extensively about them. The ideas in this appendix are based on their excellent work.

182

What are some unspoken rules? If a person is always afraid to speak up when talking with other people, if this person never offers an opinion different from the people around him, if he is asked to do a favor but never says "no," he is letting unspoken rules rule him. Think of the pressure that these rules are applying. Literally, they are dictating his lifestyle. We can infer—from his behavior—some of these rules including, *I must never get anyone angry at me, I must please everyone, and I must never think of my own needs—only the other person's.* Since this person lives according to the rule, I must never get anyone angry with me, a lot of his behavior will be influenced by that rule, and he will pay a price for that. For example, anyone who gets angry (or even threatens anger) will dictate to him. And while he spends time doing what pleases others and avoiding what might anger them, he is neglecting his own needs and wishes. That priority (which results from his unspoken rule) puts pressure on him and decreases his personal resources for coping with that pressure. Here are other common unspoken rules:

I must never make a mistake.

I must never fail.

I must never look foolish.

I must work very hard at all times.

I must never get angry.

I must always play it safe.

We also have unspoken rules for other people. These are our expectations about how other people should behave toward us:

People should never treat me unfairly.

People should never disappoint me.

People should do what I ask.

People should be reasonable toward me.

People should not ask me to do what I don't want to do.

Usually, the rules for ourselves consist of "musts"—I must do this, I must be that. The rules for others consist of "shoulds"—he should do this, she should be that.

We feel distressed when these rules are broken. When we break rules we have set for ourselves, we usually feel either anger or guilt. We can also experience shame, discouragement, anxiety, depression, or embarrassment. Anger is the most common response when other people break rules that we have for them.

Think of a situation where you have been angry or guilty, or experienced some other stressful response. See if you can discover the unspoken thought process that led to that emotional response. It could be something like this:

I made a mistake yesterday. That's terrible. *I must never make a mistake.* If I make a mistake, that means that I am stupid or foolish. Maybe it means that I'm weak. People will think less of me. *Other people should always think the best of me. Other people should never know my weaknesses.* I feel terrible; I can't stand it.

When we think (self talk) like this, it leads to toxic personal consequences. We begin to feel unpleasant emotions—like anger, guilt, and embarrassment. Also, we begin to act in unproductive ways—like withdrawing from other people. Also, we begin to see ourself differently—like someone who is a "poser."

An example of how these unspoken rules impact our relationships with others is as follows. Suppose that someone promises to take a trip with you but backs out of that promise shortly before you are to leave; your self talk could sound like this:

He lied to me. *People should never disappoint me.* He made a promise, and so he should keep it—he has no right to change his mind. He's someone that I could never trust again. *People should always keep their promises to me.*

Again, when we think (self talk) like this, it leads to toxic relational consequences. We begin to feel negative emotions toward that other person—like anger. Also, we begin to act in unhealthy ways—like confronting the other person. Also, we begin to see the relationship differently—like one that we no longer want to be involved in. Often, when we are upset with other people, it is because they have broken one of our unspoken rules.

Anxiety is another emotion that results from the unspoken rules we have about ourselves and others. Think of a situation that makes you anxious and ask yourself, "Why am I so anxious?" As you think about it, you will probably discover an unspoken rule. Many of these rules are so impactful that even the prospect of not keeping such a rule can cause tension. You may be thinking, *I must never do this,* or *This should never happen to me.* You may be believing that you couldn't stand it if this rule was broken or this need was not met. As an example, if a person is anxious because he must speak before a group of strangers, it is probably because he believes a number of unspoken rules. Among them could be the following:

I must not make a mistake in public.
People must think well of me in this situation.
I must not let people know that I worry and feel fear.
I must never appear to be inadequate in front of others.

Rules help us live efficiently and effectively. We could not do without them. Certain rules, however, get us into difficulty and these need to be revised. Usually, these are the "musts" and the "shoulds." When we think that something *must* be, or *should* be, or *has to* be, we get upset when life doesn't fit our demands. A rule is a demand—a demand that we and other people be, act, and think in ways that *we* consider right.

People who suffer most from stress reactions are not necessarily those who have many external demands placed upon them; if, however, these people also place (internal) demands on themselves, they are very likely to experience distress. These internal demands can be the hardest to bear. For example, an executive who must make all the decisions, must always be in control, and never delegate responsibility is under much more pressure than another executive with equal responsibility but different unspoken rules.

The amount of pressure that a person experiences also results from how that person uses these unspoken rules. Unspoken rules tend to convert hopes and preferences into needs. So, something that we prefer would happen gets converted to what *must* happen— so pressure is intensified. Also, unspoken rules can feel very important, so we tend to overemphasize and exaggerate the results of breaking those rules. And, maybe most impactful of all, we tend to criticize ourselves and others for breaking these rules.

All of us would like to succeed at every task we undertake. There is nothing wrong with that hope. But when a person converts this hope or preference into a need, then the unspoken rule, *I must succeed at everything all the time,* becomes part of that person's software. There is a huge difference between preferring to do well and thinking, "I *must* do well." If I prefer to do well but find I have failed at a given task, I might be concerned, disappointed, and maybe a little sad, but it won't be a catastrophe. If I believe the rule, *I must always do well and succeed at everything all the time,* then—when I fail at any given task— I become angry at myself, ashamed, guilty, and even depressed. Converting the *preference* to do well into a requirement results in intense pressure and (consequent) stress reactions.

Unspoken rules are often accompanied by all-or-nothing thinking. If I obey the rule, then all is well. If I break the rule, then all is terrible. So, a person with all-or-nothing thinking will think that he's great when he keeps the rule but will think that he's stupid or terrible when he doesn't. Those who live by the rule, *People should never disappoint me,* think of you as a great friend as long as all is going well but conclude that you are no friend at all as soon as the first disappointment appears. This swinging to extremes in our thinking compounds our distress.

We often exaggerate or overemphasize the importance of these unspoken rules. Notice your experience when you break one of them. If you don't have what you think you

must have, then you'll think it's terrible to be without it—not disappointing or unfortu-
nate to be without it—but *terrible.* The person whose rule is, *I must never make a mistake
in public,* feels it is intolerable when he/she makes one. For that person, the very prospect
of making a public mistake generates anxiety because he says to himself, "I couldn't stand
it; I couldn't live with myself." This is a real but exaggerated reaction to breaking an unspoken rule. As a matter of fact, there are few things that we couldn't stand or couldn't
live with.

Perhaps most serious is the tendency to put down ourselves and others when unspoken rules are broken. We think less of ourselves and others if we do not keep these rules.
If your rule is, *I must never lose my temper,* then—when you do lose it—you might tell
yourself that you are a bad or terrible person. If your rule for others is, *People must always
anticipate my needs,* then you might think of them as bad or evil when they don't.

How can we reduce the distress caused by these unspoken rules?

First, become aware of them. As noted earlier, we often take these rules so much for
granted that we hardly notice their existence or impact. Start to examine each distressing
situation you experience—particularly those involving unpleasant emotions like anger,
anxiety, guilt, or depression—and look for the unspoken rules behind your emotional
reactions. Look for the "musts" and the "shoulds." Ask yourself, "Why do I feel as I do in
this situation? What demands am I putting on myself? What demands am I putting on
others?" You may have to think about a situation for a while (or talk about it with a good
friend) before discovering your unspoken rules, but after you have practiced a few times
you will become skilled at identifying them.

Second, examine the thinking that accompanies your rules. Notice the all-or-nothing
thinking and the exaggeration of importance that accompanies your unspoken rules. Notice, when you don't keep one of your rules for yourself, to see if you have negative talk (toward yourself). Write down that negative self talk. Do the same, when someone else does
not keep one of your unspoken rules.

Third, talk it over with "safe" friends. Share your rules with them and get their feedback. Have them share their rules with you, if they so choose. Just speaking these rules
out loud can help because that exposes their unreasonableness and allows you to be more
aware of them and of their impact on you.

Fourth, challenge these rules. Ask yourself, "Why must I think this way? Who says
that I must live up to this rule? Where did I learn this rule? Why must I demand this of
myself? Why must I demand this of others?" Another series of questions goes like this:
"Is it terrible if I don't live up to my rules? Am I a failure if I don't always live up to the

demands I place on myself? Are other people terrible if they don't do what I want or behave as I wish they would? Is it possible that my reactions are really over reactions?" These rules often come from deeply held beliefs, and they won't be changed quickly or easily, but asking these questions begins to challenge them.

Fifth, revise your rules. Substitute a more reasonable, less harsh rule for the one you are now following. For example, suppose your rule is, *I must always do my best.* Behind that rule is usually this one, *It would be terrible if I didn't do my best.* Revise this rule, making a more reasonable one, such as, *I prefer to do my best. I feel better when I do my best, but it isn't always possible. It isn't the "end of the world" when I don't meet my goal. I will forgive myself and move on.*

Here are several unspoken rules and their revisions:

UNSPOKEN RULE	REVISED RULE
(1) I must never make a mistake in public. I couldn't stand it if people saw me doing something stupid.	(1) I would prefer not to make a mistake in public, but if I do, it's not the end of the world. I won't like it when people see me make a mistake, but I can stand it.
(2) People must think well of me. It would be terrible if others don't like me.	(2) I like it when others think well of me. I certainly don't like it when they don't. But if some people don't like me, I can live with that. Furthermore, I can like myself even when someone else does not.
(3) People should never disappoint me. People who disappoint me have no right to do so. Something is wrong with people who disappoint me.	(3) Life is easier when people keep their promises and react as I prefer. I know that at times people won't do this. I accept their faults just as I hope they will accept mine. I can't expect others to be what I want them to be.
(4) People should not ask me to do what I don't want to do.	(4) I prefer that people not make unwanted requests, but I can't expect them to know what I want and don't want. When they make unwanted requests, I will evaluate them and respond on my terms, not theirs. I can say "no" or "not now" or "let me think about that" as well as "yes."

Generally, it is helpful to revise our rules in order to change the "musts" and "shoulds" into preferences. Also, we acknowledge that, when things don't go our way, the result is a situation which we don't like but can live with. It is not terrible, horrible, or something we just can't stand. (You can practice revising unspoken rules by completing exercise 1 at the end of this appendix.)

Sixth, notice the difference it makes when you think according to your revised rules (rather than the original unspoken rules). As you notice how much better you feel about yourself and others when you think in terms of the revised rules, you'll find it easier to substitute those rules for your original unspoken ones. (The second exercise at the end of this appendix helps you to do this.)

EXERCISES

1. Select four situations which are distressing for you. Specifically, select one resulting in anger, one resulting in guilt, one resulting in anxiety, and one other of any type. Describe each situation in a few sentences. Then think through each situation carefully, asking yourself, "Why do I react as I do?" and "What am I saying to myself that contributes to this reaction?" Keep asking these questions until you discover the unspoken rule which contributes to your reaction. Remember that unspoken rules are sometimes difficult to uncover. Use the examples in this appendix to help you. Record the unspoken rule; then write out a revision of that rule which is more reasonable and less apt to result in a stress reaction.

   Situation 1. Anger: _____

   _____

   _____

   _____

   Unspoken rule: _____

   Revised rule:_____

   _____

   Situation 2. Guilt:_____

   _____

   _____

   _____

   Unspoken rule:_____

   Revised rule:_____

   _____

   Situation 3. Anxiety: _____

   _____

Unspoken rule:_____

Revised rule:_____

Situation 4. Other: _____

_____

_____

Unspoken rule:_____

Revised rule:_____

1. Seat yourself comfortably in a chair, close your eyes, and imagine yourself in one of the situations described in Exercise 1. Visualize that situation for a few minutes, experiencing it as vividly as you can. Remind yourself of your revised rule, and imagine yourself in the situation believing the revised rule rather than the original unspoken rule. Note how differently you react with this new rule. Repeat for all the situations in exercise 1, and record your reactions below.

Reactions to this exercise: _____

_____

_____

_____

_____

_____

_____

_____

Appendix H

STRATEGIES FOR BUILDING UP YOUR GENERAL HEALTH

Our state of mind and the condition of our body continually interact with each other. People who experience considerable distress, who are in poor mental health, or who worry and fret more than others have an increased risk of physical illness. Experts have studied the relationship between physical illness and emotional well-being extensively, and while there are many unanswered questions in this complicated subject, there is no doubt that our emotional well-being does affect our general physical health. Increasingly, we are learning that excessive experience of stress leads to illness and disease. In fact, many experts feel that there is a mental or emotional component in most physical illness.

People frequently overlook the fact that the opposite is true as well; namely, that our physical condition affects our mental state. When we are tired and run-down, we are more prone to overreact to stressful situations than when we are well rested. If a person fails to get enough sleep and exercise, she or he will become angry or upset more easily than otherwise. When we work without taking time to relax and let go for awhile, tensions can build, and we can then explode at some insignificant event. Recent studies suggest that our eating and drinking habits play a larger role in how we feel about ourselves and relate to others than most of us realize. Have you seen the television ads that portray the coffee drinker as irritable and easily upset? There is truth in those ads. Data on the effects of caffeine implicate that substance in a variety of unpleasant personal reactions.

You are probably aware of the fact that there are times when you are more easily irritated and angered. Today's traffic jam nearly put you into a rage, while yesterday's presented no problem at all. You became very angry when you felt your wife wasn't listening to you at home but understood her preoccupation with her interests at another time. There are many reasons why we respond differently in different situations and at different times, and our physical condition is one of the most important of them. The more we push ourselves, sleep erratically, eat improperly, and exercise irregularly, the more we will find ourselves tense, irritable, and unreasonable, and the more we will overreact to stressful situations.

What can we do about this? We can learn to take care of ourselves. If we get into the habit of looking after our health, of letting go, of taking it easy once in a while, and of slowing down, we can reduce our stress considerably.

Unfortunately, people who most need to learn to take care of themselves are the most apt to resist doing so. People who complain that they are pressured, hassled, and overworked also feel that they don't have the time to stop and relax. The woman who rushes frantically from activity to activity to meet the demands of her career and her family understandably argues, "I have no more time." And looking after yourself does take time. The grade-conscious college student, anxious about his/her abilities, feels that every minute spent relaxing is lost from studying. The person heavily involved in community projects, who already feels overworked and overburdened exclaims, "What? You want me to take time out to relax?" Often I have given a relaxation tape to people complaining of always feeling tense and tired, only to have them tell me months later that they didn't have time to play the tape!

You may sincerely believe that you do not have the time to take care of yourself, but that belief must be challenged. We don't find time for this purpose—we *take* time. We must decide that slowing down and letting go are important. Can you make it a priority for yourself? If you do, then you will make the time to do those things that are required.

You might find it easier to establish taking care of yourself as a priority if you realize that, in the long run, it saves you time rather than costs you time. When we have been frantically busy for a long period of time, we tire and begin to lose our efficiency. We think less clearly, we take longer to do our work, and then we worry about our reduced effectiveness and respond by working even harder and even less efficiently. A person who is tired and run-down—and worried about work—can do much less in an hour than a person who's refreshed and rested. If you take the time to let go and become refreshed, when you return to your activities you will more than make up for "lost" time.

Overwork also affects the way we think about ourselves and relate to others. As noted earlier, when tired and frustrated, we become short-tempered, irritable, hard to get along with—you know the "song and dance." When something goes wrong, it upsets us more than usual, and that only makes the situation worse. People who say they don't have the time to relax are kidding themselves if they believe that they can keep up a hectic pace without paying the price.

Get Adequate Rest (as well as sleep)

If we are to prevent ourselves from being overly tired and run-down, we need to get adequate sleep and rest. We can lose sleep for short periods without suffering noticeable harm, but adequate sleep is essential in the long run for physical and mental health. Since different people need different amounts of sleep, each of us needs to experiment until we discover what "adequate sleep" means to us. Don't overlook the need for adequate rest, too. Take a few minutes during each day to rest. When working on long projects, take a short break every hour or two. The student who studies for fifty minutes and then rests for ten will study longer and learn more than one who crams for four hours straight. So too, with the executive writing a report. Work that requires heavy concentration (like memorizing) needs more frequent breaks. Other work, such as planning sessions that involve interaction with other people, might need less frequent breaks, although a short break usually perks up the participants. Since "a change is often as good as a rest," taking a break may simply mean moving to another activity for a few minutes.

Slow Down

When you notice yourself rushing and getting tense, slow down deliberately. Take any activity and do it slowly and carefully. You might try taking twice the time to get washed and dressed in the morning. Or, when walking, walk slowly. All of us would benefit if we would take our time at meals, eating in a relaxed and easy manner. Instead we take our problems with us to our meals, hold meetings at lunch, pay no attention to what we are eating, and leave the table as tired as we began. Select some regular activity and decide to engage in that activity slowly and deliberately each day. You will also need to practice the internal component to slowing down—saying the things to yourself that give you permission to slow down. For example, "The best way to refresh myself, right now, is to just ease through this activity."

Relax

While many methods of taking care of ourselves qualify as relaxation, some are designed specifically to produce a quiet state of deep relaxation. Options that help you to develop the skills for getting to that state are found in appendix C.

Develop Present Awareness

You will understand the idea of present awareness better if you will now put this guide down, take a short walk around the room, and then come back to this page. ... Did you do it? What went through your mind as you walked around? Perhaps you were thinking,

"I wonder what this is all about? This is silly. This is fun." Or maybe your mind turned to other things and you found yourself thinking about something you must do tomorrow or something that happened to you in the past. The point is that most of the time there is a constant chatter going on in our heads. We are always thinking about something—talking to ourselves. Much of the time we are either thinking about (and worrying about) the future or reminding ourselves of (and often regretting) the past. While we are letting our thoughts wander to the past or the future, we are not fully in the present. You know how you can take a long drive and not even notice where you are going. At other times we eat a meal but never even pay much attention to the food. This tendency to be somewhere other than the present creates difficulty for us in two ways:

1. This constant inner chatter takes energy and contributes to our distress.
2. The problems of the future and the past interfere with our enjoyment of the present.

Suppose that you could take a walk around the room and be totally in the present—not thinking about the past, future, or anything at all but just experiencing all that was in the room. That would be a great experience! You would be very relaxed because nothing at all would be bothering you; since you were just experiencing the present, no problem or difficulty would be on your mind. Even if you faced a stressful situation tomorrow, if you developed this present awareness, you would not fret over it today. Also, the mistakes of the past cannot bother you if you are totally in today's present.

Being totally in the present all the time is not possible for us, nor is it advisable. But developing the ability to be more in the present than we usually are, can be an effective means of relaxing and renewing ourselves.

How can you increase your present awareness? The awareness exercise (on pages 142-144) is an excellent tool to use.

You can also practice awareness with your eyes open and while you are engaging in some daily activity. To begin, select some routine activity which you do alone, (for example, taking a shower). As you shower, try to be as aware as you can of yourself, your surroundings, the water falling on you, and all other present sensations. Each time your mind wanders and you begin to think about what you must do later in the day or begin to worry about some problem, let those thoughts go and return to just being aware of yourself in the present. Don't strain to be aware; let all sensations come to you. You might also try this present awareness as you eat your breakfast, drive to work, or engage in some other routine activity. Another very good time is one brief period spent lying in bed right after waking up or just before going to sleep. Gradually you will expand the time when your mind is not cluttered with endless chatter, and you will find yourself becoming more relaxed and less stressed.

Remember that present awareness is easy as long as you don't push it too far. That is, there is no way in which we can be totally in the present without our minds wandering to some extent. Expect that to happen and don't let it upset you. Just gently turn your attention to the present whenever you find this happening—which will be every few seconds. Let this be an easy exercise: if you set out to free your mind of all thoughts, you will fail and then be angry with yourself and increase your stress. If, on the other hand, you set out to increase your present awareness even a little, you will succeed and enjoy the success. This is a powerful and effective exercise; it's worth practicing. Since you are doing it while engaging in some routine activity, it takes no extra time at all.

Develop A Daily Routine

An effective means of slowing down and letting go is that of developing a routine of some sort which takes about one-half hour and which we can engage in daily. Most people find that they can work a routine into their lives on a regular basis even if they can't do it every day. For example, one person might end each day by taking a shower and listening to music for twenty minutes or so. Another might read the newspaper after returning from work and before dinner. Another might have a friend that could be called each day for a chat. The possibilities are limitless, but the idea is always the same: develop some reasonably quiet, enjoyable routine which takes about a half hour and try to engage in that routine at the same time each day.

Watch Your Physical Health

The previous strategies that we have looked at in this appendix are all ways of letting go. This strategy for taking care of yourself is to take care of your physical health. As previously mentioned, good physical health is important in any stress management program. This section is not designed to give you a program to follow to be physically healthy—you will need to consult other sources for that. It is designed to invite you to make your physical health a priority. Here are some relevant questions to ask yourself:

• Am I engaging in "good and sufficient" physical exercise?
• Am I eating properly?
• Am I getting sufficient sleep?

We cannot cheat on our physical health without paying for it (with less years in our life and less life in our years). To look after ourselves physically is a crucial long-term investment.

Exercises

A. Review your daily routine and ascertain if you are letting go as frequently as you want/need to. Notice which of the methods you are already using (and check that box).

1. Get adequate rest.   ❏
2. Slow down.   ❏
3. Relax.   ❏
4. Develop present awareness.   ❏
5. Develop a daily routine.   ❏

Next, put an asterisk (*) beside the number of each method that you are already using sufficiently. (So, all you have to do is keep doing what you are already doing in order to get the benefits you want.)

Next (for every method without an asterisk beside it), underline every method that you want to improve your application of.

Next, (for each method that you want to improve your application of), write—below—when, where, and how you will implement that application. Think in terms of the next step that you need to take in order to apply that method (rather than the ideal and perfect application strategy).

Get adequate rest:_____

_____

_____

Slow down: _____

_____

_____

Relax: _____

_____

_____

Develop a daily awareness:_____

_____

_____

_____

Develop a daily routine: _____

_____

_____

_____

_____

_____

_____

_____

B.   Review your daily physical health practices—as it relates to physical exercise, eating and sleeping. Since all of us could ongoingly improve how we do these practices, we could make this a never ending pursuit. Here, however, we will focus on only one change (but one that will get you the best "bang for your buck"). Answer the following question in the spaces below.

"If I could do one thing differently that would most improve my application of this practice, what would it be?"

As it applies to exercise: _____

_____

_____

_____

As it applies to eating: _____

_____

_____

_____

As it applies to sleeping: _____

_____

_____

_____

Appendix I

STRATEGIES FOR BUILDING UP YOUR SUPPORT SYSTEM

A major source of help in times of stress is support. Anyone experiencing distress needs to seek out and utilize all needed sources of support. In this guide, *support* means (1) knowing that someone cares for you, understands you, and is there to help you and (2) obtaining information and assistance from other people and organizations.

Gaining support is knowing that someone is on your side, that you are not alone. Unfortunately, people who experience distress often suffer in silence. They don't tell others about their fears, anxieties, guilt, or stress, and this silence only makes their troubles worse. You are not alone in this world, and when you realize that fully, that realization in itself can help you manage stress.

How do we obtain support? There are six basic methods for obtaining and utilizing support in times of stress. (Look for and use your one or two key applications—often these small changes can make a big difference.)

Talk It Out

The first of these methods is very simple: share your distress with others. Talk about it. Tell others how you feel. Don't keep it to yourself.

Over the years, I have repeatedly seen, in my work as a psychologist, the benefits of people sharing their struggles with me. Often, I have been the first person whom they have shared those burdens with. These benefits, often obvious after a single session, are not because I have given such great responses (sometimes, all I have done was to listen carefully and respectfully). Actually, there are a number of reasons why talking to another person is valuable:

- It lets you know that you are not alone. People were built to be in community so, when they are alone, they carry a double burden—loneliness as well as the burden of stress. When they tell another person (in other words, enter into community) they feel relief (in part because they experience community).

- It lets you know that you are valued. When a person shares a struggle, and the receiver of that information listens carefully and respectfully, the person with the struggle feels valued and cared for. That's because high-quality listening—in and of itself—is a demonstration of valuing and caring for. ("Just listening" is just about the most important caring skill you can develop. It is even more valuable, of course, because of what you learn when you listen well). About this issue, Mills (in *Coping With Stress*) says:

Talking it out gets it off your chest. After talking for a while, you feel as though you have put down a great burden. Have you ever experienced grief or anger and, after talking it over with someone, found that the grief or anger was lessened? That's the release that comes with support. Many times people who tell me about their situation begin by talking quite rapidly in a tense voice. I've learned to remain relatively quiet and let them continue. After a while, once they feel safe and know that they are with someone who cares, they burst into tears. All the anguish that has been building up inside comes out. They have a good cry, and they feel better. Feelings that do not find some expression build up inside us and can create all kinds of havoc. The release gained through support is not only comforting, but also helps prevent further difficulties from developing.[18]

- It lets you organize and clarify your experience. When a person shares a struggle, he/she must first organize and clarify that struggle sufficiently within him/herself in order to be able to communicate it to me. Many times, after a session where I primarily listened and helped the person organize and clarify his/her thoughts and feelings (usually via high quality questions: " . . Then what happened? … Can you tell me more? … Can you give me an example of that? … What were you feeling at that time? … What were you saying to yourself? …), the person had a sense of what his/her next step needed to involve. Sometimes, he/she has given me credit for that insight; in fact, I only helped him/her to arrive at his/her own insight. Related to this reason, Mills adds: "Another benefit from sharing is a broadened perspective. When we talk out our problems with others, we understand them better—we see them in a different light. All too often, frustrations, angers, and disappointments that are not shared fester within us, and soon we lose all sense of proportion and perspective. A problem that I keep to myself is frequently distorted and looks worse than it is. When I share it with another person, I see it better myself."
- It gives you the opportunity to receive feedback. Feedback is what you get back from the person that you have "talked it out" with. Typically, feedback is thought

of as advice—and this is part of what feedback includes (along with resource provision and answers to questions). It is much more than that, however, and that
"more" includes support ("I'm glad you've talked to me about this; now I can be
here for you"), encouragement ("You've got a good understanding of what is pressuring you"), empathy ("What I hear in your voice is … "), clarification ("What
were you saying to yourself when she said … ?"), focusing ("If you were going to
change one thing about X, what would it be?"), and challenge ("It sounds like X is
your contribution to the problem; what could you do to get past that?")

• It gives you an opportunity to find a "fellow traveler." Obviously this doesn't
always happen, but sometimes when you talk to another person (and enter into
community) you find someone whose life journey is enough like yours that you
begin to travel together as friends (long after the stressor you initially talked about
is history). A client of mine, who struggled with alcohol consumption, checked
out and joined—with my encouragement—a local chapter of Alcoholics Anony-
mous. Initially, he did that with reluctance but found, in his relationship with his
sponsor there, a "kindred spirit" who has become a best mentor/support/friend.

My career involves working with people who "talk it out" with me. From my training
and research and experience I have discovered a number of ways to enhance the value of
such conversations. So, if you plan to talk to someone, look for the following "ingredients"
in that conversation (and "move on" if you don't find enough of them; keep looking until
you find a relational fit):

(i)   The person you talk to comes to feel like a "safe" person. Such experience of safety
      may not happen immediately, but you know that the person you are talking to is a
      fit if there is a growing sense of safety or comfort. Such experience is recognized in
      a number of ways:

      (a) When you feel accepted

      (b) When you know that your conversation will be kept private

      (c) When you sense caring

      (d) When you know that you are being accurately understood

      (e) When you feel like the person you are talking to is with you (not against you) or
          is on your team

      (f) When you sense that this person is "unshockable" and will respect you as a per-
          son (whether or not they agree with or like your thoughts and/or behavior)

(ii) The person you talk to comes to help you to "normalize" your behavior. Normaliz-
      ing (the process by which you find out that other people have the same experiences

and struggles that you have and that there are ways to manage or resolve these experiences and struggles) is especially valuable if you feel that your situation is unique or overwhelming or hopeless. When you discover that other people have been through what you are going through and that they have found constructive ways to deal with this kind of struggle (and just because you feel overwhelmed doesn't mean that you are overwhelmed), your hope … and energy … and perspective … will return. If the person you are talking to has personally faced and come through such a challenge, that is uniquely helpful because that person is living proof that you don't need to be trapped by this issue forever. About this consideration, Mills says:

> Sharing your stress with anyone is helpful. Sharing it with someone you care for and respect is more helpful. Most helpful of all is sharing with someone who has experienced or is experiencing the same type of stress as you. A recent television program told of a telephone network for children suffering from terminal cancer. These children could make long-distance calls to other children in similar difficulty and just talk. They didn't always talk about their illness. They talked about things any child would talk about. But that sharing and that support did wonders for the children.
>
> There are many examples of people finding support by sharing with others having similar difficulties. In many high schools, children of divorced parents meet periodically to talk about their experiences. Alcoholics Anonymous was founded on the principle of one alcoholic helping another. Now we have Al-Anon and Al-Ateen to bring families of alcoholics together for mutual support. The number of "anonymous" groups is growing: Gamblers Anonymous, Parents Anonymous (for child abusers), Neurotics Anonymous, and many more.[19]

(iii) The person you talk to is living out the fruit of the Spirit. When you find someone who is showing these characteristics—love, joy, peace, patience, kindness, goodness, faithfulness, gentleness, and self-control—in a noticeable way, you have found someone who (in all likelihood) can be constructive as you dialogue with him/her.

So far we have discussed our "talking it out" in relation to other people (some of whom are paid for their involvement, some not). There are other (sometimes overlooked) ways to talk it out that can be just as valuable (and even more valuable if you can't access other individuals when you need them).

One of these "other" ways is to talk it out—with an author. When we are stressed, we can find a "fellow traveler" who is an author, read his/her input on the issue at hand, select the helpful ideas that he/she has suggested, and develop an action plan for applying these ideas in our life. For anyone reading this material, this will not be an overlooked method because—if you are following my suggestions—you are doing these steps with this book. Some books (like this one) try to promote dialogue by providing application exercises; others provide questions or workbooks for that same purpose.

Another of these "other" ways is to talk it out with yourself. Initially, the idea of talking it out with a person that you need to go inside yourself to dialogue with may sound contradictory. When you put that dialogue on paper or tape or disk, however, you immediately get new understanding and perspective on what was (until recently) behind your eyes and silent to your ears. I have been journaling for decades (in part because confidentiality surrounds the content that I need to process and in part because—as a "visual" learner—I have to "trap it where I can see it"). I can attest to the relief it brings, the clarity it provides and the solutions it reveals. Often my journaling has helped me to access my experience—my fears, my sadness, my frustrations, my "pain"—so that I could begin to acknowledge and download that burden. (For those of us with "macho" training—where the training program was "how to rack, pack, and stack your feelings"—self-permission to "feel your feelings" has been an enlightening option.)

As I have learned to "feel my feelings," I have also learned that (when such experience rates a "ten" on the "unpleasant" scale) I can access and use self-soothing skills. These skills are high quality painkillers that help me to get through the most intense and negative of my experience. Such skills don't have the side effects of the low quality painkillers that some of us are familiar with. Again, the skills that help you may be substantially different from the skills that help me (no "new news" here). All of us, however, would benefit from having a list of such skills at our fingertips (or, at least, our mental fingertips). Among the discussions of self-soothing are Edmund Bourne's book *Healing Fear*[20] (which looks at these skills in the context of dealing with anxiety) and David Schnarch's book *Passionate Marriage*[21] (which looks at these skills in the context of doing a relationship).

In light of what has already been written in this chapter, it won't surprise you to find that, among the other ways to talk it out, I include talking it out with God. The infinite and personal God of the Hebrew and Christian traditions is the one I am referring to. (For some reason) He wants a relationship with us and (so) is willing to listen to us and help us when we come to Him to talk. There is a long tradition of people bringing their struggles to God; nowhere is that more clear than in the Psalms. Recently, when I was studying Psalm 31, I came across a comment and a prayer about that Psalm (in Eugene Peterson's book *Praying With The Psalms*) that provided a window into that tradition:

> The agonizing loneliness of pain and suffering is alleviated when we place each detail before God who is a sympathetic listener. The prayer process enables us to see suffering as God sees it and to begin to participate in his redemption of it. The prophet Jeremiah, who suffered extensively and prayed passionately, used part of this psalm in his prayers (Jeremiah 20:7-18).
>
> PRAYER: O God, because of Gethsemane and Calvary, I know there is neither humiliation nor pain that is beyond the power of your resurrection; I place every hurt before you in the sure hope of your salvation. Amen.[22]

This tradition can also be our present reality. God, who assures us that He is "a very present help in a time of trouble" (Psalm 46:1) is waiting to hear from us.

The exercises at the end of this appendix—that are related to "talking it out"—are designed to help you to identify and use a larger group of "supporters."

Seek Counsel

In the "talk it out" section, the focus was on the benefits that came with the talking. In this section, the focus is on the benefits that can come from the responses you receive. (This was touched on in the discussion of "feedback.") Depending on who you talk to, responses vary: person-specific feedback from another person, non-specific feedback from an author, insightful feedback from yourself or from God. To get the most benefit from such feedback, it is important to listen carefully to it (if you are like I am, that would include taking notes) and to evaluate it carefully. To evaluate feedback implies that you may not take and implement that feedback into your life. Sometimes feedback is relevant and practically useful (a "fit"); sometimes it is not relevant—but it is always helpful. Some of the best feedback I ever received was feedback that I did not agree with or make use of directly; it was useful because it helped me to clarify what I wasn't going to do and what I would do, instead. In other words, seeking counsel doesn't mean that you will necessarily take and directly apply the counsel you receive. You seek counsel as *input*—that which will inform your decisions. To evaluate feedback also implies that you are not abdicating responsibility for the things—including counsel—that you put into your life. (You would be abdicating responsibility if you were to *unthinkingly* accept and use that counsel; seeking counsel is not constructive if it is used to avoid personal responsibility.)

When you evaluate counsel (which is the step between *listening* to counsel and *using* the counsel), it is helpful to keep in mind the options you have for applying (using) that feedback. These options include the following:

1. Accepting the counsel (as when the feedback is a fit for you—it feels right, makes sense, stays within your circle of biblical options, has no major downside)

2. Rejecting the counsel (as when the feedback is not a fit for you—it doesn't feel right, doesn't make sense, doesn't stay within the circle of biblical options for you, has a prohibitive downside)

3. Modifying the counsel (as when you change the counsel in ways that—for you— move it into the "acceptable" category)

4. Holding the counsel in abeyance (as when you do nothing with that counsel—"just put it on the shelf"—with the understanding that it may be useful in the future)

When you accept counsel, you maximize its benefit by developing an implementation plan, a plan for applying it into your life in a way that makes a "real" difference. (A "real" difference is one that would be seen on the tape of a television camera that was recording your behavior twenty-four/seven.) When you reject counsel, you use it to identify what is unacceptable about it and (so) what an acceptable alternative would look like. When you modify counsel, you use that process to design an acceptable alternative (which can then be implemented). When you hold counsel in abeyance, you use it to lay down (possible) tracks into the future and to clarify what you will do now. Any of these processes will reduce a stressor.

The exercise at the end of this appendix will help you to clarify your game-plan for seeking counsel.

Utilize Resources

It is extremely likely that, as you got feedback from others, you also received (as part of that feedback) resources that they felt would contribute to your stress management. Sometimes, however, you may need to find those resources directly. About this method of obtaining support in times of stress, Mills says: "We not only have other people to help us, we also have a world of resources. The person who knows how to locate and utilize resources has a much easier time of handling difficulties and managing stress."

Resources are available to you for almost any stressful situation you can encounter. There are various ways to locate these resources, including:

• Libraries
• The internet
• Agencies or organizations relevant to your area of distress

Librarians can help you to gain access to a host of resources, as can your friendly internet search engine. Sometimes, specialized organizations have specialized resources that you can access. In an information rich culture, quantity of resources will rarely be a problem but quality (and fit) of resources can be. So, finding someone (an expert or fellow learner in the area or a person with relevant experience) who can help by evaluating the quality of your information and tailor make an application of it for your life can be crucial. As I have said elsewhere, stress management isn't about knowing a hundred new things, it is about doing two or three crucial things differently.

The exercise at the end of this appendix will help you decide how to seek and utilize resources.

Create a Support System

The need to create a support system in an urban environment is not high. It is more likely that you will need to find a more specialized sub-group within an already existing support system. For instance, many of us, as part of our faith journey, have found small groups or fellow travelers (where struggles and questions can be shared) to be a vital complement to the Sunday services of our church.

In a more rural environment, however, the need to create a support system may be greater. Such a support system may be no more complicated than finding one other person to interact with—in person or online. Many good things happen, including stress reduction, when two or three (people) are gathered.

Another way to create a support system is to find and develop a hobby or a vocation that can be "taken on the road." By that I mean developing and doing something that you have passion about participating in and finding other people, who share that passion, to participate with. Groups of people who connect with each other around a shared interest are, by definition, a support system because just doing that activity together can be highly stress reducing. A friend of mine cycles with other enthusiasts; they don't talk much, but he finds the tours highly refreshing. Sometimes, such groups become excellent "fishing holes," places where you can find a fellow traveler (literally, if you are a cyclist) who becomes a friend. Over the years, I've met many people who have found a primary support system as they participated with others in activities they loved to do: sports, working out at the gym, fixing cars, taking courses, painting, being in a book club, doing computer games, developing gourmet meals, raising and showing dogs, watching movies, watching sporting activities, birding, wine-tasting, and the list goes on.

Some of the above activities contain unique opportunities for developing multiple support systems. For example, raising and showing dogs (in addition to connecting you with "like-activitied" people) can also enable you to develop another support system—with the dog him/herself. A few years ago, our family got a puppy—who is now an 80 pound family member with unlimited play potential and unswerving devotion to members of his pack. Gryphon (our black lab) has single-handedly (actually, "single tonguedly") raised the playtime in every member of our family (which is no small stress-management achievement in a work-oriented family).

The exercise at the end of this appendix can help you to specify the process for creating a support system.

Participate In Ritual

About this way of obtaining support, Mills says: "Participation in ritual and ceremony is a source of considerable support. It is no surprise that societies establish rituals for most crucial (and therefore stressful) moments in life. Retirement parties, graduation ceremonies, weddings, funerals, and more informal ceremonies help by bringing us into contact with others, providing us with guides on how to react, and helping us share the experience and wisdom of others."[23]

You will notice that each of the rituals he mentions occurs at the time of (and helps a person through) a *transition*—a time when a person is moving from one "chapter" of his/her life to the next. At such times of change—when the old chapter is "dying" and the new chapter is just "being born"—people often feel disoriented and anxious, even if they are positively anticipating the upcoming chapter.

John Gottman, in his book *The relationship Cure*, provides excellent insights about how sharing rituals can help you build stronger bonds with others (and thus experience support) as well as specifying what kinds of rituals can be stress reducing:

> A ritual of emotional connection provides structure in your life to ensure that bids for connection happen on a regular basis. A ritual of emotional connection is the one place you can count on having a significant exchange with somebody you care about. A regular evening meal with your family can be a ritual of emotional connection. So can a couple's annual romantic getaway, or the office staff's quarterly retreat. A ritual can be as casual as saying hello to your coworkers each morning. Or it can be as elaborate as a royal wedding.

Like routines, rituals are repeated over and over, so they become predictable. Everybody knows what to expect, and everyone knows what his or her responsibilities are in the ritual. But there's an important difference: Rituals have symbolic meaning. Brushing your teeth in the morning is a routine, kissing your kids good-bye as you leave is a ritual. The difference is, the kiss carries the meaning, while the tooth-brushing does not. The kiss says, "I love you, and I'll think about you, even when we're apart.[24]

Rituals of emotional connection, when enacted with people who have our welfare at heart, are powerful stress antidotes.

By doing the exercise related to rituals at the end of this appendix, you could clarify what existing rituals you would benefit from maintaining or enhancing. You could also clarify where in your life a ritual—if you were to develop one—would help to manage stress.

Share in the Experiences of Others

About this method of obtaining support, Mills says: "We can gain much strength and comfort in times of stress by learning that other people have had difficulties similar to ours and have successfully overcome them. Seeing how other people manage their stress gives us ideas for handling our own. Knowing that other people have had some of the same concerns as we do helps eliminate the feeling that we are somehow strange or different."[25]

People in our family of origin (primarily our parents, usually) were the source of our first stress management strategies—learned as we lived with them. In other words, learned as we shared in their experiences of surviving (and, hopefully, thriving) in life. For my mother, work was the cure for many ills; no wonder I've tried to apply that strategy to the issue of stress management. As we grew and began to transition out of our family of origin, the world got larger—in the sense that we found and shared in the experiences of a broader range of people. My guess is that you (like me) can still remember the "culture shock" of your first days of going to school. As our world has continued to expand, we have learned how to access the experiences of others directly, indirectly, and virtually—with great potential for stress enhancement or stress reduction. Since our focus here is on stress reduction, let's look at the (familiar) means that we can use for obtaining support and managing stress.

- Find a coach. Many people have, for example, found listening to a fellow "recoverer" in a twelve-step program to be a life changing experience.
- Read. Who hasn't found something helpful in *Readers Digest*?

- Watch movies. In my library, I have a book called *Rent Two Films and Let's Talk in the Morning*.[26] It is designed to use movies, intentionally, in the process of helping people deal with what they are facing.
- Watch T.V. Who hasn't seen a documentary that gave you both strength and comfort?
- Go online. Divers in that ocean of information have discovered resources of deep relevance.

The exercise (at the end of this appendix) that is related to this method of obtaining support, will help you to specify the "what" and "how" of your application of sharing in the experience of others.

Exercises
For "Talking It Out"

(a)
- In the left-hand column of the chart below—using a few key words—list situations, worries, or concerns which are stressful for you. In the top row of the chart, name people with whom you come in contact regularly. Then place an X beside each stressful item and under the name of each person with whom you have talked about your feelings on the item. When you have done this, the remaining empty spaces represent opportunities to seek further support. As you look at each "stressful item" you've listed, select the person that you think would be most helpful to talk to (about that item). Put a "1" in their blank space.
- If you identify a person that you haven't listed, but who would be uniquely relevant for a particular stressful item (for example, a boss at work for a work related stressor), write his/her name in column "6" (beside that stressful item).
- If it helps you to put a time frame around talking to these people, write in the date (in the appropriate square, with a different colored pen) by which you will have talked to them.

PEOPLE

	1.	2.	3.	4.	5.	6. Unique Situation Supporter
a						
b						
c						
d						
e						
f						
g						
h						
i						
j						
k						

(b) If you want to "talk it out" with an author, answer the following questions:
  • Do I know a book that would help me to deal with one of my "Stressful Items"? (Look at the Stressful Item's list from exercise a.)
    – If "yes," write it below and get it ...

  _____

  _____

    – If "no," ask "Who could I talk to, for a recommendation of such a book?"(Write that name below; contact that person; get the book...)

  _____

  _____

(c) If you want to "talk it out" with yourself consider the following:
  • Decide on the method for doing so that suits you best; (check one of the following):
    ❑ Journal on paper
    ❑ Journal on computer
    ❑ Talk on CD/digital recorder
    ❑ Answer the questions in a workbook

- Insure confidentiality, so you know that your only audience will be you (otherwise you might start to internally edit your conversation to fit it to your bigger audience).
- After "unpacking your head" about this item(what happened, what am I feeling, what am I thinking …), you may draw a blank in answer to the question, "What could I do about this?" It sometimes helps to record your responses to the question, "If I had a good friend who was going through what I am, what would I say to him/her?"

d) If you want to identify and use self-soothing skills (to moderate painful experience), fill in the following:
- List skills that I *know*, from my experience, will help me through times of pain.

_____

_____

_____

_____

- List skills that I *think* will help me through painful times (and which I will "road test" when feasible).

_____

_____

_____

_____

(e) If you want to "talk it out" with God, consider the following:
- Talk to Him by prayer. That prayer can be written/typed, internal-verbal (thought), external-verbal (voice), second-hand (using someone else's prayers), via Scripture (using scriptural content to fashion prayers), or via someone else (having someone pray for you) …
- Listen to Him. That listening can be by intuiting His response: noticing what becomes meaningful in your conversations, reading, dreams, circumstances; noticing what becomes meaningful as you read the Scriptures; noticing what changes occur after you ask Him to give you "eyes to see and ears to hear" what He is showing you and talking to you about.

For "Seeking Counsel"

- In the space provided, list, using a few key words, stressors that are now of concern to you. These may include some of the items used in Exercise a. After each stressor, state at least one person to whom you can go for counsel.

• Then, in the last column, indicate the date by which you will seek that counsel.

PROBLEM	RESOURCE PERSON	DATE

For "Utilizing Resources"

• Identify three issues which are of concern to you and which you believe might be better handled if you had more information. (List them below):

1._____

2._____

3._____

• Decide how you will *access* that information. (Check one or more of the following for each issue):

ISSUE: (1) (2) (3)

    ❏ ❏ ❏ library

    ❏ ❏ ❏ internet

    ❏ ❏ ❏ specialized agency or organization

    ❏ ❏ ❏ personal resource person

    who? _____

• *Gather* information on each issue.

• Decide how you will *evaluate* and *apply* that information for each issue/stressor.

Issue (1)   How will I *evaluate* that information? (Check one):

    ❏ ❏ ❏ by myself

    ❏ ❏ ❏ with others

    who? _____

How will I *apply* that information? (Check one):

    ❏ ❏ ❏ by myself

    ❏ ❏ ❏ with others

    who? _____

Issue (2)   How will I *evaluate* that information? (Check one):

❏ ❏ ❏   by myself
❏ ❏ ❏   with others
who? _____

How will I *apply* that information? (Check one):

❏ ❏ ❏   by myself
❏ ❏ ❏   with others
who? _____

Issue (3)   How will I *evaluate* that information? (Check one):

❏ ❏ ❏   by myself
❏ ❏ ❏   with others
who? _____

How will I *apply* that information? (Check one):

❏ ❏ ❏   by myself
❏ ❏ ❏   with others
who? _____

For "Creating a Support System"

• List the *interests* that you have developed (or want to develop further) that could become a means to connecting with others (and, so, create a support system).

(1) _____

(2) _____

(3) _____

(4) _____

(5) _____

(6) _____

(7) _____

• Circle the number of the interest that is a "best fit" for you now (taking into account what activity is most valuable for you to develop, what activity most interests/intrigues/energizes you, what activity already has an infrastructure in the place you live, and what activity has health and stress-reducing benefits that are most needed by you …).

- Having chosen that area of interest, list the next four things you will do in order to turn that interest into a support system. (For example, who will you phone; what resource option—like the catalogue of Adult Learning—will you track down; what step will you take, to actually connect with another "like-activited" person.)

  (1) _____

  (2) _____

  (3) _____

  (4) _____

- Remember: beyond doing/enjoying your area of interest with others, you are (also) looking for a person in this group who will become a more "significant other."

For "Participating in Ritual"

- As I stated in this chapter, rituals help us to get through (among other things) a time of transition in our life. Carter and McGoldrick, in their book *The Changing Family Life Cycle*,[27] identify these times of transition throughout our life span. They do this for the "Intact, Middle-class, North-American Family Life Cycle" (outlined in table 1), for the "Divorce Life Cycle" (outlined in table 2), and for the "Remarriage Life Cycle" (outlined in table 3).

TABLE 1: THE STAGES OF THE FAMILY LIFE CYCLE

Family Life Cycle Stage	Emotional Process of Transition: Key Principles	Second-Order Changes in Family Status Required to Proceed Developmentally
1. Leaving home: Single young adults	Accepting emotional and financial responsibility for self	a. Differentiation of self in relation to family of origin b. Development of intimate peer relationships c. Establishment of self around issues of work and financial independence
2. The joining of families through marriage: The new couple	Commitment to new system	a. Formation of marital system b. Realignment of relationships with extended families and friends to include spouse
3. Families with young children	Accepting new members into the system	a. Adjusting marital system to make space for child(ren) b. Joining in childrearing, financial, and household tasks c. Realignment of relationships with extended family to include parenting and grandparenting roles
4. Families with adolescents	Increasing flexibility of family boundaries to include children's independence and grandparents' frailties	a. Shifting of parent-child relationships to permit adolescent to move in and out of system b. Refocus on midlife marital and career issues c. Beginning shift toward joint caring for older generation
5. Launching children and moving on	Accepting a multitude of exits from and entries into the family system	a. Renegotiation of marital system as a dyad b. Development of adult to adult relationships between grown children and their parents c. Realignment of relationships to include in-laws and grandchildren d. Dealing with disabilities and death of parents (grandparents)
6. Families in later life	Accepting the shifting of generational roles	a. Maintaining own and/or couple functioning and interests in face of physiological decline; exploration of new familial and social role options b. Support for a more central role of middle generation c. Making room in the system for the wisdom and experience of the elderly, supporting the older generation without over-functioning for them d. Dealing with loss of spouse, siblings, and other peers and preparation for own death; life review and integration

**TABLE 2. DISLOCATIONS OF THE FAMILY LIFE CYCLE REQUIRING ADDITIONAL STEPS
TO RESTABILIZE AND PROCEED DEVELOPMENTALLY**

	Phase	Emotional Process of Transition Prerequisite Attitude	Developmental Issues
Divorce			
1.	The decision to divorce	Acceptance of inability to resolve marital tensions sufficiently to continue relationship	Acceptance of one's own part in the failure of the marriage
2.	Planning the breakup of the system	Supporting viable arrangements for all parts of the system	a. Working cooperatively on problems of custody, visitation, and finances b. Dealing with extended family about the divorce
3.	Separation	a. Willingness to continue coopera-tive co-parental relationship and joint financial support of children b. Work on resolution of attachment to spouse	a. Mourning loss of intact family b. Restructuring marital and parent-child relationships and finances; adaptation to living apart c. Realignment of relationships with extended family; staying connected with spouse's extended family
4.	The divorce	More work on emotional divorce: Overcoming hurt, anger, guilt, etc.	a. Mourning loss of intact family; giving up fantasies of reunion b. Retrieval of hopes, dreams, expecta-tions from the marriage c. Staying connected with extended families
Post divorce family			
1.	Single-parent (custodial household or primary residence)	Willingness to maintain financial responsibilities, continue parental contact with ex-spouse, and support contact of children with ex-spouse and his or her family	a. Making flexible visitation arrange-ments with ex-spouse and his family b. Rebuilding own financial resources c. Rebuilding own social network
2.	Single-parent (non-custodial)	Willingness to maintain parental contact with ex-spouse and support custodial parent's relationship with children	a. Finding ways to continue effective parenting relationships with children b. Maintaining financial responsibilities to ex-spouse and children c. Rebuilding own social network

TABLE 3. REMARRIED FAMILY FORMATION: A DEVELOPMENTAL OUTLINE

Steps	Prerequisite Attitude	Developmental Issues
1. Entering the new relationship	Recovery from loss of first marriage (adequate emotional divorce)	Recommitment to marriage and to forming a family with readiness to deal with the complexity and ambiguity
2. Conceptualizing and planning new marriage and family	Accepting one's own fears and those of new spouse and children about remarriage and forming a stepfamily Accepting need for time and patience for adjustment to complexity and ambiguity: 1. Multiple new roles 2. Boundaries: space, time, membership, and authority 3. Affective Issues: guilt, loyalty conflicts, desire for mutuality, unresolvable past hurts	a. Work on openness in the new relationships to avoid pseudo-mutuality b. Plan for maintenance of cooperative financial and coparental relationships with ex-spouses c. Plan to help children deal with fears, loyalty conflicts, and membership in two systems d. Realignment of relationships with extended family to include new spouse and children e. Plan maintenance of connections for children with extended family of ex-spouses(s)
3. Remarriage and reconstitution of family	Final resolution of attachment to previous spouse and ideal of "intact" family; acceptance of a different model of family with permeable boundaries	a. Restructuring family boundaries to allow for inclusion of new spouse stepparent b. Realignment of relationships and financial arrangements throughout subsystems to permit interweaving of several systems c. Making room for relationships of all children with biological (noncustodial) parents, grandparents, and other extended family d. Sharing memories and histories to enhance stepfamily integration

- Look at these tables, circle any stage, phase, or step that you are presently participating in (you may be participating in just one or in more than one).
- As Gottman specified, rituals of emotional connection are to be (intentionally) repeated. For some transitions in our life, however, it is crucial to "let go" and "move on" (as in the "launching children and moving on" stage—where parents must let

go of "parent-child" styles of interacting and move on to "adult-adult" styles of interacting). That also applies in the "divorce" phase of the divorce process—where the person going through this process must give up fantasies of reunion. Rituals that are helpful in facilitating these kinds of transitions are one-time rituals (like writing a "good-bye" letter or attending a "new beginning" week-end).

For each stage you are participating in, choose a ritual that is appropriate. (Some may have been suggested in this chapter and some may be obvious as you look at the "Developmental Issues" involved in your transition.) If no meaningful ritual is readily apparent, you may want to talk with someone who can help to clarify what would be helpful. Also, you could choose to design a tailor-made ritual. The following steps for doing so are adapted from Bill O'Hanlon's book *Do One Thing Different*:

(i) Clarify what the purpose of the ritual is (connection or letting go/ moving on).

(ii) Prepare for the ritual by deciding what symbols you will use, when you will perform the ritual, who else will be included, what you will wear, where you will perform the ritual, and what you need to do to get ready— emotionally and psychologically.

(iii) Perform the ritual.

(iv) If it is appropriate, arrange for friends, significant others, or family members to attend a celebration of the completion of the ritual.[33]

If these steps are not "good and sufficient" for you (to design a ritual), reading O'Hanlon's book (chapter 11) would be helpful.

For "Sharing in the Experiences of Others"

• Look at the list of "Stressful Items" that you generated in exercise a. Choose one of those items after saying to yourself, "If I knew how others faced and handled an item like this, that information would (probably) help me too." (Write that item below.)

Item: _____

• Look at the (following) list of ways to access the experience of others (concerning that item).

❑ Find a person who has experience in this area (for example, a therapist, someone who is leading a training program, or someone you know who has been through this issue).

❑ Find someone who has written about this item (for example, in a book, magazine, or periodical).

❑ Find a relevant movie (for example, from a movie critic).

❑ Find a relevant T.V. program (for example, a documentary).

❑ Find a relevant website (for example, by your own skills or those of someone else).

• Checkmark (✔) the ways you will use in order to access the experiences of others.

• In front of each checkmark, write out the first step you will take in that pursuit.

ENDNOTES

[1] Mills, J., *Coping with Stress*, New York: John Wiley and Sons, 1982, p. 18.

[2] Mills, p. 19.

[3] McGaw, Phil, *The Ultimate Weight Solution*, New York: Simon and Schuster Inc., 2003, p. 64.

[4] Lloyd-Jones, D.M., *Spiritual Depression: Its Causes and Cure*, Grand Rapids, Michigan: W.B. Eerdmans Pub. Co., 1965, p. 277.

[5] Russell, Bertrand, "Do We Survive Death" in *Why I Am Not a Christian*, London: Unwin Books, 1967, p. 70–73.

[6] Mills, p. 93–104.

[7] Neidhardt, E.J. and Conry, R.F., *Quieting*, Vancouver, B.C.: Western Centre Health Group, 1982, p. 27–28.

[8] Davis, M. Robbins Eshelwan, E. McKay, M. *The Relaxation and Stress Reduction Workbook*, Oakland, California: New Harbinger Publications, 1982, p. 23–26.

[9] Shakespeare, William, *Hamlet*, Act 2, Scene 2, Line 259.

[10] I Peter 5:7.

[11] Psalm 46:1.

[12] Isaiah 30:21.

[13] John 15:15.

[14] Revelation 5:8.

[15] Gurtov, M., *Making Changes: The Politics of Self Liberation*, Oakland: Harvest Moon Books, 1979.

[16] http://www.sk.lung.ca/content.cfm?edit_realword=diaphragm, retrieved July 29, 2006.

[17] http://www.merck.com/mmhe/sec04/ch038/ch038e.html, retrieved July 29, 2006.

[18] Mills, p. 134.

[19] Mills, p. 135.

[20] Bourne, E., *Healing Fear*, Oakland, California: New Harbinger Pub. Inc., 1998.

[21] Schmarch, D., *Passionate Marriage*, New York: Henry Holt and Co., 1998.

[22] Peterson, E., *Praying with the Psalms*, New York: Harper Collins Publishers, 1993, February 26.

[23] Mills, p. 138.

[24] Gottman, J., *The Relationship Cure*, New York: Three Rivers Press, 2001, p. 221–222.

[25] Mills, p. 138.

[26] Hesley, J.W. and Hesley, J.G., *Rent Two Films and Let's Talk in the Morning*, (Second Ed.), New York: John Wiley and Sons, Inc., 2001.

[27] Carter, B. and McGoldrick, M., (Editors), *The Changing Family Life Cycle*, (Second Ed.), New York: Gardner Press, 1980.

[28] O'Hanlon, B., *Do One Thing Different*, New York: Harper Collins Pub. Inc., 2000, p. 187.

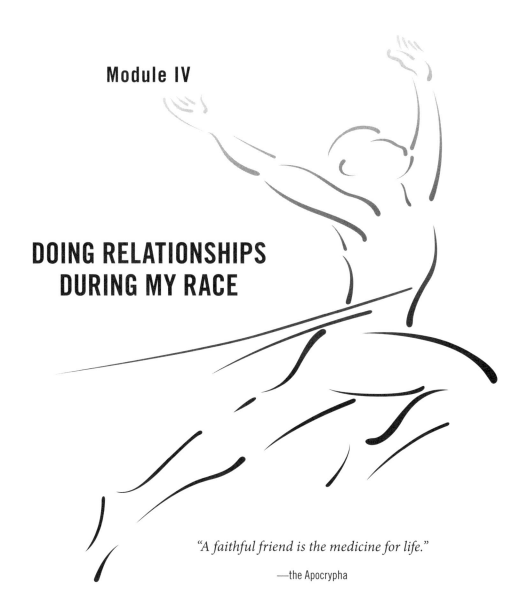

Module IV

DOING RELATIONSHIPS
DURING MY RACE

"A faithful friend is the medicine for life."

—the Apocrypha

INTRODUCTION

As we run the multi-demand marathon, we have in us and around us a host of people. Those who are for us include God's Spirit (saying "I'll be with you until this race is over … Draw on my strength …This is the way …"), our constructive and renewed self talk (saying "Keep your eyes on the prize … pace yourself … follow your preparation plan …"), confidents/companions (saying some version of "You can do it … I'm with you …Here's some water"), friends (saying some version of "Go for it … [aside] He looks tired"), and acquaintances (saying [aside to another spectator] "Which runner is he again?") And, if that was not enough, there are also those who are against us. They include kingdom of darkness spirits (saying some version of "Did God really say this was the way?…Do you think that a poser like you can really do this …?"), our old and destructive self talk (saying some version of "Is that the best you can do?…You never were very good at running!"), and non-friends, possibly posing as friends (saying some version of "I need to ask you a question …I'll have a chair for you at about the 20th mile, when you hit the wall …This is a huge investment of time and energy; I wonder if you will find it to be a good investment …?") Navigating in and through this interpersonal environment (without getting grounded or sunk) is a major accomplishment for a human being—an accomplishment that won't be achieved without taking on some water more than once. "Well, if it is that risky," someone might say, "why don't you find a safe harbor and permanently anchor down or, better yet, permanently put your boat in dry dock?" The answer to that question, of course, is that boats weren't built to sit on (or beside) the water but to move across the water—as people are built to be in relationships with other people. And, so, we collide with one of the paradoxes of living in a fallen world: we were built to be in relationships (in fact, the qualities that most clearly distinguish us as human beings—like languages and love—can only be actualized in our life as we live in relationships), but relationships have the greatest potential of anything in our environment to hurt and to destroy us. (All of humankind's inhumanity to mankind is simply a demonstration of our ingenuity at doing relationships destructively). Relationships are necessary business … and risky business. Relationships are exciting and entrancing… and scary and painful. As Bruce Cockburn puts it, "…When your hands are full of thorns, but you can't quit groping for the rose …"

My purpose in this chapter is to provide you with a simple navigational map. It is a tool for identifying the kinds of relationships that you must deal with. (And deal with them you must, since the costs of trying to avoid these relationships become, as time passes, greater than the costs of facing them.) We can never really avoid involvement in relationships. It is also a tool for determining how to make these relationships more constructive/less destructive. I will illustrate the principles involved by looking at how our Lord handled the relationships that surrounded His life. When we are able to identify the kinds of relationships that we must deal with and determine how to make these relationships more constructive/less destructive, we will be better able to stay on course and reach our finish line.

In light of what God has revealed to us, we see that—from His perspective—relationships are of central importance. One of the implications of being made "in His image" is that we are capable of having and doing relationships—with God, with others, and with ourselves. When Jesus was asked about which commandment was greatest, He replied: "Love the Lord your God with all your heart and with all your soul and with all your mind. This is the first and greatest commandment. And the second is like it: Love your neighbour as yourself" (Matt. 22:34–40).

These commands are all relational: to love God … and your neighbor … and yourself. There are different kinds of relationships at different levels. Having and doing these relationships constructively is necessary to our surviving and thriving.

The following *model* is my navigational tool for doing relationships:

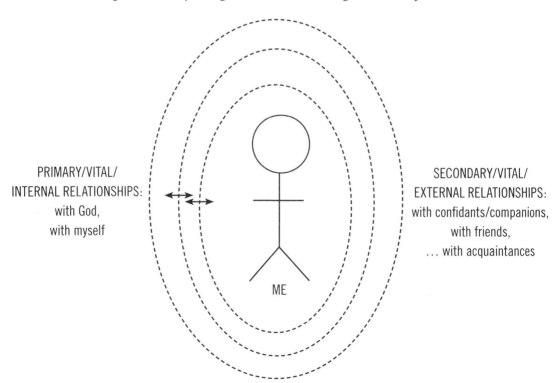

PRIMARY/VITAL/
INTERNAL RELATIONSHIPS:
with God,
with myself

SECONDARY/VITAL/
EXTERNAL RELATIONSHIPS:
with confidants/companions,
with friends,
… with acquaintances

ME

PRIMARY/VITAL/INTERNAL RELATIONSHIPS

The primary/vital/internal relationships are the relationships at the core of my life. They are (both) twenty-four/seven relationships with the potential to nourish and grow me in ways that no other relationships can. These relationships are foundational to how I run the rest of my life, so I will reap many benefits if I make them a functional priority in my life—which involves continuing to maintain and enhance them. Since these are internal relationships, there is a sense in which they are "behind my eyes" and "behind the scenes," so they can be ignored and neglected. (Indeed, some of us were taught—via behaviorism—that such relationships were only pseudo-relationships, with no more independent reality than a dream has after we wake up.) If we neglect these relationships, however, we do so at our peril—like neglecting the playbook and the conditioning and practice sessions before the game. If we neglect these relationships, we will not have what it takes to finish the multi-demand marathon, the "race set before us."

After Jesus had talked about the importance of establishing, maintaining, and enhancing a relationship with God, He said:

> Therefore everyone who hears these words of mine and puts them into practice is like a wise man who built his house on the rock. The rain came down, the streams rose, and the winds blew and beat against the house; yet it did not fall, because it had its foundations on the rock. But everyone who hears these words of mine and does not put them into practice is like a foolish man who built his house on sand. The rain came down, the streams rose, and the winds blew and beat against that house, and it fell with a great crash (Matt. 8:24–27).

MY RELATIONSHIP WITH GOD

Much has been said and written about establishing and growing a relationship with God that I will not repeat here. About "doing" such a relationship, however, I will mention the following:

- The dynamics for doing this relationship are fundamentally the same as for doing any other relationship. The key dynamic is that of dialogue (speaking to Him and Him speaking to you). Obviously, the "how" of this dialogue is different from that of other relationships (since Jesus is no longer here in "flesh and blood") but learning that "how" is fundamental.

- You must leave some of your beliefs about Him at the door, when you embark on this (relational) journey. (The only beliefs that you initially need are (1) that He exists and (2) that He shows up when you earnestly seek Him. Other understandings will grow as you continue the journey.) If you don't suspend your beliefs—or those of others—you run the risk of creating Him in your image (rather than getting to know Him). That same "suspension of possible relational knowledge" must be made when we enter into any relationship. If I, in the process of getting to know you, don't suspend who I think you might be or who someone else told me you were, and let you speak and act for yourself, I will only know about you (or think that I know about you) without actually knowing you. Some of what we believed or were told may actually prove to be accurate, but it needs to be accepted as a result of our gaining experiential knowledge (which "proves" some of what we thought or had been told). Some people come to God holding on to inaccurate beliefs, like this one: He is there to give them what they ask for. Such beliefs can negatively affect the development of their relationship with Him.

- Your relationship with God, like any relationship, develops and changes as time passes; it is progressive and developmental. When I tell people that I've been married four times, I sometimes get surprised looks—until I explain that each marriage has been to the same woman, but that the dynamics of our relationship have changed as time and circumstances have changed. (So, we have had a "couple before children" marriage, a "couple with children" marriage, a "couple with young adults" marriage, and a "couple after young adults" marriage. In each "marriage," we have had to modify the explicit and implicit agreements that we had made, in order to get those agreements to better fit our new circumstantial realities.) As we learn more about God—both theoretically and experientially—the dynamics of our relationship with Him will change: we will know and be better able to rest in His promises; we will be better able to distinguish His voice; we will get more comfortable talking to Him ongoingly; we will be better able to notice and enjoy His presence; we will be becoming more unconditional in our faith (in Him). This progress scenario, however, isn't inevitable. Because a relationship is the interaction between living beings, a regress scenario is also possible: where our questions remain bigger than our perception of God's promises (so we continue to experience anxiety), where we don't learn to distinguish voices (so we are blown around by every new voice), where our expectations don't get modified (so we end up only talking to Him in anger or disappointment or demand), where we don't learn to turn toward Him for comfort (so we turn away from Him—to some other source of comfort—when we are struggling),and where we have not grown our faith (so we live in fear of circumstances that are—in our belief system—too big for God). Fortunately, we have a say in the kind of relationship we have with God. (How's that for a consequence of having the ability to choose?) We can "taste and see that the Lord is good" and, as a result of that nourishment, can become"… like a tree planted by streams of water, which yields its fruit in season and whose leaf does not wither" (Ps. 1:3).

• You must prevent your (chosen) relationship with God from degenerating into obligation. As is the case with any relationship, if you lose the sense that you have chosen this relationship and that this relationship can take you to new and exciting and interesting places ("within" and "without" yourself), you will lose the wonder of connecting with this other Being. Instead, you will experience this relationship as a burden (to be endured or to be gotten out from under). To see every relationship as a "gift" (not always pleasant or easy to deal with but always profitable in the sense that it gives us something to grow with) is a constructive perspective, in this fallen world.

• You must let God set the boundary conditions of your relationship. He has specified these conditions: you enter into relationship by accepting and receiving the gift that Jesus provided; your relationship grows as you follow the guidelines that He has laid down; your relationship is restored as you confess … and so on. Some people consider such conditions to be confining (and so design their own boundary conditions). Other people, myself included, see these conditions (properly understood and applied) as what enables us to be who we were created to be. In the same way that I don't find the owner's manual for my 4Runner to be confining (otherwise I might treat that vehicle in a destructive way), I don't find His boundary conditions to be confining. For people who want to be in control of God, however, it is necessary to make him according to their specifications (in their image). An advantage of having a created god is that he won't direct their path. A disadvantage is that they don't have a relationship with anyone who can direct their path. (And who doesn't need direction through the outer and inner environments that we must traverse?)

The information and exercises(in appendix A, at the end of this chapter) are designed to help you identify your "growing edges" in your relationship with God.

MY RELATIONSHIP WITH MYSELF

The other "primary/vital/internal" relationship—my relationship with myself—operates most constructively when it is informed by my relationship with God. This twenty-four/seven relationship operates on the basis of how it has been informed by significant others (parents … teachers … cultural heroes—any influential others in our personal histories, whether or not these influences were constructive). By the process of introjection, (taking in the input of these significant others and making it our own), we learn to treat ourself the way others have treated us. And this process (which happens long before we could reach the stage of cognitive development that would enable us to reflect on what is happening) remains out of consciousness, operating much like the glasses that we have worn for many years (remaining unnoticed on our face but influencing everything that we see). When we call attention, however, to the fact that we are wearing glasses (which I just did), we can begin to notice the glasses. When we begin to become aware of the fact that we had "significant trainers" in our past, we can begin to notice (and specify) the content of that training. As we do that, it becomes possible for us to modify that training (we can't change what we aren't aware of) by replacing it with personally chosen training. If I discover that some of that old training is "destructive"—keeping me from actualizing my potentials, putting me into physical or emotional pain, telling me lies about myself or others or God—I can begin to replace it with constructive training. Doing so enables me to become more of who I was created to be, to get to "places" of rest and peace, to tell myself the truth about myself and others and God. In my economy (which the model in this chapter reflects), the best place to look for the constructive training program (to modify old, destructive training) is in my relationship with my heavenly Father. He treats me, in light of His Son's work, with forgiveness and generosity and grace and instruction and discipline and encouragement. He also treats me, in light of His Spirit's work, with love and joy and peace and patience and kindness and goodness and faithfulness and gentleness and self-control. Certainly He treats us this way in order to show us who He is and what He is like, but He also does this in order to provide a model or to be a model for us, to help us learn to treat ourself constructively. It's as if He says to us, "Imitate Me; learn to treat yourself the way I am treating you, then you will be nourished and will be able to treat others that way, too." For people like me, who have an old training program that includes harshness and perfectionism and competition and performance orientation, God's coming into my life was revolutionary (like light coming into a dark place). That revolution was followed by God staying in my life and—in an evolutionary way—teaching me how to begin to transcend the toxic training that had been poisoning me (like walking in the light, so as to have "fellowship" with Him and myself and others). To the extent that I have been able to introject this new training program—by His instruction and in His power and by my choices and efforts toward obedience—I have become progressively more constructive toward myself and others and a better servant in His kingdom. For me, this aspect of the "Good News"—that I could progressively transcend the training program that kept me (to quote Paul) "doing the evil I don't want to do"—has been a source of real hope and, as I've seen progress continue, a source of real thanksgiving. (It is a thanksgiving that I am sure is echoed by my wife who, more than any other person, has had to live with me.)

I can almost hear someone saying, "The view of God that you have just given bears little resemblance to the view of God that I have." To that person, I'd say, "Look back, and look into where you got your views of God." God has been enlisted in the service of all kinds of agendas: to justify personal choices (… of course God would not be against anything that feels so right to me …); to enhance compliance (… I love you and have a wonderful plan for your life; the first step of that plan requires that you …); to justify power and control tactics (… God will get you, if you …); to promote the building of my kingdom (… since God has blessed me, I will tear down my old store houses and build bigger ones …); to meet personal needs (… of course God won't let me suffer; after all, He loves me …). So, if you got your views of God from a person or community that promoted seeing God as a servant to their agendas (rather than seeing Him as the King and seeing their role as learning to obey His agendas), you will have some distortions in your view of Him. And, of course, "your viewing, influences your doing" … and "your doing, influences your experience." If you see God, for example, as your servant, it will influence how you relate to Him (very likely with the expectation that He should give you what you want and with anger when He doesn't comply). In turn, such "doing" will influence the quality of your experience of Him and with Him (very likely with little intimacy but with a lot of blame). If you discover such distortions (by seeing them in the light of what God wants us to know about Himself, as He showed Himself to us through Jesus), you need to correct them, even if some people might feel offended when you do that.

What, functionally, does it mean to treat myself the way that my heavenly Father treats me. In other words, "what does that look like?" The most useful way that I have found to answer that question, is to treat myself in the way that I would treat a close friend (a "confident" or "companion" in the model I am outlining). In other words, be for myself rather than *against* myself—like God is, toward me (Rom. 8:31). Let me illustrate an application of this principle from my journey. My background training (family and culture) was harsh and conditional—my acceptance was based on my performance, and I was only as good as my last performance. If I did not perform up to the expectations of my "trainers," I was taught that I should be ashamed of myself and should be harsh with myself (as others were) until my performance met minimally acceptable standards (which, for some of my trainers, was "error free"). Fortunately, I had ability to perform—both athletically and academically—well enough to meet (at least) some of these expectations most of the time. (I have no idea of where I would be now if I hadn't been able to perform.) As a consequence of that training, I internalized it and began to drive myself—as mercilessly as I had been driven—to reach acceptable performance levels (including being "error free"). In other words, I learned to be my own "harsh taskmaster," often demanding of myself that I "make more bricks with less straw." Such a "life management program" is not without consequences; in my case, they included migraine headaches, free floating hostility, "hurry up" sickness, and a willingness to sacrifice relationships for results.

When I connected with God, however, the seeds that would grow to overthrow the tyranny of my harshness training were sown. I learned about God's unconditional love for me (what a concept!—that nothing, not even my failures of performance, would separate me from His love). I began the long journey of thinking through and living out the implications of this truth, one of which is that I am to become unconditional in my self-support. Now, when I don't perform up to expectations—mine, others, God's—I am able to resist the urge to drive myself. (Some old training dies hard; I have to keep putting it to death.) Instead I forgive myself (on the basis of God's forgiveness of me). I *gently* hold myself to biblical standards, focusing on *learning* from every instance where my performance isn't meeting minimally acceptable standards so that I can do better next time. This is my attempt to cooperate with God in working all things—including my performance deficits—together for good and to focus on planning *how* I will do better (improve my performance) next time. So, instead of being harsh and punitive of myself (and, so, putting myself in pain), I am able to focus on growing my skills (without the interference caused by self-inflicted wounds).

In order to specifically illustrate the dynamics involved in treating myself like a confidant, I'll use a recent event in my life:

> Situation: I had a counselling session in which I did not meet minimally acceptable performance standards (according to me). I tried too hard, tried to do too much (as usual), repeated myself too frequently, didn't properly pace my responses ("hurry up" sickness dies hard), didn't pay sufficient attention to what my client was showing me, didn't properly integrate information

and insights from past sessions into this session, didn't stay on the client's "wavelength," didn't bring the session to a comfortable close, and on and on ... When the session (finally and mercifully) ended, I was "fit to be tied."

Interruption of Old Training
(Behavioral Emphasis)

Following my old training program, I began to "power up/adrenalize," get ready for "fight or flight" (except the only person to fight was me) and to berate myself. However, following my new training program, I immediately disabled my self-fighting by saying to myself (as I have practiced), "I refuse to be harsh with myself ... being harsh with myself and a dollar will get me coffee ... Do I want to add the problem of self-inflicted pain to the problem of having performed poorly? ... Do I want to treat myself as my heavenly Father treats me or as Satan treats me (with accusations)? ... Do I want to focus on the problem (of performing poorly) or on the solution (of how to deal with this now and how to do better next time)?"

[This doesn't represent everything I said to myself to prevent myself from directing my energy toward myself in a destructive way, but it does give a sample of my pattern interrupt.]

Interruption of Old Training
(Cognitive Emphasis)

Then, in order to disable my old training program, of self-berating, I used the "Two Column Technique" (where, on one side of the page, I wrote down what my old training has taught me to say to myself in circumstances like these).

[Such self talk will always, to some extent, be my first reaction. I must eliminate my expectation that I should be able to eliminate such self talk. What I can expect of myself is that I will not believe such "lies," that I will challenge such beliefs, and that I will replace such self talk with new programming that is more congruent with treating myself as a confidant. In this way, I've hooked up a second reaction that will disable, but not erase, my first reaction].

On the other side of the page I wrote my rebuttals—based on my new training program—to that old training.

Here is my application of the Two Column Technique:

OLD (DESTRUCTIVE) SELF TALK	NEW (CONSTRUCTIVE) SELF TALK
What a terrible session!	It wasn't terrible, but it was certainly a session that didn't go well. [Decatastrophizing]… I'll just rev down for a minute or two [relaxation practice]…Everybody, sooner or later, has a poor session [normalizing]… It isn't the end of the world [gaining perspective]…If it is as big a mess as I feel it is, I'll just do whatever it takes to clean it up [getting solution focused].
…You incompetent loser …	I'm not incompetent, and I'm not a loser; I won't take on either of those labels [protecting my identity from destructive labels]…The evidence is that I have been making progress and my track record—over many years—is that people grow (as we work together) and, for the most part, are happy with their results … [using hard data to challenge these potential labels].
…You should be ashamed of yourself …	Here is a "blast from the past" that I used to let swamp me; now, I am going to get my sail out of that wind [that was then; this is now]… Having a poor session is nothing to be ashamed of, unless I believe that I should never have a poor session [challenging perfectionism]… If I had a close friend who had a poor counselling session, I would encourage him/her to F.I.P.P. the session—Forgive him/herself, Investigate what happened, Plan what to do better next time, Practice those improvements into his/her life [getting solution focused]… I would not suggest that he/she be ashamed of him/herself. Now, I get to practice being a good friend to myself [getting a constructive focus].

Continued

...What is wrong with you?...	This question assumes that something is wrong with me. That is a nonsequitor—such a conclusion doesn't logically follow from having a poor session. Maybe I don't have all the skills I need, maybe I don't always apply the ones I do have in a helpful way, but that doesn't mean that there is something wrong with me [making a distinction between what I do and who I am].
What will [client] think of you after a session like that?...	Actually, I don't know what [client] thinks of me in light of that session, and I refuse to fantasize about that (avoiding mind reading)... I will pay attention to any "fallout" from this session, when I meet with him next time. If needed, I will bring that issue up and discuss it with him (with the purposes of using that discussion to build my rapport with him and to clean up any mess from the last session). If not needed, I will use what I learned to adjust my approach in ways that will be a better fit for him. I want to model for him how to face and handle situations that don't go well (including admitting that I messed up).... If he is so impacted by that session that he doesn't want to work with me further (the "data" I have so far would not suggest that, but it is possible), I will be prepared to refer him elsewhere. As long as I keep, as my top priority, his getting the best service that I can provide, I will have little trouble doing this—since referral is the best service that I can provide now [constructive game-planning].

For those of you who are curious about what happened when I met this client (at our next session), here is the update: The client came as usual and made no reference—verbally or non-verbally—to the last session. By all the data-gathering means that I use, I picked up nothing that indicated that he had been negatively impacted (as I had been). This certainly illustrates what all therapists know: that clients are from Mars, and therapists are from Venus, and that meeting on earth requires a stretching of everyone involved in order to develop shared/understood territory. Therefore, I did not refer to the last session but focused on staying with the agendas that he was showing and presenting. Because I had processed my stuff, I was able to focus on his next steps and, because I was very prepared (which is one of the by-products of getting my ability to analyze/obsess to work for me), this next session—at least according to my perceptions—went well.

Was all my work of staying self-supportive, therefore, unnecessary? As I see it, without "staying on my own team," I would have been in no place to make the next session helpful for him. Without that work being done, my responses could have ranged from self-blood-letting to defensiveness to referring him *before* the next session.

Having given a specific instance of what self-support looks like, I now want to focus on what is involved (and not involved) in *walking* in self-support.

Initially, I want to clarify (at a conceptual level) what I mean (and don't mean) by "self-support." I've already talked about self-support as learning to treat myself as my heavenly Father treats me and as I would treat a close friend. I also see self-support as "self-nourishment," where I learn to build up/encourage/strengthen myself. I do self-nourishment in each of the dimensions I was created with: physical, emotional, cognitive, spiritual, relational. As a consequence, I create an internal environment that promotes personal growth. Self-support or self-nourishment is in contrast to "self-indulgence," where I would give to myself at the expense of others and/or give to myself in a destructive way—as when I feed an addiction. Self-support or self-nourishment is also in contrast to "self-abuse," which occurs when—in its passive form of "self-starvation"—I deprive myself of the ingredients necessary to promote growth (for example, depriving myself of sleep or healthy food or time to connect with others). Self-abuse—in its active form of "self-hurting"—occurs when I treat myself in ways that block personal growth (for example, putting my fist into a wall or calling myself a name or breaking a constructive relationship). When Scripture talks about "self-denial" (for example, Luke 9:23), it could mean that I am to deny my sin nature (Rom. 6:1–14) or that I am to deny putting my agenda before God's agenda (Luke 22:42). It could also mean that I am to discipline myself (1 Cor. 9:24–27) but do so in the way that a good coach would. Such a coach would instruct me—in an edifying way—to improve mental and physical performance. A good coach would not instruct me the way a critic would—tearing me down by sitting in judgment on my present mental and physical performance.

Walking in self-support involves the following.

- *Walking in self-awareness and self-honesty; not walking in image management.*
  When I am on good terms with myself, I am able to face those parts of myself that I struggle with and to find options for dealing with those parts in inclusive

or non-rejecting ways. No part of who I am gets excluded or marginalized. I don't have to suppress part of myself into the basement. So, when I turn to face the outside world—whether the people out there are for me or against me—I am a united front and can deal with what that dimension of reality "serves up," with coherence and integrity. I can be honest in that public setting because I have been honest in my private setting with myself. When I am not on good terms with myself, however, the internal power struggles (rather than getting resolved with acceptance and respect and inclusion) get resolved with rejection and judgment and exclusion. With one part of me sitting in judgment on other (unacceptable) parts of me, I am a house divided against itself. In order to protect myself from external reality—where, I assume, other people are as much against me as I am—I do a cover-up of my internal fractures and present a "together" front to the external world. In order to maintain that "mask," I have to do image management, as a skilled model must do when performing a "photo shoot" on a rainy day. During one interaction, Jesus said to the Pharisees, " …You are like whitewashed tombs, which look beautiful on the outside but on the inside are full of dead men's bones and everything unclean. In the same way, on the outside you appear to people as righteous but on the inside you are full of hypocrisy and wickedness" (Matt. 23:27–28). Jesus advocated internal cleanliness as well as external cleanliness, which is why He said that the righteousness of His followers needed to exceed that of the scribes and Pharisees. For the scribes and Pharisees, it was good enough to look good.

• *Walking in forgiveness; not walking in judgement.* When I am on good terms with myself, I will be walking in the harmony that comes from having received and given forgiveness toward God, my neighbors, and myself. Those of us who have a relationship with God understand that that relationship was established by receiving forgiveness from God—through what Jesus did for us—for our sins. In order to draw closer to God, we may also need to affirm our forgiveness of God. There are those (like Lewis Smedes) who suggest that we intentionally forgive God (as well as receive His forgiveness).[1] I approach this issue in a different way. When I have been angry at God (or disappointed in Him or distressed by what He was allowing), it has always helped me to identify the distorted belief that I have been carrying (which has been generating that anger or disappointment or whatever) and to change that belief (thereby changing my expectation). However, if following Smede's suggestion works best for you, please do it. I believe that you (and I) should do whatever it takes to (both) gain and maintain walking in harmony with God.

As it relates to receiving and giving forgiveness with other people ("my neighbors"), receiving their forgiveness can only occur if they choose to give it (and that is their choice to make). If they choose to not forgive me, no reconciliation is possible. I don't, however, need their forgiveness (as much as I might appreciate it) to carry on with my life. Where I can extend forgiveness, I should take that initiative. (It is clear from Scripture—for example, Colossians 3:13—that I am to do everything in my power to walk in forgiveness.) Like me, you may have been (or are) in a situation where you are called to forgive, but the recipient of your forgiveness is not repentant and might even see your forgiveness as an opportunity for further exploitation. In my practice, for example, I (periodically) encounter someone who benefits from my services but refuses to pay. When that occurs, I am required to forgive him/her, whether or not he/she is repentant (and that repentance will occur, if at all, by the work of God's Spirit, not by what I do or don't do). I choose to forgive, both because God asks me to and because I value my health and well-being. (If I chose to not forgive, I would be planting seeds that would lead to a root of bitterness growing in my life.) Such forgiveness, however, can remain private and will not lead to reconciliation unless that person chooses to pay what he/she owes me. (Reconciliation requires the participation of both parties. Without such participation, my forgiveness brings our relationship to a constructive end—I don't seek vengeance [although I might seek justice], and he/she can't seek further exploitation.) For me, forgiveness is necessary; for us, reconciliation is optional.

As it relates to receiving and giving forgiveness toward myself, this way of thinking about forgiveness still applies, if I understand that one part of me can sit in judgement on another part of me (and, so, create a toxic internal environment). If that has been/is happening, I need to negotiate a new deal with myself: one in which I ongoingly forgive myself (not so that sin can grow and flourish in my life, but so that I can grow and flourish—toward being the person I was created to be). So, when I sin, I need to confess that sin … and repent of that sin … and make restitution for that sin (if necessary). Having received God's forgiveness for that sin (as 1 John 1:9 promises), I can now—on the basis of His forgiveness of me—forgive myself and walk under His mercy. As I do this, I am (in fact) treating myself the way He treats me. As I do this, I can spend little time in self-abuse and much time in learning from that situation and putting that learning to (future) uses. (For those of you who are interested in a more in-depth look at the issue of forgiveness, see appendix A, (6) at the end of this chapter.)

If, however, I choose – unwisely – to walk in judgement, the dynamics are different. Those dynamics are illustrated in the following senerios: I do not sit in direct judgement of God, but I use His standards to sit in judgement of others, and I try to get God to rubber stamp my plan for my life (showing that I am indirectly judging His plan to be inferior to mine). Sometimes when I am sitting in judgement of others, it leads to self-judgement (if I value fairness). Sometimes when I am sitting in judgement of others, I exempt myself (if I value the power to be able to rewrite the rules). In either case, however, internal toxicity is brewed—harshness in the first scenario, arrogance in the second scenario. These dynamics all illustrate being against others. Such dynamics cannot build relationships—only damage them. And, ultimately, my relationship with God is also damaged (see Matthew 6:14–15).

In the final analysis, the issue of self-support points us toward contrasting ways of doing our relationship with God: the way of grace and the way of law. The way of grace, illustrated and articulated by (ex-Pharisee) Paul, sees God as unconditionally for us and recognizes that our relationship with Him finally depends on Him. So, we walk with Him, secure in His promise to us that nothing will separate us from His love (Rom. 8:35–39). The way of law, illustrated and articulated by (other) Pharisees, sees God as conditionally for them and recognizes that their relationship with Him finally depends on their obedience to His laws. So they walk with Him, insecure in their ability to earn His love and denying (to themselves) their hypocrisy. No wonder they hated our Lord—who exposed their hypocrisy when He called them "whitewashed tombs."

The information and exercises (in appendix B, at the end of this chapter) are designed to help you identify and take the next steps for growing your relationship with yourself.

I have contended (as I have looked at these two core relationships) that the core of my being is strongest when I am on "good terms" in both of these relationships. ("Good terms" means when I am experiencing unconditional support—consistently through time— from both relationships.) I access that support, in my relationship with God, by receiving (through faith) His provisions for me. I access that support, in my relationship with myself, by learning to treat myself as God treats me. As I become more able to walk in this support (through practice over time), I experience core strength when I require it.

As we look at the documents that give us a glimpse into our Lord's life, we can see dynamics there that hint at these *core relationships in His life.*

Jesus' relationship with His Father is the ideal—which we wish our relationship with our father was/is and toward which we aspire in our role as father. When Jesus talks about His relationship with His Father, two themes emerge: (1) they had a love relationship with each other, and (2) they had a harmonious working relationship with each other. The love relationship theme emerges in John 15:9–10 (where Jesus encourages his followers to obey His commands and [so] remain in His love, as He has obeyed His Father's commands and remains in His love) and in Mark 14:32–36 (where, in the most challenging of circumstances, Jesus turns toward His Father—calling Him "dad"—and putting His life in His [Father's] hands). The harmonious working relationship theme emerges in various passages: Matthew 11:27, John 10:29–30, John 14:10–11, John 14:24, John 15:15, and Revelation 3:21. Then there are passages where both themes emerge (John 14:31 is an example). Possibly the most dramatic window into the love and harmony in this relationship was given when—during Jesus' transfiguration (Matt. 17:1–8)—His Father spoke (to Peter, James, and John) saying, "This is my Son, whom I love; with Him I am well pleased …" Ongoingly, Jesus drew on the support of His Father.

When we look at Jesus' relationship with Himself, there is less data to work with, and some can only be arrived at by inference. I once heard a speaker say that he wished that he could have been on the road to Emmaus, where "…Beginning with Moses and all the Prophets, [Jesus] explained to them what was said in all the Scriptures concerning himself" (Luke 24:27). This speaker said that, if the content of that conversation had been recorded, our understanding of the Scripture would be much enhanced. In the same way, I wish I could have talked with our Lord, while He was here, and asked Him what He said to Himself for encouragement during His three years of public ministry. During those years, it seemed that everyone wanted something from Him or was trying to trap Him or was trying to find a way to misunderstand Him. If I could have had that conversation, my understanding of self-encouragement would be much enhanced. I'm sure He would have used the Scriptures for encouragement. Perhaps He was encouraged by the anointing of the Spirit when He read from Isaiah 61 at his home synagogue in Nazareth (Luke 4:14–21). Although the Scripture records little of our Lord's inner dialogue, it does tell us that He loved and continued to love (John 15:9–12), that He (ongoingly) experienced joy (John 15:11), that He (ongoingly) experienced peace (John 14:27), and that He (ongoingly) experienced hope (John 17:13). We discover this about our Lord because, in the most looming of circumstances, He prays these lovely and practical gifts into His follower's lives.

In these glimpses of His inside life and His outside life, we see Someone whose experience and behavior is incompatible with a person divided against himself. There was no "shadow of turning" in His life; He was ongoingly self-nourishing (see Mark 6:31, Mark 6:46, Mark 4:38). He could not have sustained His giving (during His years of public ministry) otherwise.

SECONDARY/VITAL/EXTERNAL RELATIONSHIPS

The Secondary/Vital/External relationships are the relationships that surround my life. In the model I use, they are depicted as concentric circles around me. The inner circle (the one closest to me) is labeled *"confidants/companions"* and contains those people (few in number, thus it is the smallest circle) who have—over time—deeply interacted with me in constructive ways. These relationships are characterized by mutual giving and receiving, established trust, flowing communication, mutual acceptance, openness, and felt affection. Examples of such relationships include marriage partners (who have grown their relationship to the harvest of intimacy) and colleagues (who have worked together over the years to build a business or a program). The next closest circle, labeled *"friends,"* contains those people whom I have a working relationship with. There is (also) mutual giving and receiving in this kind of relationship, but not at such a personal level. There is (also) trust in this kind of relationship, but it will not be as deep or as extensive (as at the confidant level). There will (also) be communication but at a less personal and extensive level; it may be confined to the area mutual interest—like the mutual work project that is in both lives. At this level of relationship, acceptance and openness and affection are nice but not required (and, so, are like butter on bread—making the interaction sweeter—but not strictly required to get the job [of nourishment, in this simile] done). Examples of such relationships include (as mentioned) the colleague who shares a project and the buddy who shares games of golf or the person who sings in the same choir. In the outer circle, labeled *"acquaintances,"* are those people who are in my life space but not in a significant way. The primary ingredient of such a relationship is (two-way) communication—usually for the purpose of satisfying some interest or need. Examples of such relationships include the people in the service department where you get your car fixed (although some people would never entrust their vehicle to anyone less than a friend); people you meet in your pursuit of food, clothing, and shelter; and people you meet in your educational, recreational, and spiritual endeavors.

Since relationships consist of the interactions between living beings, those interactions change—sometimes growing, sometimes withering—the connection between the people. Every interaction between people—verbal or nonverbal—gives data that informs the recipient about the present status of the relationship and about the most appropriate direction (in light of that data) for the relationship to take. So, relationships migrate toward us (becoming more deep and personal) as the result of certain kinds of interactions and migrate away from us (becoming less deep and personal) as the result of other kinds of interactions. In this way, some people who start out as acquaintances (as everyone does) become friends and (possibly) confidants—a thrilling and enjoyable journey. Some people who have made that migration toward us can, by choosing to interact differently, move away from us (even back to being an acquaintance)—a sad and painful journey. Such migrations (like many processes in and around our lives) occur whether or not we are aware of them. As we become aware of them, we can make choices that influence these processes to work for us. What I advocate (and practice) that helps to get this process to work for me, is the intentional gathering of data (as I interact with the people around me) and the consequent assignment (and reassignment) of those people to one of my relational categories (on the basis of that data). This means that I am letting the kind of relationship that I am having with other people be assigned (into the categories of "confidant/companion" or "friend" or "acquaintance") on the basis of the kinds of interactions that I am *actually* having with them. "So what?" you may ask. "Because [I would answer] that is a higher quality way of assessing relationships than is usually used." (And, whether we are aware of it or not, we are ongoingly assessing relationships—so we can decide who to trust, who to protect ourself from, who to spend time with and so on.) Typical ways that people use to assess relationships rely less on data and more on theory. For examples, "You can trust family" or "Marriage partners must be each other's best friends" or "Our relationship will get better if I work harder on making it so" or "If she looks attractive to me, I want a relationship with her." In fact, every family of origin (which is a culture) has taught us some rules for assessing relationships. In the family I grew up in, one of those rules was "If someone is too friendly to you too quickly, you shouldn't trust that person because they are after something." Whenever my father (who was the exponent of this rule) mentioned this rule, he illustrated its value with reference to his time as a soldier in World War II. (He had left a farm in Saskatchewan—where relationships in those days were defined by geography—and had entered into a [military] culture, where interactions with strangers were ongoing.) So, that rule may have helped him at that time, but it didn't add to my social skills (except my caution). In the model that I am advocating, I am suggesting that we give ourself permission to modify our theories on the basis of what is actually happening. So, for example, if you are finding family members treating you in an abusive way, you can modify your theory that "you can trust family" (to, possibly, "you can trust *some* family members"), even if family members are advocating that theory. Then, you can begin to treat family members differentially—on the basis of the data that they have given you, rather than on the basis of what they are saying. (Where I come from, talk can be part of a con to distract you from protecting yourself from their agendas.) This model is also helpful as we make future relational investments (for example, what relationships we are going to invest in and what relationships we are going to stop investing in). As we go through life, some relationships we participate in will grow and some will wither; I am advocating that we intentionally participate in that process—watering those relationships that contain constructive dynamics and not watering those relationships that contain destructive dynamics. As we do this, we become more relationally *proactive*; being relationally *reactive* means that we are letting others tell us what kind of relationships we will have.

I realize that, for some of you reading this, what I have written may sound "bizarre" or "cold-hearted" or "blasphemous." If so, you have just assessed that this (interactional data gathering) approach to lessening/maintaining/enhancing relationships is not a primary fit for you. Indeed, there are other ways of assessing relationships—letting your heart lead you or letting your intuition lead you or letting someone else lead you—that will give you different (and possibly "better fit") data. There may still be, however, value in using this approach in a supplemental way; having more than one data stream (like more than one income stream) can be helpful.

As I have used this model, I have found it to be less helpful if I emphasized precision as it relates to the criteria for inclusion in a category. Everyone has his/her own criteria and will weigh each criterion differently, so there can be no "across-people" precision as it relates to the category that a person is in. (When a person is in transition, it seems, sometimes, that he/she is between categories.) I have found this model to be more helpful if I emphasized the trends that were developing in the relationship. (For example, "It seems like, during our last few conversations, we have had less to say to each other" or "It seems like, as we have talked recently, there is a growing sense of enjoyment"). These trends are based on data: what the other person shows me (verbally and non-verbally), what the dynamics are between us, and what my mind and heart and body are telling me. When I have gathered enough data to establish a trend, I can assign the person (for now) to the category that most accurately reflects this trend. (For example, "As I consider my last conversations with 'Jim,' not only have we had less to say to each other, but also I have felt a growing tension between us and a distancing within me—like things aren't so safe between us anymore. I think this trend has become established, so I will now consider 'Jim' to be an acquaintance, rather than a friend. I'm not sure, yet, whether or not I will talk to him about what I am picking up on, but (for now I will move away from taking initiatives to grow our relationship and move toward just letting things be what they will be between us ….") For those of you who would respond to this example with "of course you should talk to him!," I would reply by saying that you have just identified a relationship rule for yourself. It is, however, sometimes less helpful to make that rule a prescription for other people. In my experience, my attempt to share my perceptions of what is going on in (our) relationship has got me "out of the frying pan and into the fire". So, for some of us, the relationship rule is "Sometimes we should talk to the other person; sometimes we should not; whether or not we talk depends on [relationship-specific criteria]…"

Each of us will weigh different aspects of relationships differently; this will individualize the amount and kind of data that each of us need in order to make decisions pertaining to the relationships that surround our life. For example, as a result of the "training program" that I grew up with, I have learned to have a sensitivity to (and dislike for) criticism. So, when I experience criticism in present relationships, I quickly begin to withdraw (in contrast to someone who learned a different training program and who finds criticism less toxic). I have the option of learning to be less sensitive to criticism. I have decided, however, not to "shut my radar down." Instead I *evaluate* all criticism that I receive (instead of buying it, which is what I did as a child) and look for anything in it that I can agree with and learn from. When I sense that the motive of the "criticizer" is my edification (rather than my compliance with his/her perspective), I evaluate that criticism more carefully (but, still, only buy it—even partially—if I can sense that there is truth in that criticism). In that way, I attempt to get criticism to work for me (rather than just defend myself against it). Criticism for me, however, still precipitates relationship "withering" more quickly than any other dynamic of relationships. As a relationship growth example (from my life), I would point to the aspect of autonomy. I highly value the exercise of my free will (thinking for myself and choosing according to my priorities). Over the years, I have said to various people, "If I'm going to make a mistake here, at least it is going to be *my* mistake." So, any person (that I am in a relationship with) who respects my views (they don't have to like those views or agree with those views or [even] fully understand those views), I see as respecting me and, immediately, feel that relationship growth is possible. As each of us becomes aware of what withers relationships and what grows relationships *for us*, we can more quickly and accurately assess whether the potential in each relationship will become actual.

As we look at the documents that give us a glimpse into our Lord's life, we can see *how He structured and handled the relationships that surrounded His life*. It is evident that Jesus had relationships at the "confidant/companion" level, at the "friend" level, and at the "acquaintance" level.

There were three people in the inner circle of Jesus' life—Peter, James, and John. This is clear from the fact that they were with Him (no doubt by His request) at His transfiguration (the high point of His ministry) and in Gethsemane (the low point of His ministry). When significant things happened in our Lord's public ministry, He brought His companions to participate with Him—to share His glory or to receive their support (as limited as it might have been). At another recorded event in His public ministry—the raising of Jairus's daughter—Jesus specifically brought these companions (and no other disciples), but we are not told about the reason(s) He had for doing so (see Mark 5:35–43 and Luke 8:49–56). From all these events, we know that these three disciples were privy to information and experiences that no one else was; it was as if Jesus was wanting to share these special events with His closest companions. The dynamics of His relationship with these confidants are only hinted at, but they include deep sharing (Matt. 26:38) and deep affection (John 17:6–19).

The information and exercises (in appendix C, at the end of this chapter) are designed to help you manage your relationship with the "confidants/companions" in your life.

Within the "friendship" circle of our Lord's life are the other disciples—those men whom He invested in during His public ministry years—and (possibly) others in his entourage (Mark 15:41). Also in that circle are the followers He sent out to tell the people that "the kingdom of God is near you" (Luke 10:1–20) and people who had connected with Him during His ministry years (Luke 10:38–42, John 11:1–44, and John 12:1–11). I also put the family in which Jesus was raised in this category. I do so because Jesus (like some of us) was not understood or supported within His birth family; He had to protect Himself from members of that family. The incident I point to as support for this view is found in Mark 3. The time context (of this incident) is the beginning of Jesus' public ministry. He was beginning to challenge the traditions of the religious leadership (v. 1–6), so they were plotting to kill him (v. 6). People were beginning to hear about Him and come to see Him (v. 7–8); they saw him both heal people (v. 10) and rid people of demons (v.11),and he had just selected the twelve disciples (v. 13–19). In verse 21 we see his family's reaction to such events: "When his family heard about this, they went to take charge of him, for they said, 'He is out of his mind.'" (To this day, people who do deliverance work are sometimes considered crazy.) The religious leaders from Jerusalem were not saying He was crazy (they no doubt had seen and heard the power encounters); they were saying that He was driving out demons by the power of the prince of demons, Beelzebub. (By mislabelling where Jesus was getting His power, they were accusing Him of being a pawn of the kingdom of darkness; this, also, is a strategy that is still being used.) When his mother and brothers arrive (v. 31), they stand outside (the house where He is staying) and send someone to call Him out. In all likelihood, this is the first step in their plan to take charge of Him; on the basis of being family, they are demanding His obedience to them—to leave His endeavors and come to them. (This power play is used by relatives to this day.) When Jesus is told, "Your mother and brothers are outside looking for you," He responds by saying (in effect), "I have chosen a new family (the disciples); whoever does God's will is my brother and sister and mother." (He has come of age—30 years of age in that culture—and must be about His Father's business. He does not let family ties bind Him and keep Him from doing what He was called/sent to do.) So, in light of this incident, I have placed His family in the "friends" category. It could be argued that, in light of subsequent events, His family came to both understand who He was and to support what He was doing (and, so, would have migrated into the "confidant" category).

The information and exercises (in appendix D, at the end of this chapter) are designed to help you manage your relationship with the "friends" in your life.

Obviously, there were many people in the acquaintance circle of Jesus' life—many were people that He had given something to (like the hungry people that He fed in Matthew 14:13–21 or the woman who was healed of a physical illness, in the account found in Mark 5:21–34 or the man who was set free from demons, in the account found in Luke 8:26–39). Also in this category are the people Jesus clashed with—primarily the religious leaders (for example, Matthew 23:1–39). Also, in this category are the people that Jesus met, like the rich young ruler (Luke 18:18–23). As we can see from these examples, acquaintances include people that we meet only on one occasion or only briefly, people whose involvement with us is limited to receiving (or giving) and people who are kept at a distance because they are against us.

The information and exercises (in appendix E, at the end of this chapter) are designed to help you manage your relationship with the "acquaintances" in your life.

As already mentioned, relationships change—either growing or withering as a result of the kinds of interactions that take place between the participants. We see such relational migrations toward and away from our Lord's life. The longest "toward" migration is seen in the life of the apostle John who, between the time he met Jesus (Luke 5:1–11), and when he was exiled to Patmos (Rev. 1:9), had become "the disciple whom Jesus loved" (John 21:20). We've already looked at some of the data that indicates that he was one of the three confidants in Jesus' life, but there are some hints that John was the closest of the three (for instance, John 13:21–26). Unfortunately, little has been recorded about the kind and quality of the interactions that produced such closeness from the years they spent together. The longest "away from" migration is seen in the life of Judas Iscariot. Judas was invited by Jesus to a place of closeness (see Mark 3:13–19),in the terms of the model that we are discussing, to the "friendship" level at least (and arguably to the "confidant" level).

As such, he had years of ongoing access to Jesus' presence as well as His teaching and His work with people. At the time of the last interaction between Jesus and Judas—at the "last supper" (John 13:1–30)—relationally significant things were happening: the Devil had prompted Judas to betray Jesus (v. 2) and Jesus knew it (v. 18–26). At their last interaction, Judas chose to do the betrayal (v. 27a), and Jesus relegated him to the acquaintance level (v. 27b), as indicated by the terse instruction to Judas, "What you are about to do, do quickly." At that time, there was no focus on their relationship (as there is with the rest of the disciples throughout the remainder of the meal—John 13:28–17:26).There is only business to finish. The longest two-way migration (toward *and* away from *and* toward again) is seen in Peter's relationship with Jesus. Peter, too, was called to closeness (Mark 3:13–19) and to special closeness (as already discussed). He also disowned Jesus (John 13:31–38), but Jesus—knowing Peter's heart—protected him (Luke 22:31–32).Although Peter distanced himself from Jesus (John 21:1–3), Jesus took the initiative to come to Peter (John 21:4–14) and to bring him back to relational harmony and closeness (John 21:15–22). In John's account of this restoration (John 21:15–19), we glimpse the "away" migration that had taken place by the fact that Jesus said (three times), "Simon, Son of John" (which is his family of origin name, not the name—"Cephas"—that Jesus Himself had given him [John 1:42] and which symbolized Simon's move to his new family—the family of God). Also, when Jesus said, "…Do you love me? …," He used—in His first two repetitions of the question—the word "agapao" (which indicates an unconditional love). When Peter answered, "… You know that I love you," he used the word "phileo" (which indicates a lesser, brotherly love). When Jesus asked "…Do you love me?" the third time, He used the word "phileo," calling into question Peter's love at this (lesser) level. When Peter heard this new question, he was hurt (verse 17) and replied, "You know all things" (a reaffirmation of Jesus being the Messiah) and "You know that I phileo you." Then (for the third time) Jesus said, "Feed my sheep." (In this way, Jesus re-commissioned Peter for his role in the family of God and reversed Peter's three denials of the Messiah.) Following this reinstatement—to role and relationship—Jesus gave Peter a glimpse of his future (as He had when He first met him— see John 1:42). He also gave Peter the same instruction that He had given him years ago, "Follow me." (To this day, Jesus—in His kindness and patience toward us—gives us new beginnings that transcend our failures.)

It is clear from the Scriptures that Jesus was intentional in His data gathering so that He would be informed in His decision to let some people come close to Him and to keep other people at a distance from Him. He not only gathered behavioral data (for example, how the person[s] acted toward Him) but also data provided by His giftedness (for example, using His gift of discernment) and data provided by His discussions with His Father (for example, praying to and listening to His Father). The most significant relationships in Jesus' life—those with his twelve disciples—were established in consultation with His Father (Luke 6:12–16). Significant friendships in Jesus' life were established by how He had been treated: in John 11:5 we read that "Jesus loved Martha and her sister [Mary] and Lazarus." We know that such a relationship had been developed by Mary's actions (John 11:2 with reference to Luke 7:36–50) and by Martha's generosity (Luke 10:38–42). Jesus kept some relationships at an "acquaintance" level because He knew (via His discernment) that they would exploit Him if He was to "entrust Himself to them" (John 2:24–25). Another example of Jesus protecting Himself from potentially exploitive followers is found in John 6. (These events go against training—that some of us were subjected to—that Jesus was available to everybody all the time, with the application being that we should run our lives likewise. Thus, some of us got inflicted with chronic people pleasing.) In this instance (of John 6), we see Jesus feeding a large number of people with virtually no food (and with much more food remaining after the meal than went into the meal). When the people saw the miraculous sign, they said, "Surely this is the Prophet who is come into the world" (verse 14) but—instead of listening to Jesus—they tried to make Him king by force (to insure their ongoing food supply). Again, Jesus knew what they intended and withdrew from them (v. 15). These were determined people, however, and they tracked Him down again (verses 16–25). (We would probably do the same, at the prospect of an ongoing free lunch.) When they found Him—on the other side of the lake—Jesus "cut to the chase," saying "I tell you the truth, you are looking for me, not because you saw miraculous signs but because you ate the loaves and had your fill." (In other words, "You love me and have a wonderful plan for my life ….") And these people (more determined than ever to get Jesus to do their will, now resort to the bargain of "What will you give us so that we will believe in you"); they say "What miraculous sign then will you give that we may see it and believe you?[As if they hadn't already seen one!] What will you do? Our forefathers ate the manna in the desert, as it is written: 'He gave them bread from heaven to eat'" (v. 30–31). It is evident that these hungry people want something that is at least as spectacular as the forty year daily handout program that they are referring to. Jesus would not give in to this manipulation—although He had already proven that He was capable of providing what they were looking for—but, instead, began to direct the interaction to the fact that He was the bread of life (which got their mouths—as well as their stomachs—grumbling). These examples demonstrate how our Lord deliberately and differentially related to the people around Him.

Because our Lord related differentially to those around Him, He knew what relationships to "water" (nourish) and what relationships to leave dry. (Like me, you may have experienced the regret of not having watered relationships that—with hindsight—appear to have been full of potential but now have withered and died. Also, (like me), you may have experienced the frustration of watering (and watering and watering and watering … a relationship without either growth or fruit developing). The differential approach to doing relationships gives us criteria for watering and for not watering, based on sense-given and gift-given and prayer-given inputs. Jesus was a great waterer of those "that His Father had given Him." In what some see as the holy of holies in the New Testament (John 13:1–17:26), we see Jesus nourishing His disciples in ways that would enable them to bloom for the rest of their lives. In the short (and sad) account of the "rich young ruler," we see Jesus choosing not to water a relationship in light of responses He was given. In Mark's version of this encounter (Mark 10:17–31), there is a sentence (in verse 21) that indicates that our Lord cared about this young man and (probably) saw his potential. This sentence—"Jesus looked at him and loved him"—provides the context for Jesus saying, "One thing you lack. Go, sell everything you have and give to the poor, and you will have treasure in heaven. Then come, follow me." (This was an invitation to relationship, given in the same words that He used to call His other disciples.) When this young man went away sad (because he had great wealth—which he wasn't prepared to give up), there may also be a trace of sadness in our Lord's subsequent responses to His followers. Jesus did not pursue this (rich, devout, young) man with information about gaining treasure in heaven as well as treasure on earth (a language which this rich man would certainly have understood). Instead He let him go (even though he looked like a more capable follower than the others Jesus had chosen). In the ensuing discussion, Jesus answers Peter's question, "We have left everything to follow you, [what about us?]" with information that there will be blessings in this world (*and* in the next world) for following Him, but He didn't try to bribe someone who had not yet chosen to follow.

We also get glimpses, from our Lord's life, about how to handle relationships at the "confidant/companion" level, the "friend" level, and the "acquaintance" level. At the *confidant/companion* level, we see our Lord making deep, personal investments and turning toward those people. Such people had drawn close to Him: Jesus talked to them behind the scenes (John 13:21–26, for instance); He invited them to see behind the scenes (Mark 5:37, for instance); He was open with them in a unique way. At the *friend* level, there is also a closeness, but the focus of that closeness was more on working together (to get a task done). The closeness that our Lord shared with his twelve disciples at their last meal together is a closeness for their benefit: for their comfort, for their information, for their clarification, for their peace, for their joy, for their preparation, for their protection. Here, the emphasis is on giving (not reciprocity) and on instruction for upcoming tasks (not relationship development). At the *acquaintance* level, our Lord constructively "touches" the life of another person as an event in and of itself. (In other words, not for relationship development or task attainment purposes.) Such "touches" are the bricks for leading to these (further) purposes, but often those bridges weren't built. For example, on one occasion when Jesus was in Capernaum, a centurion from the Roman army came to Him, asking Him to heal one of his servants. (There are two accounts of this encounter—Matthew 8:5–13 and Luke 7:1–10.) It was a remarkable encounter and a remarkable demonstration of faith, which Jesus used at the time for teaching purposes, but no further mention of this gentile is ever made.

Relationships develop (grow more significant and close in the lives of the people involved) or dissipate (grow less significant and close in the lives of the people involved) as a consequence of the kinds of interactions that occur. (So, in the model—on page 221—there are two-way arrows [⟷] between the concentric circles that surround the individual.) Development happens only by the mutual (constructive) participation of both people; dissipation happens if either person does not do his/her part (no matter what the other participant wants/says/does). It takes two (people) to make a relationship work; it takes one (person) to stop it from working. Either participant can initiate a constructive (or destructive) input toward the other participant. When the other person responds (and such initiatives and responses can be verbal or non-verbal, direct or indirect, and so can be clear or unclear, sufficient or insufficient), an interaction has occurred. As individuals interact, a dynamic of mutual influence is set up—where each person's input influences the other person's (subsequent) response. People vary significantly in their interactional styles (some being more outgoing and direct, others being more reserved and indirect, for instance). People also vary in their interactional vigilance (some being less vigilant because they spend a higher proportion of interactional time in participant mode, others being more vigilant because they spend a higher proportion of interactional time in spectator mode). People also vary in the amount of interactional data they need in order to bring about a level shift on the relational grid. As people move toward higher interactional vigilance (paying more attention to how the inputs of the other participant are impacting them rather than just focusing on their own inputs), they become more able to relate differentially to the relationships that they are engaged with. This also happens when people choose to lessen the amount of interactional data required to make a shift of level on the relational grid (by assigning higher impact value to each interaction, for instance). The

more they are able to differentiate between confidants/companions and friends and acquaintances and the more they can identify the relational trends (toward or away from),
the more they will know what relationships are valuable to water and what relationships
are not valuable to water. The general rule for watering is: "Give water to relationships that
bear fruit." ("Watering" is a metaphor for the investment of time, energy, and resources
toward another person.) Some people will make a larger investment toward relationships
that are already bearing fruit, so that a (known) harvest will continue. Some people will
make a larger investment toward relationships that they sense (via sense-given and/or gift-
given and/or prayer-given data) will bear fruit, so that a (new) harvest will begin.

To me, these considerations are related to "stewardship," to spending our life well. I
am advocating a considered and (growingly) intentional approach to doing relationships.
I am *not* advocating that this is the only way to do relationships. So, if you find this approach helpful in your relational pursuits, use it (in whatever adapted way that would
make it tailor-made for you). If you do not find this approach directly helpful, then I'd
suggest that you use it only to help you clarify (by contrast) what you are doing (and,
thereby, improve *your* approach).

Appendix A

INFORMATION AND EXERCISES FOR ENHANCING MY RELATIONSHIP WITH GOD

As I approached this (most important) topic, I asked myself, "What could I possibly say that hasn't already been said (by people with more intelligence and insight and devotion than I have)?" My answer is, "Not much—except as it relates to *my* journey/struggle to have a relationship with God." Hopefully, you will find information here that will encourage your journey/struggle.

When I came into God's family, during my first year at university, I was almost completely ignorant of who God was and how He had operated/was operating in this world. I did have, however, a deep desire to know Him better and so began my journey toward Him and into the Christian community that I had (also) discovered. That community talked about being a family—God's family—and about what being a good family member involved (and the teaching I received was that, if I was a good family member, that would please God and benefit my relationship with Him). I was an earnest youngster (since I saw this family as the replacement for the dysfunctional one that I had grown up in) and an eager pupil (since I was committed to doing what God wanted). The training that I (subsequently) received was both helpful and unhelpful; I have spent a significant amount of time struggling to apply (and "unapply") what I was taught. During those struggles (which have occurred intermittently throughout my next thirty years), I have refined that teaching. So, the format for this appendix is as follows:

    (a) What I was taught (with apologies to any of my teachers whom I have misrepresented)

    (b) What I have come to believe and practice in my journey toward God

    (c) My questions to you (the reader) concerning what next step(s) you might want to take—as it relates to the aspect of teaching (for growing your relationship with God) that we have just considered.

BIBLE STUDY

From the day I heard about Jesus, I also heard about the Bible. I was told that it was God's "love letter" to me, that it was written by God's Spirit (as He worked in and through people who had a relationship with Him) and that it was the final authority on issues related to God. I was encouraged to read it, study it, memorize it, quote it, and obey it.

I remain deeply appreciative to those people who gave me this emphasis. The Scriptures have become (and remain) "a lamp to my feet and a light for my path." I have come to accept the view that the Scriptures reveal God's heart to us, that they are God-breathed and that they give us unique information on how to draw closer to Him and how to evaluate that journey. On my journey toward knowing the Scriptures and obeying the Scriptures, however, I have had to learn some things that I wasn't taught and unlearn some things that I was taught. I share these with you now—in the hope/prayer that they will make your journey a little easier and a little more fruitful.

Although I was encouraged to read and study Scripture, there was little discussion about reading for different purposes (and how you read depends on the purpose you have for reading). I was encouraged to read the entire Bible in a year (and was given a guide for doing so), but the purpose (implicit in that approach) emphasized "quantity" and "destination," not "quality" and "learning while on the journey." So, I did not find it to be helpful (and don't recommend it, now). I was encouraged (even commanded) to read the Bible every day. Such a command contained the (implicit) purpose of making Scripture reading an end in and of itself (rather than a means of getting to know God better). When Scripture reading becomes an obligation (something that I have to do, rather than something that I choose to do), it becomes a way to manage guilt or to score "religious superiority" points; as such, it becomes hazardous to my faith. I am not against reading the Scriptures daily; I am against reading them in such a way that our relationship with God is harmed rather than enhanced. I was encouraged to memorize the Scriptures. (Again), if Scripture memorization becomes an end in and of itself, it can be a source of spiritual pride. What has worked for me (and what I suggest for your consideration), is that you study the Scripture. (For me, "studying" involves answering these questions: what does this text say? [understanding]; what does this text mean? [interpretation]; how can I obey this text? [application]). In my experience, by the time I had finished studying the text, I had (as a by-product) memorized that text. When memorization is done in that way, it won't be an end in and of itself, and knowledge of the text (historical, theological, and personal) will be wedded to your memory of the text. (Otherwise, you could "know" the text but not know what it means or what it means to you or how it applies to you — a "knowledge" that any parrot could duplicate.)

Here are some purposes to put on (like eye glasses), through which to look at the Scriptures. They include the following:

Read to broaden your understanding of who God is. God is obviously much more than He has revealed to us, but it is our responsibility to grow in our knowledge of Him as far as His (general and special) revelation and our reason can take us (so that we will be better able to "get with His program"). And when we get to the limits of reason, we don't assume that we have discovered all there is to know about Him (nor do we assume that reason, in the hands of limited creatures, can fairly or completely judge the Infinite Creator). Instead, we look for other ways of knowing, that complement reason, (like intuition and personal dialogue with Him) in order to get to know Him better. He promises that "...We will find Him, when we search for Him with all our heart and all our soul" (Deut. 4:29). That process is not one that uses reason exclusively.

Read to discover how God related/relates to people. This includes those He has a personal relationship with and those He doesn't have a personal relationship with. Obviously, God has a relationship with every person (a Creator-to-creature relationship), but He makes a big distinction between people who have used their (God-given) free will to personalize their relationship with Him and those who have used their free will to stay out of relationship with Him. It is fascinating to discover what becomes available to us as we enter into a relationship with God, and just as fascinating to walk in the process of actualizing—in our lives—the gifts that He has made available.

Read to learn to see life through the glasses of biblical presuppositions. Every worldview has (scientifically unprovable) presuppositions that create the glasses through which the "wearer" (of those glasses) interprets his experience of life. That interpretive framework determines the "wearer's" response to each life event. For example, people will have very different responses to difficult/stressful/painful life circumstances depending on the interpretive glasses through which they are looking at these circumstances. God's revelation of Himself (to His "chosen people" and documented in their accounts of His interactions with them) supplies us with such an interpretive framework. That framework begins, for example, with the presupposition that God made us (rather than one prevailing view in our present culture, that we made God). When we are able to see life from the perspective of this framework, we will begin to know how to respond to everything that we face on our journey through this life. (My interpretation that life in this world is a journey—with a beginning, middle, and end—and that there is a "real" (created, material) world surrounding us and actual events that we must interact with, is a result of that framework. The understanding that we (humans) are also "real" and that there is another world that we enter into after this one, is also a by-product of that framework.)

In addition to reading the Bible with specific purposes in mind, I have also found it valuable to bring specific *attitudes* to that reading.

Bring the attitude of valuing rationality without becoming rationalistic. Reason is a powerful tool to bring to Bible study. People who can reason inductively and deductively will find the Scriptures to be a treasure house. At the same time, it is not helpful to make reason our final authority (it is just one way to gather knowledge, and it has its limits). The distinction that I am trying to make here is illustrated in these famous verses:

> Trust in the Lord will all your heart and lean not on your own understanding; in all your ways acknowledge him and he will make your paths straight (Prov. 3:5–6).

- "Trust" is a response to God that involves my will and my emotions as well as my thinking; it is a holistic response. I get information about (and from) God because I am in relationship with Him that I would not get if I was only learning about Him. (The same dynamic applies to any relationship.)
- My own understanding (based on reason) is not sufficient to know what I need to know...
- As I line up my life with God's directives (acknowledging Him in all my ways), He will involve Himself with me (for example, guiding me).
- This process of "getting with His program," however, necessarily uses reason (for example, it is involved in acknowledging Him).

Bring the attitude of humility. When we bring this attitude to our study of the Scriptures, we will be teachable (not taking a "know-it-all" stance) and curious (not taking a judgmental stance) and open to what the Scriptures say to us (not taking a defensive stance). An (ex)colleague of mine used to say to his students, "Don't be 'down' on something that you are not 'up' on." This attitude of humility will help us to keep learning and to keep our evaluations from becoming judgments. Some of my teachers were so vehement in defending their views on theology and Bible study that questions concerning their position were seen as personal attacks (and were responded to with counter-attacks). I have come to believe that, since none of us has the "immaculate perception" of the Scriptures, humility is in order.

Bring the attitude of anticipating the work of the Holy Spirit. Bible study needs to include my interaction with the text (and, via sermons and books and other resources, the interactions of fellow studiers), but it needs also to include my discovery of what the Holy Spirit is saying to me about that text. In other words, His interaction with me is a necessary dimension of bible study. At times, some of my teachers forgot about listening for the voice of the Spirit and so began to act like—if they had consulted more commentaries than other people—they were the final authority on that text. (By doing that, they demonstrated how to turn a study of the Scriptures into a power struggle—as if our world didn't already have enough demonstrations of that dynamic.) When I invite the interaction of God's Spirit, I notice—sometimes subtly, sometimes dramatically—a change in the quality of my interaction with the text. Sometimes I am startled by the clarity of a new insight from a familiar text; sometimes I realize new connections between texts; sometimes I am gripped by the relevance of this text for the circumstances or struggles that I am presently facing; sometimes a promise or a perspective "comes to me" with a force that impacts and changes my present experience. When these changes occur—when the written word becomes the living word to me—I experience the work of God's Spirit in a way that edifies me and turns study into adventure.

Bring the attitude of developmental growth. In Psalm 119:130 the text says, "The unfolding of your words gives light." The concept hinted at here is that of progressive development. Like a flower that progresses from bud to blossom to fruit, God's word unfolds to us (as we study it) in ways that help us to move from thinking like a child to thinking like an adult (as Paul mentions in 1 Corinthians 13:11). Some of my teachers saw the Scriptures as a dead text that, once understood, was to be adhered to without modification. They did not see it as a living text which, as we ingest it, nourishes and grows us—enabling us to see further new dimensions and applications to pursue and enter into. Show me a person who doesn't have an attitude of ongoing growth (as it relates to the study of the Scriptures) and I will show you someone who has never progressed from the milk of the Word to the meat of the Word (although they may have progressed to having a detailed understanding of that Word).

Bring the attitude that there is a circle of biblical truth. This concept, which I first heard from Francis Schaeffer many years ago, has been helpful (as I have studied the Scriptures) in deepening my understanding that different ways of looking at the text may both be correct (in other words, within the circle of biblical truth). This is in contrast to the view that there is just a "point" of biblical truth (where there is just one correct perspective; all other perspectives are incorrect). Obviously, there are times when we affirm an exclusive position (for example, "There is only one mediator between God and mankind" [1 Tim. 2:5]), and there are times when we affirm an inclusive position (for example, the Trinity is both

One and Three). I am prepared to concede that, in heaven, we will know the truth (in all its complexity), to the limits of what we can grasp (so, even there, there will be a circle of truth; the inclusive point of truth exists only in God). I am not prepared to concede, while on earth, that anyone (Jesus excluded) has reached that point.

Recently, I read a story in Margaret Silf's book *One Hundred Wisdom Stories from Around the World* that illustrates the point that I am trying to make.

God's Hat

One day, God took a walk across the earth, disguised as an old tramp. He made his way through the fields, where a group of friends were working, and decided to have a little joke with them. He put on a hat that was red on one side, white on the other, green on the front and black at the back.

As the friends walked home to their village that night, they talked about the old tramp: "Did you see that old man in the white hat walking through the fields?" asked the first.

The second replied, "No, it was a red hat!"

"Don't tell me that," retorted the first. "It was definitely white!"

"No, it wasn't," argued the second. "I saw it with my own two eyes, and it was red!"

"You must be blind!" said the first.

"There's nothing wrong with my eyes," snapped the second. "It's you! You must be drunk!"

"You're both blind," chimed in a third. "That fellow's hat was green!"

"What's the matter with you all?" rejoined a fourth. "It was a black hat. Anyone could see that! You were obviously half asleep when he walked past. What fools you all are!"

And so the argument continued, and before they knew what was happening to them, the group of friends had become a band of enemies.

And the strife continues. To this day, the descendants of those former friends still go on arguing. The White Hatters versus the Red Hatters, the Green Hatters versus the Black Hatters—each party believing that it knows, beyond any doubt, the colour of God's Hat.

As for God, he still walks the fields in disguise, saddened now. But the Mad Hatters are too fiercely embroiled in their arguments to notice.[2]

Bring the attitude that knowledge needs to produce change. In the German language there are two different verbs related to the concept of knowledge. One verb conveys the idea of "knowing about" something; the other verb conveys the idea of "knowing" something in the experiential sense. For example, I know about New York, but (since I have never been there) I have no experiential knowledge of that place. I believe that New York exists (since I have seen pictures, the Dave Letterman Show, and so on), but I do not have the same knowledge (nor would I use that knowledge in the same way) as a person who had visited New York or who was living there. I have had teachers who approached Bible study as if knowing about the Scriptures was good and sufficient. I have come to believe that—in the same way that faith if not accompanied by action is dead (James 2:17)—knowledge if not accompanied by change (external and/or internal) is dead. What I have come to believe (and practice) is that it is not good and sufficient to have a detached observer perspective toward knowledge. I must come to have an involved participant perspective, and when I achieve that perspective, change (in one form or other and at some time or other) is inevitable. If I was dying of thirst in a desert and came upon an oasis, I could perish while sitting beside the water knowing the fact that it could quench my thirst. If, however, I acted on that knowledge (in other words, let that knowledge bring about a change of behavior) and drank some water, I would get the benefit of that water.

Next steps:

The following questions will (hopefully) help you to specify your next steps of improvement in the area of Bible reading and study.

1. Is there any *purpose* for which I should read the Scriptures that could help my faith journey?

    _____
    _____
    _____

    Is there any *attitude* that I should adopt as I read the Scriptures, that could help my faith journey?

    _____
    _____
    _____

2. What else could I do/not do that would improve my practice of Bible reading and study?

    _____
    _____
    _____
    _____

3. If I was to apply what I have just discovered, what would my "application plan" include? (Write it out, below; it is helpful to keep it simple and short so that you could use it as a bookmark in your Bible.)

_____

_____

_____

_____

_____

_____

Prayer

From the day I heard about Jesus, I also heard about prayer. My teachers, at that stage of my journey, told me that prayer was talking to God. I remain grateful for that teaching and, looking back on it, I realize that I continue to affirm some of the implications—that God is Someone independent of me, that God is Someone who listens, and that God is Someone that I can have a relationship with. In subsequent years, I learned that there are other views of prayer (for example, prayer is meditation; prayer is connecting with my higher consciousness; prayer is transcending my ego; prayer is actualizing my dreams; and so on), but as I looked at the Scriptures it became obvious that the view of prayer implied and stated *there* supported my initial training.

I was also taught that I should set aside time during the day (preferably in the morning) and, following a game-plan like ACTS (Adoration → Confession → Thanksgiving → Supplication), should talk to God. Supplication (asking for things) should involve asking for what others need/want as well as asking for what I need/want. I was also taught that God has already given me His answers through the Scriptures. (Part of my early teaching was summarized as, "I talk to God through prayer; God talks to me through the Bible.") Because such teaching was given with the implication (and explication) that this approach was the "right" way, I spent far too long trying to fit in with that teaching (before I gave myself permission to adapt that teaching to fit me). Subsequently, I have modified that teaching in the following ways:

1. Because I try to run my life like a military operation, I like game-plans—but not if they take me out of the game. For me, ordering my conversation with God according to ACTS kept my connection with Him too formal—I felt like I was giving a report to my CEO rather than talking with "Abba." I also found myself, during the day, saying to myself, "I'll have to remember to pray about that (during my

set-aside time)." Then, when I got to that time, I experienced the frustration of try-ing to remember the various issues that I had mentally flagged. As I began to pur-sue what worked for me (having come to understand that "The Sabbath was made for man, not man for the Sabbath"), I found my prayer life moving toward more informality. I began to talk to God throughout the day, in no particular sequence of topics and about whatever was going on in my consciousness (which included many topics not covered by ACTS). As a consequence of this shift, I experienced a burden lifting and a friendship with God growing. I also began to get a glimpse of how "pray without ceasing" (a statement that Paul made in 1 Thessalonians 5:17 and which had confounded me) was possible.

2.   As obvious as it may be to you, early in my faith journey, I never made the connec-tion that supplication included purposes that were bigger than presenting God with my "shopping list." (That gap in my understanding and practice may have been due to my "missing the obvious" as well as the poor teaching I received.) I (literally) had lists of prayers—for myself and others—that consumed my prayer time. I saw these lists as the means to get these needs/wants met by God. As I became more familiar with the Scriptures—and with verses like, "God knows what you need before you ask Him" (Matt. 6:8)—I began to wonder about the value of these lists (which, to me, were beginning to sound like "vain repetitions"). Finally, one day I said to the Lord, "If you are as bored with these lists as I am, You'll be asleep." (At the time, I wasn't sure if God would be accepting of that kind of honesty. Since then, I've come to believe that He values honesty—because it promotes relationship development. I've also come to understand that He doesn't sleep; I'm not sure if He gets bored.) That prayer started me on a new journey—to find a way of doing prayer that would bring me to life, not death. (At that time, I said to myself, "I don't know where this quest will take me but, if I continue to do what I am doing, I will condition myself to hate and avoid prayer.") That quest has led me to discover that prayer is not just about getting things from God; it is also about giving things to God, "Lord, what would please You, in this situation?"..."Lord, I invite You into this situation"..."Lord, how can I do Your will, in this situation?" As this new dimension to prayer un-folded, so did my discovery that prayer was not just about getting "marching orders"; it was also about relationship development. *Everything* that I experience— what I consider, feel, struggle with, feel conflicted by, rehearse (to show others), strategize about—is "discussable" with Him. All of a sudden, I realized that this is (in part) what it means to have a "Friend who is closer than a brother."

3. As I followed the teaching that "God talks to me through the Bible," I began to re-alize that many of my questions (like "Should I marry and, if so, who?" or "What career should I pursue?") could not be specifically answered. (Yes, the Scriptures give guidelines about such issues but not answers.) When I came to realize that Scripture speaks truly—but not exhaustively—into my life, I quit looking for the chapter with my name on it. Even when I experienced God's Spirit making the written Word, the living Word (for me), the questions that were of central importance to my development at that stage of my life were not addressed. The Scripture, however, did inform me that "...The Counselor, the Holy Spirit, whom the Father will send in my name, will teach you all things..." (John 14:26). I also learned that some believers could actually hear from God—directly and person-ally (John 10:1–18, for instance). This instruction put me on a search, to become a "sheep who could hear the Shepherd's voice." This search resulted in learning skills that enabled me to transcend the poor teaching that I had received—which was keeping my relationship with God in poverty. Later, I realized that the people who initially taught me did not have listening skills, so they could not teach me how to dialogue with God.

As I look back on my faith journey, this discovery (of how to listen to God) has been among the most exciting and nourishing and relationship-developing of all. The risks of learning to have "ears that hear" are certainly matched by the risks of not learning to lis-ten. In this fallen world—where risk assessment and management is inevitable—I suggest that you choose to draw closer to God by learning to listen to Him and that you see the risks involved in this process as skill refinement opportunities. For example, the risk of mistaking His voice is lessened as you practice listening (This includes hearing a "voice," interpreting that voice, applying that voice, and getting feedback on your "hearing/inter-preting/applying" from God, others [seen and unseen], self, and circumstances.) As I have made/am making this journey, my toughest struggle has been/is managing my old train-ing program of perfectionism. This training pushes me toward expecting that I will have perfect communication with God and pushes me toward despair when I discover that my communication has been less than perfect. An aspect of this (perfectionistic) irrational thinking is what has been called "all or nothing" thinking. Applied to this issue, it would state "Either I achieve perfect communication with God [which can be trusted one hun-dred percent of the time] or I want nothing to do with communicating with God [since that communication cannot be trusted one hundred percent of the time]." It would be a silent world if we applied that criterion to all our relationships! "But," you might say, "God is perfect—so perfect communication is achievable." "But," I would say, "You [or I] are not perfect—so perfect communication is not achievable, but substantial communication is." Seeing substantial communication as "good enough" will only happen if I manage my perfectionism, rather than letting it manage me. I can get my perfectionism to work for me, however, by using it to glimpse what communication in heaven will be like. Yearning for such rapport and intimacy is not delusional within the Christian worldview, but it is (delusional) if I expect to achieve it in a fallen world. If I see substantial communication (moving toward excellent communication) as the achievable communication goal in this world, I can expect mistakes and, when they arrive, use them as feedback to refine my skills for drawing closer to God.

On this journey (of learning how to listen to God), I have discovered a number of books that have acted like roadmaps for me. Since I haven't the clarity (yet) or the space to give you my roadmap in these areas, let me supply you with the maps that helped to navigate me (roughly in the sequence that they helped me):

- Joyce Hugget's *The Joy of Listening to God*[3]
- Richard Foster's *Meditative Prayer*[4]
- John Powell's *He Touched Me*[5]
- Richard Foster's *Celebration of Discipline* (2nd Ed.)[6]
- Richard Foster's Prayer: *Finding the Heart's True Home*[7]
- Jack Deere's *Surprised by the Voice of God*[8]
- Dallas Willard's *In Search of Guidance: Developing a Conversational Relationship with God* (later entitled *Listening To God*)[9]

NEXT STEPS

The following questions will (hopefully) help you to clarify your next steps of growth in the area of prayer.

1a) Is there *any aspect* of how I am presently doing prayer that I need to *change* (in order to make it a better fit for me)?

a) _____

b) _____

c)_____

d) _____

1b) My *game-plan* for making each of these changes is as follows (for each aspect of prayer identified):

a) _____

_____

b) _____

_____

c)_____

_____

d) _____

_____

2a) In my journey of learning how to listen to God, my next steps are:

a) _____
b) _____
c)_____

2b) My game-plan for taking each of these next steps is as follows:

a) _____

_____

b) _____

_____

c)_____

_____

GOD'S LOVE

When I first heard about God and His love, I was an exponent of the rule, "If it sounds too good to be true, it probably is." Here, I found an exception to that rule. When I heard the story—especially the part where God sent His only Son to earth as a demonstration of His love for us—I was shocked. (Where I came from, people with power sent family members to "lord it over" people with less power.) Within weeks of opening my life up to God, I faced the biggest crisis of my life. During that crisis I received a demonstration of God's love to me; I have never recovered from that experience. Consequently, the issue of God's love (for me) was settled. The soil had been prepared for the teaching that "Nothing...in all creation, will be able to separate me from the love of God that is in Christ Jesus our Lord" (Rom. 8:39). During my crisis, that teaching took root in my life. However, as time passed, I heard some disturbing rumors about the possibility of being separated from God's love. I learned that, if I committed the "unpardonable sin," I would be separated from God's love. (So, I resolved not to do that—and found some comfort in the understanding that my concern about having committed this sin was proof that I hadn't done so.) I also learned that I could choose to take myself out of God's love (for me, this was only a hypothetical issue; what prospector would choose to dig elsewhere if he had just hit the mother lode?) I also learned something that was a challenge to me—the teaching that sin would separate me from God and His love. The people who taught me this perspective, used verses like Psalm 66:18"If I had cherished sin in my heart the Lord would not have listened" and Isaiah 59:2"But your iniquities have separated you from your God; Your sins have hidden his face from you, so that he will not hear. "They taught me that there was an absolute cause and effect relationship between sin and God not listening; it always and inevitably happened. In other words, this wasn't just one of God's responses, depending on the people and the circumstances. It always happened. As I view it now, that teaching implies that sin controls God. From what I know of these teachers, I believe it is accurate to attribute positive motives to them (for instance, they wanted me to understand the seriousness of sin). However, I do take issue with their strategy of teaching a half-truth to influence my thinking/behavior toward a constructive end. For a time on my faith journey, I attended a church where the pastor, who was highly concerned about the misuse of alcohol, taught that the only biblical position on the issue of alcohol consumption was abstinence. To support that position, he (also) taught that the wine Jesus made (at Cana) was non-alcoholic (although the word for wine in that passage is the same word that is used in passages referring to wine with alcoholic content). To me, this is another example of misusing the Scriptures in order to achieve a constructive goal.

I have come to believe that God loves me unconditionally. When I sin and confess it, God forgives me and cleanses me from that sin (I John 1:9); that dynamic enables me to walk in the light (with Him) and to experience fellowship (1 John 1:7). When I sin and don't confess it ("cherish it," as Psalm 66 puts it), God still loves me but He changes His ways of relating to me. One change that He may make is not responding to my communication to Him. From my point of view, this could be interpreted as "He won't hear me." (An all-knowing God, I believe, cannot go against His character by becoming ignorant of what I may say to Him while I am cherishing sin. He can, however, "respond" to me as if

He hadn't heard.) Any change of response (toward me) will flow out of His love for me and will reflect an opportunity for my growth that He wants me to benefit from. In this situation (where I am cherishing sin and where God chooses to not respond to my communication to Him), He may have chosen this response in order to sensitize me to the change in relationship that my holding on to sin has precipitated. Because of His love for me, He responds differently so that I will become aware of this new dynamic and might begin to search for what I need to do in order to restore the old dynamic (of His responding to me). His change of response could be interpreted as Him punishing me or withdrawing His affection from me or making me respond correctly, but I don't see God as a destructive parent (who punishes rather than disciples; who withdraws love rather than flexibly continuing to love; who tries to control rather than honoring choice). I see Him as the model to which all parents aspire. As I have looked in the Scriptures, I have noticed that God expresses His love in a broad range of ways that are person-specific. (In other words, God has multiple ways of relating to me, whether I am cherishing sin or cherishing righteousness.) Some of these expressions (of His love) are seen as such; some are less obvious (but who are we to limit our perceptions of His love to what we understand or like or appreciate?) Here is a (non-exhaustive) list of ways that Scripture depicts God showing love (I've arranged these from "more obvious" to "less obvious"):

1. By blessing us (Eph. 1:3–14).
2. By guiding us (Ps. 23).
3. By strengthening us (Isa. 41:10).
4. By protecting us (Ps. 91).
5. By being with us now (John 14:15–24).
6. By being with us in the future (John 14:1–4).
7. By reminding us (John 14:25–28).
8. By warning us (Jer. 1:4–10).
9. By disciplining us (Heb. 12:1–13).
10. By sending trials (James 1:2–8, 12).
11. By allowing temptations (James 1:13–15; 1 Cor. 10:13).
12. By allowing person-specific difficult circumstances (2 Cor. 12:1–10). In this situation, God allows a messenger from Satan (v. 7) to ongoingly torment (v. 7) Paul. So, in this sense, it is both a trial *and* a temptation.
13. By allowing sickness (1 Cor. 11:27–32).
14. By allowing death (1 Cor. 11:27–32).

These are among the strategies that God allows/initiates toward His family members. As such members, we know that He has our best interests at heart, so we let these strategies do their good work in us—including the work of preventative maintenance (as is the case with 13 and 14).

God has other strategies for people who have made turning away from Him into a lifestyle (for instance, Jeremiah 3 and 4, especially 3:8 and 4:5–9) and for people who have never had a relationship with Him and don't want one (for instance, Romans 1, especially verses 24, 27, 28).

NEXT STEPS

The following questions will (hopefully) help you to clarify your next steps of growth in the area of God's love.

1a) Is there some belief concerning God's love that is hindering my ability to walk in that love? If so, what is that belief? (State it, below.)

_____

_____

_____

1b) What will I need to do so that I am not letting that belief hinder me from experiencing and walking in God's love?

_____

_____

_____

_____

2a) Is there any circumstance in (or around) my life that I am not interpreting as a learning opportunity that God is giving me (out of His love for me)? If so, what is that circumstance? (State it, below.)

_____

_____

_____

_____

2b) If I was to see this circumstance as being within the context of God's love, what growth opportunities emerge?

a) _____
b) _____
c) _____

3) If I wanted to *understand* more about God's love, what "next steps" would I take? (For instance, who would I talk to? what resources would I access?)

a) _____
b) _____
c) _____

If any of the following resources sound relevant, check it off and track it down.
- ❏ *Does God Really Love Me*—Earl Wilson[10]
- ❏ *The Love Language of God*—Gary Chapman[11]
- ❏ *The Epistles of John*—John R. W. Stott[12]
- ❏ *The Bible in Counselling*—Waylon Ward (studies on God's Love, God's Child, and God Loves You)[13]
- ❏ *Love Beyond Reason*—John Ortberg[14]
- ❏ *The Sacred Romance*—Curtis and Eldridge[15]

4) If I wanted to *experience* more of God's love, what next steps would I take? (An example is praying Romans 5:5 to be your experience or taking a pilgrimage to be in the presence of someone who has grown in and is showing God's love.)

a) _____
b) _____
c) _____

GROWING (MY) FAITH

From the day I heard about Jesus, I (also) heard that there were things that I must do to grow my faith. I remain thankful for such teaching (since it is in contrast to the unhelpful teaching that some converts received—namely, that conversion is followed by an [effortless] "magic carpet ride"). Consequently, I eagerly sought those things that I should do (many of which make up the sections of this appendix) and began to incorporate them into my life. Some of these inclusions occurred without a lot of sweat; some required not only sweat but blood; some didn't occur even after blood, sweat, and tears. At that stage of my journey, I interpreted my application struggle as my fault, as something wrong with me. After all, this was what God wanted me to do and, since He was helping me, there should be no reason for "failure" other than my own doing (or being). What intensified my struggle was the truth that God would never ask me to do what wasn't possible. I had already begun to move toward being a "whited sepulchre" (a person who looked good on the outside/publicly but was covering up private struggles/shortcomings) when I "discovered" (God revealed to me) that the "failure" had been in my training (not in me). My trainers had helpfully focused on *what* I should put in my life but, when it came to how I should put it in my life, they had emphasized a "one size fits all" approach (usually, that meant that whatever had worked for them, they laid on me). They had (obviously) assumed that there was just one "right" way to implement that discipline into my life (and that was the way that they had discovered). In summary, they made a *description* of what worked for them a *prescription* for me. It began to dawn on me that the "blood" I had been losing was a result of sandpapering myself to fit the application strategies that I had been given; I was a square peg who was determined to fit into that round hole. My journey from that time of distress until now (where I see my relationship with God as being unique and where I have given myself permission to discover and design and use tailor-made [to me] ways of growing my relationship with Him) has had many steps. I will, however, only focus on one issue, in order to illustrate the paradigm shift I had to make. It occurred when a friend of mine, who was teaching a Sunday school class on prayer in the church I was attending, asked me to help him. I had been talking to him about some ideas in this area and he, being the more practical person, asked me if I would "road test" one. I accepted his invitation and decided to share the essentials of Michael and Norrisey's book *Prayer and Temperament* with the class. Basically, this book uses the Myers-Briggs Type Indicator (a psychological tool that helps people to discover their preferences on four fundamental bi-polar traits; more on this tool to follow) to help people identify (in light of these preferences) what style of prayer would be a "best fit" for them. The class members were intrigued with this approach to prayer (as I was); they practically demanded to take the MBTI and find out what it would show them concerning their prayer preferences. When that information got in their hands, and they had time to apply the recommendations to their prayer life, almost without exception they expressed how practically helpful it had been for them. This tool, far from hindering their prayer life, actually helped them to focus their prayer life and to do prayer in a way that they found preferable to what they had been doing.

This experience sent me on a search to discover other refinements that would allow me to grow my faith in ways that fit how I had been created. To discuss some of these discoveries, I need to introduce you to the Myers-Briggs Type Indicator. The theory behind this tool states that each of us has a preference (between the two options given) in each of the four traits measured. A *summary* of the tool is as follows:

1) Extravert (E)   or   Introvert (I)
   (showing where we get our energy, how we are revitalized)
2) Sensor (S)   or   iNtuitive (N)
   (showing how we take in information)
3) Thinker (T)   or   Feeler (F)
   (showing how we process information)
4) Perceiver (P)   or   Judger (J)
   (showing whether we prefer a lifestyle that is open-ended or closure-oriented)

Definitions of the *terms* used in this tool (which don't always agree with the definitions of these words as used every day in our culture) are as follows:

1) Extravert (E)   or   Introvert (I)

- If you are an Extravert, you will tend to be energized by events, situations, or people outside of yourself. If you are an Introvert, you will tend to find these activities tiring and need to regain your energy from within yourself, while alone.

- If you are an Extravert, you will tend to speak first and then think about what you have said—you do your thinking while talking out loud. If you are an Introvert, you sort out your thoughts in your mind before you speak.

- If you are an Extravert, you probably know lots of people, have a lot of friends, and enjoy being with them, going places and doing things. You are likely to know quite a lot about them—their thoughts and details concerning their personal life. If you are an Introvert, you will not know quite so many people, and they certainly will not know too much about you and your personal affairs. You will not "wear your heart on your sleeve." You will probably prefer your own company or that of just one or two close friends. An Extravert goes for breadth of relationships; an Introvert goes for depth of relationships.

All of us have both Extravert and Introvert skills. In different situations, we will tend to use the skill set that that situation calls for, but we all have an innate preference for one of these traits. We feel more at home when operating in that mode. It is not better to be extraverted rather than introverted (or vise versa); they are just different!

      2)   Sensor (S)   or   iNtuitive (N)

- If you are a Sensor, you prefer things to be specific and detailed. If you are an iNtuitive, you get bored with detail and prefer the broad, generalized picture.
- Sensors like specific, manageable, and separate "blocks" of information, work, or activities. INtuitives prefer information to be interrelated in some way—they like a "big picture."
- If you are a Sensor you will prefer to do something rather than merely think about it. INtuitives prefer thoughts to actions—and they are often not as proficient when it comes to being practical.
- Sensors think that "seeing is believing" and prefer things to be grounded and rooted in the present tense. INtuitives, on the other hand, are more concerned about the future (than the present); they like dreaming and imagining possibilities.
- If you are a Sensor, you will have a keen eye for color and for detail. If you are an iNtuitive, these things can pass you by without you noticing them.
- If you are a Sensor, you will enjoy using skills that you have already learned more than learning new skills. If you are an iNtuitive, you will enjoy using new skills more than practicing old skills.
- If you are a Sensor, you will tend to be patient with details but impatient if the details get complicated. If you are an iNtuitive, you will tend to be impatient with details but more patient if the situation is complicated.

We all have both Sensor and iNtuitive skills; in different situations, we opt for using one skill set rather than the other. However, we all have an innate preference for one of these approaches. Our preference feels normal for us (like handedness). It is not better to be a sensor rather than an intuitive (or vise versa); they are just different (providing each of us with unique strengths and unique challenges).

      3)   Thinker (T)   or   Feeler (F)

- If you are a Thinker, you probably prefer to settle disputes on grounds that are fair and objective rather than on what makes people happy. If you are a Feeler, you probably prefer to decide things on the basis of what is likely to be most harmonious.
- If you are a Thinker, processes are important to you, and you will tend to believe that you cannot have a good conclusion or end result if it is not built upon good, logical, and reasonable foundations. If you are a Feeler, you just know that what is

important is the end result of peace, harmony, acceptance—and this is more important than being concerned about the process.

- If you are a Thinker you tend to be more firm-headed than tenderhearted. If you are a Feeler, you tend to be more tenderhearted than firm-headed.
- If you are a Thinker, you probably prefer to see things from the outside, as an onlooker. Feelers prefer to see situations from the inside, as though they were involved.
- If you are a Thinker, you value justice more than mercy. If you are a Feeler, you value mercy more than justice.
- If you are a Thinker, you tend to pay more attention to ideas or things. If you are a Feeler, you tend to pay more attention to human relationships.

We all have Thinker and Feeler skills; in different situations, we can/will use different skill sets. However, we all have an innate preference for one of these traits rather than the other. Again, it is not better to be a Thinker rather than a Feeler (or vise versa). It is easy to see how each could make a unique contribution to making a decision.

4) Perceiver (P)   or   Judger (J)

- If you are a Judger, you are usually on time for appointments and prefer things to have their own time and place. Perceivers, on the other hand, are less sensitive to time constraints and prefer to "go with the flow" (rather than scheduling).
- If you are a Judger, you probably make lots of lists, and keep to them. Perceivers don't think in terms of lists, or if they do, they seldom keep to them.
- Judgers tend to appreciate organizations, hierarchies, rules, and regulations (not necessarily for their own sake, but because they allow and enable things to happen, to be achieved). Perceivers are less appreciative of organizations or set procedures or formalized structures. They prefer a more informal and autonomous climate.
- Judgers like things to be well organized, and they like to know where they stand in relation to situations. Perceivers are more likely to "fly by the seat of their pants," to see things as being provisional, and to change their mind if something else seems more appropriate.
- Judgers like to have plans and to have decisions made in advance; Perceivers like to stay flexible and leave their options open.
- Judgers are looking for closure; Perceivers are looking for new information.
- Judgers want to be right; Perceivers want to miss nothing.

We all have both Judger and Perceiver skills. However, we all have a natural preference for one trait rather than the other. It is not better to be a Judger rather than a Perceiver (or vise versa); they are just different!

Each of us will have an innate preference for one option as it relates to each of these four traits. This means that our "type" (which is the pattern made by the four letters that specify our four preferences) will be one of the 16 possible combinations of letters. These 16 "people type" combinations are as follows:

ISTJ	ISFJ	INFJ	INTJ
ISTP	ISFP	INFP	INTP
ESTP	ESFP	ENFP	ENTP
ESTJ	ESFJ	ENFJ	ENTJ

Knowing our "type" gives us valuable insight into how we were created. Although much more can be said about each type, the following are minimal snapshots of each of these 16 profiles.

SENSING TYPES WITH THINKING (ST)   SENSING TYPES WITH FEELING (SF)

ISTJ	ISFJ
• Serious, quiet, earn success by concentration and thoroughness • Practical, orderly, matter-of-fact, logical, realistic, and dependable • See to it that everything is well organized • Take responsibility • Make up their own minds as to what should be accomplished and work toward it steadily, regardless of protests or distractions • Live their outer life more with thinking, inner more with sensing	• Quiet, friendly, responsible, and conscientious • Work devotedly to meet their obligations • Lend stability to any project or group • Thorough, painstaking, accurate • Their interests are usually not technical • Can be patient with necessary details • Loyal, considerate, perceptive, concerned with how other people feel • Live their outer life more with feeling, inner more with sensing

Continued

ISTP	ISFP
• Cool onlookers, quiet, reserved, observing and analyzing life with detached curiosity and unexpected flashes of original humor • Usually interested in cause and effect, how and why mechanical things work, and in organizing facts using logical principles • Live their outer life more with sensing, inner more with thinking	• Retiring, quietly friendly, sensitive, modest about their abilities • Shun disagreements, do not force their opinions or values on others • Usually do not care to lead but are often loyal followers • Often relaxed about getting things done, because they enjoy the present moment and do not want to spoil it by undue haste or exertion • Live their outer life more with sensing, inner more with feeling
ESTP	ESFP
• Good at on-the-spot problem solving • Do not worry, enjoy whatever comes along • Tend to like mechanical things and sports, with friends on the side • Adaptable, tolerant, generally conservative in values • Dislike long explanations • Are best with real things that can be worked, handled, taken apart, or put together • Live their outer life more with sensing, inner more with thinking	• Outgoing, easygoing, accepting, friendly, enjoy everything and make things more fun for others by their enjoyment • Like sports and making things happen • Know what's going on and join in eagerly • Find remembering facts easier than mastering theories • Are best in situations that need sound common sense and practical ability with people as well as with things • Live their outer life more with sensing, inner more with feeling
ESTJ	ESFJ
• Practical, realistic, matter-of-fact, with a natural head for business or mechanics • Not interested in subjects they see no use for, but can apply themselves when necessary • Like to organize and run activities • May make good administrators, especially if they remember to consider other people's feelings and points of view • Live their outer life more with thinking, inner more with sensing	• Warmhearted, talkative, popular, conscientious, born cooperators, active committee members • Need harmony and may be good at creating it • Always doing something nice for someone • Work best with encouragement and praise • Main interest is in things that directly and visibly affect people's lives • Live their outer life more with feeling, inner more with sensing

Continued

INTUITIVES WITH FEELING (NF)	INTUITIVES WITH THINKING (NT)
INFJ • Succeed by perseverance, originality and desire to do whatever is needed or wanted • Put their best efforts into their work • Quietly forceful, conscientious, concerned for others • Respected for their firm principles • Likely to be honored and followed for their clear convictions as to how best to serve the common good • Live their outer life more with feeling, inner more with intuition	**INTJ** • Usually have original minds and great drive for their own ideas and purposes • In fields that appeal to them, they have a fine power to organize a job and carry it through with or without help • Skeptical, critical, independent, determined, sometimes stubborn • Must learn to yield less important point in order to win the most important • Live their outer life more with thinking, inner more with intuition
INFP • Full of enthusiasms and loyalties, but seldom talk of these until they know you well • Care about learning, ideas, language, and independent projects • Tend to undertake too much, then somehow get it done • Friendly, but often too absorbed in what they are doing to be sociable • Little concerned with possessions or physical surroundings • Live their outer life more with intuition, inner more with feeling	**INTP** • Quiet and reserved • Especially enjoy theoretical or scientific pursuits • Like solving problems with logic and analysis • Usually interested mainly in ideas, with little liking for parties or small talk • Tend to have sharply defined interests • Need careers where some strong interest can be used and useful • Live their outer life more with intuition, inner more with thinking
ENFP • Warmly enthusiastic, high-spirited, ingenious, imaginative • Able to do almost anything that interests them • Quick with a solution for any difficulty and ready to help anyone with a problem • Often rely on their ability to improvise instead of preparing in advance • Can usually find compelling reasons for whatever they want • Live their outer life more with intuition, inner more with feeling	**ENTP** • Quick, ingenious, good at many things • Stimulating company, alert and outspoken, may argue for fun on either side of a question • Resourceful in solving new and challenging problems, but may neglect routine assignments • Apt to turn to one new interest after another • Skillful in finding logical reasons for what they want • Live their outer life more with intuition, inner more with thinking

Continued

ENFJ	ENTJ
• Responsive and responsible	• Hearty, frank, decisive, leaders in activities
• Generally feel real concern for what others think or want, and try to handle things with due regard for the other person's feelings	• Usually good in anything that requires reasoning and intelligent talk, such as public speaking
• Can present a proposal or lead a group discussion with ease and tact	• Are well-informed and enjoy adding to their fund of knowledge
• Sociable, popular, sympathetic	• May sometimes appear more positive and confident than their experience in an area warrants
• Responsive to praise and criticism	• Live their outer life more with thinking, inner more with intuition
• Live their outer life more with feeling, inner more with intuition	

Like many other people, I was shocked by the accuracy of my profile when I took the MBTI. The following are my illustrations of how this tool helped me to design a tailor-made way of growing my faith.

Each time (over the years) that I have taken the MBTI, my Introversion preference has been very strong. (This built-in preference was enhanced by growing up on a farm as an only child; environment always interacts with heredity to modify the strength of a trait.) Early in my Christian life I was taught (obviously by extraverts) that growing my faith was about being involved with people, especially witnessing to them. As I tried to carry that teaching out, I found it both exhausting and frustrating. The insight (that I was an introvert) helped me to give myself permission to stop trying to operate like an extravert and to see private time as more than a waste of time. I now believe that the gift of evangelism will usually be given to extraverted people (who get energized by person-to-person interaction) and that it is best to find and develop the gifts God gives me (rather than following people who think that everyone should have and develop the gifts that they have and value). For me, some of the sweetest times (and growing times) in my spiritual life are when I am on a personal retreat (if I can resist the invitation—from extraverted others—to start interacting with other people).

Initially, when I took the MBTI, I scored as an "S." Fortunately, I had friends (and a wife) who said to me, "You may have scored that way but you don't function like an 'S.'" So I used the "best fit" procedure related to this tool and discovered that I was an "N" with dominant "S" skills. This situation (of skills overriding preference) had been developed by growing up with "S" parents and in a (farming) environment that demanded a practical, specific, here-and-now lifestyle. (Certain environments can push us to develop skills that are not in line with our natural preferences.) As I have given myself permission to let the intuitive mode of gathering information develop (my parents had seen little need for "dreamers" on our farm), I have been able to identify, affirm, and grow gifts that God has given me (like discernment) which require that data-gathering style. To this day, intuitive data-collection seems somewhat suspect to me, but I have learned that whatever God gives me I should use (rather than burying it [Matt. 25:14–30]).

Each time I have taken the MBTI, it has identified a strong "T" score. Since "Thinking" is my lead system for interacting with the outside world, this preference has long been seen by others as well as myself (so it has become an established insight). In light of that insight, I have learned (in my ministry to others) to balance—with empathy and kindness and patience—my natural tendency to say to people, "Get off your sofa and do the right thing." In light of that insight, I have also learned (in my ministry toward myself) to only say that which edifies (Eph. 4:29). My tendency is to emphasize justice; I need to grow in my ability to give (and receive) mercy.

Each time I have taken the MBTI, it has indicated a strong "J" score, so it isn't surprising that I run my life (spiritual and otherwise) like a "military operation." This tool has sensitized me to the insight that "Js" like things "nailed down" (organized, scheduled, clarified, specified) but "Ps"—around "Js"—feel "nailed down." Consequently, I have encouraged people with a "P" style to keep their options open. Toward myself, however, I have given myself permission to organize for all the efficiency and all the effectiveness that I can get from my (multiple) planning tools.

The following books are those I have used to help me apply the MBTI as a spiritual growth tool; if this sounds like a profitable direction for you to take, these may help:

- *Knowing Me, Knowing God*—Malcolm Goldsmith[16]
- *God's Gifted People*—Gary Harbaugh[17]
- *Personality Type and Religious Leadership*—Roy Oswalt and Otto Kroeger[18]
- *Life Keys*—Jane Kise, David Stark, and Sandra Krebs Hirsh[19]
- *Looking at Type and Spirituality*—Sandra Krebs Hirsh and Jane Kise[20]
- *Your Personality and the Spiritual Life*—Reginald Johnson[21]
- *Prayer and Temperament*—Chester Michael and Marie Norrisey[22]
- *Finding Your Way: Personalized Practices for Spiritual Growth*—John Ackerman[23]

*These are the books that primarily informed my description of the Myers-Briggs Type Indicator in this appendix.

NEXT STEPS

The following questions will (hopefully) help you to specify your next steps of improvement in the area of growing your faith.

1a) Is there *any aspect* of how I am presently growing my faith that I need to *change* in order to make it a better fit for me? (Areas where you feel frustrated or discouraged or confused are good areas to focus on...)

a) _____

b) _____

c) _____

d) _____

1b) My game-plan for making each of these changes is as follows:

a) _____
_____

b) _____
_____

c) _____
_____

d) _____
_____

2a) If you have used the Myers-Briggs Type Indicator to help design your way of growing your faith, the following questions may be helpful:

a) In light of your (E)/(I) preference, what changes would be profitable to make?

i) _____

ii) _____

iii) _____

b) In light of your (S)/(N) preference, what changes would be profitable to make?

i) _____

ii) _____

iii) _____

c) In light of your (T)/(F) preference, what changes would be profitable to make?

i) _____

      ii)_____

      iii) _____

  d) In light of your (P)/(J) preference, what changes would be profitable to make?

      i) _____

      ii)_____

      iii) _____

2b) Now, in relation to *each* of the preferences, put an asterisk (*) beside the change that is most valuable to make at this time.

2c) Now, in relation to each of these selected changes, write out (below) what you will do to put each of these changes into your lifestyle.

In relation to the selected (E)/(I) change, I will do the following to make it part of my lifestyle:

      i) _____

      ii)_____

      iii) _____

In relation to the selected (S)/(N) change, I will do the following to make it part of my lifestyle:

      i) _____

      ii)_____

      iii) _____

In relation to the selected (T)/(F) change, I will do the following to make it part of my lifestyle:

ii) _____

      ii)_____

      iii) _____

In relation to the selected (P)/(J) change, I will do the following to make it part of my lifestyle:

      i) _____

      ii)_____

      iii) _____

OBEDIENCE

From the day I heard about Jesus, I heard (and intuitively knew) that obedience to Him was a "big deal." So I began, with the instruction of the church I had become a part of, to walk in obedience. Initially, that took the form of changing where I spent my time and energy—going to church, getting involved in the church, going to Bible studies, tithing and so on. (For me, it also involved going to Bible college, since I knew very little of what the Scriptures said or about the culture that I had entered.) I will always remain grateful for that initial teaching—that obedience to God is to be the centerpiece of my life (in contrast to teaching that I have since run across which says, "I have a relationship with God but my will, not His, be done").

As I grew from childhood to adolescence in this new family, I moved from unquestioning obedience (to what my mentors had told me) to a questioning obedience. I began to ask questions like, "Since there are differing views on this issue, who should I be obedient to?" and "It is true that some people strongly assert that they are right, but maybe they are just vocal (but) blind guides; do they really have the immaculate perception on this issue?" and "Some of the people who are instructing me are not, themselves, obedient to the Scriptures; so should I trust their instruction to me?" and "There are differing interpretations of Scripture on this issue; what do I do with those differences?" When I went public with those questions, I either got answers that created more questions (easy answers make life hard) or I got labels—"rebellious," for example. Fortunately, I had already learned that asking questions, although it can be a sign of rebellion, can also be a sign of wanting to learn, so the label of "rebellious" didn't stick to me. These experiences pushed me toward a private search for my answers and God, who works *all* things together for the good of those of us who love Him and have been called according to His purpose, has used that search to both inform me and to draw me closer to Himself. (I don't suggest such a private journey for others, except maybe those with an INTJ personality type [see previous section of this appendix]. Some of us need to get off the "beaten track" to find our good and sufficient answers.)

Now that I have been on the journey of obedience for many years, I'll let you look at (and evaluate) my "roadmap" for that journey:

Obedience to God is essential; obedience to a human being is optional. When we want to know and do what God wants (obey Him), we have various sources of information that can help us: The Scriptures (that claim to be written by God working through humans); the Holy Spirit (who lives in us—if we have a relationship with God—and who has promised to lead us into the truth as we ask and interact with Him); other people—who are seeking to obey God—but are not in my time or space (they can be accessed by books or videos or television or internet); other people—who are seeking to obey God—and are in my time and space (they can be accessed by the local church community or meetings or telephone). Although the process of God leading us differs from person to person, He will help us find a way (usually via a combination of the above sources) of knowing what He wants, as we trust Him to show us. At the same time that we are to "diligently seek" Him, we are also to evaluate the data that we are getting from these sources: Scripture can be twisted, Satan—who can show up as an angel of light—can imitate the voice of the Holy Spirit, and other people (in our time and space or not) can be wolves in sheep's clothing or blind guides in sheep's clothing. The biblical command to "Test everything. Hold on to the good" (1 Thess. 5:21) has, in my theology, a range of application that covers all the sources mentioned. So, we need to learn to "correctly handle the word of truth" (as Paul instructed Timothy in 2 Timothy 2:15), to discern between voices (so we can distinguish between the voice of the Holy Spirit and a voice from the kingdom of darkness or the voice of someone else or our own voice), and to evaluate the fruit (both doctrinal and be-havioral) in the life of other believers.

When people ask us to "obey" them (to see the world as they do or to spend our life as they suggest), evaluation is in order:

- Does Scripture endorse their perspective and their request? (Is this request within the circle of biblical options?)
- Does the voice of the Spirit endorse this perspective or request—for me? (A re-quest to do a "good thing" is different from an endorsement to do a "God thing.")
- Does this person's fruit indicate that he/she is walking in obedience him/herself? (Be more careful about obeying someone who is not, him/herself, walking in "obedience.")
- What do people—that I have built a trust relationship with—say to me about this perspective and/or this request? (The input of such people can be very helpful, but the final decision is mine to make.)

When the "lights are green" from such an evaluation (In other words, all sources of data endorse an affirmative response), then obedience needs to be given (at least until disconfirming data shows up). When the "lights are red" (especially on one or both of the questions related to Scripture or the voice of the Holy Spirit), then obedience should not be given. When the "lights are yellow" (in other words, it is not clear if we should proceed or not), then obedience should be delayed (until more data can be gathered). When the person requesting our obedience becomes more insistent on our cooperation (in other words, his/her request for obedience takes on a "demand for obedience" quality) or he/she speaks with increasing certainty that he/she knows that this is the right thing for us to do (in other words, he/she knows God's will for our life, as it relates to the issue being consid-ered), these are "proceed with caution" signals (like a flashing yellow light). Our response is to thank this person for his/her input, but to inform him/her that we must turn (finally) to God for His input (confirmation or disconfirmation) on how we are to respond. If the person is upset with this response, that reaction gives us data that he/she may be wanting to play God in our life. Since we should never cooperate with those who propose idolatry, we should employ a "moving on" strategy (and we should never cooperate with those who propose idolatry).

All obedience, in the kingdom of light, is chosen obedience. God could make us obey Him (all He would need to do is show up in power, or have one of His angels get in our face and threaten us), but He respects us (as beings who—because we are made in His image—have the ability to choose) and so does not overwhelm us. Our obedience to God must come from us—from our choosing to do what He wants. This is not a once-for-all-time choice but a moment-by-moment choosing which, if sustained, makes up a commitment to obey. (So, beware of any teacher who encourages you to make some once-for-all-time choice so that, for instance, the Holy Spirit can "possess" you and make you do the right thing from now on.) It is the kingdom of darkness that endeavors to take away our ability to choose and (so) make us puppets to what that kingdom wants. Beings from the kingdom of darkness treat us differently from how beings (and the Being) in the kingdom of light treat us because they don't care about having a relationship with us—they only want us to be "hewers of [their] wood and drawers of [their] water" (Josh. 9:21). So, beware of any teacher who encourages you to see your relationship with God in terms of slavery. We are to *choose* to operate as His servants—remembering that our Lord said, "I no longer call you servants … instead I have called you friends …" (John 15:15). We have one Boss, who (legitimately) requests our obedience; our service to others is a result of our obedience to Him. When He says "Don't give here," we are not to give. To heed contrary instructions—even if the sources of those instructions are saying that they are speaking for Him—is idolatry.

Obedience is dynamic. Because obedience is an aspect of my response to God's kindness and generosity to me, it will develop as my relationship with Him develops. When I was a child (in my relationship with God), I thought and acted like a child and my obedience consisted primarily in finding out what the rules were and following them. As I became a young adult, I began to seek the reasons behind the rules; that involved more dialogue with the rule-Maker. Obedience moved from an unquestioned obedience to a questioned obedience. (God is fine with this change and says to us—in effect—"Come, let's reason together" [Isaiah 1:18]. Sometimes, however, *people* are not so concerned with our growth, just our compliance.) This change reflects a relationship change—from parent-child dynamics to adult-adult dynamics. Now that I am an older (and hopefully more mature) adult, my obedience (again) looks different. It has moved (again) from a questioned obedience to an expanded obedience. Expanded obedience (based on the answers I have received) focuses on applying those answers to every dimension of my life. Consequently, this stage of my life becomes my "magnum opus" (my best work in His kingdom). Again, this change reflects a relationship change—from the mentoring emphasis of my early adult years to the collegiality of my later adult years. At this stage, as we strive to become all that God wants us to be, we have come to a place in life where we can be more entrusted by God (and, so, have a deeper and closer relationship with Him). At earlier stages, we were deeply loved by God, but He may not have been able to entrust us as deeply.

What I have been outlining here is a developmental view of obedience. The following points help to define this view:

- This view sees obedience like a book—with several chapters, each building on the previous chapter. As with a book, you could decide to only read the last chapter, but (as you may know if you have taken that shortcut) you will lose the meaning and the coherence of the story. (In other words, the results of going through the stages are cumulative; shortcuts only cut the benefits of the journey short.)
- This view sees obedience as progressive—with mistakes providing feedback, so we will be able to know/do better, next time. (In other words, mistakes are seen as a refining tool.) Soon after I became a believer, I was told that "If Jesus isn't Lord of all, He's not Lord at all." That sounded very spiritual to me—and very discouraging (since I had already recognized that making Him "Lord of all" was going to involve a long and bloody battle). Now, I see that slogan as training in perfectionism—"either obey God perfectly or fail." I (now) believe that God, in His mercy, gives us a training program (including severe mercies) for our growth toward maturity; He doesn't expect my immediate and absolute obedience. One illustration of progressive obedience (from Scripture) that I have found encouraging is Paul's relationship with Barnabas as it relates to John Mark. This account begins in Acts 13 when, as mutual participants in the community of believers in Antioch, Paul and Barnabas were called by the Holy Spirit to work together. In their subsequent journey together (outlined in Acts 13–15), John Mark (a companion on this journey), deserted them and returned to Jerusalem (Acts 13:13). Later, when Paul wanted to visit the believers (who had become Christians during that journey), he and Barnabas disagreed over whether or not they should (again) take John Mark. (Tough-minded Paul said "no"; tenderhearted Barnabas said "yes.") The Scriptures say, "They had such a sharp disagreement that they parted company. Barnabas

took Mark and sailed for Cyprus, but Paul chose Silas and left [for] Syria and Cilicia …" (Acts 15:39–41). The following chapters of Acts follow the journey of Paul and Silas, so we don't hear anything about John Mark until Paul—now a prisoner in Rome and about to be executed there—mentions Him in his "prison" letters (in Colossians 4:10 and 2 Timothy 4:11). In these references, we see Paul going out of his way to affirm and encourage John Mark (in contrast to his earlier words and actions). Earlier, Barnabas was the only one to affirm and encourage John Mark. To me, this illustrates Paul's progressive obedience (from a performance-oriented ex-Pharisee who wasn't prone to give a second chance, to a more gracious and experienced leader who—like his Lord—was prepared to give a second chance).

I realize that this change of "viewing and doing" toward John Mark could also be accounted for by John Mark's growth (from deserter to helper in Paul's ministry), but I believe that it (also) had to do with Paul's growth of obedience.

The goal of obedience is pleasing God and developing my maturity (not my perfection). My obedience to God is a way of saying "Thank you" to Him for what He has done/is doing/will do for me. Such obedience is not a wearing down/wearing out process (as it is when working for a harsh taskmaster—who wants "more bricks with less straw"), but is a building up process, a training program that grows me toward maturity. I can almost hear someone objecting to this view by saying (something like), "If a goal of obedience is maturity, not perfection, then why did Jesus say "Be perfect as your heavenly Father is perfect?" (Matt. 5:48). Because (I would answer) the Greek word that is translated as "perfect" in English is "teleios." "Teleios" does not mean "flawless"; it does mean "complete" or "fully developed." In other words, it means "all God made you to be" (which is a good definition of maturity). So, one way of understanding maturity is found in 2 Peter 1, where we are instructed to "… make every effort to add to your faith goodness; and to goodness, knowledge; and to knowledge, self-control; and to self-control, perseverance; and to perseverance, godliness; and to godliness, brotherly kindness; and to brotherly kindness, love. For if you possess these qualities in increasing measures they will keep you from being ineffective and unproductive in your knowledge of our Lord Jesus Christ" (v. 5–8).

Obedience is (sometimes) imprecise. By that I mean that we are not sure, sometimes, what obedience looks like in a particular situation. For various reasons (including the world, the flesh, and the Devil), the road of obedience gets "fogged in" and we "see through a glass darkly" (which, being translated, means that we don't see much and what we do see is unclear). When there is no light, we wait (in prayer) until some light comes and we are able to walk in that light. When we can't see far ahead, we (carefully) take the steps that are clear. When the fog lifts, we (joyfully) move ahead at the pace we sense God setting (being careful not to run ahead of Him in presumption or lag behind Him in unbelief). When we discover that we have taken a wrong turn (off the path of obedience), we endeavor to get back on track in several ways: (a) We see this situation as a learning opportunity—so that we can do better next time. (b) We clean up any mess that getting off the path caused. If the disobedience was willful, that clean-up will include getting forgiveness from God, others, and myself. If the disobedience was a result of ignorance or misinformation or deception—so that it was more like a mistake—clean-up will include praying to God. He knows that our heart intended to serve Him but that our skills let us down, so He will work that mistake together for good. (c) We ask for His guidance (in the future) and so develop a game-plan for improving our "serve."

A recent example (of many I could choose from) of imprecise obedience occurred as I worked with a lady in my practice. She had shared with me a dream she had—in which a daughter that she had adopted was healed by God of conditions that child had sustained before adoption. My client wondered if God was asking her to do her part—through prayer—to bring this healing about. I said that I would pray about it—and did so with a friend of mine who is also a prayer partner. Both of us "heard" that she (and us) should pursue this healing (which we did). We were also told that the healing would not be instantaneous, but would take place over a period of time and would be finished by a specific date. However, when we met again—after that date had passed—my client reported that there was no change in her daughter's condition. I find such "results" difficult to deal with (to say the least). But, since I am committed to learning/growing (rather than ignoring or "losing heart" or letting a root of bitterness grow), I told God that I choose to see this situation as a learning opportunity and that I need eyes to see and ears to hear what He wants to teach me. I also met (again) with my client, at which time I shared my confusion and disappointment and frustration and embarrassment. I also gave her an opportunity to process her thoughts/feelings (after all, she was my client; I wasn't hers). We talked about ways of understanding this result and about what our next steps would include. (This was my attempt to clean up the mess.) To this date, I remain on good terms with my client. Her daughter's condition remains the same, and I have not received any insight or instruction about what happened in this situation or what I need to do differently next time. Since I have put this situation in God's hands—which is part of my game-plan for improving my serve—I am waiting (not in limbo but in anticipation) for His light (to walk in). If He chooses not to supply that light (which is His prerogative), I remind myself that many situations will not be clarified or restored this side of heaven and that I will have all the time I need (in heaven) to view all the relevant videos, since then I will know as I am now known. (As you may guess, I value understanding and closure.)

To those of you who are wondering if this view of obedience fits within the circle of biblical truth, I'd suggest that each point that I have made (in this section) is either stated or implied in what Paul says to us in Philippians 3:12–17. Here is my thinking about this, for your evaluation:

I have suggested that obedience to God is essential (but) obedience to a human being is optional. In verses 12–14, Paul talks about "pressing on toward" (twice) and "straining toward" a goal. The imagery here is of a race, where the runners are coming down the home stretch, flat out. (Do you remember Donovan Bailey coming down the stretch to win gold in the one hundred meters at the 1996 Olympics? That is the kind of concentration and effort that I think Paul is talking about, here.) And what is this goal that Paul is striving to attain? It is to reach the goal that God called him to attain. For Paul, it is about doing what God wants him to do. And what about obedience to (and from) other humans? In verse 15, he says—talking to those who have made progress in spiritual growth (he says different things to the immature)—"And if on some point you think differently, that too God will make clear to you." He isn't implying that God will always support his view, but that He will always bring clarity that will lead to consensus (and, in the meantime, unity without agreement can be maintained). So, Paul isn't adamant about people obeying him; he asks the mature believers to turn to God and obey His input. (In following that process, Paul asks these people to follow his example.)

I have suggested that all obedience, in the kingdom of light, is chosen obedience. Even a cursory reading of this letter alone (in other words, without reading his other letters), will show that Paul's obedience to God was chosen. Earlier in this letter, he says

"… But whatever was to my profit I now consider loss for the sake of Christ. What is more, I consider everything a loss compared to the surpassing greatness of knowing Christ Jesus my Lord, for whose sake I have lost all things" (Phil. 3:7–8).

However, someone might argue, "What kind of choice did Paul have? Wasn't he knocked off his horse and made to believe?" (Acts 9). In response, I would say that Paul (then, Saul), being a Pharisee, would understand instantly—when "a light from heaven flashed around him" and a voice spoke to him—that he was in the presence of Deity. (After all, he would be familiar with experiences like those of Moses.) So, when Saul responded by saying, "Who are you, Lord?" he knew that he was talking to God; he just wasn't sure of anything else. To me, Saul's question is parallel to Moses question when God called him (Exodus 3 and 4): "Suppose I go to the Israelites and say to them, 'The God of your fathers has sent me to you; and they ask me, "what is his name?" Then what shall I tell them?'" In the case of Moses, God said "I am who I am. This is what you are to say to the Israelites: I AM has sent me to you." In the case of Paul, God said, "I am Jesus, whom you are persecuting." From that moment on, I would suggest, Saul knew who God was and chose to serve Him—with the same zeal that characterized his commitment to Judaism. Notice that, within three days of his encounter with Jesus, Saul was already praying to Jesus and had received an answer, in the form of a vision(Acts 9:11–12).

Another characteristic of Paul's chosen obedience was that (to quote Eugene Peterson) it was "a long obedience in the same direction." In other words, it was a moment-by-moment commitment to obey, and it was sustained through time—including difficult times. The circumstances in which Paul wrote this letter (to the believers at Philippi) were that he was in jail in Rome, facing death. (To notice how his faith and obedience transcends circumstances—even death—see Philippians 1.)

Another characteristic of Paul's chosen obedience was that it was free from his past. In other words, Paul had resolved his past so that it was not a weight that he had to carry as he raced to do what God wanted. In verse 13–14, Paul says:"… But one thing I do: forgetting what is behind and straining toward what is ahead, I press on toward the goal to win the prize for which God has called me heavenward in Christ Jesus."

When Paul says that he "forgets what is behind," I would suggest that (contrary to other points of view) Paul hadn't become unable to remember the past (as if he had chosen a lobotomy). Earlier in Philippians 3 (in verses 4–6), he talks about his past, so we know that he is not using the word "forget" in a literal sense. Nor do I believe that Paul is advocating suppressing or repressing his past. (In other words, he didn't advocate burying his past alive and walking away from it.) Paul clearly recommends that we resolve our past (see, for instance, Ephesians 2:1–22) so that we can bury it dead. (When you bury your past alive, it keeps kicking you; when you bury it dead, you have peace.) I contend that Paul had gone through the process of resolving his past (since he was a man who walked his talk, who followed his own recommendations). And, if ever there was a past that needed resolution, it was Paul's. We first hear about this Pharisee (who studied under Gamaliel—Acts 22:3) when he took the role of coat-check boy at the stoning of Stephen (Acts 6:8–7:60). Saul approved of Stephen's murder (Acts 8:1). After that event, we know (by his own words—Acts 22:2–5 and Acts 26:1–11) that he persecuted the followers of Jesus, putting some in prison and killing others. And, when he was knocked off his horse, he was on his way to Damascus to do more of the same (Acts 9:1–2). Notice that the first question Jesus ever asked Paul was "Why do you persecute me?" (So we know that Paul had been walking his talk.) When Saul faced his Lord, he was a multiple murderer. How did he get from that place to the place where he could affirm that his past was behind him? In his letter to the believers in Rome (which contains his most systematic treatment of the "Good News"), we get a glimpse of Paul's answer (Rom. 4:23–5:11).How he personally applied that answer, we have no record. Presumably, that was done during the time after his conversion(Gal. 1:15–18). It is no coincidence, however, that Paul's writings give us the most thorough and insightful treatment of God's grace to us. He had first-hand experience of that grace, which gave him peace with God (and himself).

I have suggested that obedience is dynamic. It grows and changes as our relationship with God grows and changes. In Philippians 3:15 Paul says, "All of us who are mature should take such a view of things." (The view that he is endorsing is found in verses 12–14.) This instruction implies that some believers are not mature and, as happened in Corinth, they fought with each other (1 Cor. 1:10–17; 3:1–23), rather than striving for personal growth and corporate unity. In his first letter to the believers in Corinth, Paul (again) indicates that obedience is developmental. In 1 Corinthians 3:1–2 he says, "Brothers, I could not address you as spiritual but as worldly—mere infants in Christ. I gave you milk, not solid food, for you were not yet ready for it. Indeed, you are still not ready." Later in this letter (1 Cor. 13:11) he touches on this theme again, when he says, "When I was a child, I talked like a child, I thought like a child, I reasoned like a child. When I became a man, I put childish ways behind me."

And, what should the mature believer do? (This is the believer who is pressing on to the goal that God has called him/her to.) He/she should (a) keep on growing (v. 12–14) rather than becoming complacent, because of thinking that he/she has already attained everything. Also, he/she should (b) seek God to clarify differences (v. 15b) rather than quarrel with each other. Also, he/she should (c) apply, in behavior, what is already clear to him/her (v.16) rather than knowing things without doing them.

I have suggested that the goal of obedience is pleasing God and developing personal maturity (not perfection). It is obvious from verses 12–14 that Paul's striving to reach the goal that God called him to is a functional definition of obedience. And obedience is the means to actualize (make actual) my growth (toward maturity). Since this process involves many steps, it is almost inevitable that I will get off track (like, if I drive a vehicle long enough, I will probably get stuck or go off the road). So, an important skill set is that of handling "getting stuck" (handling disobedience) and of getting "back on track" (getting back to walking in obedience). I have attempted to address this issue on pages 12–26 in The Introduction. I once heard a man lecture for an hour (or maybe it just felt like an hour) on how, because of Jesus' work and the work of His Spirit, believers don't need to sin. That lecture has proven (for me) to be about as helpful as a lecture on walking in outer space; it hasn't been relevant to me because I have never been there. (Of much more relevance to me has been 1 John 1:9.) I suggest, therefore, that we focus less on what might be theoretically possible (unless, of course, we are training to be an astronaut) and focus more on what is practically necessary.

I have suggested that obedience is (sometimes) imprecise. As we look (again) at Philippians 3:15b—… "And if on some point you think differently, that too God will make clear to you."—we see that mature believers will differ (in other words, there will be imprecision as they all seek to obey God). To me, this imprecision has been a hassle: I've worked with people who were immobilized because they wanted to obey but didn't know what that obedience, in that particular situation, looked like; I've worked with people who were sure they knew what obedience looked like, but were proven to be wrong; I've worked with people who became discouraged with trying to obey and gave up (and sometimes those people were me). As a result of these experiences, I have come to see the imprecision of obedience as a "trial" (in the biblical sense of the word). Such trials are to be handled by the instructions given to us in Hebrews 12. In that chapter, our instructions include what not to do and what to do.

There are three things that we are *not* to do, three attitudes that we are to avoid, in order to respond to trials effectively:

1. We are not to *take lightly* the trials that come into our lives (Heb. 12:5). We are to avoid this attitude because they are a means God uses to grow us. We can take trials "lightly" by denying them (by doing "motivated forgetting" to get them out of conscious awareness) or by ignoring them (usually by choosing to focus on other things) or by minimizing them (by how you talk to yourself about them). If we run our trials through any of these cognitive processes, we change our responses to these trials in ways that make these trials less beneficial to us (as would be the case if we ran our ham sandwich through the washing machine before eating it).

2. We are not to *lose heart* when trials come into our lives (Heb. 12:5). There are many ways to lose heart. Among these ways are getting discouraged (by telling ourself that these trials will be permanent and pervasive and caused by ourself) or getting panicky (by telling ourself that these trials will overwhelm us) or running from them (by telling ourself that these trials must be avoided). If we lose heart in any of these ways, we make it difficult for these "personal trainers" to do their work in our lives.

3. We are not to let a *root of bitterness* grow in our lives when trials come (Heb. 12:15). Trials can produce endurance (James 1:2–4) but they can also produce bitterness, depending upon our response to them. There are many ways to grow bitterness; one of the best is to ask ourself (low-quality) questions like:

    • Why me?

    • God knows that I don't deserve this, so why would He do this to me?

    • How can God love me if He does this to me?

        If we ask ourself low-quality questions, they put our focus on issues that don't facilitate our cooperation with the trial (and our cooperation is essential if the trial is to do its good work in our life).

Hebrews 12 also identifies four things that we are to do in order to respond to trials effectively:

1. We are to "fix our eyes on Jesus" (Heb. 12:2). The context of this verse indicates that we should do this because Jesus provides us with the ideal role model for going through trials (verses 2–4). Another dimension (of what it means to fix our eyes on Jesus) is to talk to Him about the trial since He is a high priest who will give us grace to help us in our time of need (Heb. 4:16). As it relates to the trial of imprecise obedience, this involves letting Him know what the situation involves—that we don't know what to do and that we are requesting His guidance.

2. We are to reset our expectations. As I see it, there are at least three expectations to establish:

    i) There will be trials, which we are to see as discipline from God (v. 7). Some believers think that God will—and should—keep us from having to go through trials. We must establish the expectation that we will face trials. With that established, we won't rail against trials or try to avoid them; we will accept them and focus on getting through them and learning from them.

    ii) Trials, in and of themselves, teach us important lessons (v. 8). Some believers don't see trials as learning opportunities. We must establish the expectation that there is something valuable to learn from each trial and (then) be on the lookout for what that lesson is. In the context of this chapter, one lesson identified is that trials indicate that we are truly God's children (verses 7–10).

    iii) Trials produce (in us) good results (v. 11). Some believers see trials as personal offenses. We must establish the expectation that trials produce valuable outcomes—if we cooperate. (This differs from the previous point, which focuses on the process itself, not the product.) The text is clear when it says, "No trial seems pleasant at the time, but painful. Later on, however, it produces a harvest of righteousness and peace for those who have been trained by it" (v. 11).

So, as it relates to the trial of imprecise obedience, we should expect such a struggle and be looking for growth lessons in both the process and the product. One process lesson is that of remaining dependent upon God's ongoing input (since it can't be figured out by leaning on our own understanding). One product lesson is that of perseverance, which is developed as we struggle to fine-tune our responses of obedience.

3. We are to "strengthen our feeble arms and weak knees" and "make level paths for our feet" (v. 12–13). At the very least, this means that we are to respond to trials in ways that empower us. Those responses include both "inside" responses (where we strengthen ourself by, among other strategies, applying truth to our life) and "outside" responses (where we strengthen ourself by, among other strategies, behaving in ways that do the truth). As these processes relate to the trial of imprecise obedience, "inside" lessons could include appropriating the truth that God will not let these trials overwhelm us and that, when the time is right (in His time), we will see what the next step (of obedience) needs to include. (That step may involve stepping out—in the dark—with the faith that we are safe and will be guided in the dark.) "Outside" lessons could include any empowering action, like designing a game-plan for getting through the trial effectively. For me, an inside response to the trial of imprecise obedience is saying to myself, "This is 'gameday'—my opportunity, before a stadium full of believers from the past (Heb. 12:1), to handle this trial in a way that would cause them to cheer. I won't miss this opportunity, so what is my game-plan for handling this trial?" And, "When I handle it successfully, what are the outcomes that I want to see?" For me, an outside response is praying with my prayer partner about what "next step" God wants me to take; writing down what He tells us; walking through a confirmation process (on what we heard); (if confirmed), acting on what we heard.

4. We are to obey what God shows/tells us to do (v. 25). This may seem obvious (and maybe it is) but I would suggest that even this step requires preparation. (For me, anyway) it is valuable to commit myself to obedience *before* I know the content of any particular trial. When the trial shows up (and it could come in various shapes and sizes), I am less tempted to evaluate what God says to

me—especially if I don't like or agree with or understand what I am hearing. Some of you may be saying, "First Willson wants us to evaluate, then he doesn't want us to evaluate, what is he trying to say?" In response to that question, I say, "There is a time and place to evaluate *and* a time and place to not evaluate." We are to evaluate whether or not the information that we are hearing (and/or seeing and/or feeling) is from God. So, I talk about a confirmation step as part of a listening process. Once we are sure (or as sure as we can be) that the information we have received is from God, we are to obey (not evaluate) that information.

As it relates to the trial of imprecise obedience, I say (concerning my options):

- "God, I am committed—as best I can—to obeying You: right now, there is no light (that I can discern from You) on this issue, so I am going to wait for the dawn" (if that is the situation).
- "God, right now, there is no light (that I can discern from You) on this issue. I need to do something, so I will step out, trusting that You will guide me in the dark as You will guide me in the light. If this is a wrong step, you know my heart (which is to obey You). Please work this step together for the good of all involved and (especially) for my edification" (if that is the situation).
- "God, right now, there is only one step that I can see ahead. There is confirmation that You have shown me that step, so I take it now—trusting that You will continue to lead" (if that is the situation).
- "God, right now, the way You want me to go is both clear and confirmed. I will move ahead as You lead me, being careful to not run ahead of You or lag behind You. Please keep me with You, hand in hand" (if that is the situation).

NEXT STEPS

The following questions will (hopefully) help you to specify your next steps of application in the area of obedience.

The following chart (graphically) summarizes what I tried to convey in the section entitled, "Obedience to God is essential; obedience to a human being is optional."

	GOD	HUMAN
OBEY	always wise and valuable (to do)	- sometimes wise and valuable (to do) _____ - sometimes *not* wise and valuable (to do)
DISOBEY	never wise or valuable (to do)	- sometimes wise and valuable (to do) _____ - sometimes *not* wise and valuable (to do)

- Is there any step of obedience, that I know God wants me to take, now?

  Step: _____

  _____

  _____

  Plan for taking that step:_____

  _____

  _____

  _____

- Is there any step of disobedience, that I know God wants me to quit taking, now?

  Step:_____

  _____

  _____

  Plan for stopping that step: _____

  _____

  _____

  Plan for replacing that step: _____

  _____

  (with what?) _____

- Is there some human being (either past or present in my life) that I am obeying but (in light of where I am in my life now) I need to quit obeying?

  Person and issue:_____

  _____

  Plan for discontinuing obedience: _____

  _____

Alternative plan (i.e. what I will do instead?):_____

_____

_____

_____

• Is there some human being (either past or present in my life) that I am not obeying but (in light of where I am in my life now) I need to choose to obey?
   Person and issue:_____

   _____

   Plan for choosing obedience: _____

   _____

These questions deal with *changes* you should make.

What you should *maintain* (in other words, what you are obeying that you should
continue to obey or what you are not obeying that you should continue to not obey) can be
strengthened by making renewed personal decisions to continue to do (these) constructive
things and to continue to avoid (these) destructive things.

If you think that an exercise for strengthening your maintenance commitments would
be valuable, the following steps outline that exercise:

(i)   On one side of a page (or hard drive equivalent), make a list of the issues
      in which you are walking in obedience. (These need to be issues where
      you are making a conscious and deliberate choice to walk in obedience.)

(ii) At the bottom of this page, sign and date the following prayer (or, if you
      don't like this prayer or want to improve on it, write your own) to the
      Lord Jesus Christ:

      * I have committed myself to doing the above.

      * Please help me to keep doing these constructive things (and, so,
         deepen my commitment to them) until I reap the harvest You want me
         to receive.

      * Please help me to refine these commitments (and so improve them) in
         the ways that You want.

      * I will continue to make these things part of the fabric of my life. I turn
         toward You for Your help in making that happen.

      Signature: _____

      Date: _____

(iii) On the other side of that page (or hard drive equivalent) make a list of the issues that you are—as an act of obedience—avoiding. (These need to be issues that you are making a conscious and deliberate choice to avoid.)

(iv) At the bottom of this page, sign and date the following prayer (or, if you don't like this prayer or want to improve on it, write your own) to the Lord Jesus Christ:

* I have committed myself to avoiding the above.
* Please help me to keep distancing myself from these destructive things (and, so, deepen my commitment to avoid them). By doing this, I am freeing myself to focus on developing constructive "fruit" in my life.
* I will continue to turn away from these things (so that they will have no roots in my life). I turn toward You for Your help in this endeavor.

Signature: _____

Date: _____

If all obedience (in the kingdom of light) is chosen obedience, what next steps of obedience do you need to identify and choose? (To help you identify these steps, look at the areas of your life that you aren't satisfied with. Ask God to help you clarify *what* that next step would look like and *how* to take that step.) Record these next steps below:

(i) My next step of obedience is _____

_____

_____

_____

I will take that step by _____

_____

_____

_____

(ii) My next step of obedience is _____

_____

_____

I will take that step by _____

_____

_____

(iii) My next step of obedience is _____

_____

_____

_____

I will take that step by _____

_____

_____

If obedience grows as your relationship with God grows, what ways of doing obedience are due for an upgrade?

(a) Is there some issue in your life that you (now) feel requires more understanding in order for your obedience (in relation to this issue) not to feel forced?

In relation to each such issue, do the following:

- Write a note (or letter) to God—talking to Him about that issue, letting Him know what you need and inviting Him to come and respond (when and how He wants).
- His role (in that scenario) will be to confirm to you the right information when you find it. Make a list of the people and resources that you will check in order to deepen your understanding of that issue.
- Do your homework.

    (God may want you to deepen your obedience in the same direction. He may, however, on the basis of listening to Him/doing your study, reveal to you that He wants you to deepen your obedience by going in a different direction. In my experience, He has asked me to do continuity and discontinuity—usually when I was expecting to do the other—so be prepared to do more of the same or something different.)

(b) Is there some issue(s) in your life that you (now) feel requires an expansion in order for your obedience not to feel confined?

In relation to each such issue, do the following:

- Write a note (or letter) to God—talking to Him about that issue, letting Him know what you are aspiring to do and inviting Him to come and enable that expansion (when and how He wants). Also, if He doesn't want you to do that expansion, ask Him to show you what to do instead.
- His role in that scenario will be to confirm to you the right information, when you find it. Make a list of the people and resources that you will check in order to outline the *what* and the *how* of that expansion.
- Do your homework.

If the goal of obedience is to please God and to develop my maturity, are there some ways that I am (presently) doing obedience that need to change (so that this goal is more fully reached)?

If you have been wondering why, both in the text of this chapter and in the above question, I have talked about having one goal (of obedience) but then have proceeded to talk about two goals (pleasing God and developing personal maturity), it is because I see these two outcomes as being the two sides of the same coin: As I seek to please God (by my obedience), I will (automatically) be working on my growth.

One way to upgrade the "please God" aspect of this goal is to commit (or recommit or ongoingly commit) to walking in obedience. If the following prayer expresses your desire to walk in obedience, then sign and date it; if you prefer to use your own words, then write out your own prayer (and sign and date it).

> Lord Jesus Christ, I know from Your word that You are pleased when I obey You—
> You tell me that my obedience to Your commands is proof that I love You and, when I
> obey, You and Your Father will love me (too) and will reveal Yourselves to me (John 14:21).
> My heart's desire is to please You (by stepping up to do Your will, by cleaning up when
> I mess up and by never giving up) and to finally come to that place where I hear You
> say to me, "Well done, good and faithful servant … come and share your master's hap-
> piness" (Matt. 25:21).

> Signature:_____
> Date:_____

If you have been going through these exercises, you will have noticed that I repeatedly suggest that you sign and date decisions you are making (or renewing). Because signing/ dating is usually associated with doing contracts or agreements, there is a sense of commitment involved with this act. What makes this action most growth promoting, however, is when it helps us to open our heart so that we can take this decision to heart. Then our passion can fuel our decision and push it toward sustained action. (We have committed to something when we are taking action—based on a decision—in a sustained way.) Deciding with just our head may leave us without the fuel to maintain that decision.

One way to upgrade the "develop my maturity" aspect of this goal is to do the following:

     (i) Identify some aspect of obedience that you are presently experiencing as burdensome; clarify that aspect by writing it below:

_____

_____

_____

(ii) See this aspect of obedience as a growth opportunity. One way to do that is to ask yourself this question: "Since God has allowed this (to impact my life), what is He wanting me to learn from this?"

_____

_____

_____

_____

(iii) Turn that question into a prayer—inviting God to show you what He is wanting you to learn. ("Learning" could include what He is wanting you to come to know, do, or change.) Write down—as a result of praying—what you think He is wanting you to learn; specify that below:

_____

_____

_____

_____

(iv) (If you still have no answer to that question) arrange your life, for the next week, to include five minutes per day, during which you will (again) ask yourself that question. (Usually, you will know within that time-frame; if not, keep doing this practice until you become clear about what you are to learn.) When you discover this "learning," write it, below:

_____

_____

_____

_____

(v) If there is any application of that learning that you need to make, specify that below:

_____

_____

_____

(vi) If there is any game-plan, for that learning, that you need to specify, write it below:

_____

_____

_____

If obedience is (sometimes) imprecise, we need ways to handle that imprecision constructively. Since I have already attempted to outline a constructive procedure for handling situations where our obedience must be imprecise (by seeing those situations as trials and [so] applying the principles of Hebrews 12), I will focus the following exercises on helping your applications of that procedure.

   (i) Of the three attitudes you must avoid (if you want to benefit from the trial), underline the one that you might still be using. Also, underline the extent to which you see yourself using that attitude.

   Attitudes:
   - Taking the trial lightly
   - Losing heart (in relation to the trial)
   - Growing a root of bitterness (in relation to the trial)

   Extent:
   - Minimally
   - A little
   - Somewhat
   - Quite a bit
   - A lot

   If you are using one of these (destructive) attitudes more than minimally, write out how you will reduce your use until it is minimal.

_____

_____

_____

_____

   (If you aren't sure how to do this, you have just identified a "growing edge" of your life that you could invest in by reading about, talking to a friend about, praying about …)

   (ii) "Fixing our eyes on Jesus" can mean a number of things. The aspect (of what that means) that I will focus on here is inviting Him into this situation (of imprecise obedience). Your invitation could include the following:
   - Talking to Him about what the situation involves.

- Asking for His guidance (by any means and any time frame that He chooses).
- Asking for "eyes to see and ears to hear" what He will be showing you or saying to you.
- Letting Him know that any action that you take (if clarity doesn't come) is just your best attempt at obedience (given the information that you have) and that such action will be changed to fit any (subsequent) data that you receive from Him.
- Letting Him know that you will never turn your requests into demands (thus "putting Him to the test").
- Letting Him know that you want to learn from this situation—even if what you learn isn't pleasant or easy or anticipated or fully understood.

  Using these categories as guidelines, either pray (out loud) to God your invitation prayer (Why, out loud?--so that you can hear your prayer with your own ears and make it more than a mental exercise) or write out your invitation prayer (below).

_____

_____

_____

_____

_____

_____

_____

_____

_____

_____

_____

_____

(iii) "Resetting our expectations" can be done in various ways. Among those ways are the following:

- Read the expectations (in the text of this chapter) that I suggest you establish.
- Think about or journal about or talk to a friend (or mentor) about any (explicit or implicit) expectations that you have, as it relates to this situation (of imprecise obedience). Evaluate each expectation (by yourself

or with a friend or mentor). Modify each expectation until each is *clear* and *realistic* (as you see it) and *tentative*.

– I suggest *clear* because unclear or vague or implicit expectations can contribute to confusion and "double mindedness."

– I suggest *realistic* because unrealistic or idealistic or perfectionistic expectations can contribute to disappointment and discouragement.

– I suggest *tentative* because firmly held expectations can contribute to inflexibility. I suggest that you make a clear distinction between your faith in God and your expectations; they are not the same.

For each expectation that you can identify, I suggest that you "run it through" the following steps:

[Step 1]

(After thinking about or journaling or discussing ...) write down (below, if you like) your clearest version (to date) of this expectation.

_____

_____

_____

[Step 2]

There are various ways to evaluate an expectation. We will do that (evaluation) here by asking ourself "high-quality" questions.

Who is this expectation directed toward?

(a) If God:

• Is this a realistic expectation of Him? (If you have an expectation of God, for example, that requires or implies that He will override the free will of someone—yourself included—that expectation is not realistic.)

• If this expectation wasn't met (by God), would this negatively affect your relationship with Him? (If it would [negatively affect your relationship with Him], maybe you are expecting God to do your will, rather than remaining flexible enough to do His will.)

I've discovered that

• just because God *can* do something doesn't mean that He *will* do it.

• His doing something in the past doesn't necessarily mean that He will do it again or, if He does it, that it will be done the same way.

- A "good thing" to do is not necessarily a "God thing" to do.
- Waiting (until I sense His permission to go ahead…) is crucial for proper timing.
- Being a "faithful" servant is not the same as being a "successful" servant.

(b) If other people:
- Is this a realistic expectation of him/her/them? (Don't confuse what they *should* do with what they *are* doing.)
- Is your expectation of them realistic in light of the following?
     (i) Their track record with you
     (ii) Their present skills and maturity
     (iii) What you have seen them do/not do with others
- If this expectation wasn't met (by others), do you have an effective way of adjusting to that reality?

I've discovered that
- I have had lots of opportunities to practice my "adjustment to unmet expectations" skills.
- It is preferable to adjust, when my expectations are not being met, rather than holding on to those expectations and waiting for others to change and meet those expectations. (This paradigm shift—to adjusting—empowers me, since I have influence over my adjustment process whereas I have little influence over the decisions of others.)
- The more specific and numerous my expectations of others are, the more opportunity I have to experience disappointment.

(c) If myself:
- Is this a realistic expectation of myself? (Don't confuse how you think you *should* meet this expectation with how you *can* meet this expectation; be realistic [rather than idealistic] with yourself. Do you have a *game-plan* for meeting that expectation? Do you have the *skills* to meet that expectation? Do you have the *desire* to meet that expectation? If you can't answer "yes" to these three questions, you aren't being realistic with yourself.)

- Does this expectation empower me to take action (within, of course, the circle of biblical options)?
- If this expectation wasn't met (by myself), would this negatively affect my relationship with myself? (Rather than driving yourself to meet that expectation—which is what a harsh taskmaster would do—I'd suggest [if you have assessed this expectation to be realistic] that you look for the knowledge, skills and motivation you need to meet that expectation and then take action—holding yourself [gently] to the goal that expectation points toward.)

(If you fail to meet that goal, you F.I.P.P. the situation—see the Introduction, pages 12–26).

I've discovered that:
- Being on good terms with myself (and [so] not burdening myself with unrealistic expectations) is as important for me as it is for any other relationship in my life.
- My background training operates automatically (and so predisposes me to certain expectations, unless I identify and evaluate and modify that training).
- My body helps me to identify self-expectations by generating anxiety or anger or depression.
- I was built to be in community—including community with myself. I decide and design whether that community will build me up or tear me down.

[Step 3]
- In light of this evaluation (step 2), rewrite the expectation being evaluated. Make this revision clear, realistic, tentative, and empowering. Write it below. (Repeat these steps for every expectation that you can identify.)

_____

_____

_____

(iv) "Strengthening our feeble arms and weak knees" and "making level paths for our feet" can be done in various ways. In the text of this chapter, I suggested that this involves "inside" responses and "outside" responses.

Inside responses (to the trial of imprecise obedience) include several points:

- Claiming relevant biblical promises (for instance, Hebrews 4:14–16).
- Rehearsing personal affirmations (for instance, I have affirmed the following: "Sooner or later, in one way or another, with God's help, I'll find a way to get through this ...")
- Praying (for instance, I have prayed: "Lord, I will face this trial the best I can [I will not try to flee it]...Please empower me ...Please give me "eyes to see and ears to hear" what You want me to learn ...Please walk with me through this; I invite You to do so ...")
- Game-planning (for instance, I have developed a list of *guidelines* as it relates to this trial):
    - "One day at a time; one step at a time" ask "What is my next step?"
    - Don't try for premature closure.
    - Journal every insight or lesson that comes; get in/stay in anticipation mode.
    - Stay curious.
    - Avoid all self talk that would move me toward avoidance.
    - Avoid low-quality questions like "why me?"
    - Remember: I committed myself to life-long learning... now is my opportunity to learn.
    - This situation will show me where I am not yet skilled enough ...
    - Adjust ... adjust ... adjust ...
    - If I fail to plan, I plan to fail.
    - I must not get the "disease" of "hardening of the categories."
- Ask high-quality questions. (For instance, I have asked myself these questions):
    - Do I have something better to do than participate in this learning opportunity? (To me, this is a rhetorical question.)
    - Am I walking in protection?
    - Is there any remaining preparation that I need to make? (Remember Maximus in *Gladiator*).
    - What do I need to mentally rehearse? (So I am getting my mind and body ready to perform.)

These categories are not separate (as I have outlined them above). So, use them as guidelines, but—as you do your internal preparation (for strengthening your feeble arms and weak knees)—let them flow into each other. Drawing on what you know that works for you, write your *internal response plan* below.

_____

_____

_____

_____

_____

_____

_____

_____

_____

Outside responses (to the trial of imprecise obedience) include the following:

- Draw on feedback from coaches. There are two kinds of coaches: "Unintentional coaches" (who usually show you what *not to* do) and "Intentional coaches" (who you choose and who will show you what *to* do). For instance, I have talked to my intentional coach(es) about several points:
  - How he/she has handled similar circumstances
  - How he/she would suggest that I handle such circumstances
  - What resources he/she would suggest that I utilize
- Draw on my support system. (For instance, I have drawn on my support system for the following):
  - Prayer support
  - Spiritual feedback (what he/she hears from God that he/she understands is for me to consider)
  - Recreational support (for constructive distractions from the trial)
- Develop an action plan. (For instance, I have developed an action plan that included the following):
  - A self-support/self-sustaining aspect that includes several dimensions:
    - A physical dimension (exercise)
    - An emotional dimension (talk to a trusted fellow traveler)
    - A cognitive dimension (reading about others who handled this kind of circumstance)

- A spiritual dimension (praying for His lessons to be clear)
- A set of behavioral steps, (the content of which is specific to the [trial] situation)
- A commitment to journal the process
- A commitment to Kai Zen (the concept of making small and ongoing changes, in light of the feedback I get from the process, so that I am ongoingly adjusting to that feedback).

(Again), these categories are not separate (as I have outlined them above). So, use them as guidelines, but—as you do your external preparation (for making level paths for your feet)—let them flow into each other. Drawing on what you know that works for you, write your *external response plan* below.

_____

_____

_____

_____

_____

_____

_____

_____

_____

_____

_____

_____

_____

_____

_____

_____

_____

_____

(v) "Obeying what God shows/tells us to do." This principle, in contrast to the other principles of Hebrews 12, is not open to interpretation—you either obey or you don't. So (as it relates to the trial of imprecise obedience) maybe the only exercise needed is that of filling out the following chart (as the next steps for handling this trial are revealed).

NEXT STEP REVEALED	RESPONSE OF OBEDIENCE
Date: _____	Date: _____
Content: _____	Content: _____
_____	_____
_____	_____
Date: _____	Date: _____
Content: _____	Content: _____
_____	_____
_____	_____
Date: _____	Date: _____
Content: _____	Content: _____
_____	_____
_____	_____

One message that echoes throughout this book is "Take and use what you find helpful; leave the rest behind." I want to repeat that message at the end of this section (especially if you feel burdened by my approach to doing obedience). My hope is that what I have outlined here will make your process of doing obedience a little clearer and a little more productive. If you find my process too complicated or formal, you may only want to use my process to evaluate (and "tweak") your process. For example, you may find an idea or an exercise that will enhance what you are already doing, so just import that improvement into your plan.

My daughter and son-in-law enjoy preparing gourmet meals. A fun activity for them is to design such a meal, preparing everything from the fresh ingredients that they have purchased (and, as a recipient of such a meal, I can say that they are not the only ones to enjoy it). In contrast to that, I prepare nothing (when it comes to food), and I eat (with the exception of my evening meal), exactly the same food everyday. (In fact, when the people in the Subway that I go to every day see me coming, they begin to prepare my sandwich automatically.) What is crucial, no matter how much our styles differ, is that we all eat. The same applies to obedience: no matter how much our styles differ (along the dimensions of formal–informal, planned–intuitive, detailed–simplified, considered–heartfelt …), what is crucial is that we all obey. (And, hopefully, we won't fight over who has the "right" style; we will recognize that every style is "right" if it is a right fit for the person using it.) May we all experience the blessings of obedience.

FORGIVENESS

The importance of forgiveness was stressed in my early training as a Christian. The emphasis (of that training) was that God—through Jesus—had forgiven me, that I should receive His forgiveness, and that (as a consequence) I should forgive others. I remain thankful for that training; it kept me from doing vengeance on people who—when I was a child—had been abusive to me. As my development as a believer grew, however, questions about forgiveness began to arise:

- Have I forgiven another person if I still am angry toward him/her?
- If I forgive someone, should I tell him/her?
- If I forgive someone, does that mean that I should "forget" what he/she has done? And what should I do if my forgiveness/forgetting leads to that person exploiting me again?
- Does forgiveness always involve reconciliation?
- Should I forgive myself?
- How do I do forgiveness (which God values) and also do justice (which God also values)?
- Does it make sense to forgive someone who is dead?
- When I choose to forgive, what understandings are contained within that choice?

These questions (among others) put me on a search for how to do forgiveness in a way that honors God, other people, and myself. As usual, I began this search by reading everything I could get my hands on and, as usual, different perspectives were presented as if each was the final word on this subject. Again (as usual), I have struggled with these views (sometimes for years) and have concluded (as usual) that I need to design a way of doing forgiveness that fits within the circle of biblical options, that answers my questions, and that fits me. My attempt to reach these goals is what follows. My prayer is that you will find something here that will grow your understanding and your practice of forgiveness.

Reasons to Forgive.

Doing forgiveness is hard work. If you are like I am, it helps to know that the "outcomes" of forgiving will be worth the effort expended. To consider that, let's look again at the heart of Christianity, at the central commands around which everything else is commentary: "Love God with all your heart, soul, mind, and strength … and your neighbour as yourself"…(Matt. 22:37).

These commands are relational: they tell us that, to do what God wants, we are to be in right relationship (by means of love) with Him, our neighbor, and ourself. I have come to realize that, without forgiveness, none of these relationships can grow. How is that for a "good enough" reason to do forgiveness?! Let me explain.

First, forgiveness is required if our relationship with God is to be established and growing. It is clear from Scripture that our relationship with God is established by our receiving the forgiveness (for our sins) that God the Father offers to us by means of the death of His only Son, Jesus Christ. When we receive that gift, our relationship with Him is secured (see Romans 5:1–11 for the benefits). Our relationship with God grows as we walk in forgiveness. James 4:7 gives us the two sides of that "growth" coin: "Submit yourselves to God" and "resist the Devil." "Submitting ourselves to God" involves doing what He wants. When He says to us,"…If you forgive men when they sin against you, your heavenly Father will also forgive you. But if you do not forgive men their sins, your Father will not forgive your sins" (Matt. 6:14–15),we know that forgiveness is a practical necessity to staying on good terms with Him. "Resisting the Devil" involves not doing what Satan wants. When Paul says, "Forgive … in order that Satan might not outwit us. For we are not unaware of his schemes" (2 Cor.2:10–11),we know that walking in unforgiveness is one of Satan's schemes that we must avoid.

Second, forgiveness is required if our relationship with ourself is to be established and growing. Initially, our relationship with ourself begins when we "introject" ("model," "replicate," "imitate") the attitudes and treatment of our "significant others" and begin to treat ourself similarly. Thus, if we had trainers who treated us harshly, we began to treat ourself harshly. If we had trainers who treated us with kindness and forgiveness (like our heavenly Parent does), we learned to treat ourself with kindness and forgiveness. For those of us who had unbiblical training (whether or not we grew up in a Christian home), we begin to establish a constructive relationship with ourself when we begin to forgive ourself. About this, Smedes says: "We feel a need to forgive ourselves because the part of us that gets blamed feels split off from the part that does the blaming. One self feels despised and rejected by the other. We are exiled from our own selves, which is no way to live. This is why we need to forgive ourselves and why it makes sense to do it: We are ripped apart inside, and forgiving ourselves is the only way we heal the split."[24] When we begin to re-parent ourself and to treat ourself like our heavenly Parent treats us (with love, patience, kindness, faithfulness, gentleness, generosity, encouragement, and forgiveness …), healing begins. If that isn't "good news" to those of us who carry an introjected critic around with us, I don't know what is! We grow our (constructive) relationship with ourself as we learn to walk in forgiveness. Walking in forgiveness (toward ourself) involves the following steps.

(i) Developing my identity on the basis of who my heavenly Parent says I am. For instance, God's Word tells me that I am chosen by God and dearly loved by Him

(Col. 3:12) and that there is no condemnation of me by Him (Rom. 8:1). Consequently, as one who is to model his Parent and show a family likeness, I need to
start to love myself ("nourish" myself, not "indulge" myself) and to stop all condemnation of myself (following the directive of 1 John 1:9 instead, when I sin).

    (ii) Moving from the role of critic toward myself (and thus being against myself) to
       the role of being a coach toward myself (and thus being for myself, as my heavenly
       Parent is. See Romans 8:31). For instance, when I make a mistake, I move away
       from critical self talk (like, "You stupid jerk, will you never learn!") to construc-
       tive self talk (like, "A mistake is not the end of the world. Remember my new
       agreement with myself: 'When I mess up, I will clean up, but I will not beat up'").

    Third, forgiveness is required if our relationship with our neighbor is to be established
and growing. Among the many factors that contribute to the establishing of a relationship, forgiveness must be included. Only when (and the sooner the better) we forgive our
neighbor for not meeting all our (ideal) fantasies of what our relationship should be, can
we begin to accept our (less than ideal) neighbor and begin to deal with the realities of our
(less than ideal) relationship. Only when we let our neighbor be who he/she really is, can
we begin to learn the lessons that God wants to teach us through this person. We grow
our relationship with our neighbors as we learn to walk in forgiveness. Notice, in Paul's
instructions to the church in Colosse, his emphasis on walking in forgiveness: "Bear with
each other and forgive whatever grievances you may have against one another. Forgive as
the Lord forgave you" (3:13).

    Walking in mutual forgiveness is the fundamental way to stay "for" your neighbor
(rather than getting "against" him or her). As you stay "for" and "with" your neighbor,
your relationship can grow and blossom. As soon as you get "against" your neighbor, your
relationship will begin to wither.

What Forgiveness Is Not and Is

    Like mud on a vehicle, many misunderstandings have "stuck" to the concept of for-
giveness. Such misunderstandings have accumulated until much of the color and beauty
of forgiveness has been besmirched. In this section, I will attempt to "run forgiveness
through the carwash" so that the clarity and beauty of this God-delivered vehicle (of grace)
is restored. I will attempt to do this by looking at a series of contrasting propositions that
follow the format: "Forgiveness *is not*…" "Forgiveness *is*…"

    *The process of forgiveness does not involve emotional change only. The process of forgive-
ness, by the time it is finished, will have touched all of who we are, as human beings.*

People have talked about this process differently. For instance, Smedes (talking about the beginning of this process) says:

> The long and short of it, however, is that in order to forgive, we need to feel an inner push to forgive. We probably won't do much forgiving unless something inside of us makes us want to do it. I am certain that people never forgive because they believe they have an obligation to do it or because someone told them to do it. Forgiveness has to come from inside as a desire of the heart. *Wanting to* is the steam that pushes the forgiving engine.
>
> We forgive when we feel a strong wish to be free from the pain that glues us to a bruised moment of the past. We forgive when we want to overcome the resentment that separates us from the person who wounded us. We forgive when we feel God's Spirit nudging us with an impulse to pull ourselves out of the sludge of our disabling resentment. We forgive when we are ready to move toward a future unshackled from a painful past we cannot undo.[25]

In contrast to that, my experience of "doing forgiveness" is that of a hard, cold choice—seen as an act of obedience to God. The only "want" I am conscious of is retaliation. For me, all physiological and emotional and social changes flow from that "choice of obedience." For me, forgiveness begins with the declaration, "God, I choose to forgive x, now."

So, is there more than one way to do forgiveness? Yes, I think that the process of forgiveness is like a four-hole golf course. It doesn't matter which hole you play first, but all holes have to be played before you've done the "round"/process.

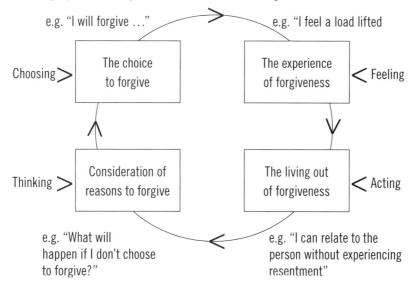

The sequence of steps is not important; the number of steps is important (for forgiveness to be comprehensive—as true forgiveness is).

So, when I need to forgive my neighbor, it must include (my) making a conscious choice—before God—to do so. (It can be a choice I say in prayer, a choice I put in my journal, a choice I verbalize to my neighbor—or all of the above.) Usually, such a choice has been preconditioned by such thoughts as, "What will it cost me if I don't forgive?" and "What are my alternatives if I don't forgive?" Subsequent to doing this, I have a change of experience—usually a melting of the anger I am prone to carry and a lessening of the pain that a recollection of the offence has been stimulating. When that has occurred, I feel free enough to draw closer to my neighbor again (rather than staying withdrawn). As I draw closer, the giving and receiving that makes up our relationship can begin to flow again.

Beware of shortcuts! There is no "quick fix" when it comes to doing the work of forgiveness.

Forgiveness doesn't depend on the response of another person. Forgiveness is a change that occurs within me as I do the correct things; it is independent of the response(s) of the recipient(s).

Our merciful God has informed us about forgiveness (through His Word), demonstrated forgiveness to us (through His Son), and equipped us to follow His example (through His Spirit). When we do follow His example, we become the first beneficiary of our obedience—without regard to the attitude or reaction of those we choose to forgive. By the time I became a believer and found out about forgiveness, some of the people who had been abusive of me when I was young (and living away from my family) were already dead. When I chose to forgive them, however, a new beginning slowly began to take place in me (and, as you might guess, they didn't respond much).

And what are the understandings that are contained within my choice to forgive? From my perspective there are three:

  i) I choose not to hold the offence against the offender. In other words, I let go of my plan for revenge, and I reaffirm that choice as many times as I need to (both to God and to myself). A frequent inner dialogue of mine has been, "I feel like responding to x in kind, but I will not act on that desire. God, I reaffirm to You my choice to forgive; I know that is what You want me to do; please empower me to carry out that choice."

  ii) I choose (ongoingly) to go on with my own agenda(s). In other words, I choose not to let the offence set my focus and attitude and direction. A painful wound (physical or otherwise) can scream for attention and response. The response I must give, as I do forgiveness, is, "I have decided to let this go, so (as I look past it) what is my next step for getting to where I want to go?" In this way, as I keep taking these steps, I am able to get that offence behind me.

iii) I choose not to bring up the offence again. In other (and more) words, I decide not to bring this offence up to the offender (unless it is part of a reconciliation process—more about that later) nor to bring this offence up to myself (so that I can rehearse the offence). In this way, I am letting go of the offence, both externally and internally. To follow through on this commitment, whenever the pictures or words or feelings that constitute the memory of this offence come back to me, I see myself putting that situation in God's hands, while saying to Him, "I give this (again) to You ... please give me Your healing and Your peace."

Forgiveness is not a one-time (four-step) process. Forgiveness is a (four-step) process that usually needs to be repeated as the healing (in the forgiver) continues.

Like salve on a burn, apply the medicine as many times as you need to. As you continue to apply it, it will take care of the wound at both the superficial and the deeper levels.

(As already implied) *forgiveness is not the passage of time. Forgiveness involves the action of the forgiver.* About this issue, Wangerin says:

"Neither is forgiveness a silent, patient waiting for the sinner's change (no matter how faithfully the wounded one may pray for that change). Even as sins do not appear by magic (they are the real stuff of human nature), so they will not vanish by magic. God himself had to do something about the sin of the world. The notion that time heals wounds may make us seem saints of patience; but in fact we are ducking a dreadful responsibility. Sinners seldom change spontaneously."[26]

Forgiveness is not the same as healing. Forgiveness opens the door to (leads to) healing. An implication of this point is that doing forgiveness precedes (sometimes by much work and a long time) the experiential results that are labeled "healing." To continue with the salve analogy, it may take a number of applications before there is pain reduction. The primary thing to remember is to keep on with the treatment program until you begin to experience the benefits. (We know that we have the right medicine—the Great Physician Himself has supplied us with it and has modeled its use for us.)

When I was a child, I lived away from home for several years. During those years, I was treated in ways that would (now) be called abusive. One result of such treatment was that I became angry and reactive. Another result of that treatment was that I distanced myself from those people. Later in life, having become a Christian, I realized that I would need to forgive these people—which I started to do (as I have mentioned) by a cold choice of obedience, against my (hot) desire to get revenge. Several years later, I attended a relative's wedding and discovered that one of my abusers was also there. (If I had known that he would be there, I'm sure that I would have avoided that event.) What was startling to me, as I sat in the same room as this person, was how calm I was. In contrast to my expectation (that I would be furious), I was not even experiencing an increased heart-rate. Then it dawned on me—my (ongoing) choice to forgive had led to my healing; my choice to forgive had set a prisoner free and (surprise of surprises) it was me. I left that event with a new appreciation for the truth that, "[God] who began a good work in [me], will carry it on to completion …," sometimes outside my consciousness.

Forgiveness is not the same as forgetting. Forgiveness involves remembering in a new way. Forgiveness leads to healing. As we heal, we move from remembering in a *pain-producing* way (where we replay the event, over and over, and feel the pain connected with that event, over and over) to remembering in a *growth-producing* way (where we begin to focus on what we learned from the event and how it has strengthened and equipped us). As we do this, our focus shifts from our painful past (a problem focus) to our potential future (a possibility focus). And, as we open the door to a possible future that our painful past had shut, we cooperate with the God who said, "I work in all things for the good of those who love me."

Forgiveness is not something that we must do. Forgiveness is something we choose to do. It is true that God asks us to forgive—even commands us to forgive—but he does not make us forgive. (God created us with the ability to choose; He continues to respect that ability, whether or not we use it constructively.) Forgiveness is always and only ours to give. If we choose not to forgive, we will live with the consequences of that choice—as we do with every choice we make. Those consequences include staying in pain and out of closeness with Him. If we choose to forgive, we are doing what God wants us to do. The consequences of this choice include beginning to leave the pain behind and beginning to deepen our relationship with Him.

Forgiveness is not "letting the other person off the hook" (in other words, absolving him/her of his/her responsibility for his/her actions). Forgiveness is "letting yourself off the hook" (in other words, dealing constructively with the pain of some offence).

For me to understand how forgiving is letting myself off the hook, I need to understand my options. About our options, Smedes says: "There are only two genuine options for responding to a personal injury that we did not deserve. One of them is vengeance. The other is forgiving. Any other way of responding is really denial. Forgetting, excusing, or overlooking the wrong that was done are all devices of denial that prevent real forgiving from happening."

From my perspective, Smedes—in this paragraph—outlines *three* "options for responding to a personal injury that we did not deserve." (Vengeance … forgiveness … some form of denial.) Consequently, I would say that there are two *active* options (where the person chooses action); all other options are passive (where the person chooses inaction). I would also say that, of all these options, only forgiving is constructive—both to my relationship with others and to my relationship with myself. The other options are destructive to my interpersonal life *and* my intrapersonal life—whether that destruction is quicker (in the case of vengeance) or slower (in the case of denial).

Smedes goes on to say:

> Vengeance is the only alternative to forgiving. It is, simply put, a passion to get even. We have been unfairly hurt. Life is out of whack. The scales are unbalanced. The only way to balance them and get life back to normal is to inflict as much pain on our abuser as he inflicted on us. An eye for an eye, wound for wound, insult for insult. Revenge—the ancient formula for undying futility.
>
> The reason getting even does not make life fairer is that it never happens. Cannot happen. Ever. Not a chance of it. Will the Tutsis ever get even with the Hutus? Will the Bosnian Muslims ever get even with the Serbs? … Never. They may go on killing each other until they are all dead, but they will never get even …
>
> The reason we cannot get even is that the victim and the victimizer never weigh pain on the same scale. One of us is always behind in the exchange of pain. If we have to get even, we are doomed to exchange wound for wound, blood for blood, pain for pain forever. Perpetual pain. Perpetual unfairness.[27]

For me, it is like holding on to a poisonous snake. My options boil down to continuing to hold onto the snake (and, like vengeance, continuing to be bit and poisoned by it) or dropping it (and, like forgiveness, beginning to recover from the poison). When I choose to "drop the snake," I empower myself—I take back my life from the internal and external costs of revenge, and I stop the prolongation of the pain of my abuser's offence. Within the context of all my relationships, that choice makes me (again) "fit for human consumption."

Forgiveness is not ignoring justice. Forgiveness is releasing the right to get even (to be judge and jury on the issue) and putting the issue in God's hands—for Him to bring about justice in His time.

About this issue, Smedes says:

> But take care. When you give up vengeance, make sure you are not giving up on justice. The line between the two is faint, unsteady, and fine.
>
> What is the difference between the two? Vengeance is our own pleasure of seeing someone who hurt us getting it back and then some. Justice, on the other hand, is secured when someone pays a fair penalty for wrongdoing another even if the injured person takes no pleasure in the transaction. Vengeance is personal satisfaction. Justice is moral accounting.
>
> Forgiving surrenders the right to vengeance, it never surrenders the claims of justice. Therein lies a key distinction. After Pope John Paul forgave a man who took a shot at him, a journalist commented: "One forgives in one's heart, in the sight of God, as the pope did, but the criminal still serves his time in Caesar's jail." Very true. Human forgiveness does not do away with human justice. Nor divine justice. Consider the Bible's book of Numbers: "The LORD is slow to anger ... forgiving iniquity and transgression, but by no means clearing the guilty" (14:18NRSV).[28]

When I forgive, I resolve to live with (and work through) the consequences of another person's hurtful choices, without seeking revenge. Also, I resolve to put the issue in the hands of the one just Judge—who will "balance the books" of justice in His own time and His own way.

Forgiveness is not the means to make an intolerable offense tolerable. Forgiveness sets us free from intolerable offenses. Since forgiving and tolerating are independent events, I can forgive the offender and, at the same time, resolve to never put up with it again. That resolution can involve an action plan designed to prevent a rerun of the offence (and that action plan is likely to be more constructive because we have "the beam out of our own eye"). About this distinction Smedes says: "Forgiving and tolerating have nothing in common. They live in different worlds. Forgiving may enable us to bear up under and even to surmount intolerable abuse that people do to us when we cannot escape it. But it can never, should never, shall never, transform intolerable wrong into tolerable pain."[29]

And so, when wronged by my neighbor, it is important (and legitimate) to both forgive him/her and to request change (from him/her to us) so that the intolerable offence is changed.

Forgiveness is not directed toward the other person's character. Forgiveness directed toward the other person's behavior. This important distinction is unpacked in this quote from Smedes:

You may have noticed that it is always our trespasses—the bad things we do, the sins we commit—that we ask God to forgive. When it comes to the sorts of persons we are, we most want God to love and accept us. It is for the deeds we do that he forgives us.

The same thing is true in our daily traffic with each other. We have no calling to forgive anyone for being a blockhead or for being ugly or lazy or arrogant or sloppy or any of the labels we pin on people to mark them as the sort of people we do not like. We are not called to forgive them for being bad people. We like them, dislike them, accept them, leave them, and sometimes weep over them and try to help them improve on their characters. But we don't forgive them.

People do not wrong us by being liars; they wrong us by lying about us. They do not wrong us by being untrustworthy; they wrong us by betraying our trust. And since forgiveness is only for wrongs people do to us, we can forgive them only for doing these wrongs.[30]

Forgiveness is not only directed toward others. Forgiveness is (also) directed toward self. If you have not been encouraged to (also) direct forgiveness toward yourself, you are likely to be carrying all kinds of burdens that you need to drop. An initial step in learning to treat yourself in the same (nourishing) way that your heavenly Father treats you, is to forgive yourself—as He does. In my experience, this has been a neglected dimension of the "good news" and so I have, in my attempt to encourage your application of it, outlined (in the "Next Steps" at the end of this section) the steps involved in doing personal forgiveness.

The next sets of contrasting propositions will clarify the connections between forgiveness (an *intra*personal event) and reconciliation (an *inter*personal event). Some of the following distinctions have already been implied; now I will spell them out.

Forgiveness does not necessarily lead to reconciliation. Forgiveness will lead to reconciliation if both parties do their part to bring it about. Forgiveness happens inside the wounded person; reconciliation happens in the relationship between people. If each person does his/her part to restore the relationship, a relational (re-) beginning starts—that is reconciliation. The relationship will never be the same again, but it can be better. When there is reconciliation between people, it can look different, depending on the kind of relationship involved before and after the offence.

To help us look at the different scenarios that illustrate the connections between forgiveness and reconciliation, let's look (again) at the model found on page 221 of this module.

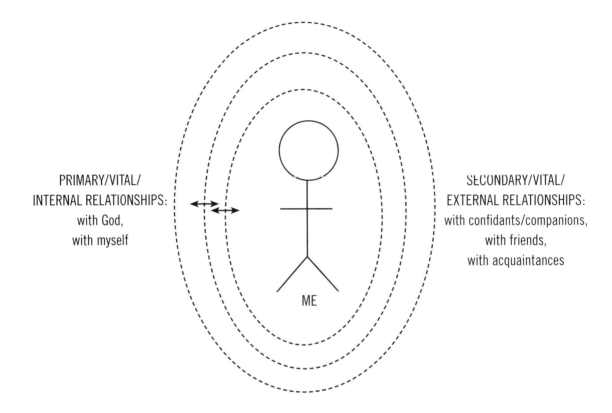

PRIMARY/VITAL/ INTERNAL RELATIONSHIPS: with God, with myself

SECONDARY/VITAL/ EXTERNAL RELATIONSHIPS: with confidants/companions, with friends, with acquaintances

ME

(You may want to re-read pages 236–241 of this module—to refresh your understanding of the "secondary/vital/external relationships" dimension of this model).

This model can inform our understanding of forgiveness and reconciliation in a number of ways:

(1) The closer the relationship we have with another person, the greater is the potential for that person to help us or to hurt us. So, when a "confidant/companion" level person wounds us, the need is greater to apply the medicine of forgiveness.

If someone at the acquaintance level wrongs us, and it is not a large or deliberate hurt (or, conversely, we hurt someone at that level in a minor and unintentional way), an apology may be sufficient to repair the damage. However, when someone we have entrusted our life to hurts us, an apology often isn't sufficient (although what one person considers an "apology sized" issue, another person may consider "forgiveness sized"). In the "Next Steps" at the end of this section, the necessary and sufficient steps for doing (interpersonal) forgiveness are outlined.

(2) This model identified the need for forgiveness and reconciliation to be directed toward self. See pages 232–234 in this module for my elaboration of this issue. See the "Next Steps" at the end of this section for the steps on how to do this (Next Step #3, pages 316–319).

(3) This model identifies the (possible) need for forgiveness and reconciliation to be directed toward God. See page 232 in this module for my elaboration of this issue. See Lewis Smede's book *The Art Of Forgiving* (pages 105–114) for his steps on how to do this.

(4) In the terms of this model, unforgiveness puts the offender outside the acquaintance circle—beyond the realm of the human and beyond our need to relate to him/her. Unforgiveness turns a person into an "it"; the offender is reduced to his/her offence. And when we do that (in order to distance ourselves from these "pain-givers"), we stop the flow of humanity within ourselves and, like stagnant water, begin to breed all kinds of diseases. About this dynamic, Smedes says:

> We filter the image of our villain through the gauze of our wounded memories, and in the process we alter his reality.
>
> We shrink him to the size of what he did to us; he *becomes* the wrong he did. If he had done something truly horrible, we say things like, "He is no more than an animal." Or, "He is nothing but a cheat." Our "no more thans" and our "nothing buts" knock the humanity out of our enemy. He is no longer a fragile spirit living on the fringes of extinction. He is no longer a confusing mixture of good and evil. He is only, he is totally, the sinner who did us wrong.
>
> As we start on the miracle of forgiving, we begin to see our enemy through a cleaner lens, less smudged by hate. We begin to see a real person, a botched self, no doubt, a hodgepodge of meanness and decency, lies and truths, good and evil that not even the shadows of his soul can wholly hide. We see a bubble held aloft by the flowing of a divine breath. We see a human being created to be a child of God.[31]

In terms of this model, forgiveness means choosing to allow the offender back into your life at the acquaintance level, back to where you can relate to him again in a human way. This does not necessarily mean talking to or interacting with the offender (after all, he/she may be dead, unavailable or dangerous).It does mean putting him/her in God's hands to do with as He chooses (in other words, treating him/her like the human being he/she is). Nor, does it mean setting yourself up for a replay of the hurt, if you do interact with the offender. As Sandra Wilson so concisely put it, "Forgiveness and boundary setting are *not* mutually exclusive."[32]

It may be that this person will never again come closer to you than the acquaintance level, no matter what level he/she was at before (which I suggest you maintain if, for instance, this person is trying to repeat his/her offence against you). It is close enough, however, for a new (and distant and boundaried) relationship to exist. In the case where the offender is not repentant (not sorry for what he/she did and not prepared to change his/her behavior) and is not prepared to make restitution (not prepared to make practical and sufficient compensation for the injury), sufficient distance (again) should remain. Smedes illustrates this distinction in the following way:

> "I believe that when a person close to us wrongs us, he throws up two obstacles between us. One of the obstacles is our sense of having been violated, which produces our anger, our hostility, our resentment. This is the obstacle that our forgiving removes. But only the person who wronged us can remove the other obstacle. And he can remove it only by repentance and, if need be, by restitution."[33]

(5) In the terms of this model, when the offender is prepared to repent and to make restitution, then the (mutual) hard work of moving the relationship toward the "friendship" level (and even toward the "confidant/companionship" level) can begin. (People have asked me how they can know if the offender's repentance and restitution are genuine—since they aren't interested in getting set up for a re-offence. I have let them know that, from my experience, the best way to find out is to embark on the process of reconciliation with one eye on gathering the data that would help them answer that question.) This journey involves the re-establishment of communication and the re-learning of trust; it involves the following steps:

   (i) Talking with the offender about his/her offence. The purpose of such talk is information (not accusation), letting the offender know that damage has been done but that you want to do your part to repair that damage in order for a new beginning to start. You discuss what—specifically—hurt you and request—specifically—what changes (in future interactions) you need, so that trust and closeness can grow. (The past events are brought up in order for them to be worked through and transcended.)

In response, the offender acknowledges his offence, says that he/she is sorry for the damage he/she caused, asks for forgiveness, and says that he/she will do what he/she can to get healing and growth started.

(ii) (Mutually) developing an action plan that will help you (both) apply the changes (and so make the relationship safe again). Such a plan answers the question, "What do we need to do in order to promote closeness again?" As this plan is followed, over time, it creates the conditions that make it possible for the offender to be admitted again into the relationship circles that are closer to you.

(iii) (Mutually) developing follow-up sessions. These sessions help monitor the action plan so that what is working well can be identified and encouraged and what is not working can be modified.

When people do the work of reconciliation, they are operating with integrity. According to O'Hanlon and Hudson, integrity has three levels: "The first involves keeping your word and staying within the agreed-upon limits. The second level requires accountability for breaking your word or violating the personal boundaries of another. On the third level you make amends when you have hurt [the other person] or damaged the trust and safety in the relationship."[34] As people do reconciliation, they are relating at all those levels. Such behavior is the key that opens the door to (restored) closeness.

The process of forgiveness does not end with clarity and precision. The process of forgiveness comes to an (imprecise) end amid relapses (into old feelings and reactions) and reaffirmations (to finish letting go). Again, I have used material from Smedes to illustrate this (last) proposition:

Where I live there is a section of Interstate Highway 5 that Californians call the Grapevine, a slow grade to about five thousand feet. It's not all that high, but it is a wearisome climb that exasperates me considerably. The road levels off deceptively at several points and tricks me into thinking I have gotten over the crest. Then I feel gypped when I discover I have more to go. I am never sure when I really have gotten to the top until after I have gotten over it a bit and the Toyota surges to the touch of my foot. Forgiving is often like this—a slow haul up a long incline. and we are often not sure we are over the hump until one day we feel a lightness in our spirits that was too long in coming.[35]

Next Steps

The following questions will (hopefully) help you to specify your next steps of application in this area of knowing and doing forgiveness.

(1) As you look over the propositions that outline what forgiveness is not and is, what propositions have clarified your understandings of forgiveness? List them below:

    (i) _____

    (ii) _____

    (iii) _____

    (iv) _____

    (v) _____

(2) In light of that clarification, what changes would you make in order to do forgiveness more effectively? If possible, think about some person to whom you have extended forgiveness, and write down (below) the improvements you would make if you were to extend forgiveness again.

    (i) _____

    (ii) _____

    (iii) _____

    (iv) _____

    (v) _____

(3) In one of the propositions, I say "Forgiveness is not only directed toward others. Forgiveness is (also) directed toward self." Below are the steps involved in *doing personal (or self-directed) forgiveness.*

    (i) Make a list of the events that you haven't forgiven yourself for:

        a._____

        b. _____

        c._____

        d. _____

        e._____

      – When you have read 1 John 1:9, check off the following box.
       ❑ DONE

      – As you ask God for His forgiveness of your attitude toward yourself as it relates to each of the above events, check off that event on the above list.

- When you have received, by faith, His forgiveness for all of the above events (if necessary), check off the following box. ❑ DONE
- When you have renounced and repented of the sin of unforgiveness (toward yourself), check off the following box. ❑ DONE
- When you have forgiven yourself, check off the following box. ❑ DONE

For some people, it helps to do one or more of the following activities in order to establish your forgiveness of yourself:

- Pray your prayer of self-forgiveness out loud. An example for such a prayer would be "Father, on the basis of Your forgiveness of me, I choose now to forgive myself for … [specific event]."
- Pray your prayer of self-forgiveness out loud, while looking at yourself in a mirror.
- Write out your prayer of self-forgiveness; sign and date that prayer; keep or file or burn the page.
- Do the equivalent of writing out your prayer of self forgiveness, on your computer.
- Talk to a (trusted) friend or mentor about forgiving yourself (using James 5:16 as an outline for that conversation).

    (ii) Write down the name of anyone who should know that you have forgiven yourself:

       a) _____

       b) _____

Make sure that you have a good reason for sharing that information and that the person is a "safe person"—who will not try to take away what God gives you.

    (iii) Write down any restitution that you need to make toward yourself:

       a) _____

       b) _____

       c) _____

Here are some examples of ways to make restitution toward yourself:

- Make an apology to yourself—out loud, in front of a mirror, on paper, on computer, with a friend—for anything that you have said or done toward yourself that you would apologize to a friend for saying or doing.

- Give yourself a gift. This gift can be seen as restitution for past treatment (for example, having been a harsh taskmaster toward yourself). It can also be seen as a peace offering with yourself or as a symbol of how you will treat yourself in the future.
- Give yourself a promise. The promise that you will learn to treat yourself as you would treat a trusted friend, is a good example.

(iv) Write down the name of anyone who might try to sabotage your self-forgiveness:

a) _____

_____

b) _____

_____

c) _____

_____

How will you deal with each of these people, so that you will remain in a state of forgiveness (and grace) toward yourself?

a) _____

_____

b) _____

_____

c) _____

_____

If you aren't sure how to protect yourself, who could you talk to or what could you read that would help you to develop a self-protection game-plan?

(v) If you were to walk in forgiveness toward yourself, what would you do? What would you *not* do?

a) _____

_____

b) _____

_____

c) _____

_____

d) _____

_____

Do not be "knowers" only but (rather) "doers" of the truth that will set you free.

(vi) If you have to re-affirm your self-forgiveness, what prayers/self talk/Scripture promises/books/sermons/audio tapes/videotapes/ compact discs would be helpful to you? Make a list of them below.

a) _____

_____

b) _____

_____

c) _____

_____

d) _____

_____

e) _____

_____

f) _____

_____

(vii) If you want to celebrate your walking in personal forgiveness, what would you do and with whom? Make a list of these people and of your celebratory acts below. (If you want to do them "impulsively," that's fine too.)

a) _____

_____

b) _____

_____

c) _____

_____

(4) Here are the steps involved in *doing interpersonal forgiveness*; I've organized these steps within the framework of what to do *before* your meeting with the other person and what to do *during* your meeting with the other person. These steps assume that mutual (or reciprocal) forgiveness is the goal of the meeting. (In other words, forgiveness will be given and received during that meeting.) It is also possible to have a meeting in which only one person extends forgiveness (and the other person receives it). It is also possible to do interpersonal

forgiveness with the other person not present. These two possibilities require an adaptation of these steps. Hopefully, you will find these steps helpful as you make the adaptations that fit your situation.

Before the Meeting:

The conversation where mutual forgiveness is done (and possibly reconciliation begins) needs to be prepared for. These preparations include the following:

(i) Have good and sufficient information about what forgiveness is and how to do forgiveness. The "what" of forgiveness has been provided in the content of this section; the "how" of forgiveness is outlined in the steps that follow.

(ii) You have applied forgiveness to your own life (so that you are walking in forgiveness toward yourself). The "how" of doing this is provided in the previous step (#3).

(iii) Pray for God's involvement … help … strength … guidance … perspective … (and whatever else you know to be in short supply). You may find some of the following prayers to be relevant:

- "Lord Jesus, help me to do the right thing, no matter how I may be feeling."
- "According to Your Word [Matt. 18:21–35], whatever I have to forgive [other person's name] for is little compared with what you have forgiven me. Help me to not be like the ungrateful and unmerciful servant that Your Word talks about but, rather, forgive [him/her] from my heart."
- "Lord Jesus, I know that the purpose of our (upcoming) time together is to listen to each other and for me to take responsibility for my contribution to this situation in order to start our healing process. [The purpose of meeting is not to blame or to inflict pain.] Please help me to be an instrument of your peace."
- "Lord Jesus, I know that things [other person's name] may say could trigger old pain in me. I realize that having unhealed pain triggered is not the same as [other person's name] causing that pain, but it is painful nonetheless. Please help me to bear that pain constructively for as long as I need to in our time together, to process it with [other person's name] and to finally put it in your hands. Please give me the awareness and the strength to do the right thing if/when that pain comes."
- "Lord Jesus, I pray for [other person's name]. Please enable him/her to be willing and able to do his/her part to bring about our new beginning."

- "Lord, please bring to my mind all the events/issues/ situations that I need to deal with. Please help me to handle each, today, in a way that pleases you."

(iv) Cultivate the following truths—so you can reap the harvest of constructive attitudes. As you bring these attitudes to the meeting, they provide a framework that will help the meeting to be constructive:

- "Although I am hurt, I want to hold onto this relationship more than I want to hold onto the hurt."
- I need to rehearse the truth that the purpose of the (upcoming) meeting is reconciliation, not blame. If I come to the meeting to dump my hurt on the other person (directly or indirectly blame him/her), I could stimulate a defensive reaction in him/her. "Letting go" of my hurt (where I share with [name of other person] what is going on inside me) is very different from "dumping" my hurt (where I interact in a way that shows that I am using my hurt for controlling purposes against him/her—punishment, manipulation, guilt-inducement—all of which will erode the relationship). If I am seeking reconciliation, I will let go of my hurt; if I am seeking some kind of control over this other person, I will use my hurt.
- "[Person's name] has contributed to my feelings of being hurt, but I am not the totally innocent one here; I have also made a contribution to this state of affairs."
- Many of us have been trained in the language of victimization: "You made me feel 'x'," "You wrecked my life," "You made me do 'x.'" In the interactional dance of relationships, this is seldom accurate. Usually both parties have made a contribution (even if unequal) to the experience of the other. So our Lord asks us to, "First take the plank out of your own eye, and then you will see clearly to remove the speck from your brother's eye" (Matt. 7:5). When our attitude involves being prepared to look at our own contribution to the mess and to acknowledge that reality, we will not only be more able to accurately assess the other person's contribution but also more willing to work with him/her.
- "I need to forgive [person's name] the way that God has forgiven me."
- "I will emphasize my description of what happened; I will de-emphasize my interpretations of what happened."

An example of a description (what could be caught on a video camera) is, "I felt hurt when you talked to Andrea for an hour at that party." An example of an interpretation (which also involves the inclusion of personal meanings) is, "I felt hurt when you ignored me at that party." The forgiveness (and possible reconciliation) process goes more smoothly when the offenses are talked about in ways that don't involve mind-reading of the other person.

- "I will not overload the process."

     When your discussion of offenses is specific (rather than vague and general) and one at a time (rather than many at once), each of you will get the "air time" you need without blocking the time needed for an adequate response.

(v) Make a list of the event(s) that you need to walk through with this other person. (Such events include those in which you have been offended or from which you have unfinished emotional business.) Start each sentence (where each sentence represents one event) as follows:

> "I felt hurt when you…" or
> "I felt offended when you…" or
> "I felt upset when you…" or
> "I felt frustrated when you…" or
> "I felt afraid when you…"

(In this way, you have captured on paper—outside yourself—those events which may have been on your mind or on your "old movie" channel for a long time. In fact, some of them may now be classic!) These sentences specify the agenda for your time together.

During the meeting

Go, together, to a private, comfortable place. (That could be your car, a coffee shop, a park bench, a hillside, a canoe, an office, or wherever …) Once you are settled there, each of you, in turn, are to do the following steps:

(i) Each person takes a turn reading one sentence from his/her list, to the other person.

     Remember: the purpose of this reading is to inform and to promote reconciliation, *not* to blame. Although forgiveness happens internally, reconciliation can only occur when these events are constructively shared and taken care of.

(ii) After each sentence, the person receiving the message says: "I'm sorry that I contributed to your pain. Please find it in your heart to forgive me."

(You may not be comfortable with these exact words—so you will need to modify them—but it is crucial to have each of these elements included in your response.)

Remember: "Forgiveness leading to reconciliation" is more than just going through the motions or just saying the words. We are to forgive "from our heart" (Matt. 18:35), not just our head. Among other things, this means that we are to do this process with *meaning* (involving our thinking and our feeling and our choosing).

Notice that I used the words, "...*contributed* to your pain ...." I am careful to not use the word "*cause*." Although I may have contributed greatly to the other person's pain, it is only rarely that I am *totally* responsible for his/her pain to have "caused" it. Usually the other person also makes a contribution to his/her pain (by, for instance, how he/she handles his/her pain). If, for example, he/she dwells on and rehearses what I did to him/her, he/she increases his/her experience of pain.

Remember: You are in this meeting to do forgiveness and reconciliation, not argue over your differing versions of the past. Therefore, it is important to recognize that the other person's recollection of the past event (that contributed to his/her pain) is valid—even if it differs from yours. It is also important to recognize that his/her experience is real—even if it is built on a memory that differs from yours. So, *from his/her perspective*, forgiveness needs to be done. Thus, when he/she reads a sentence, "I felt x when you *y*...," you need to respond with, "I'm sorry that I contributed ..." rather than, "That isn't what happened!" In so doing, you adopt the other person's frame of reference, while he/she talks about where his/her hurts are. (You don't have to agree with his/her version of past events—just that his/her version is valid and his/her pain is real.) By the way, *neither* of you have the "immaculate perception" of what happened back there. The other person will (reciprocally) adopt your frame of reference when you begin to talk about your hurts.

As you work together in this way, you are co-creating unity and promoting healing within and between yourselves (whether or not you have agreement about the past event). If one or both of you are determined to fight over whose perspective is "totally true," I would suggest to you that you are having a "delusion of grandeur"—since only a Being who is all-knowing and everywhere-present—could comprehend and integrate the many facets of that (past) event.

If you are like I am, this explanation could leave you unconvinced, so I'd suggest the following visualization:

See yourself and the person you are going through this process with, walking out to your vehicle. When you get there, you sit in the driver's seat while the other person stands outside the vehicle. Now, you both write down a description of what you are seeing. Since you are inside the vehicle, you probably will be describing the steering wheel and the instrument panel; since the other person is outside the vehicle, he/she will probably be describing the tires and the fenders or doors of the vehicle. Now, let me ask you, "Which description of the vehicle is the correct one?"

I'd suggest that the answer is that you are both correct—given your perspective of the vehicle. I would also suggest that only a Being who could see that vehicle from every angle at once could have a totally true and complete perspective on that vehicle. Since we aren't that Being, I'd suggest that we give credibility to perspectives that cut a different slice out of the pie of reality than we have cut. When we do that, we can forgive without feeling that we have accommodated the lie of the other person's "wrong" perspective.

(iii) In response (to the receiver's request for forgiveness), the person reading his/her sentence says: "I do forgive you and, with God's help, I will not bring this issue up again … I consider it finished now."
(Again, you may not be comfortable with these exact words, so use your own—making sure to include each element specified above.)

Remember: When God forgives us, He doesn't bring the issue up against us again but acts toward us as if He has forgotten it. Contrary to the opinion of some, I suggest that He does not actually forget (since that would go against His character—of an all-knowing God—His character being the moral absolute of the universe). Since we are striving to be like Him, we should strive to put the issue away (from between us), too.

If, *within* us, the issue comes up again (later), we need to backup:

- Reaffirm our forgiveness—to God and ourselves
- Put the issue, again, in His hands (by means such as personal prayer, journaling, or prayer with a pastor or counselor)
- Get focused, again, on the tasks at hand

    Do this as many times as it takes, for this issue to stay in His hands.

(iv) When each person has worked through everything on his/her list (by the reciprocal following of steps i—iii for each issue), the participants have extended mutual forgiveness.

(v) After both people have worked through their lists (literally), they need to take care of their lists (symbolically).

Working together to take care of both lists (symbolically) can be beneficial in a number of ways:

1. It can bring closure (and thanksgiving) to a time which may have been difficult and emotionally draining.
2. It can stimulate the healing process (which is a special by-product of doing forgiveness).
3. It can help to re-focus the relationship away from where it has been and toward where it could be.

Taking care of your lists involves both of you choosing (together) how to dispose of the lists. The options can be creative:

- (Each of you) writing "paid in full" across your list and (then) giving it to the other person
- Exchanging lists, tearing them up together and (then) throwing them away
- Arranging (then or later) to burn them
- Exchanging lists, so that each of you can file them in the "finished business" file
- Praying together (for instance, that God will help you to keep the commitments you made in this process) and then doing any of the above.

Once you have had this meeting, you have given each other the gift of forgiveness and (possibly) of a new (relational) beginning.

SERVICE

Early in my walk as a Christian, the emphasis on service (giving to others) was given. The content of that emphasis was that I was to pass on what Jesus had given to me. Scripture verses like Matthew 10:8 (" …Freely you have received, freely give …") and Acts 20:35 ("In everything I did, I showed you that by this kind of hard work we must help the weak, remembering the words the Lord Jesus himself said: It is more blessed to give than to receive"), were used to validate that emphasis. As I grew in my understanding of Scripture, I realized that whole books of the Bible (Ephesians, for instance) clarified that emphasis. I remain appreciative of that early training, but (as usual, for me) I began to encounter situations in which advanced training (on how to give and on how to survive giving) was required.

One (seven year) chapter of my life consisted of teaching at a Bible College. Although I had a great time with the students there (and, I think, a few of them had a great time with me), the opportunities to give were greater than my abilities (at that time) to manage my giving. I had grown up on a farm, where the (implicit) giving policy was: work until the work is finished. (It wasn't a helpful policy for a context in which the work was never finished and where "JOY" was defined as **J**esus first, **O**thers second, and **Y**ourself, last.) After several years of working eighty plus hours a week, my body informed me—in a rather forceful way—that I needed to do my giving differently. (Without recognizing it, I had become a "JO-boy" for the agendas of others and had lost myself in over-giving.) I had received "early warning" signals previously (like the look I got from a stress management course instructor when he returned my results—my scores were off the top of the chart!), but it took a stay in the hospital to get my attention and my action. Subsequently, I have learned to include myself in my giving (an application of "loving my neighbor *as myself*") and to protect myself from over-giving. (I have tried to include what I have learned in the module on stress management.) I have also learned to make the distinction between a "good" act of service and a "God" act of service (and to live out that distinction). There are many good ways to give in this world. God permits these acts of service—there is no law against doing these things. There are also God-directed ways to give in this world. God calls us to these acts of service—these are the top priority (and non-negotiable with other people) activities that are to become the centerpieces of our life. When I was young in the faith (and couldn't distinguish between a "good" activity and a "God" activity because I wasn't familiar with His voice or His leading), I gave to every need that showed up. As I grew in my relationship with Him, I became more focused and selective in my giving (choosing the best rather than the good). If I hadn't become selective, I would have died on burnout road (because trying to give to all good things, when we are finite, will crush us). Unfocused giving also leads to idolatry (because we will be listening to many guides, rather than the Guide). It took me a long time to discover and to enter into doing (primarily) the activities that God calls me to do. But I should never settle for anything less (since, to settle for something less, is to build with wood, hay, and straw rather than gold, silver, and precious stones.; 1 Corinthians 3:10–15 may help to explain what I am talking about). Since I had been trained to be a human "doing" (rather than a human being), I was highly vulnerable to every "wind of giving" opportunity that blew through my life. Although I was slow to get past over giving, I have learned to hear and obey His voice with regard to giving (and to resist other voices that tempt me to dissipate my giving). As I have been walking in obedience to His calls in my life, I have discovered a new joy and a new energy (which comes from doing what I have been designed to do). This is in sharp contrast to the exhaustion of doing never-ending good things or the discouragement of trying to make "more bricks with no straw." I am not saying that this journey has been or is (or will be) easy; I am saying that there is a joy on this journey that indicates His presence and His pleasure. (He is not a "harsh task master" but a coach, who says "Come to Me, all you who are weary and burdened, and I will give you rest" [Matt. 11:28].)

As I have sought to deepen my understanding of giving—of what perversions of giving look like as well as what authentic versions of giving look like—I have discovered the following (from Matthew 23):

JESUS' WARNINGS— TO HIS DISCIPLES— OF THE PHARISEE'S PERVERSIONS OF SERVICE	PERVERSION OF SERVICE	CORRECTION OF PERVERSION
(a) "They tie up heavy loads and put them on men's shoulders, but they themselves are not willing to lift a finger to move them" (23:4).	Their acts of service (explaining the law) had the net effect of burdening the students; these teachers would not help to lighten that load. If you have felt burdened by some biblical teaching, and spiritual leadership has not helped in the lightening of that load, you know (experientially) about what is being talked about, here.	Do giving so that it "builds up" the giver (as well as the receiver). Steps to promote this include the following: Consciously choosing the act of giving (rather than giving out of obligation) Only giving in areas where you have a calling to do so Continued

(b) "Everything they do is done for men to see: They make their phylacteries wide and the tassels on their garments long; they love the place of honor at banquets and the most important seats in the synagogues; they love to be greeted in the marketplaces and to have men call them 'Rabbi.' "But you are not to be called 'Rabbi,' for you have only one Master and you are all brothers. And do not call anyone on earth 'father,' for you have one Father, and he is in heaven. Nor are you to be called 'teacher,' for you have one Teacher, the Christ. The greatest among you will be your servant. For whoever exalts himself will be humbled, and whoever humbles himself will be exalted" (23:5–12).	Their acts of service (prayer and teaching) were done to impress other people. (In other words, they were striving to build their reputation.) If you have seen spiritual leadership saying/doing things for the effect of impressing you, you know (experientially) about what is being talked about, here.	Do giving with the focus on the recipient, not the (human) audience. Steps to promote this include the following: Remembering that you are called to give with humility (v. 11) Remembering that God is the One we seek to please (v.12)
(c) "Woe to you, Teachers of the law and Pharisees, you hypocrites! You shut the kingdom of heaven in men's faces. You yourselves do not enter, nor will you let those enter who are trying to" (23:13–14).	Their acts of giving (unspecified here) had the effect of "shutting the kingdom of heaven in people's faces."	Do giving in a way that opens the kingdom of heaven/makes it available. Steps to promote this include: Modeling the truth that, "God is for us, not against us" Modeling the truth that "God loves you" Modeling grace (not judgment) Giving in a "non-condescending" way

Continued

(d) "Woe to you, Teachers of the law and Pharisees, you hypocrites! You travel over land and sea to win a single convert, and when he becomes one, you make him twice as much a son of hell as you are" (23:15).	Their acts of service (evangelism) were done to produce clones of themselves. If you have seen spiritual leadership saying/doing things in order for you to become like them (not just "do" like them), you know (experientially) about what is being talked about, here.	Do giving in a way that frees the recipient to become who God created him/her to be. Steps to promote this include the following: Promoting self-knowledge (as a way to help the person discover his/her God-given uniqueness) Model the freedoms (as well as the boundaries) of the Christian life Teach/model listening to God Teach a distinction between biblical truth and the messages of the surrounding culture
(e) "Woe to you, blind guides! You say, 'If anyone swears by the temple, it means nothing; but if anyone swears by the gold of the temple, he is bound by his oath.' You blind fools! Which is greater: the gold, or the temple that makes the gold sacred? You also say, 'If anyone swears by the altar, it means nothing; but if anyone swears by the gift on it, he is bound by his oath.' You blind men! Which is greater: the gift, or the altar that makes the gift sacred? Therefore, he who swears by the altar swears by it and by everything on it. And he who swears by the temple swears by it and by the one who dwells in it. And he who swears by heaven swears by God's throne and by the one who sits on it" (23:16–22).	Their acts of service (teachings on oaths) had the effect of creating distinctions where distinctions shouldn't exist. (These false distinctions fostered the belief that a person could get around the carrying out of his/her promises.) If you have seen spiritual leadership teach in a way that allowed them to 'get around' legitimate responsibilities (like the Pharisees did with the issue of "corban"), then you know (experientially) about what is being talked about here.	Do giving in a way that demonstrates that everything is under God's jurisdiction. Steps to promote this include the following: Teaching/modeling that all of our life is a gift from God and that He is pleased when we return it to Him as a "thank offering" Encouraging people to face/deal with their responsibilities (not try to avoid meeting them) Encouraging the attitude that "Your will, not mine, be done" Asking the question, "What do I need to do, in this situation, to fulfill my responsibility?"

Continued

(f) "Woe to you, Teachers of the law And Pharisees, you hypocrites! You give a tenth of your spices—mint, dill, and cumin. But you have neglected the more important matters of the law—justice, mercy, and faithfulness. You should have practiced the latter, without neglecting the former. You blind guides! You strain out a gnat but swallow a camel" (23:23–24).	Their acts of giving (tithing) became "trivial pursuit." They focused on trivia while neglecting the important issues of faith. (As Jesus so vividly put it, "You strain out a gnat but swallow a camel.") If you have seen spiritual leadership spending time and energy on inconsequential issues while important issues are left unaddressed, you know (experientially) about what is being talked about here.	Do giving in a way that addresses both the important and the small issues (v. 23). Steps to promote this include the following: Getting "outcome driven" (develop clear goals … make sure that intermediate strategies move you toward these goals), in the context of God's word and God's Spirit having chosen those goals Inviting feedback from people outside the "in-group" (in order to avoid "group think") Doing personal evaluation: … Am I playing trivial pursuit (in my spiritual life)? … Am I keeping my eyes on the prize? … Am I clear about what God considers important issues?
(g) "Woe to you, Teachers of the law And Pharisees, you hypocrites! You clean the outside of the cup and dish, but inside they are full of greed and self-indulgence. Blind Pharisee! First clean the inside of the cup and dish, and then the outside also will be clean. Woe to you, teachers of the law and Pharisees, you hypocrites! You are like whitewashed tombs, which look beautiful on the outside but on the inside are full of dead men's bones and everything unclean. In the same way, on the outside you appear to people as righteous but on the inside you are full of hypocrisy and wickedness" (23:25–28).	Their acts of giving (described as "cleaning the outside of the cup," but unspecified) were for the purpose of "image management" (looking good). There was no focus on cleaning up their motives. If you have seen spiritual leadership saying/doing things to look good (but with no regard for their motives, for why they are doing what they do), you know (experientially) about what is being talked about, here.	Do giving in a way that focuses on clean motives, so that the (consequent) behaviors will also be clean (v. 26). Steps to promote this include the following: Emphasizing doing the right thing for the right reason Discovering and using the (clean) motives that energize you … (for example, obedience, as a way of saying "thank you") Confessing destructive motives; installing constructive motives

Continued

(h) "Woe to you, Teachers of the law and Pharisees, you hypocrites! You build tombs for the prophets and decorate the graves of the righteous. And you say, 'If we had lived in the days of our forefathers, we would not have taken part with them in shedding the blood of the prophets.' So you testify against yourselves that you are the descendants of those who murdered the prophets. Fill up, then, the measure of the sin of your forefathers! You snakes! You brood of vipers! How will you escape being condemned to hell? Therefore I am sending you prophets and wise men and teachers. Some of them you will kill and crucify; others you will flog in your synagogues and pursue from town to town. And so upon you will come all the righteous blood that has been shed on earth, from the blood of righteous Abel to the blood of Zechariah son of Berekiah, whom you murdered between the temple and the altar. I tell you the truth, all this will come upon this generation. O Jerusalem, Jerusalem, you who kill the prophets and stone those sent to you, how often I have longed to gather your children together, as a hen gathers her chicks under her wings, but you were not willing. Look, your house is left to you desolate. For I tell you, you will not see me again until you say, 'Blessed is he who comes in the name of the Lord'" (23:29–39).	Their acts of giving (building tombs for the prophets and decorating the graves of the righteous) were put in the service of gaining righteousness by association. (They aligned themselves with the prophets and disassociated themselves from the actions of their forefathers—while actually doing the same as their forefathers; see verses 33–39).

If you have seen spiritual leadership saying/doing things to build themselves up by associating with established "heroes" and by cutting others down, you know (experientially) about what is being talked about, here. | Do giving in a way that expresses a hungering and thirsting for the growth of personal righteousness.

Steps to promote this include the following:
Remembering that growing (inside) righteousness is how we meet our Lord's requirement: (which is) that our righteousness exceed the righteousness of the Pharisees.
Asking the question, "What would doing the right thing, in this situation, involve?"
Praying, "Lord Jesus, please gather me under your wing …." |

As you may have guessed, I believe that Pharisaism is still alive and influential. Although I have not done so in this section, I could illustrate (from my journey in the religious community) every perversion of giving that we looked at in Matthew 23. Consequently, Jesus' warning to "Be on your guard against the yeast of the Pharisees …" (Matt. 16:6) is still relevant ("yeast" meaning the "teaching" of the Pharisees [Matt. 16:12]). As we have looked at that teaching in this section, it isn't hard to see why Jesus said of them, " … Do not do what they do, for they do not practice what they preach." (Matt. 23:3).

The following questions will (hopefully) help you to specify your next steps in improving your serve.

NEXT STEPS

1. In this section, I have made the distinction between "good" acts of service and "God" acts of service. Is there any good act of giving that needs to be "pruned" out of my life? (I use the word "pruned" with reference to John 15:1–8—where the Gardener prunes every branch that does bear fruit so that it will be more fruitful.) As we listen to Him (and obey Him), we will be pruning lower quality giving out of our life so that the sap of our time/energy/ability can be redirected into higher quality giving. Make a list (below) of the (good) giving that needs to be pruned from your life.

    (i) _____

    _____

    (ii) _____

    _____

    (iii) _____

    _____

    (iv) _____

    _____

    Make a list (below) of the (God-directed) giving activities that need to become greater recipient(s) of my time/energy/ability.

    (i) _____

    _____

    (ii) _____

    _____

    (iii) _____

    _____

What are the next steps for bringing that about?

(i)_____

_____

(ii) _____

_____

(iii)_____

_____

(iv) _____

_____

Remember: The Gardener is the one to do such pruning, so only do this process as you sense His leading …

2. (In light of "burdensome" training that I have received), is there any way that I am burdening myself (or others—for example, family members) with my applications of that teaching? In relation to such teaching (which could include perfectionistic teaching or the belief that God is a policeman), fill out the following:

(a) Content of burdensome teaching   Recipient(s) of burdensome teaching

(i) _____   (i) _____

(ii) _____   (ii) _____

(iii) _____   (iii) _____

(b) My game-plan for lightening that burden:

(i) _____

_____

_____

(ii) _____

_____

_____

_____

(iii) _____

_____

_____

_____

(3) (In light of "seeking to impress" training that I have received), is there any way that I am seeking to impress myself (or others) with my applications of that

teaching? In relation to that teaching (which could include focusing *only* on my "successes" or speaking about only my "successes"), fill out the following:

(a) Instances of "seeking to
   impress" behavior   Who am I trying to impress
   (i)_____   _____
   (ii) _____   _____
   (iii)_____   _____

(b) My game-plan for changing that behavior (and the thinking that maintains that behavior):
   (i)_____
   _____
   _____
   (ii) _____
   _____
   _____
   (iii)_____
   _____
   _____

(4) (In light of "shutting the kingdom of heaven" training that I have received), is there any way in which I am shutting the kingdom of heaven on myself (or others) with my applications of that teaching? In relation to that teaching (which could include cutting off promises to myself or others, cutting off blessings to myself or others, or making the entrance requirements impossible to meet), fill out the following:

(a)Instances of "shutting the
   kingdom of heaven" behavior   Recipient(s) of that behavior
   (i) _____   (i) _____
   (ii) _____   (ii) _____
   (iii) _____   (iii) _____

(b) My game-plan for changing that behavior (and the thinking that maintains that behavior):
   (i)_____
   _____
   _____

(ii _____
_____
_____

(iii)_____
_____
_____

(5) (In light of "evangelism" training that I have received), is there any way in
which I am trying to make converts in my image through my applications of
that teaching? In relation to that teaching (which could include making a description of what works for me a prescription for the convert/trainee or promoting to the convert/trainee that my culture or traditions must be "taken to heart"
along with doctrinal truths), fill out the following:

  (a) Instances of "cloning" behavior   Recipient(s) of that behavior

      (i) _____   (i) _____
      (ii) _____   (ii)_____
      (iii) _____   (iii) _____

  (b) My game-plan for changing that behavior (and the thinking that maintains that behavior):

(i) _____
_____
_____

(ii) _____
_____
_____

(iii) _____
_____
_____

(6) In light of "teaching on oaths" training that I have received), is there any way in
which I am trying to circumvent (by-pass or get around) any promise that I have
made or responsibility that I have taken on (and am I trying to get someone else
to do the same)? In relation to any instance of that teaching, fill out the following:

  (a) Instances of "promise-breaking"
behavior   Recipient(s) of that behavior

      (i) _____ _____   (i) _____

       (ii) _____   (ii) _____

       (iii) _____   (iii) _____

(b) My game-plan for changing that behavior (and the thinking that maintains that behavior).

       (i) _____

       _____

       _____

       (ii) _____

       _____

       _____

       (iii) _____

       _____

       _____

(8) (In light of "image management" training that I have received), is there any way in which I am trying to look good to myself or others without regard to personal integrity. (As Jesus puts it, "on the outside you appear to people as righteous but on the inside you are full of hypocrisy and wickedness.") In relation to any instance of that teaching, fill out the following:

  (a) Instances of "looking good" behavior   Recipient(s) of that behavior

       (i) _____   (i) _____

       (ii) _____   (ii) _____

       (iii) _____   (iii) _____

(b) My game-plan for changing that behavior (and the thinking that maintains that behavior).

       (i) _____

       _____

       _____

       (ii) _____

       _____

       _____

       (iii) _____

       _____

       _____

(9) (In light of "righteousness by association" training that I have received), is there any way in which I am trying to gain associated righteousness by aligning myself with someone that I want to look like (or unalign myself with someone that I don't want to look like). Also, who am I modeling this behavior to? In relation to any instance of this teaching, fill out the following:

    (a) Instances of "associated righteousness" behavior   Recipient(s) of that behavior

        (i) _____   (i) _____

        (ii) _____   (ii) _____

        (iii) _____   (iii) _____

    (b) My game-plan for changing that behavior (and the thinking that maintains that behavior).

    (i) _____

_____

_____

_____

    (ii) _____

_____

_____

_____

    (iii) _____

_____

_____

_____

CHURCH INVOLVEMENT

On the same (twenty-four hour) day that I became a Christian, the emphasis on getting involved with the church was given. The understanding of "church" that I received could (roughly) be put into two categories:

CHURCH AS ORGANIZATION	CHURCH AS ORGANISM
• The church is a culture—including an environment with a focal point (the church building) and a structured program throughout the week (worship services, prayer meetings, Sunday school meetings, small group meetings, and so on). • This organization has beliefs (for example, "If this organization grows bigger, that's a sign of success") and roles (for example, "I need to discover where I am gifted so that I can play an effective role in this organization") and rules (for example, "Everyone should contribute to this organization") connected to it.	• The church is the family of God—including leaders (pastors, elders) and followers (who come for instruction, support, encouragement, direction, and so on). • This family has beliefs (for example, "Members of this family make up the body of Christ") and roles (for example, "The leadership in this family are like parents; the followers are like children") and rules (for example, "Members of this family are to build one another up") connected to it.

Although my early training sometimes emphasized that the organization was to be in the service of the family (or person) and sometimes emphasized that the family (or person) was to be in the service of the organization, I soon came to agree with the former emphasis (an emphasis that I still hold). At that time, my choice was influenced by my belief that, in this family, I had discovered a replacement for the dysfunctional family that I had grown up in (and had escaped from). That belief—like many other new beliefs that I learned at that time—was endorsed by the leadership of the church I was involved in. My subsequent experiences (over the next thirty years) in this family (of God) have taught me that—like families-of-origin—some are primarily functional, some are somewhat functional (and somewhat dysfunctional), and some are primarily dysfunctional. On this (thirty year) journey, I have been told that there is no perfect church. That statement has usually been spoken in the context of encouraging me to accept this organization/family for where/who they are (and I agree that I should set my expectations of that family at a realistic level or I will be setting myself up for disappointment). What I have needed to (also) learn over these years (in addition to the truth that there is no perfect church) is how to relate to such (less than perfect) organizations/families. The following information outlines what I have discovered (and am discovering) in relation to two items:

i) Identifying where, on the "functional/mid-range/dysfunctional" continuum, a particular church is.

ii) Responding differentially to each of these three "kinds" of churches. (Growing up on the prairies in Canada, I have learned to dress differentially—I wear different clothing during different seasons of the year. I'm suggesting that we also think and act differentially in relation to the church organizations/families that we are involved with.)

Since a church is an organization and a family (like a family-of-origin—all successful families-of-origin have a structure and organization that maintains and enhances their constructive, relational interactions), the tools for distinguishing healthy families from unhealthy families can be used to distinguish healthy churches from unhealthy churches. The following criteria can help to make that distinction:

Use of Power

A primarily functional church will use power in a (primarily) constructive way. The following statements define what that constructive way includes:

- Leadership uses their positions of authority and their expertise to encourage the growth and development of the members of that community. (So, leadership empowers the followers—by teaching, modeling skills, and demonstrating lifestyle—to actualize the potentials that God created them with and to seek His plan for their lives.)

- Leadership is flexible in their application of power. (So, even bids for power by followers are handled with respect and with dialogue; such encounters are even seen by the leadership as growth opportunities for all involved and as relationship development opportunities.)

- Leadership is clear about (and open to others about) the boundary conditions on their power. (So, they inform the followers about who they, as leaders, are accountable to; they specify the areas where their power doesn't apply; they invite questions from followers about the reasons for the rules [rules being the way in which leadership power is applied].)

- Leadership abides by the same rules that they are asking their followers to adhere to. (So, leadership models what they want followers to do; they are *not* saying, "Do as I say, not as I do.")

- Leadership applies power in ways that maintain or enhance the relationships of the people involved. (So, the followers involved will sense that the leaders involved are working *with* them, not *on* them.)

A primarily dysfunctional church will use power in a (primarily) destructive way. The following statements define what that destructive way includes:

- Leadership uses their positions of authority and their expertise to encourage the growth and development of obedience (to the rules of the community) in the members of that community. (So, leadership promotes "followership" in the members of that community, so that the hierarchical power structure is maintained.)

- Leadership is inflexible in their application of power. (So, all bids for power by the followers are seen by the leadership as "rebellion" [or something negative] and handled with escalating demonstrations of leadership power and control. Such bids for power are seen by the leadership as threats to the established order in the community.)

- Leadership is not open (to community members) about the boundary conditions on leadership power. (So, power is concentrated in a "decider subset" of leaders and decisions are made "behind closed doors." Only the products of those discussions are given to the followers; the process by which those decisions are made is not given to the followers. Because these leaders may want to be "a law unto themselves," they design structures so that they are not accountable to anyone else. Because these leaders may want influence over every aspect of the follower's lives, they don't specify any limits. Because these leaders may see questions as a threat to the status quo [a status quo that serves the leaders well], they do not encourage questions—or any kind of dialogue—about the rules of the organization.)

- Leadership—at an overt level—may seem to be abiding by the same rules that they ask their followers to adhere to, but—at a covert level—there may be a different set of rules for leadership. (So, there is a "double standard" and a belief that they are "above the law"—especially if they have the power to rewrite the laws of the organizations that they lead.)

- Leadership does not apply power in ways that maintain or enhance the relationships of the people involved. (So, followers involved will sense that the leaders involved are working on them, not with them. The main goal of such an organization is to maintain or enhance the power of the leaders [not maintain or enhance the growth of the members]. Manipulation tactics or deceptions [or whatever means] can be used. In such organizations, the ends [of power maintenance] justify the means. And relationships are sacrificed in that process.)

In mid-range churches, there is a mixture of functional and dysfunctional uses of power so that it is difficult to label such a church as "functional" or "dysfunctional."

Closeness

A primarily functional church will "do" closeness in a particular way. The following statements outline what that looks like:

- There are various ways that closeness can be shown in a church organization/family. The following chart outlines some of these ways:

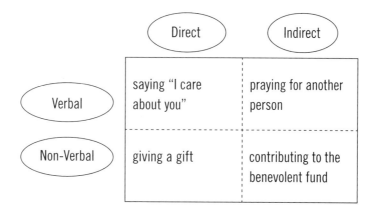

	Direct	Indirect
Verbal	saying "I care about you"	praying for another person
Non-Verbal	giving a gift	contributing to the benevolent fund

Different churches will have different emphases (in regard to how they show closeness); all styles are legitimate. In a functional church, closeness will have the following features:

- It will be real and heartfelt (not fake and put-on).
- It will respect the boundaries of the recipient. (In other words, it will be done in a way that is respectful of the recipient; it will take into account what the recipient is comfortable with/not comfortable with; it will flex to what the recipient finds meaningful/helpful.)
- It will invite and appreciate different expressions from different people.
- It will be a gift (not a loan).

- Closeness will be promoted without regard to the response of the recipient. (In other words, expressions of closeness will be seen as ends in/of themselves; they will not be seen as means to modify the behavior of the recipient.)

Some ways of doing closeness are constructive (as just outlined); some ways of doing closeness are destructive (as about to be outlined). In a primarily dysfunctional church, closeness will have the following features:

- It will have a quality to it that could be described as "fake" or "put-on" or "insincere."
- It will not respect the boundaries of the recipient. (A term that has been used

to describe this feature of destructive closeness is "enmeshment"—where "closeness" has a "smothering" quality and a tendency to reduce privacy, where "acts of closeness" are actually demonstrations of what the giver wants to receive in return, and where "closeness" has a "demand" quality).

– There will be (implicitly or explicitly) approved methods of doing closeness; these are often prescribed.

– It will be a loan (not a gift). As a "loan," it will be a means to some end. It is an investment that is looking for a return (on that investment). Some of the "returns on investment" that such acts of closeness are looking for, include the following:

  * Reciprocity ("Let me return your generosity")
  * Appreciation ("What a generous person you are!")
  * Emotional engagement ("I've finally found someone who can give without my asking")
  * Obligation ("I am indebted to him/her/them")

• This kind of closeness has been called "closeness with strings attached."

(Again), in mid-range churches there is a mixture of constructive and destructive features of closeness, so that it is difficult to label such a church as "functional" or "dysfunctional."

Goal-Directed Negotiation

A primarily functional church—as it follows the process of working toward resolving an issue—will do so in a particular way. That particular way has three components:

  (i) *Tracking.* A functional church will identify the issue and will stay focused on that issue throughout the process.

  (ii) *Involvement.* A functional church will encourage and solicit participation from a high percentage of its membership.

  (iii) *Resolution.* A functional church will bring the issue to closure—in a "win-win" way or "win-win somewhat" way (otherwise known as "compromise").

In a dysfunctional church, this process will look different; as it relates to the three specified components, it will involve the following:

  (i) *Tracking.* A dysfunctional church will have a less clear understanding of the issue and the process will meander (get off issue, bring in other issues, stop for a "soap-box" speaker, and so on).

(ii) *Involvement*. A dysfunctional church does not encourage membership participation (except to endorse what the "decider-subset" has already decided). So, membership feels less invested in the process and in the decisions.

(iii) *Resolution*. A dysfunctional church may not bring the issue to closure, so it remains an "open wound" waiting for another "go around" or it may bring the issue to premature closure (by "fiat" or other less democratic means).

(As usual), a mid-range church will show a mixture of functional and dysfunctional components of that process.

Responsibility

In this context, responsibility refers to the degree to which members acknowledge and take personal responsibility for their own past, present, and future actions.

A primarily functional church will provide an environment within which members are encouraged to take personal responsibility. The following features characterize the interactions within this kind of environment:

- Members will voice personal responsibility statements (often starting with "I") and other members of this community will not punish members for acknowledging personal responsibility when mistakes occur. (Such communities will, however, deliver consequences for the behavioral aspects of these mistakes.) Relationships in this community are characterized by openness, trust, and respect.

A primarily dysfunctional church will provide an environment within which members are not encouraged to take personal responsibility. The following features characterize the interactions within this kind of environment:

- Members will avoid personal responsibility statements (often speaking in the third person, for example, "Everyone else does ...") and will use the (responsibility) avoidance tactics of blaming someone else, attacking someone else, or scapegoating someone else.
- Any attempt to acknowledge personal responsibility will be accompanied by fear and anxiety, because punishment, love withdrawal, or severe "disappointment" could be consequences.

(As always), a mid-range church will show a mixture of these features.

Handling the Unresolved

All groups of people encounter issues on which members do not all agree. A primarily functional church will handle such unresolvable issues as follows:

- Members are clear and direct in expressing and understanding their differences, but these differences are viewed as different perspectives (rather than personal attacks). So, relationships are less likely to be negatively impacted by these differences.
- Members can tolerate higher levels of ambiguity (which differences contribute to). So, they are more likely to "agree to disagree" or to hold the differences in abeyance until something changes.

A primarily dysfunctional church will handle such unresolvable issues as follows:

- Members harbor grudges (in relation to past unresolvable issues).They may be vocal and confrontational about such issues or they may be quietly seething in a tense silence about such issues, but there always will be a sense of being against the members who are on the other side of the issue. So, relationships are more likely to be negatively impacted by such differences.
- Members are more likely to take these differences personally and to either attack or withdraw from people who embody these differences.

(Again), a mid-range church will show a mixture of these styles.

What I have attempted to do here is to provide you with criteria for evaluating the church (the organization/family) that you are involved with. This evaluation is along the
FUNCTIONAL — MID-RANGE — DYSFUNCTIONAL
continuum. Now, I will attempt to outline how to relate (differentially) to each of these styles of community.

If you have the good fortune to be involved in a functional church, then you have something everyday to be grateful for (in the same way that, if you grew up in a functional family-of-origin, you have something to be grateful for every day). Your responses to/in such a community (in addition to gratitude) could include the following:

- *Intentional participation.* Such a community produces enough safety and respect and support to facilitate growth, so participation will produce constructive growth in you.
- *Learning from the leadership.* The architects of such a community have constructive things to teach, so modeling how they do the various dimensions of their life (as children model their functional parents) would be highly profitable. As it relates to issues where differences exist, give the leadership the "benefit of the doubt," since they have proven themselves to be trustworthy.
- *Intentional giving.* As you are able, look for ways to contribute to this community. (If you have ever been part of a successful sports team, you will have experienced

how every member proactively looked for ways to contribute to the team; that is what I am suggesting in this context.) The well-known categories of time, talent, and treasure can help you to look at dimensions of your contribution.

- *Find fellow-travelers.* This community facilitates acquaintances becoming friends and friends becoming confidants/companions, but it is also your (individual) responsibility to look for "God-sends" (people that God sends into your life) and to do what you can to draw close to those people. Often when we find such people there is a sense of fit (for instance, people say, "I feel like I have known this person all my life"). Often it is apparent how each person is building into the life of the other. Such relationships are precious gifts. (We are wise if we treat them as precious.)
- *Include others.* Such communities are "things of beauty and nourishment." They will nourish all who come, so it is helpful to invite those who are in need of nourishment (in the same way that you might invite someone into your functional family-of-origin to share a meal).

If you are involved in a mid-range church, then you are in a community that can teach you valuable lessons (but you will need to work harder to receive them, and you may experience less enjoyment than if you were in a functional church). Your responses to/in such a community could include the following:

- *Selective participation.* There will be places and people in this community with whom you will experience safety and respect and support, but you will need to look for/find them. (If you grew up in a mid-range family, you learned how to connect with those family members who were "for" you and to disconnect from those family members who were "against" you; those same skills are relevant for this community.) If you don't have these skills, this is a great context within which to learn them. This learning will be helped by your acceptance of this community for being what it is (a mixture of constructive and destructive people). This is preferable to your adherence to the (idealistic) belief that harmony with everyone is required for growth to occur or that it is your job to get those people to start meeting your expectations of how this community should operate. Since I have already talked about some of the dimensions of connection (in the "functional church" section), I'll talk (here) about some of the ways to disconnect. People to get/stay disconnected from come in various shapes and sizes—some "love you and have a plan for your life," some want to use you, some want you to look after them, and so on. When you begin to get this kind of data from these people, (through your interactions with them), it is advisable—using the terms talked about in this chapter—to keep them at the "acquaintance" level. As you do this (with applications of your boundaries, by focusing on your game-plan, by explicitly or implicitly declining their invitations to "dance to their tune," and so on), it is crucial to do this (disconnecting work) with kindness and gentleness and patience. Doing it this way, the people involved sense your respect for them and don't see your interactions with them as "put-downs." Since the leading of God's Spirit is an "override" of my plans, if I sense that He wants me to get more deeply involved with someone that I would choose to stay disconnected from, I will facilitate that involvement. (At the same time, I would be managing my involvement with that person so that it remains as constructive as possible for both of us. If I have heard accurately from God, it will be a "learning" relationship—although maybe not easy—for both of us.) Obviously, different people have different tolerance levels and skills and gifts and callings to facilitate their involvement in such circumstances. My only suggestion (here) is that the "how and how much" of such involvement be done in the context of God's leading (rather than generalized guilt motivation or leaning on your own understanding—or that of others—to specify how you should be relating to each person in this community).

• *Learn (carefully) from the leadership.* Since there will be good things to learn as well as good things to stay away from, your nourishment in this community will involve both swallowing the meat and spitting out the bones. To do that, you will need to "evaluate all things and hold on to what is good" (1 Thess. 5:21) and to "avoid [let go of] every kind of evil" (1 Thess. 5:22). The work of such evaluation, which includes praying/listening, reading about what other leaders say, talking to people who are experienced in these matters, comparing the practices of this community to scriptural principles and practices to see if community practices are within the circle of biblical options and personally deciding what to ingest and what to spit out, can be arduous. But, like many difficult processes, can also be very educational. Hebrews 5:14 states "But solid food is for the mature, who by constant use have trained themselves to distinguish good from evil"; this evaluation is the way that training gets done. So, in this community, unthinking loyalty to the leadership is "a luxury that you can't afford" (whereas it would be safer to do so in a functional church community). When you can agree with the leadership, you can actively support what they are doing (and so can encourage them, invest in their program, ingest what you are learning from your participation, and enjoy the edifying journey). When you can't agree with the leadership, you can passively support what they are doing (and so can wish them well in their venture, not invest in their program, and continue to be on good terms with them [but] from a spectator, rather than participant, perspective). Functional leaders will be able to accept your non-participation (especially if you let them know that you have come to this conclusion by—among other means—consulting with a High Authority). Dysfunctional leaders will be less able to accept your non-participation (possibly because they may consider themselves to be that Higher Authority).

- *Intentional (and selective) giving.* We are to be a good steward of our life (taking responsibility for and carefully using the time, talent, and treasure that we have been given). In a mid-range community (more than in a functional community) there are times and places to "spend" our life that are not beneficial. In 1 Corinthians 10:23, Paul says, "Everything is permissible—but not everything is beneficial." In this context, we need to seek and find the beneficial. (Remember, of course, that what we find beneficial or not is not a prescription for anyone else; it is the work of the Holy Spirit to direct each person to what is beneficial for him/her. So, if I am convinced that someone is not being a good steward of his/her life, my first step is to pray for him/her, not try to play the role of the Holy Spirit in his/her life.)

- *Find fellow-travelers.* Although it is more risky in this community (than in a functional church community) to look for "fellow-travelers" (or, in the terms of this chapter, "confidants/companions"), it is always appropriate to do so. We were built to be in community so we are always searching to belong (unless some destructive experience has stopped our search). How we do that search, however, needs to differ from community to community. Here, it is appropriate to assume that "not all that glitters is gold," and (so) the work of finding and extracting the precious metal (of a constructive relationship) is necessary.

- *Include others in this community* (but only if it would be constructive for them). If you have found a constructive sub-group in this community (a family or a Bible study or a ministry group), that is the (constructive) context to invite others into.

If you are involved in a dysfunctional church, then you are in a community that can teach you valuable lessons (but it will be difficult to stay and, if "push comes to shove," one of your lessons may be on how to exit. I recommend that you stay long-term only if you sense direction from God to do so). Your responses to/in such a community could include the following:

- *Carefully selected participation.* If you have chosen, as an act of stewardship, to make the bulk of your interactions with other people constructive, then you will need to search for a person/people (in this community) with whom that (constructive interaction) can occur. As you know (if you have grown up in a dysfunctional family), you won't have to go searching for destructive interactions—they will come searching for you. And when such interactions find you, there will usually be (explicit or implicit) demands/requests that you accommodate those demands/requests. An example of an explicit demand for your compliance would be someone in leadership saying to you, "I have heard from God about issue X … He has told me Y … (so) if you don't go along with what I am saying, you are disobeying God." An example of an implicit request for your compliance would be someone in leadership saying to you, "What was amazing about the church in the book of Acts was that they sold their possessions and gave to anyone who had need. We are following that principle in our church, as it relates to the pastoral retirement fund." We have various response options to such demands/requests:

(i) Going along with such demands/requests (and facing the results of those choices—if we sow compliance we reap the harvest of consequences).

(ii) Confronting that demand/request (and dealing with the resulting demand escalations – "How dare you challenge God's anointed …").

(iii) Trying to negotiate a win-win agreement in response to that demand/request (and experiencing the futility of trying to negotiate with someone looking for compliance).

(iv) Bringing in a mediator to respond to that demand/request (and seeing the focus of the interaction shift to the issue of who has the authority to choose the mediator).

(v) Backing away from that demand/request (and suffering the "slings and arrows" of outraged demanders, who tend to see such withdrawal as rebellion or faithlessness).

Depending upon the (external and internal) circumstances, any of these options could be your best response option (but, as you can see, none of these options—in a destructive environment—is very effective). If you can't find people in this community with whom to have nourishing interactions, it is valuable to ask yourself why you are staying in this community.

• *Learn from the leadership—about what not to do.* Every leader (like every parent) is our teacher: Some teach us about what we should do; some teach us about what we should not do. As we learn about what not to do, we have the opportunity to learn how to be a "hard target." (A "hard target" is a person who can live in a war zone and, although gets shot at, can avoid terminal wounds.) Such a survivor will need to have (and be developing) the following skill sets:

i)   Have (and be developing) a relationship with God that does not depend primarily on other people. In a nourishing environment (like a functional church), learning from others is a part of the growth process. In a toxic environment (like a dysfunctional church), interactions with others can be how the toxicity spreads. So hearing (directly) from God and protecting your relationship with Him is necessary. (When in a war zone, don't advertise your location.)

ii) Related to the previous skill set, is that of being able to focus on and keep following the game-plan that you have received and developed, for staying in this community. In part, this involves becoming unprovokable—so you won't be provoked or pulled into another agenda. In part, this involves getting time alone with your Commander and reviewing your marching orders. (When in a war zone, hold your survival plan close.)

iii) Have (and be developing) self-support skills (specified in other modules in this book). Such skills are beneficial in any environment; such skills are crucial in a toxic environment. Related to self-support skills are self-soothing skills—for times when you have taken a (relational) hit. (When in a war zone, use your emotional first aid kit.)

iv) Have (and be developing) your "reading between the lines" skills, so you can identify the hidden agendas that may be informing what another community member says to you. Related to that skill is your "flexibility of response" skills, which reflect your ability to respond to different people in different ways so as to tailor-make responses that (simultaneously) keep the peace and maintain your boundaries. (When in a war zone, fly below the "overt conflict" radar.)

If these skill sets need further development in your life, it is easy to see why you might be directed (at least for a season) to be involved in a dysfunctional church. Such a community presents you with unique trials (opportunities). If, however, your skills are not a match for the games the dysfunctional leaders are playing, you may need to "beat a hasty retreat."

• *Intentional giving—to individuals and to self.* In a toxic environment, the broader your context of giving, the more likely you are to be "aiding and abetting" some part of an organization that doesn't reflect your values. So, good stewardship of your resources is more likely if you constrict your giving to individuals (thus by-passing the organization) and to yourself (thus providing what the organization is not providing).

- *Find fellow-travelers.* As the church environment becomes more toxic, the importance of finding a fellow-traveler increases. Matthew 18:20 says, "For where two or three come together in my name, there I am with them." In this New Testament definition of the church, we see that a community must contain at least two people. If you are in an organization/family where you can't find one person with the potential to become a confidant/companion, then I'd suggest you begin to pack your bags. If you find such a person, give that relationship a top priority investment. If you begin to suspect that it is your toxicity that is stopping relationship growth, then find someone with the skills to help you to detoxify (and do whatever it takes to get that outcome).

- *Do not invite others into this community.* Living in a fallen world will (by itself) provide people with enough challenges. We don't need to add to those challenges by getting people into toxic environments.

I would be surprised if you have (previously) heard what I have said in this section. Consequently, my perspective may be hard to chew and harder to swallow (and some of you may be saying, "I think that I'll have to 'throw up' what that guy is trying to feed me"). So, to (hopefully) help with your digestion, I will (now) provide you with some principles that have shaped my perspectives.

1. I am working toward unconditional loyalty to God; I believe (however) that there are limits on my loyalty to (God-ordained) institutions—like the family or the church. When these institutions become destructive, when the processes of such institutions have been perverted to the extent that their participants are more harmed than helped, I no longer owe allegiance to such organizations. (Indeed, to remain loyal to a destructive organization is to aid in the spread of that destruction.) Probably all of us have seen or experienced how a family-of-origin (which was designed to nurture its children) can hurt these children, through physical or emotional or sexual abuse. When that happens, the children can be (and, I believe, should be) removed, in order to give them a chance (elsewhere) to survive and thrive. When the church (which was designed to edify its members) hurts these members, through whatever processes, the option of my leaving begins to be preferable to staying. My support of this organization begins to end. (In other words, I am loyal to this institution only as long as it is carrying out—at least minimally—its original mandate.) Over the years, I have been told (more than

once) to stay within the church and work (from within) for change, if I was dissatisfied with how things were. Being someone who is rarely satisfied with the status quo (of others or of myself), I have done all I knew how to do, to promote change from within—with little effect. I have come to conclude that, in dysfunctional organizations/families, power is concentrated within a sub-group of that organization/family and that to get into that (decision-making/change-making) sub-group, a person must espouse the views of that sub-group (which don't advocate change). Consequently, someone (like me) who advocated change, could not get to a position where change from within could be brought about. (Obviously, when I was a "baby" in such organizations I wasn't advocating change, I was just eating whatever that organization dished out. As I became an "adult" in such organizations, my unconditional loyalty began to end.) The experience of other people (for instance, those more socially skilled) may be very different from mine. They may have discovered and contributed within functional churches; they may also have been heard and heeded within dysfunctional churches—I hope so. My experience, however, has led me to conclude what I have said in this section and to prioritize the seeking and finding and nourishing of relationships with "fellow-travelers" above working for organizational development (when both are not feasible). This conclusion is a departure from the training I have received and is bound to have its critics (who, obviously, have a right to disagree). I take some comfort from the fact that our Lord—who didn't build a single organization—invested (instead) in the lives of twelve fellow-travelers.

2. I take personal responsibility for the way that I relate to the organizations/families that I am involved with. This involves avoiding over-responsibility (where I feel and take responsibility for aspects of the organization/family functioning that I have no authority over). For example, trying to get the leadership to adopt my views on X, rather than seeking God's direction and asking the leadership to do the same, so that a move toward consensus via the Spirit's leading can be facilitated. This also involves avoiding under-responsibility (where I take no responsibility to pray and think through the issue(s) that face the organization/family). For example, letting others decide for me as it relates to the issue(s) at hand, rather than seeking God's direction for any input that He might want me to bring to the issue(s). Appropriate responsibility involves being responsible to the organization/family but not responsible for it. It involves giving my input (as I sense God's leading) and adjusting my responses, according to where on the "functional/

mid-range/dysfunctional" continuum, my organization/family is. Appropriate responsibility also involves investing my time/talents/treasure when I sense God's leading to give to that organization/family and the leadership endorses my giving in that endeavor. To modify a saying from my family-of-origin: "[I am to] put my money (and my time and my energy) where my mouth is."

3. In Romans 12:18, Paul says "If it is possible, as far as it depends on you, live at peace with everyone."

    Notice how Paul qualifies his directive to live at peace with everyone:
    (a) "If it is possible"—implying that, sometimes it will not be possible.
    (b) "As far as it depends on you"—implying that others will have to do their part, too, if "living at peace" is going to happen. (In other words, it is not entirely up to me to make peace happen.)

The following is how I see this scriptural instruction applying to the issue of church involvement:

In a functional church, it will be (relatively) easy to live at peace. In this kind of community, where the majority of people are (also) seeking to live at peace, it will—to a substantial (and a growth-promoting) extent—occur. In this kind of community, you can work with the other members.

In a mid-range church, it will be (relatively) hard to live at peace. In this kind of community, where some people are seeking to live at peace, you can work with them. In this kind of community, where some people are not seeking to live at peace, you can work around them. To the extent that you can do both, you will be living at peace in this kind of a community.

In a dysfunctional church, it will be very hard to live at peace. In this kind of community, where the majority of people are not seeking to live at peace, you will need to find at least one other person who is seeking peace, in order for you to be living at peace. When this minimal requirement for community cannot be met (for whatever reasons—theirs or yours), the best way to live at peace is to work without them.

The following questions will (hopefully) help you to specify your next steps in relation to your church involvement.

NEXT STEPS

1. As it relates to the organization/family (church) that you are presently involved with, what rating would you give that community—on the following dimensions? (Circle the category that most accurately identifies the level of functioning, for each dimension).

(a) Use of Power:

        Functional ... . Mid-Range ... . Dysfunctional

(b) Closeness:

        Functional ... . Mid-Range ... . Dysfunctional

(c) Goal-Directed Negotiation:

        Functional ... . Mid-Range ... . Dysfunctional

(d) Responsibility:

        Functional ... . Mid-Range ... . Dysfunctional

(e) Handling the Unresolved:

        Functional ... . Mid-Range ... . Dysfunctional

2.   In light of these ratings, where does your community fit—on the (following) "Overall Rating Scale"? (Circle one of your seven options).

	Closer to functional	Closer to mid-range		Closer to mid-range	Closer to dysfunctional	
FUNCTIONAL	FUNCTIONAL-MID-RANGE	MID-RANGE-FUNCTIONAL	MID-RANGE	MID-RANGE-DYSFUNCTIONAL	DYSFUNCTIONAL-MID-RANGE	DYSFUNCTIONAL

3.   (If your overall rating is between the distinct categories—of "Functional" or "Mid-Range" or "Dysfunctional"—read both categories in this section, when planning your response.) Then, develop (below) your game-plan for responding to your community. Be as specific as possible about the following (if relevant):

• How will I participate in this community?

_____

_____

_____

_____

• How will I relate to (a/each specific leader)?

_____

_____

_____

_____

_____

How can I give to this community? (Remember: giving out of your strengths and gifting is the most effective and nourishing way.)

_____

_____

_____

• What do I need from this community?

_____

_____

_____

• Who are my actual fellow-travelers, here? (Remember: these are the relationships of high priority in your life. Do what it takes to nourish them.)

_____

_____

_____

• Who are my potential fellow-travelers, here? (Remember: finding such people is like finding gold, so don't spare the digging.)

_____

_____

_____

Since a community is a living organism, your involvement with it will change over time. Your answers (to the above questions) are only a present snapshot, but they can help you take personal responsibility for your involvement.

Since you may not have immediate answers to these questions, they may start you on a search for these answers. The process of exploration (to find these answers) may be very enlightening.

Since your involvement with your church community needs to be directed by God's Spirit, I'd suggest that you pray for God's confirmation of the aspects of the above game-plan that are within His directed will and for His disconfirmation of those aspects of the above game-plan that are not within His directed will.

RESPONSIBILITY

Shortly after becoming a Christian, two (seemingly contradictory) themes—about what I was responsible to do—began to emerge. In fact, they were two different views of how to live as a believer, two different views of how to grow my relationship with God.

One view—that I will call the active view—encourages me to "work out my salvation with fear and trembling" (Phil. 2:12) and to "Evaluate all things; hold fast to that which is good" (1 Thess. 5:21). This view emphasizes my work and my choices in growing toward maturity. This view sees me as being mature when I can choose—moment by moment—to be obedient to God's will for my life. In Romans 12:2, I am instructed to "... not conform any longer to the pattern of this world, but be transformed by the renewing of your mind. Then you will be able to test and approve what God's will is—his good, pleasing and perfect will." Involved in this shift (from conforming to being transformed) is my effort; here it sounds like my choices make a difference. Again in 2 Peter 1:5–9 it says"... Make every effort to add to your faith goodness; and to goodness, knowledge; and to knowledge, self-control; and to self-control, perseverance; and to perseverance, godliness, and to godliness, brotherly kindness; and to brotherly kindness, love. For if you possess these qualities in increasing measure, they will keep you from being ineffective and unproductive in your knowledge of our Lord Jesus Christ."

Phrases like "make every effort" and "... in increasing measure" speak to me of concentrated effort, directed over time, to bring about growth.

The other view—that I will call the passive view—encourages me to "let go and let God," to "... commit your way unto the Lord; trust also in him; and he will bring it to pass" (Ps. 37:5). This view emphasizes God's sovereignty and love for me and tells me to "open your mouth wide, and I will fill it" (Ps. 81:10). This view sees me as being mature when I can consistently get out of the way so that God can work through me. This view sees me as being mature when I am a "channel only" of God's work. In Matthew 25:31–46 we get a glimpse into the future—when Jesus returns (as King) to separate the sheep from the goats. In His dialogue with the sheep, we discover that those who had done the right things were unaware of their good deeds, presumably because they had "let go and let God" live His life through them.

For years, as these two themes grew in my awareness, so did my tension. I knew, growing up on a farm, that you "reap what you sow" (and that sowing takes effort).But I also knew that I could sow destructively (see Galatians 6:8a) and that the only guarantee of a good harvest (read "fruitfulness") is to be connected to Jesus "as the branch is to the vine" (John 15:1–8). Then, His sap would flow through me (no effort, other than "remaining in him," required). I saw this increasing tension as a "bad" thing. I had been told that I would have peace if I "surrendered all." But, since peace wasn't coming, I concluded that I must still be "unsurrendered." I (ongoingly) told the Lord that I surrendered all, but I was interpreting my experience (of tension) as a "disconfirmation" of my words. (And I certainly knew that just saying the words was no guarantee that my heart or my feet were going in the same direction.) So, I was (to use modern psychological jargon) experiencing "cognitive dissonance." In these days, when "mysteries" confront me, I pray that God will use them in my life in the same way that a grain of sand is used in the life of an oyster—to produce a thing of beauty (even if it is uncomfortable for the oyster). In those days, however, I went around and around on this issue, like a dog chasing his tail.

As years have passed, a new way of looking at this dilemma (of my effort or God's power) has begun to emerge. I began to realize that both these perspectives were clearly taught in the Scriptures and (so) it wasn't fair to the Scriptures if I let go of either perspective (or prioritize one over the other). I began to think "both/and" rather than "either/or"; This ended my debate about which wing of the airplane was the most important. (This "paradigm shift" has become my "pearl"—since many scriptural issues have seemingly contradictory perspectives, all of which need to be embraced in order for the multidimensionality of the biblical perspective to be glimpsed.) I discovered that these new "both/and" glasses had been tried on before; Pascal says:

> There are then a great number of truths, both of faith and morality, which seem contradictory, and which all hold together in a wonderful system. The source of all heresies is the exclusion of some of these truths; and the source of all the objections which the heretics make against us is the ignorance of some of our truths. And it generally happens that, unable to conceive the connection of two opposite truths, and believing that the admission of one involves the exclusion of the other, they adhere to the one, exclude the other, and think of us as opposed to them. Now exclusion is the cause of their heresy; and ignorance that we hold the other truth causes their objections.[36]

Part of what I understand from this quote is that problems and perversions occur when people think "either/or", when they choose one theme to the exclusion of the other. (In my analogy, they are trying to fly the airplane on one wing.) When we choose to embrace both themes, we have to face the issue of how to let both themes do their good work in our life. Adopting a "both/and" perspective can solve one problem (Is it my effort or God's power that brings the harvest?) and, at the same time, create another problem (How do I apply both of these themes in my life?) As it relates to the issue of responsibility, the following extract (from Virginia Mollenkott's book *In Search of Balance*) outlines how, at a functional level, that question can be answered. (The following discussion is in relation to Proverbs 3:5–6— a Scripture in which both the themes of my effort and God's power are laid out.)

But it is because the Bible paradoxically emphasizes both poles of truth that I am likely to fall into error if I think of the one without the other. Thus when I seek to trust in the Lord with all my heart, and not lean on my own understanding, I must not repudiate my own insights, nor must I refuse to make responsible decisions. Instead, I must judge a human situation as carefully as I can, at the same time reminding myself of my human limitations and the possibility of my own error. I must pray for God's guidance; I must consciously open my thoughts to the influence of the Holy Spirit; I must try to see things as I think God might see them, all the while aware that I am *not* God and that ego and self-interest might be skewing my judgment. As I swing into action, doing the thing which seems to be right in the situation so far as I can assess it, I must do so in reliance upon God's guidance and mercy; but I must not assume my own infallibility … So I am *simultaneously* resting in God and making responsible human choice.[37]

Thinking in a broader context, Mollenkott goes on to say:

…When I commit my way to the Lord, I put forth all possible human effort to achieve the goal I have set for myself. But my trust is not in my effort; for all the while I know that no amount of effort will bring my goal to pass unless God so permits. If my goal is truly His will, there is no doubt that it will come to pass. But God is not my accomplice, under obligation to bring about just any goal I happen to set my mind on. There is always the margin of human error. I may think I am trusting purely in God, I may think my way is wholly committed to Him, yet be fooling myself completely. Redemption will cover such unconscious sin, for Christ "is able also to save them to the uttermost that come unto God by him, seeing he ever liveth to make intercession for them" (Heb. 7:25).

On the other hand, I must not assume that my every successful venture constitutes proof that God was in it. Psalm 37:5 does not promise tangible success, but only the fact that if I *will* to commit my way to God, He will bring about *genuine* commitment in my heart. He will take what was unreal and unaccustomed and turn it into a very real and meaningful habit: "he shall bring it to pass. And he shall bring forth thy righteousness as the light, and thy judgment as the noonday" (Ps. 37:5–6) … God's power? Human effort? When man is at his best, they cannot be distinguished. And in submission to the polarities of scriptural truth, I vow that I will not stress either factor to the exclusion of the other. For "according to Christian morality God is on both sides of the line; the will of God works *in* the wills of those who love him; and the grace of God is made known in the ability to love him." [A. Boyce Gibson, "Discussion of the views of P. H. Newel-Smith," in Christian Ethics and Contemporary Philosophy, ed. Ian T. Ramsay (London: SCM Press Ltd., 1966), p. 123.] Paul expressed the paradox in these words: "But by the grace of God I am what I am: and his grace which was bestowed upon me was not in vain; but I labored more abundantly than they all: yet not I, but the grace of God which was with me" (1 Cor. 15:10).[38]

And when I return to texts that I used earlier in this section to illustrate the "my effort" theme, I find the other theme (of God's power) also in those texts. For example, I quoted Philippians 2:12: "… Continue to work out your salvation with fear and trembling… ." If I carry on (into verse 13), I read, "For it is God who works in you to will and to act according to his good purpose." For another example, if I look again at 2 Peter 1—from where I quoted the list of things that we are to add to our faith—I notice (in verses 3 and 4) the other theme: "His divine power has given us everything that we need for life and godliness through our knowledge of Him who called us by his own glory and goodness. Through these he has given us his very great and precious promises, so that through them you may participate in the divine nature and escape the corruption in the world caused by evil desires. For this very reason, make every effort to add to your faith …"

And when I return to the texts that I used earlier in this section to illustrate the "God's power" theme, I find the other theme (of my effort) also in these texts. For example, in Psalm 37, I quoted verse 5.As I go further through that psalm (to verses 7 and 8), I see instructions—which will require my effort—that inform me about what I need to do in order to cooperate with the Lord as He brings about His will. These instructions include: "… be still … wait patiently … do not fret … refrain from anger…." (I don't know about you, but some of these instructions for me will require much effort.)

Some of you may be asking, "Is this practical in some way or is this just a trip into "concept land?" (I can imagine people, from the culture that I come from, saying, "I don't care if you milk the cows, or if you milk the cows in God's strength—or if God milks the cows—as long as they get milked.") To such practical people, I would reply that the "both/and" perspective works better as human circumstances get tougher. (Is there a better test for practicality than that?) I draw my example from the writings of Dietrich Bonhoeffer, who knew something about being in tough circumstances. (This quote is taken from *Letters and Papers from Prison*.)

"Responsibility implies tension between obedience and freedom…. The man of responsibility stands between obligation and freedom: he must dare to act under obligation and in freedom; yet he finds his justification neither in his obligation nor in his freedom but solely in Him who has put him in this (humanly impossible) situation and who requires this deed of him. The responsible man delivers up himself and his deed to God."[39]

As I have worked to "add to my faith …" and as I have trusted Him (which is also a developmental process because—as He has demonstrated His faithfulness to me—I have been able to trust Him in a deeper and a more comprehensive way), I have come to realize that this dynamic is the crucible in which my relationship with Him is developed. As I have said elsewhere, God is into relationships; these dual processes facilitate relationship growth.

As you consider this way of doing responsibility, you may discover that your preference for one theme (and your distaste for the other theme) is rooted in a personal advantage that you can see flowing out of that preference. For example, you may be emphasizing the "my effort" theme (and deemphasizing the "God's power" theme) because you want your will (not God's) to be done, and you don't want God messing with your plan for your life. For another example, you may be emphasizing the "God's power" theme (and deemphasizing the "my effort" theme) because you want to be looked after, you want to be the perpetual child who gets perpetually carried around and who never has to experience the pain of learning how to walk (which includes falling down). I'm not sure that God, being a good parent (who has our growth as a priority), will cooperate with such "songs and dances," but He certainly gives us the freedom to evaluate such theology (by allowing us to sow it in our life and discover what fruit it produces).

The following questions will (hopefully) help you to specify your next steps in relation to doing responsibility.

NEXT STEPS

My contention, in this section, is that you need to be thinking and doing "both/and"—as it relates to the scriptural themes of "my effort" and "God's power."

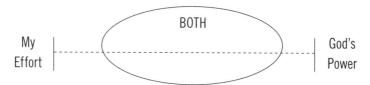

(a) Identify your present practice regarding responsibility by placing an "x" on the (above) continuum. For example, if your present practice has a much larger emphasis on trusting God's power than it does on exercising personal effort, you would place your "x" toward the right end of the continuum.

(b) If your "x" was placed within the "Both" circle, congratulations! (since your walk involves both themes).

(c) If your "x" was placed outside the "Both" circle (toward either end), make a list (below) of what you will say to yourself and will do so that you are moving your way of doing responsibility toward (and into) the circle. For example, if your "x" was placed toward the "my effort" end of the continuum, one thing that you might put on your list (of things to say to yourself) could be:

- "I am not sufficient for all of life's circumstances; I must invite God into the process …. Lord, please come …"

One thing that you might put on your list (of things to do) could be:

- Write a letter to God, claiming Hebrews 4:14–16

For (another) example, if your "x" was placed toward the "God's power" end of the continuum, one thing that you might put on your list (of things to say to yourself) could be:

- "God expects me to walk in obedience, to keep in step with the Spirit. He expects me to do the walking. He isn't going to carry me."

One thing that you might put on your list (of things to do) could be:

- "Make a list of next steps that I need to take in order to accomplish 'y' ['y' being something that you're sure God wants you to do]."Prioritize those steps, putting a "1" beside the first thing to do, a "2" beside the next thing to do, and so on …

Your List

❏ To say to self
❏ To do   (1) _____

❏ To say to self
❏ To do   (2) _____

❏ To say to self
❏ To do   (3) _____

❏ To say to self
❏ To do   (4) ____   _____

❏ To say to self
❏ To do   (5) _____

❏ To say to self
❏ To do   (6) _____

(Have at least two "to say to self" boxes checked and at least two "to do" boxes checked.)

Appendix B

INFORMATION AND EXERCISES FOR ENHANCING MY RELATIONSHIP WITH MYSELF

I have talked about the importance that I put upon my relationship with myself in the text of this module (pages 225–235). Here is a brief summary of the points that I attempted to make:

– We treat ourselves as we have been treated by the significant others in our life.

– We can change that "programming."

– The best relationship to model, in order to acquire a constructive training program, is our relationship with our heavenly Father.

– As we learn to treat ourself in the same ways that God treats us, we facilitate our growth (toward becoming who He created us to be).

I have also talked about the importance of walking in forgiveness toward myself (as well as toward others) in the introduction of this book (pages 12–20) and in the text of this module (pages 232–234). A procedure to follow—in order to establish forgiveness toward myself—is outlined in the "Forgiveness" section of appendix A of this chapter (see #3 of "Next Steps," called "Doing Personal or Self-Directed Forgiveness," pages 316–319).

In this appendix, I will outline the exercises that will (hopefully) help you to develop an ongoingly constructive and nourishing relationship with yourself (which is an often overlooked relationship on our journey toward wholeness).

Basically there are three ways that a person can relate to him/herself:

1. You can be against yourself.
2. You can be conditionally for yourself.
3. You can be unconditionally for yourself.

These categories are not discrete and specific; they are ranges of response toward self. So, if you usually speak and act toward yourself in a negative and critical or pain-producing way, you are in the "against yourself" category. If you usually speak and act toward yourself in a positive or supportive or pain-reducing way, you are in the "conditionally for yourself" category. If you speak and act toward yourself in a positive or supportive or pain-reducing way no matter what circumstances you are facing, you are in the "unconditionally for yourself" category. As I see it, our journey toward whole-ness needs to involve moving toward treating ourself with unconditional support (as our heavenly Father does). For those of you who see such a goal as disguised perfectionism, I would say that if I don't (proactively) always treat myself supportively, but always (reme-dially) clean up any "mess" that I make toward myself, I am (still) walking in uncondi-tional self-support (since no condition or circumstance is keeping me on "messy" terms with myself).

If you are walking in "against yourself" mode, then you are putting/keeping yourself in pain (since you keep "shooting yourself in the foot" during life's race). Many people in this mode talk about the "relentless internal critic" who sits in judgment on all that they do and on all that they are. Consequently, such people are also walking with anxiety or depression or guilt or rage or discouragement or … (and these aren't pleasant fellow travel-ers). Many people continue to listen to this critic because this, for them, is the normal state of affairs (such programming having been taught to them by a "significant other" early in this victim's life) and because they believe that such interaction "drives" them to get things done. In fact, such interaction creates a toxic internal environment, pushes these victims to find some kind of painkiller and contributes to these people limping through life—unable to run to the speed that they would be (otherwise) capable of. When such people decide to be "for" themselves and to begin to reprogram themselves accordingly, they begin to de-velop a nourishing internal environment, begin to find their painkillers of choice to be less necessary, and begin to glimpse the joy of pain-free running.

If you are walking in "conditionally for yourself" mode, then you are being a "fair-weather friend" toward yourself. (A "fair-weather friend" is someone who is with and for you as long as things are going well—in other words, as long as the weather is pleasant. If, however, things in relation to you are not going well—in other words, if relational storms come—the person does not sustain his/her stance of being with and for you.) Similarly, if things are going well with yourself—you are meeting your expectations of yourself and your life circumstances are pleasant—then your self talk will be positive. If, however, you aren't meeting your self-expectations and/or your life circumstances become unpleasant, you don't sustain your self-support but, rather, become critical of yourself. Consequently, you will (periodically) walk with anxiety or depression or guilt or rage or discouragement or…. When you decide to be unconditionally for yourself and to begin to reprogram your-self accordingly, you will find yourself running with different fellow-travelers—peace and joy and hope and encouragement and….

If you are walking in "unconditionally for yourself" mode, then you are being a "trusted friend" or "confidant" toward yourself. (A "trusted friend" or "confidant" is someone who can be trusted to be with and for you whether or not things are going well between you. In other words, their stance—to be with and for you—does not depend on circumstances.) Such people will not be able to carry out this commitment perfectly—as God does. But when they revert to being against you (even for a moment), they will take responsibility for this relationship breach, will change their behavior (back to being with and for you), and will do what it takes to repair that breach. By doing so, they (again) prove that they can be trusted unconditionally to be a constructive fellow traveler. Similarly, as you walk in "unconditionally for yourself" mode, you will treat yourself as a trusted friend or confidant no matter what the circumstance and, when you get against yourself, you will do what it takes to clean up that relational "mess." So, for instance, let's suppose that you are walking in this mode but—in a moment of mindlessness—you do something that reverts you back to being critical of yourself and (in that mode), you call yourself a name, like "stupid." The remediation program (for getting back to being a confidant toward yourself) includes these steps (although the content of these steps could vary widely):

(i)   Acknowledge what you've done, by saying (something like): "What I did was "stupid"—in the sense that it goes against my goals and my values— but I am not stupid. Yes, I feel stupid for having done that, but that does not make me stupid."

(ii) Change your approach toward yourself, by saying (something like): "Actually, I am very capable but—like everyone else—I make mistakes. I forgive myself for getting critical with myself. I know that that criticism comes from the (distorted) belief that I should never make a mistake. I get back, right now, to being a trusted friend with myself. I want to resolve my struggles, not make them worse by staying against myself."

(iii) Repair this breach, in your relationship with yourself, by saying (something like):"I will change that old belief—that I should never make a mistake—to 'when I make a mistake, I will clean it up and will learn from it.' I will write down the changes I will make—if these circumstances came up again—so that I will be prepared to handle them more effectively next time. Right now, I apologize to myself for calling myself 'stupid.' I will notice and enjoy the peace and harmony I feel as a result of getting back on my own team."

It is essential to commit yourself to the process of learning how to be a trusted friend with yourself and to staying in that mode. The following exercise helps you to move toward the "trusted friend" mode.

Since goal attainment is strengthened by a commitment to the process of reaching that goal, it is more probable that you will reach the goal of becoming a trusted friend/confidant with yourself if you commit yourself to the process of accomplishing that. One way to do that is to write a letter of intent/commitment. Such a letter can be addressed to yourself or to God. It should focus on the process that you will follow—both preventatively and remedially. The following is a sample letter:

From: myself
To: myself
Sent: (date)
Subject: letter of intent/commitment
      I realize that I haven't been a trusted friend to myself. I have followed my early training program of tolerating myself only as long as I performed acceptably and of criticizing myself when I didn't. Not only has that put me at odds with myself, it has also put me against others (who I treat like I have treated myself). Hurting myself (and others) has not got me where I have wanted to go (toward better performance and better relationships). I have been like a person, walking east, looking for a sunset. Now, I need to turn around and do differently—so I commit myself to becoming a trusted friend to myself. Doing that will look like the following:
- I will direct all frustration/anger *away* from myself (not toward myself). For example, I will run, cycle, chop wood, lift weights. I will not hit my head or my hands on anything.
- I will not call myself any derogatory name. If I do, I will apologize to myself.
- I will ask God to help me become a trusted friend to myself (even if I feel that I shouldn't have to ask for anyone's help).
- I will seek the help of others who have knowledge or skills or attitudes that will help me move toward my goal. Since I believe that "no person is an island," I give myself permission to build bridges.
- I will replace any self talk that isn't encouraging or supportive or hope-producing with self talk that is. For example, "You should have handled that better!" is replaced by "I didn't do that as well as I wanted to …If I were to do that better next time, what would I say/do differently?"

- I will be on the lookout for all destructive self talk. I will write it down when I identify it and will write out what I would say to a trusted friend if he/she was struggling with the same self talk (in order to replace it with something constructive). Since I want to treat myself like a trusted friend, I will take my own advice.

- I will do the F.I.P.P. steps (see pages 12–26 of introduction for elaboration of these steps) whenever needed.

- I will focus less on outcomes and deadlines (which tend to put more pressure on me) and will focus more on the process and on next steps (which tend to put less pressure on me).

- I will make a list of things that nourish me for each of the following dimensions of my life—spiritual, cognitive, emotional, physical, relational—and will attempt to do one thing from that list, daily, for each of these dimensions. (And, since I want to practice taking pressure off myself, I will be kind and patient and gentle with myself when I don't accomplish this goal.) Conversely, when I notice anything that I am doing (in any of these aspects of my life) that is destructive or "against me," I will stop doing it and will plan how to do it, next time, in a way that is nourishing.

- I will, when I face a situation that I am not sure how to handle, ask myself:

  (a) "What would I say to a trusted friend who is going through this same situation?" (Then, take my own advice.)

  (b) "Who could I talk to, so that I can benefit from their knowledge or experience or expertise?" (Then, evaluate what I am given, use what fits. I will make sure to ask a trusted friend, if possible, or at least someone who is not against me.)

- I will check out (and use, when appropriate) what others have written, about this journey (for example, *The Self-Esteem Workbook*—Schiraldi).[40]

As you write your letter, use any of the above points if they are "a fit" for you. Add any other point that will help to clarify or "flesh out" your next steps.

The previous exercise was designed to get you to "unconditionally for yourself" mode. The following exercises are designed to help you to stay in "unconditionally for yourself" mode. These exercises are categorized into (1) exercises that develop a nourishing internal reality and (2) exercises that develop a nourishing external reality. In practice, you will notice that both dimensions are involved (so this categorization is more about what dimension is emphasized).

Exercises that emphasize our internal dimension

This exercise (adapted from Schiraldi, 2001) is for the purpose of disarming beliefs that will (otherwise) shoot our unconditional self-support. At other places in this book (module IV pages 228–230; module III, appendix G), I have talked about and demonstrated the "two-column" strategy for detoxifying self talk. We will use that same strategy here but with different content. The following are examples of this application:

BELIEF THAT IS TOXIC TO SELF-SUPPORT	REVISED BELIEF: THAT IS COMPATIBLE WITH SELF-SUPPORT
(a) I must be loved or approved of by everyone that I consider significant.	(a) I want to be loved or approved of by people, and I will act in a manner—kind, gentle, patient, respectful—that will make that more likely. It is inevitable, however, that some people (for their own reasons) will not like or accept me. This is difficult for me but not the "end of the world." I didn't "cause" this, and I can't "cure" it. My self-esteem doesn't (and can't) depend on the attitudes or actions of others. I will like and support myself whether or not others do.
(b) I must be thoroughly competent and adequate in everything I do. I should not be satisfied with myself unless I'm the best or am excelling.	(b) I will strive to do my best rather than to be the best. I can enjoy doing things even if I'm not particularly good at them. I will learn to try things where I might "fail." (In fact, I only "fail" if I quit or I don't learn something. Otherwise, I will call such circumstances "not getting the result that I want, yet.") When I try and don't get the results that I want, that doesn't mean that I am an incompetent person. It does mean that I have identified a "growing edge" in my life, and I will work to handle that situation better next time (in light of what I learned this time). It may feel risky to try new things (where I have no experience), but I am courageous enough to "step out" here. I know that doing this is a necessity if I am going to grow and to grasp life's opportunities.

Below is a list of other beliefs that could move you out of "unconditional self-support" mode. In order to disarm any of these beliefs (that are sniping at you), do the following steps:

    i. Circle the number of any belief that you are presently holding onto.

   ii. Using the "two-column" strategy, dispute each of these beliefs. (If you need to upgrade your rebuttal of any of these beliefs, you may want to talk to a trusted friend or mental health professional in order to get their feedback.)

  iii. Use this same strategy to challenge any additional beliefs that get exposed in this process.

Notice how many of these beliefs make an external condition a requirement for being on good terms with yourself.

1. It's wrong to think well of myself.
2. I can't feel worthwhile unless a certain condition is met.
3. I'm entitled to happiness (or success, health, self-respect, pleasure, love) without having to work for it.
4. One day when I make it, I'll have friends and be able to enjoy myself.
5. Work should be hard and in some way unpleasant.
6. Joy is *only* gained from hard work.
7. I am inadequate … (or) incompetent … (or) ugly … (or) _____.
8. Worrying insures that I'll be prepared to face and solve problems. So, the more I worry the better. (Constant worrying helps prevent future mistakes and problems and gives me extra control.)
9. Life should be easy. I can't enjoy it if there are problems.
10. The past makes me unhappy. There's no way around it.
11. There's a perfect solution, and I must find it.
12. If people disapprove (reject, criticize, mistreat) of me, it means I'm inferior, wrong, or no good.
13. I'm only as good as the work I do. If I'm not productive, I'm no good.
14. If I try hard enough, all people will like me.
15. If I try hard enough, my future will be happy and trouble free.
16. Life must be fair.
17. I have messed up, so I deserve to be hard on myself.
18. I can't accept myself unless (condition) _____.
19. If I approve of myself, I will quit striving…

This exercise (adapted from Schiraldi, 2001) is for the purpose of developing and strengthening the kind of beliefs that will help you to stay in "unconditional self-support" mode. (A house divided against itself will fall; this is a way to strengthen the foundations.)

Your involvement in this exercise is as follows:

(i)   Sit in a quiet place, well supported in a chair, where you will be comfortable for about twenty minutes.

(ii)   Close your eyes. Take two deep breaths and relax your body as deeply and as completely as possible. Prepare yourself for, and expect, a pleasant experience. If desired, add the other steps to this process that I outlined on pages 84–87 of the module called "Paying Attention to the Holy Spirit's Input."

(iii)   Open your eyes long enough to read the first statement (below). Then close your eyes and *concentrate* on that statement. Repeat it to yourself three times slowly, allowing yourself to feel as though that statement was very relevant to you. You might wish to imagine yourself in a situation where you are actually receiving and evaluating that statement. Use all your senses to experience the situation.

(iv)   Spend more time/focus on any statement that you sense applies to you. Don't allow negative or pessimistic thoughts to distract you or undermine your progress. Accept whatever actually happens, without demanding perfection. See this as practice time, as a planting time that prepares you for good things (like inner harmony) to come.

(v)   Repeat step (iii) for each statement listed.

(vi)   Repeat this activity each day for six days.

(vii)   Each day, after doing this activity, notice how you feel. Many people notice that with practice the thoughts begin to feel more and more comfortable, becoming like trusted friends.

The statements to focus/meditate on are as follows:

1. I think well of myself. It is good to view and treat myself as God does.

2. I accept myself because I realize that I am more than my foibles, mistakes, or any other externals.

3. Criticism can be helpful. I examine it for ways to improve, without concluding that the criticism makes me less worthwhile as a person.

4. I can evaluate my own behavior without questioning my worth as a human being.

5. I notice and enjoy each sign of achievement or progress, no matter how insignificant it may seem to myself or others; every step of growth is a worthwhile step.

6. I notice and enjoy each sign of achievement or progress that others make, without concluding they are more valuable than I am as a person. To compare the progress of others with my progress is like comparing apples and oranges.

7. I am generally capable of living well, and of applying the time, effort, patience, training, and assistance needed to do so. As I recognize my need to take "next steps" in the process of living well, I will take these steps. I will (ongoingly) ask God to help me.

8. I expect others to like and respect me. If they don't, that can be difficult, but they have a right to relate to me as they choose. I, also, have a right to respond—in a way that is constructive and appropriate (for all involved).

9. I can usually earn people's trust and affection through sincere and respectful treatment. If not, that's okay.

10. I generally show sound judgment in relationships and work; I'll keep refining these skills.

11. I can influence others by my well-reasoned viewpoints, which I can present and defend effectively; I'll keep refining these skills.

12. I like to help others to enjoy themselves and to grow.

13. I enjoy new challenges and don't get upset when things don't go well right off the bat.

14. The work I do is generally good quality, and I expect to do many worthwhile things in the future, with God's help.

15. I am aware of my strengths and respect them and am thankful for them.

16. I can laugh at some of the ridiculous things I do sometimes; I am laughing with myself not against myself.

17. I can make a difference in people's lives by what I contribute; I will ask God to help me.

18. I enjoy making others feel happier and glad for time we share.

19. I consider myself a valuable and worthwhile person; I am made by God—He doesn't make junk.

20. I like being a one-of-a-kind portrait. I'm glad to be unique.

21. I like myself whether or not I compare myself with others and whether or not others compare themselves with me.

22. I feel stable and secure inside because I rightly regard my worth.

23. Others: _____

    _____

    _____

    _____

This exercise—called "Changing Channels"—is a variation of the "Two Column" strategy. Here, we use this strategy to deal with toxic self talk that occurs at the statement (not belief) level (although beliefs are implied in these statements).

Your instructions, for doing this exercise, are as follows:

- When you notice yourself thinking or making (demeaning and degrading) comments (examples of which are below), immediately tell yourself, "Stop!." (Say that word to yourself patiently and kindly and clearly; say this to yourself as you would to a trusted friend.)
- (Then) "change channels." Changing channels means thinking and speaking about yourself respectfully—in ways that demonstrate self-support and encourage personal growth.
- (After changing channels), notice and identify the emotional shift that occurs when you change channels.

TOXIC SELF TALK	STOP!	NEW CHANNEL
(1) I'm only/just a _____ (teacher, nurse, etc.).		(1) I am a _____ (teacher, nurse, etc.). I have chosen this work, and I see value in doing it. I find satisfaction in being a _____. I am looking to learn and grow and advance as a _____.
(2) I'll never succeed.		(2) Right now, I don't feel like I will succeed, but I know that if I stay on course and keep my feet moving, I will be moving closer to where I want to arrive. Right now, what is a next step that I could take on this journey?
(3) If only I'd _____.		(3) Next time, I'll _____.

(4)	I hate this about me!	(4)	What an interesting quirk. I'm going to work on this until I feel more comfortable with this. I'll feel better about myself as I notice progress in my way of dealing with this.
(5)	I'll probably blow this.	(5)	I might blow this and I might not; if I do, it still doesn't reflect on my worth as a person—that makes it easier to give it a try …
(6)	I'm fat.	(6)	I have extra weight. I am working on losing that extra weight.

- Using this "Two Column" format, record each instance of toxic self talk that you catch yourself making over the next seven days.
- Then (in the New Channel column) replace each piece of toxic self talk with encouraging self-support statements. (If you need to upgrade the quality of what you say to yourself, you may want to talk to a trusted friend or mental health professional—live or on-line—to get his/her feedback.)
- Each time you identify a piece of toxic self talk, say you yourself (something like), "I'm glad that I got that stumbling block into the light," rather than, "What an idiot I've been for carrying that around for years!"

The commitment to nourish yourself is a decision that you make every day; doing this exercise is a practical way to live out that commitment.

Previous exercises focused on detoxifying beliefs and statements that had been learned (and so are part of your software). *This next exercise (adapted from Schiraldi, 2001) is focused on giving you a tool for staying self-supportive when someone delivers toxic waste to your door and is looking for you to agree to be a "dump site."* (In the computer analogy, this would be more like a virus.)

We want to be able to acknowledge and respond to unpleasant circumstances (even some of our own making) without condemning our (essential) selves. People who are less skilled at staying self-supportive tend to use the "Because … therefore" thought construction. For example, "Because of (some circumstance), therefore I am no good as a person." Obviously, this kind of thought will move you out of self-support mode. In contrast to the "Because … therefore" thought construction, the following construction provides a realistic, positive, and immediate response to invitations (that we all get) to move out of self-support mode. It is the "Even though … nevertheless" thought construction. This construction allows you to acknowledge negative circumstances or behaviors or skill applications, while separating those externals from your worth as a person. It looks like this:

Even though _____nevertheless _____

        (some condition or   (some statement of worth—stated

        circumstance)   or implied)

For example:

"Even though I botched that project, I am nevertheless a worthwhile person."

        (performance)   (explicit statement of worth)

If you are like I am, it is easy to conceive of a work situation in which it may not be appropriate to be explicit about both parts of the previous example. (Your boss, for instance, may be interested in your performance and wants you to improve it, but he/she may not be interested in hearing about your personal efforts to remain self-supportive.) In this situation, therefore, you can modify the "Even though … nevertheless" construction as follows:

"Even though I botched that project …

    (a) To boss …   "nevertheless I will do what I can to clean it up."

                     (explicit statement of improving performance)

    (b) To self …   "nevertheless I'm still a worthwhile person."

                     (implicit statement of personal worth)

The next part of this exercise is for the purpose of giving you practice at using the "Even though … nevertheless" thought construction when faced by someone saying negative things to you:

- Get a partner.
- After explaining this exercise to him/her, ask him/her to say negative things to you (without regard to whether he/she considers them to be true). If needed, show your partner the following list, to choose from:
    - You really blew it!
    - What is wrong with your face …?

- You bug me!
- Will you never figure it out?
- I think you are wrong …!
- You are just dumb …!

• Formulate your response within the "Even though … nevertheless" construction. For example, if someone calls you "dumb," you could respond by saying "Even though I behave in a dumb way sometimes, nevertheless …"

• Here are guidelines as you practice:
- Vary the construction, sometimes making an explicit statement of worth, sometimes explicitly focusing on the criticism and making an implicit statement of worth. You can use the "Even though … nevertheless" construction without using these specific words.
- Use humor, if feasible, to lighten the situation.
- If you haven't a partner available, practice your response to each of the criticisms on the list. If you can't quickly think of an "even though … nevertheless" response to one of those criticisms, design a response by writing it out (so it is at your mental fingertips, for future availability).
- Remember something that you found challenging to your self-support when it was said to you (in the past). Design a response to that input so you have a way of staying self-supportive (but not necessarily out of pain) if it was said again.

It is helpful to evaluate your own behavior as long as you do it from the role of "coach"—someone who is helping you to improve your skills. If you do it from the role of "critic"—someone who is not on your team and who is trying to "break you down," it is not profitable. You don't evaluate who you are, as a person; instead, you accept and value yourself because God has made you, and He accepts and values you. In other words, you choose to accept His evaluation of you.

The next part of this exercise is for the purpose of giving you practice—in the flow of daily life—at staying self-supportive.

• For the next seven days, be on the look-out for any events—verbal or otherwise—that might knock you off your self-support horse. When you experience such an event, use the following format to manage that event (so that you can keep riding). Keeping a written record can be helpful to (a) heighten the clarity of your response and (b) identify your areas of vulnerability.

DESCRIPTION OF EVENT/ SITUATION	"EVEN THOUGH … NEVERTHELESS" STATEMENT USED	EFFECT - ON HOW YOU FEEL - ON YOUR BEHAVIOR
(1)		

This exercise makes explicit a commitment that the experts on self-support make with themselves. This commitment flows out of the truth that, even when a situation can't be changed, your mental frame of reference can. To illustrate this point, let me ask you the following questions (adapted from Borysenko, 2001):[41]

- Is your busy day a nightmare, or is it evidence that your business is thriving?
- Is your assertive two-year-old a monster-in-the-making, or does she just have a mind of her own?
- Is a traffic jam so annoying that you need to lean on the horn and yell, or can it be a time to relax, breathe, and listen to a CD?
- Is the dirt in the front hall a reason to whine, or is it just part of having a dog with large, muddy paws that loves you dearly?

The content of this commitment is that every interpretation that is made is designed to protect the interpreter's relationship with him/herself, every frame that is put around a circumstance is chosen to maintain or enhance self-support. (Since we get to choose from the various interpretations of any event, I am suggesting that the choice we make include the criterion of self-support.) Recently, I had a conversation (with one of my clients) that illustrated what I am asking you to consider. This client is a very intense, driven, angry, capable woman ("Type A" would be a summary description). As she talked to me about what she was discovering about herself, I could see and sense her frustration rising. She said (something like) "…When I reacted this way … I was left with this mess … I just hate that about myself!" In response I said, "It sounds like, when you notice how you are handling some situations, you immediately judge your performance." (Her response to my comment was the non-verbal equivalent to, "Now, that's about as helpful as a rubber crutch!") So, I hastened to add, "You are making real progress at noticing your family-of-origin programming. But, instead of acknowledging that progress, you are hard on yourself for having that programming in your life—programming you didn't even put there. When are you going to start to be reasonable with yourself—by acknowledging progress and also acknowledging that you are not responsible for having that old training, just for changing it—which you are already on the way to doing?" (Yes, that sounds quite pushy; it was my attempt to match strength with strength, in the context of our [positive] working relationship.)

She was able to hear me; I hope that you are also understanding what I am saying—about always being able to choose the glasses that we look at our circumstances through (and having those glasses tinted for self-support).

In order to practice your application of that (self-support) commitment, I'd suggest the following steps:

    i.   Identify any interpretation you make—of any circumstance in your life—that states (or implies) that you are against yourself. That could include being critical of yourself, judgmental of yourself, angry with yourself, unkind to yourself …

    ii. Design a new interpretation of that circumstance so that you will be able to maintain self-support. (When you do this, you not only get on better terms with yourself, you also challenge the belief that there is only one "right" way to look at an event—usually the way that you have been taught in childhood.)

When we look at … interpret … resond to any life circumstance in ways that maintain self-support, we have learned how to be unconditionally self-supportive. If this seems new/strange, it may seem less so if we think about it as it relates to our relationship with God—where we try to live every circumstance of our life in a way that maintains or enhances our relationship with Him. When we don't do that preventatively (by obedience), we can do that remedially (by confession … repentance … restitution). I'm suggesting that we apply that same thinking to our relationship with ourself.

One well-traveled road that leads to inner peace and well-being (essential to developing a nourishing internal life and to walking in self-support) is identified by the road sign "GRATITUDE." In Robert Emmons and Joanna Hill's book, *Words of Gratitude*, they quote (in the introduction) the following from David Steindl-Rast:

> "A Chinese proverb popped into my mind the moment I read the opening question of this book, 'What is gratitude?' The proverb answers: When you drink from a stream, remember the spring. Remember! Be mindful! Think! Thinking and thanking spring from the same root—in the realm of language as well as in the soul realm. Only

the thoughtful are thankful. Our proverb caught it all in one image: remembering the source as we drink from the stream; this is gratitude."[42]

This quote helps us to see contrasting views of gratitude (both of which promote thinking). The Buddhist view of gratitude emphasizes the process of moving toward the place of total peace, the cessation of all thought, where the drinker and the stream are one (and all the functions and experiences that we have seen as evidence of being a "self" are transcended). The Christian view of gratitude emphasizes that, when we drink (or do any nourishing thing), we are also nourished if we start a dialogue with the Creator of all nourishing things by saying to Him, "Thank You!" The peace and well-being (thus) arrived at is truly relational—since there is really Someone there (other than ourself) to hear us. This dialogue grows a relationship that is not transcended—even through eternity—but is just deepened. As a person who has put his faith eggs in the Christian basket, the following quote (from Thomas Merton) deepens my understanding of gratitude:

> To be grateful is to recognize the Love of God
> in everything He has given us—and He has given
> us everything. Every breath we draw is a gift of His love,
> every moment of existence is a grace, for it brings with it
> immense graces from Him. Gratitude therefore takes
> nothing for granted, is never unresponsive, is constantly
> awakening to new wonder and to praise the goodness
> of God. For the grateful person knows that God is good,
> not by hearsay but by experience. And that is
> what makes all the difference.[43]

Dimensions of gratitude are looked at, in the following quote from Emmons and Hill:

> Gratitude is a sense of thankfulness and joy in response to receiving a gift—
> whether the gift be deserved or not, whether it is a concrete object or an abstract
> gesture of kindness. Gratitude can be a moment of at-oneness that is evoked in the
> presence of natural beauty or in the silence of the soul, a moment when the world—
> with both its abundance and its challenges—makes perfect sense, when its gifts can be
> seen and appreciated in whatever wrappings they come in.

Gratitude can also be a conscious, rational choice to focus on life's blessings rather than on its shortcomings; it can be developed into a spiritual practice to create a positive outlook on life. It is a feeling, a moral attribute, a virtue, a mystical experience, and a conscious act, all in one. Gratitude is a universal human experience that can be either a random occurrence of grace or an attitude chosen to create a better life.[44]

The exercise that I suggest for developing the "attitude of gratitude" is found in Joan Borysenko's book, *Inner Peace for Busy People*. She says:

> This week when you find yourself awfulizing, try focusing on gratitude for all the things that are right. Years ago, I learned an exercise from the Benedictine monk, Brother David Steindl-Rast, author of the beautiful book, *Gratefulness, The Heart of Prayer*. He suggested that every night before bed, you say thanks for something that you've never thought about being grateful for before. It's easy for the first few weeks, but then you really have to think to come up with something new. If you continue the exercise (which takes almost no time, you'll be happy to realize) for a few months, you'll begin noticing things to be grateful for throughout the day, knowing that you'll need something new to be thankful for that night. This simple exercise makes you mindful and has the power to change your life.[45]

This exercise (adapted from Schialdi, 2001) is for the purpose of experiencing yourself in "unconditionally for yourself" mode. The steps of this exercise are as follows:

i. Find a quiet place to relax undisturbed—either lying or seated—for about ten minutes.

ii. Once you have settled in, visualize yourself sitting in the presence of a very trusted and very loving being—a confidant, a loving family member or God. (No matter who you see yourself involved with—if it isn't God—remember that the love you experience is a reflection of God's love toward you.) This being sees you realistically and very lovingly. Begin to see yourself through this being's eyes—the eyes of love.

iii. As you begin to see yourself through the eyes of love, notice what there is to appreciate. Look carefully and thoroughly.
   – Is there something pleasing or attractive physically?
   – Notice all the pleasing personality or character traits such as intelligence, brightness, insightfulness, laughter, humor, integrity, peacefulness, good taste, or patience.

- Recognize all talents and skills.
- Note the appearance beyond pure physical attributes, such as the countenance, expression, or smile.

iv. As you behold yourself through the eyes of love and appreciation, enjoy that experience for a few minutes.

v. Then, as you leave that connection, notice the feelings (of love and appreciation and …). Continue to feel warm, happy, at ease, secure.

vi. Say to yourself, "I am blessed to experience this love," and notice those feelings (of love and appreciation and…) growing inside you.

Exercises that emphasize our external dimension

Being on good terms with yourself will lead to changes of behavior and to the development of structures that reflect that good relationship. In turn, those behaviors and structures will sustain that relationship. Such circular causality (as graphically represented here) is characteristic of all relationships.

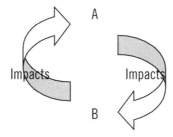

The following exercises emphasize the behaviors and the structures that flow out of unconditional self-support.

After you have made your inside environment a safe and nourishing place, having a place in your outside environment—sometimes called a "refuge"—that is safe and nourishing can be vital to maintaining your health and well-being. About such a place, Borysenko (2001) says:"A refuge … can be a powerful part of your self-care strategy. It's a warm and welcoming place where the demands of life recede and stillness takes over. Like the eye of a hurricane, your refuge space is perpetually calm. When it's filled with meaningful items that bring back memories and associations that are peaceful or sacred, just sitting there is a balm for the soul."[46]

Both my wife and I have a refuge. In our house, Verlyn has what she calls her "prayer corner." It is just a corner of our computer room but it has many objects of comfort and significance in it. For instance, the centerpiece of that corner is a rocking chair. On one side of that chair is a tape/CD player and various music tapes and CDs (highly significant to her, since she teaches music and sings in a choir). Beside the CD player is a night table, on which are family pictures, a teapot, and cup (in her favorite color) and a candle (which she lights during prayer times). On the other side of the chair is a book shelf (from her grandmother) full of books and projects and her prayer journal. (For her, reading and journaling are ways to nourish her inside life.) On the ledge that runs under the window are other objects and pictures. On the walls of that corner are pictures that have "spoken" to her, including one of a pathway that she found and loved while we were in England.

My refuge—located in the basement of our house—is as different from Verlyn's refuge as I am from her. My refuge consists of two adjoining rooms. One room is a study, with all the walls covered by books and with various piles of books, slowly moving toward the ceiling. (To me, books are friends; I try to surround myself with them.) A narrow path through that room leads to a desk (that I have had for all my professional life) piled on and around with signs, projects, souvenirs, and reminders. For example, above a bookshelf on the right-hand side of my desk, is a picture of Jesus knocking at a door; it reminds me of my need to keep inviting Him into the decisions of my life. (Some people suggest that refuges be free of clutter; I suggest wall-to-wall clutter—making the point that designing your refuge to fit you is essential.) The other room contains a T.V. (another "no-no" for some people), a treadmill, weight training equipment, and a reclining chair. Since exercising is crucial to my well-being, I have equipment available day or night (which, given my biorhythms, means late at night). Television is a good companion for my cardio/weight-training/stretching routines. The recliner serves various purposes—catnapping; relaxation practice; and watching (selected) movies, training tapes, or programs (like sporting events). For me, television can be a waste of time if I slide from "selected" watching to "unselected" watching (especially since I have trained myself to "do" curiosity) but, on the whole, its "pros" outweigh its "cons," so (for now) it stays. I have given myself permission to continue to change this environment as needs and/or circumstances change, so my refuge (like my life) is in flux.

If you don't have such a refuge, I'd suggest that you create one. It doesn't have to be big or complicated, just personally designed and useable. For some people, it will be a place to retreat from the flow of life; for others (like me) it is a place to retreat for nourishment and to design my game-plan for the challenges of the next day. Your design of this refuge will need to fit the purpose that fits you; each object in that place should promote that purpose. Often, this becomes the place (especially if you are introverted) where the core work of your life gets done.

A refuge may be the place in which you design your self-care plan. That plan is most effective when it focuses less on managing life and focuses more on managing yourself. Most of us have been taught about how to manage tasks; what I'm suggesting is that we also focus on managing and preparing ourself for doing these tasks. As we do this, we will be more grounded and balanced and clear about priorities, as we take on those tasks.

We all have to carve out time for the meaningful things that help us to stay centered. Some people cut out such things in the name of busyness. But if you don't take care of yourself, no one else will do it for you. Without boundaries, the tasks and the people in your life will swamp you. It's up to you to choose those things that will keep you centered—even when they appear to make life busier. I have said to people that I work with (and to myself), "If you are so busy driving your vehicle down the road—carrying work and family and commitments to their destination—that you don't give yourself permission to stop at the gas station once in a while, it is only a matter of time before you are stranded somewhere, unable to carry others or yourself. So, what may feel like a waste of time (stopping the journey in order to get gas), will prove to be a real time saver." The same is true for those "stops" that put nourishment and energy in your life.

Borysenko (2001) says the following about these considerations and suggests an *exercise* that I agree with: "This week, review your priorities. If self-care is not one of them, think of an activity that you would really enjoy and add it to your to-do list. This may seem like it will make you even busier, but the truth is that it will actually generate more productive time. Feeding your soul with the things you love creates happiness and gives you energy. Taking the time to enjoy life is one of the most important secrets of busy people with inner peace."[47]

And, when you are on the journey of doing your to-do list, you need a "gas gauge" for monitoring what you have—at this moment—in your tank. One simple and elegant way to do that is to draw a line on a sheet of paper. On the left end of the line put a "1" (with the word "empty" under it); on the right end of the line put a "10" (with the word "full" under it)—as below:

    1 _____ 10
    (Empty)   (Full)

Then, ask yourself this question, "Right now, where am I on this scale?" ("Empty" means tired, low energy, achy muscles, everything feeling like a task, low concentration, in survival mode, and the like; "Full" means high energy, refreshed, joyful, creative, focused, in growth mode, and the like.) Put a mark on this line that (graphically) indicates how full your tank is (where "2" is "almost empty," "4" is "some gas," "6" is "quite a bit of gas," and "8" is "lots of gas")—as below:

			where you are		
1	2	4 ⟵ ⏐ ⟶	6	8	10
(empty)	(almost empty)	(some gas)	(quite a bit of gas)	(lots of gas)	(full)

This "gas gauge" is a tool for helping you to take care of yourself. As you ask the "Right now …" question, it allows you to take a step back from the tasks and to pay attention inside. As you answer that question, you have new awareness of whether or not you need gas, right now. (And, as we know, awareness is a prerequisite for change.) This question can be asked, on paper or in your head, several times a day, as needed.

As you gather this data over a few days, you will discover that there is a "cut-off" number (unique to you), above which you cruise down the road but below which you begin to feel the engine sputter. This number (when you take a reading) tells you when to begin to look for a "gas station". In my truck, a light comes on in my dashboard when the gas in my tank has drained to a certain level; we are talking here about how to install such an "early warning signal" in your life. When your energy has drained to your "cut-off" number, a red light—indicating "stop" … "pay attention" … "get gas"—needs to come on, inside. There are two ways to get gas: (1) doing the immediate things that "put gas in your tank" and (2) developing life-style strategies that both preserve and restore gas. The short-term list (which to some extent, will be unique to each of us) could include stretching, taking a walk, doing a different task, adjusting your breathing, talking to a friend, taking a shower, pulling a card from your fun deck, or (a favorite of mine) playing with your pet (especially with an eighty-pound black lab whose mission statement includes getting pack members to play). If you have looked at the module on "Learning from My Stressors," you may have noticed, under the heading of short-term strategies for building up my general health, other items on my list.

The long-term strategies (which, again, have to be tailored to your unique needs) will include items that nourish you physically (for example, exercising), emotionally (for example, holidaying with a trusted friend), cognitively (for example, taking a course on …), spiritually (for example, taking a prayer retreat), and relationally (for example, scheduling a regular coffee time with a trusted friend).

A simple exercise—that could help you to keep track of and manage your gas level—is as follows:

• Use the "gas gauge" (which we talked about) three times a day, to keep track of your gas/energy.

- Identify the "cut-off" point at which you begin to sputter.
- When you reach that "cut-off" point, take action quickly to do what will replenish your gas. Do this by selecting one (or more) option from your short-term list and doing it. Notice what revives you quickly and well (and put a star beside that item).
- Enjoy (again) the "cruise down the road."

I've already quoted Borysenko (2001) in relation to including activities in your life that will bring renewed energy (to balance your energy consumers). Here, I want to quote her (more extensively) in relation to including activities in your life that will enable you to be a human being (not just a "human doing"). She does it this way:

> I must hear the self-help advice: "Secure your own oxygen mask first, before you help anyone requiring your assistance" at least twice a week. It's based on the actual announcement that flight attendants make before take-off, which I also hear about twice a week. And while the phrase is overused as analogies go, the reason for its popularity is that it hits the mark. If you're so busy trying to save the people around you that you black out, all of you are likely to die ... Securing your oxygen mask means different things to different people. Other than your work—even if you love it—what are the things that nourish you and bring out your best self?
>
> In no particular order, mine would include playing golf, skiing, hiking, being with my grown children, intimate conversations with my husband, sex, prayer, mystery novels, inspiring movies, singing, sharing time with friends, massages, laughing, playing word games, romping with our four dogs (Mixer, Sasquatch, Gremlin, and The Squeezirat), sitting by a fire and listening to music, being outside and taking in the silence, dancing, craft projects, cooking for friends, horseback riding, hanging around in my bathrobe until lunchtime reading magazines and staring at the ceiling, yoga, exploring new places, long road trips, foreign cultures, and hot fudge sundaes.
>
> I get to some of the things on the list pretty regularly, others hardly at all. Six months ago, I made a commitment to get a massage every week. It has increased my energy, reduced my stress, and made me feel ten years younger.[48]

Although I can't relate to the huge list of activities that nourish her (maybe because I grew up on a farm—where much of my day was set for me—so I have never focused on discovering a myriad of activities like those), I can relate to the understanding that we sometimes don't give sufficient priority to the "important but not urgent" (to quote from Stephen Covey) activities in our lives—like self-care.

An exercise that will help you to make self-care a functional priority in your life is as follows:

- Make an "oxygen" list.
- Choose something from this list that you would like to make a more regular part of your life. (You'll know what activity has the "richest mix" of oxygen for you by asking yourself, "What activity do I most look forward to doing?")
- Commit yourself to doing it. (That commitment could include making that commitment public or getting rid of the roadblocks to doing it or … For me, that means getting it into my daily planner, my "portable memory"; everything else is just a good intention.)

Another structure that we can put around our life so that self-nourishment is promoted (and self-nourishment is evidence of a person being on good terms with him/ herself) is that of Sabbath. Like me, you may be very familiar with the Judeo-Christian account of creation—where God made the world in six days and, on the seventh, He rested—blessing the day and making it holy. In the commands that He gave Moses on Mount Sinai, He said, "Remember the Sabbath day by keeping it holy. Six days you shall labor and do all your work, but the seventh day is a Sabbath to the Lord your God. On it you shall not do any work …" (Exod. 20:8–10). Obviously, God did not rest on the seventh day because He was tired (The energy Source for the universe does not run out of energy). His rest was more like a celebration of the completion of His creative work, a time to enjoy what was "very good." His directive to us (to keep the Sabbath) may include the purpose of our recovery from the exhaustion of the six previous days of work, but it is also for the purpose of celebration—to give us time to savor and say "thank you" for the good things that He has given us. These good gifts—which all come from Him—encompass all the dimensions of who we are: physical, cognitive, emotional, spiritual, and relational. (So, such gifts include "daily bread" and meaning and security and His Spirit's involvement with us and our relationship with others.)

Because God commanded that the Sabbath be kept holy, people in Jesus' day (and ours) have labored to turn that command into an obligation—a set of rules the enforcement of which they could use to gain power over others. (Indeed, one of the biggest points of conflict between Jesus and the Pharisees was His freedom to do things on the Sabbath—like healing a person—that violated their rules. See, for instance, Mark 3:1–6.) So, it may seem strange to see the Sabbath as a time for celebration, rather than a time for specifying what we can't do. Nevertheless, I am suggesting that it is within the circle of legitimate biblical options to actively nourish yourself on the

Sabbath. (Notice, for instance, what Jesus says about this in Mark 2:23–28.) "What would that look like?" you might ask. (Maybe) you could invite some friends over; (maybe) you could play music or sing or dance (or if you have my talent, you could watch or listen, and enjoy); (maybe) you could have conversations about things of beauty and meaning; (maybe) you could read to the children (or each other) or play games; (maybe) you could take extra time to talk with God; (maybe) you could walk in the country; (maybe) you could celebrate what went right with the previous six days; (maybe) you could savor simple pleasures—like playing with the dog or watching the birds or sitting where you can see the sun do its thing.

Related to the issue of implementing a Sabbath while living in a culture that has never even heard that word, I find what Joan Borysenko (2001) says, to be insightful:

> For years I thought about adopting a weekly Sabbath, but since the majority of my work is done on weekends, it isn't feasible. I might rest, but I might also starve. This is the line between work and rest that many of us walk. So, I went to see a wise and offbeat rabbi. His advice was to take the Sabbath I *could*, not the one that I *couldn't*. Four hours on a Wednesday afternoon might do for a start. The intention to rest—and a reasonable plan that could work—was more important than adhering to the letter of the law.[49]

To keep the spirit of the law (rather than adhering to the letter of the law) can sometimes enable an application of the law to be made with personal relevance and joy. There are various scriptural examples of our Lord doing that (Mark 2:1–12 or Mark 2:23–28 or Mark 3:1–6 or Mark 3:20,31–35 or Matthew 15:1–20 or John 4:1–42 or Luke 7:36–50), so I doubt that He would be upset if you were to "take the Sabbath that you could—not the one that you couldn't."

A personally relevant exercise is that of designing the Sabbath that you can carry out. The parameters of that exercise include:
- Who will it include?
- When can you do it?
- Where can you do it?
- What will it include? (A Sabbath can include an emphasis on your relationship with God or others or yourself; the celebration activities will vary, depending on the emphasis that you choose.)

NEXT STEPS

The following considerations will (hopefully) help you to specify your next steps of application in the area of enhancing your relationship with yourself.

  (1) Looking at the exercises in this appendix, choose those that will be most relevant to your growth. Choose at least one exercise from the internal dimension emphasis and at least one exercise from the external dimension emphasis; list them below:

INTERNAL DIMENSION EMPHASIS: **EXTERNAL DIMENSION EMPHASIS:**

_____   _____

_____   _____

_____   _____

_____   _____

  (2) Within each dimension, put a 1 beside the exercise that it would be valuable to do first; Then, do that exercise.

  (3) Enjoy the journey of (intentionally) deepening your relationship with yourself.

Appendix C

INFORMATION AND EXERCISES FOR MANAGING MY RELATIONSHIPS WITH CONFIDANTS/COMPANIONS

If you would find it helpful to review what I have said about the "Secondary/Vital/ External" relationships that surround our lives, that information is found on pages 236–246 of this module. The pages that speak specifically to the "confidant/companion" level of relationships are 236, 239–240.

Doing relationships is the quintessential "high risk/high reward" activity. This is never more true than with relationships at the "confidant/companion" level, where the depth and vulnerability of relationships is at its deepest. Another way of talking about confidants/ companions is to say that they are the trustworthy and trusted friends whom you have let into the "inner rooms" of your life. These are the people who have, over time, migrated to the place of "treasured closeness" in your life. Often, such people have been called "god-sends"—as Jonathan was for David.

How do you enhance such relationships? Within the context of the model I am using, these relationships are already enhanced. Whatever factors have led to this closeness (such as being on the same team, being in the same church community, being fellow soldiers, sharing the same passion), they have already worked their magic. And, for some people, it feels magical—the acceptance, the synergy, and the rapport generated by such relationships is a magic carpet ride. For some people, the boundaries that usually give personal space and definition can begin to blur; at such times, some people feel like they have merged with this "soul mate"—the world as they know it, changes. At such times, some people have ecstatic feelings, they find it effortless to change and to give themselves to this other person. Obviously, if the relationship is constructive, such experiences produce transformational growth. (Such experiences are the human equivalent of "conversion experiences"—to use that old fashioned term—that some people have had when they first encounter God.) If the relationship is destructive, (for example, if the other person isn't as impacted by the relationship and exploits your vulnerability), it can lead to some of the most excruciating pain known to humankind. In such circumstances, the impacted person can make the mistake of continuing to give everything that he/she is able to (under the influence of the mistaken belief that, if he/she just gives enough, the other person will begin to reciprocate). Some of these people contend that they can not help themselves. When that happens, a danger (while trying to enhance a "confidant/companion" relationship) appears—that of idolatry. Idolatry is the practice of prioritizing any relationship above our relationship with God. By doing so, the "idolater" considers this other relationship to be most important and acts accordingly. By so doing, the idolater has put another "god" in his/her life and is in violation of the first and second commands given by God (Exod. 20). An idol can be anything that replaces our primary allegiance to God (Matt. 6:24). When, however, "confidant/companion" relationships are reciprocal and not idolatrous, the people involved "flower" in ways that give us a glimpse of what the pre-fall world was like (and of what heaven will be like).

How do you *maintain* such relationships? The short answer to that question is "Keep doing the things that enabled this relationship to develop to the depth that it has already reached." If you are serious about having intentional relationships, make a list of – and do – those "things" that move the relationship in the directions you want. It is analogous to cooking: if you, one day, made a wonderful food dish, you would be wise to write down how you did it—both the content (for example, ingredients) and the process (for example, cooking time)—so that you could replicate that dish whenever you want to experience it again. In the same way, if you write down the ingredients and the dynamics that have contributed to this deep relationship, you have a "recipe" for maintaining it. If you are not intentional about doing relationships, such an exercise may seem strange—especially if you believe that relationships should just "happen." (Consequently, I'd suggest—as I have throughout this book—that you do what works for you.) Whether or not you are intentional, notice that I am limiting such intentionality to the maintenance of an already-close relationship. I am not suggesting that you try to develop a "confidant/companionship" relationship by design (since, many "intangibles" go into that development process).

A longer answer to that question is "apply biblical principles—for both intrapersonal and interpersonal growth—to this relationship." Actually, this is a lifelong answer, since our applications of what the Scriptures direct us to do in these areas will require ongoing refinement. A valuable exercise to start this process is to read through the New Testament, highlighting everything it says about how you are to treat others. Having done that, you would have all the information needed to maintain the closest of relationships. (However, you would also need to ask for the empowering of God's Spirit, in order to constructively apply that information.) Because we live in a world where each and every good thing can be perverted, the "good thing" of knowing and doing the biblical principles of relationship maintenance can be perverted, if you broaden the application of those principles beyond yourself. As long as you are striving to apply these principles (by the power of His Spirit) to yourself, as it relates to the relationships in your life, it will be a constructive process. As soon as you begin to evaluate the applications of these principles in the lives of others (the "confidants/companions" in your life, for instance), the process can become destructive. If you are able to evaluate how well another person is applying those principles, without becoming judgmental, that process will remain constructive and you will be able to maintain your closest relationships. If you are not able to evaluate how well another person is applying those principles without becoming judgmental, that process will become destructive, and you will not be able to maintain your closest relationships. An example of "evaluating …*without* judgment" after noticing how the other person has applied the principles to his/her life, is saying to yourself, "I see that, in relation to X, his/her application is better than mine (in relation to whatever criteria you are using); I will notice how he/she is doing this, so I can improve my applications. I also notice that, in relation to Y, my application is better than his/hers (again in relation to whatever criteria you are using); I will pray for him/her, so that his/her application growth in this area will continue." An example of "evaluating …*with* judgment" after noticing how the other person has applied the principles to his/her life, is saying to yourself, "I see that, in relation to X, his/her application is better than mine (in relation to whatever criteria that you are using); that's because he/she was born with a silver spoon in his/her mouth. I wonder how I could get him/her to gag on that spoon; he/she definitely needs to be taken down a peg. I also notice that, in relation to Y, my application is better than his/hers (again, in relation to whatever criteria you are using); that's because he/she is not as smart as I am. He/she will probably continue to act as dumb as they are." (Notice how, in the "evaluation without judgment" example, the evaluator focused that evaluation on what he/she could do—to improve his/her behavior or to support the other person. Notice how, in the "evaluation with judgment" example, the evaluator focused that evaluation on how he/she could be against the other person—by tearing that other person down or by inflating self.) The former example gives you a look at part of the training program for becoming a trusted friend; the latter example gives you a look at part of the training program for becoming a Pharisee.

Maintaining "confidant/companion" relationships needs to be seen as a high priority action. Since such "fellow travelers" arrive only rarely in our lives, they need to be valued as the precious people that they are and kept in our lives by all legitimate means.

How do you *lessen* such relationships? Within the context of the model that I am using, these relationships should never be lessened. (And, in heaven, where the ideal becomes real, they never will be.) In this place, where the real can become unreal, high-quality relationships can be damaged or destroyed if either party takes initiative (knowingly or unknowingly) to do so. I won't focus here on the initiatives that you could take to lessen close relationships (since this book is not about how to shoot yourself in the foot during the race of life). I will focus on what you can do if the other person takes that initiative. If the other person does something damaging, but unintentional, it is a relatively simple matter (even if you are feeling hurt) to talk with this friend and get the issue resolved. (Such a process will deepen your relationship and establish a safety net—of what not to do and what to do [instead], next time.) What remains hurtful (and often excruciatingly so) is the circumstance when a trusted friend does something damaging and, upon investigation, you discover that the damage was done intentionally. "Betrayal" is a word that is often used at such a time. In Psalm 41, David talks about such an experience this way:

> Even my close friend, whom I trusted,
> he who shared my bread
> has lifted up his heel against me. (v. 9)

Because this friend has had your trust, you are usually "blindsided" by his/her destructive action (and, like in football, the hit that does the most damage is the one you never see coming). Consequently, a sense of shock and bewilderment often accompanies this event (followed by other emotional reactions that people experience in the face of significant loss). This is a significant loss (sometimes worse that a death, since it has no finality to it) because it is multifaceted. The facets of loss include loss of companionship, loss of trust, loss of enjoyment, loss of harmony (some people ruminate obsessively over what happened, why it happened, what they could have done …), loss of predictability (the world is never the same), loss of feedback, to name a few. Most people begin their response to this betrayal with "Why" questions: "Why did he/she do it?" "Why me?" "Why did God allow this?" "Why didn't I see this coming; I must blind?" Although the answers to these questions are situation-specific, there are some general answers that can shed light on such tragedies. The Scriptures tell us that, in this world, we have three enemies: the world, the flesh, and the Devil. The "world" refers to the culture that we are in. As a fish is surrounded by water, we are surrounded by culture (the smallest unit of which is our family-of-origin). This culture provides us with language, traditions, values, and priorities—literally, a way to "see" the world. When the culture that we are immersed in prioritizes other things above relationships, then members of that culture may follow those priorities (sometimes to the detriment of relationships). So, a trusted friend may prioritize something over our relationship and sacrifice our relationship to that priority. In my experience, a trusted friend valued money over our relationship and (so) sacrificed our relationship for the priority of financial gain. Although this happened many years ago, I still find it baffling (which goes to show that only God can look at the heart of a person and [so] know for certain why he/she behaves as he/she does). The "flesh" refers to a tendency or nature that we have inherited, as members of a "fallen" race. (When our ancestors chose to break the harmonious relationship that they had with their Creator and to actualize sin, they changed the world. Subsequent generations were born out of relationship with God—fallen from harmony with Him—and with a predisposition to relate destructively toward God, toward other people and toward self. That predisposition has been labeled as the "flesh.") Since each and every person has this tendency within him/her, the potential to act destructively toward another person (even a trusted friend) is always there; it is only one choice away from being actualized (as it was with our ancestors). In my practice (as a psychologist), I have been involved with many people going through divorce (the uncoupling of their closest human relationship). Sometimes, such circumstances have given me a glimpse of humankind's destructive tendency. "The Devil" refers to an angelic being who (like humankind) chose to break his harmonious relationship with God and to establish his own kingdom. At this time, he is seeking to tear down God's kingdom (central to which are the harmonious relationships within and between God and all levels of His creation) and to build his own (based on his power and control over everything therein). So, there is an outside "force" which seeks to destroy harmonious relationships—like those of trusted friends. I have experienced this (qualitatively different) force enough to understand something of what the Scriptures talk about. This analysis—which is an articulation of the historical Christian worldview—makes it clear that we live in enemy territory. (This is not pleasant information to receive, but it is very valuable to receive it if, in fact, it gives us a window into why things are occurring in this world and what we need to do to avoid becoming casualties.) In fact, the Scriptures are clear about what we must do in order to deal with each of these enemies. The primary strategies (for dealing with these enemies) are glimpsed in the following passages: the world (see 1 John 2:15–27, 4:1–21, 5:1–20), the flesh (see Romans 5:12–8:17 esp. 8:12–13), and the Devil (see Ephesians 6:10–18). If you haven't incorporated these strategies into your lifestyle, doing so would be a valuable exercise to follow through on.

Although these general answers can put the betrayal that we have experienced in context, we may never get enough information to know, specifically, the "why" of this betrayal. As anyone with experience knows, there are many mysteries in this world (and in our internal world). Consequently, we stumble along—like the families who have a member "missing in action"—not sure about our next step: should we hold on to the hope of getting this betrayal clarified (or even resolved) or should we kill and bury such hope and move on, grieving our loss? In my experience, there has not been restoration following such betrayals. In the terms of the model I am using, I moved these "confidants/companions" back to the "acquaintance" level where, although I might "do business" with them, I never again trusted them or let them close to myself. (This does *not* mean that I haven't forgiven these people; it does mean that reconciliation—which sometimes follows forgiveness—has not happened. In section 6 of appendix A, I have elaborated on the distinctions I make around the issue of forgiveness.) These results are in part because I subscribe to the belief, "Betray me once, shame on you; betray me twice, shame on me" and because I (also) subscribe to the belief that—for restoration to take place—the betrayer needs to initiate a discussion for the purpose of providing restitution. (In my experience, this has not happened, so the door to reconciliation has remained locked.) Consequently, my "moving on" and "grieving" skills have had more workouts over the years than have my "restoration" skills. However, I know people who have successfully restored a relationship—after a betrayal—so I know that such a journey is possible. For me, these restorations look (so far) like they will happen in heaven—during the ultimate reconciliation process.

Sooner or later, following an unreconciled betrayal, the "why?" questions (which seek understanding) begin to be replaced by "what?" and "how?" questions, like "What do I need to do, now?" and "How do I move on?" (which seek solutions). The following points (briefly) outline what I have said and what I have done to help myself move on:

- I give myself permission to move on. Some of us are able to hang on to the hope of getting reconciliation or justice or … long after the feasibility of reaching these outcomes is gone. So, I have learned to ask myself the question (which, apparently, comes from Native American wisdom literature): "What should I do, when I discover that I am riding a dead horse?" The answer (which focuses me on the practical action that I could overlook in such circumstances) is "dismount." Implied in this answer is the understanding that, if I don't dismount, I won't be getting anywhere (except stuck).

- I value the process. When a betrayal remains, the outcomes that I value won't be reached; the process, however, can be valuable. Betrayals are "trials" (in the biblical sense of that term) that contain lessons—about God, others, and my-self—that can't be learned any other way. When I see that a betrayal is a unique educational opportunity, I turn that betrayal into a meaningful betrayal. So that betrayal—responded to in that way—becomes a "personal trainer" in my process of (skill and character) growth.

- I forgive. If I forgive, I start the process of getting over that betrayal; if I don't for-give, I start the process of letting the betrayal get over me.

- I draw closer to safe people. In the face of betrayal, I find it comforting to enjoy the people who are still on my team. One thing worse than betrayal is letting that betrayal negatively impact other relationships. (For instance, it would be easy for me to generalize from that betrayal and to conclude that nobody is to be trusted. This is the foundational belief in the process of becoming isolated from other people.) I am delighted to report that—among my safe people—I can include my-self (because I have done the work of becoming a good friend to myself) and God (because I have accepted His invitation to be reconciled with Him). In my experi-ence (which may be different from yours), I have found these relationships to be the most helpful in my "moving on" journey.

- I look after myself. As part of being a good friend to myself, I treat myself with patience and kindness and gentleness and support in post-betrayal times. It takes energy to grieve, so I take more time to rest. Feeling loss is painful, so I make sure to do things that are comforting. Betrayal is a hope killer, so I reaffirm my hope in things that betrayal cannot take away. Betrayal can focus me on experiential reali-ties that are urgent, so I renew my practice of nourishment activities (like eating well and exercising and doing activities that bring me joy) that are important but not urgent. Betrayal can foster a negative internal dialogue, so I develop and use constructive "dialogue-interrupts." (For example, my negative internal dialogue with my betrayer, where I give him a "piece of my mind" [as if I had extra], is in-terrupted when I ask myself, "Will this dialogue move me toward the outcomes that I want?" and [so] realize that my outcomes are to walk in forgiveness and to get this tragedy to work for me. Once I know my outcomes, I can craft all strate-gies to move me toward those outcomes: I can reaffirm my forgiveness of my betrayer; I can invite God into the process, seeing myself putting this issue into His hands and asking Him to work it together for good in my life. I can also ask Him to show me anything else that I need to do in order to cooperate with His plan. I can also ask to experience His healing … and comfort … and peace. By so doing, I have detoxified my internal environment.) Betrayal can get me into "pay back" mode, so I reaffirm to myself that "pay back" is God's job (not mine). I also reaffirm to myself that my job is to live the abundant (but not the painless) life. Betrayal can foster a large range of feeling (sometimes at intensities that I haven't experienced before), so I let myself feel my feelings without self-judgment but with self-control. (Feelings are neither right nor wrong; they just are. What I do with these feelings determines their destructiveness or constructiveness.)

• I take steps to bring this process to completion. As I have already indicated, in one way my betrayal won't be fully dealt with until Jesus—as Righteous Judge— deals with it. In another way, however, I can deal with it—here and now—so that it doesn't become the never-ending story in my life. For example, I have written a "progressive" letter to a betrayer ("progressive" meaning that it is written over a period of time, as relevant things to say come to mind). Obviously, this letter is not sent to the betrayer; it is written so that I have a place to say all that never got said (but I wish could have been said). It is a way to externalize my "unfinished verbal business" as related to the betrayer/the betrayal. For me, this tool is not so much an opportunity to "dump" on this other person as it is to talk about what I hoped would have happened and to express (and feel) my sadness over the loss.

• I give myself permission to get through this process at whatever pace it takes, for as long as it takes. If I put time frames or deadlines on myself for getting through this process, then I am putting pressure on myself to control a process which, in fact, I have little control over. This is like saying that I will be running on my broken ankle by the end of the month. (Sometimes, turning wishes into goals compounds the problem.) A more effective approach is to affirm that "This is not a race; it is a healing …Since my process of healing is unique to me, I will let it progress as it will …It is so important that I will give it all the time required … I will not let conditions imposed by others (or myself) override the built-in pacing of my body, but I will do everything that I can to co-operate with my body's healing mechanisms."

And how will I know when this "moving on" journey is substantially finished? Here are some indicators:

• When the pain involved is less intense, less frequent, and less enduring
• When this issue no longer occupies much of my thought life
• When there is a sense that it is more "history" than "current events"
• When it is easier to stay focused in the "here and now" and to make decisions

- When energy levels are returning to pre-betrayal levels and when motivation to do things is returning
- When any disruption to eating or sleeping patterns has reduced
- When the feelings of sadness and discouragement have diminished
- When the experience of guilt has abated
- When the future looks/feels brighter

And do I ever return to "normal"? No, events like these change us forever (so we never return to where we were before.) But, if we handle these events in constructive ways (as specified above), we will move to a "better" place ("better" meaning "stronger" and "with better skills" and "with more experience" and "with more developed character"). That place is our "new normal."

The following questions will (hopefully) help you to specify your next steps in managing these (most close) relationships.

NEXT STEPS

1. Make a list of the "confidants/companions" who are presently in your life.

_____

_____

_____

_____

_____

(2a) Evaluate *each* of these relationships, specifying *one thing* that I could *think* or *say* or *do* that would *maintain* this relationship. Write below (beside that name) what that "one thing" is.

NAME	ONE THING
(i)_____	_____
(ii)_____	_____
(iii)_____	_____
(iv)_____	_____
(v)_____	_____

(2b) Evaluate *each* of these relationships, specifying *one request* that I could make of each of these trusted friends that would *maintain* our relationship. Write below (beside their name) what that request is.

	NAME	ONE REQUEST
(i)	_____	_____
(ii)	_____	_____
(iii)	_____	_____
(iv)	_____	_____
(v)	_____	_____

(3a)   Evaluate *each* of these relationships, specifying one thing that I could *think* or *say* or *do* that would *enhance* this relationship. (To enhance a relationship is to change that relationship, to invite it to grow or develop or stretch. Therefore, it may feel uncomfortable to one or both of you. All growth is disruptive.) Write below (beside their name) what that thing is.

	NAME	ONE THING
(i)	_____	_____
(ii)	_____	_____
(iii)	_____	_____
(iv)	_____	_____
(v)	_____	_____

(3b)   Evaluate *each* of these relationships, specifying *one request* that I could make of each of these trusted friends that would *enhance* our relationship. Write below (beside their name) what that request is.

	NAME	ONE REQUEST
(i)	_____	_____
(ii)	_____	_____
(iii)	_____	_____
(iv)	_____	_____
(v)	_____	_____

(4)   Below is a list of activities that you could do for each relationship in order to *protect* these (precious) relationships.
   (a) Check off any activity that will help to protect that relationship.
   (b) Using the (unique) content of that relationship, write out how you will apply that activity to it.

- ❏ Pray for your confidant; pray for our relationship; pray for the protection of the relationship.
- ❏ Manage your expectations (so that you are not carrying an expectation that could generate disappointment or distancing or…).
- ❏ Balance our together time and our apart time (so that we are having a good time when we are together *and* a good time when we are apart).
- ❏ Find win-win agreements (so that we can *both* live with agreements that we make).
- ❏ Kill the relationship killers when they are small (so that there is no issue that will grow to the place where it could get us against each other).
- ❏ Adjust to changing circumstances (so that our relationship adapts quickly to new realities).
- ❏ Apply a biblical principle (so that we are meeting our specific need or issue or concern with a relevant scriptural truth).

Here are my *prayers* for _____ (Confidant):

_____

_____

…For our relationship:

_____

_____

_____

…For the protection of our relationship:

_____

_____

_____

Here are my *expectations* for _____ (Confidant) that have been causing me some inside discomfort (disappointment, frustration, anxiety, confusion):

    (i)_____

    (ii) _____

    (iii)_____

Here are the modifications that I have made to each of these expectations so that my discomfort is reduced:

(i)_____

(ii) _____

(iii)_____

Here is the *information* that I will give to _____ (Confidant) so that he/she is aware of my expectations and is able to respond to these expectations:

(i)_____

(ii) _____

(iii)_____

Here is what I need to do in order to improve *together* time with _____ (Confidant)

(i)_____

(ii) _____

Here is what I need to do in order to improve my time *apart* from_____ (Confidant) (so that I do not become dependent and demanding of him/her).

(i)_____

(ii) _____

Here are the issues that _____ (Confidant) and I have not (from my perspective) yet reached *win-win agreements* on:

(i)_____

(ii) _____

(iii)_____

Here is my *game-plan* for bringing each of these issues up with _____(Confidant) (a game-plan includes what … when … where … how …):

(i)_____

_____

_____

(ii) _____

_____

_____

(iii)_____

_____

_____

Here are the *issues and/or dynamics (interactions) that concern me.* If these grow between _____ (Confidant) and me, they will start to destroy our relationship.

(i)_____

(ii) _____

(iii)_____

(iv) _____

(v) _____

Here are my *initial steps* for dealing with each of these concerns. (These steps could include a personal change of behavior, a request to your trusted friend for his/her behavior change, a discussion of the issue [to be sure that we understand each other], a problem solving discussion, a personal deprioritizing of the issue [letting my confidant know that this is an issue that I will let go of], among others.)

(i)_____

(ii) _____

(iii)_____

(iv) _____

(v) _____

Here are the changes in our *circumstances* (some changes have arrived; some changes are coming) that we need to adapt our relationship to fit. (Such changes could include moves, changes of roles [for example, getting married], work related changes [for example, change of work schedule], and unexpected changes [for example, a sickness].)

Changes that have arrived:

(i)_____

(ii) _____

(iii)_____

Changes that are coming:

(i)_____

(ii) _____

(iii)_____

Here are my *initial steps* for addressing/dealing with each of these changes:
Changes that have arrived:

(i) _____
(ii) _____
(iii)_____

Changes that are coming:
(i) _____
(ii) _____
(iii)_____

Here are the specific *biblical principles* that will protect my relationship with
_____ (Confidant) :
(i) _____
(ii) _____
(iii)_____

Here is what it will look like (in other words, how the relationship will be different, how I will be different) when I have *applied* this principle. (Do this step for each principle.)
(i) _____
_____
_____

(ii) _____
_____
_____

(iii)_____
_____
_____

To those of you who are feeling tired just looking at all you could do in these relationships, let me say this:

• It is not necessary to do each of these next steps formally with each confidant/companion. My intent is to give you an evaluation process for nourishing these quality relationships—which could be done by just identifying and dealing with one or two issues or interactions. Recently, I got my 4 Runner running smoothly again by simply putting air in the tire that had lost some. If that is all your relationship needs, then that is all that you need to do. These "next steps" are here to help you to identify the "tire" that needs attention.

- If you have read appendix A, section 4 of this module, you will know that I am a long-range planner. As such, I am intentional about how I do relationships (and that gets reflected in the content and process of these chapters). If you do relationships differently, I encourage you (if you are satisfied with your results) to keep doing your relationships your way and only use my ways to supplement what you are doing.

- Relationships (like vehicles) require maintenance, but the work of maintenance is not an end in itself but (rather) a means to the enjoyment of the relationship. So, do the necessary maintenance work but focus on (and bask in) the enjoyment and enrichment that comes from having trusted friends.

Appendix D

INFORMATION AND EXERCISES FOR MANAGING MY RELATIONSHIPS WITH FRIENDS

If you would find it helpful to review what I have said about the "Secondary/Vital/External" relationships that surround our lives, that information is found on pages 236–246 of this module. The pages that speak specifically to the "friends" level of relationship are 236, 240–241.

In the model I am using, the "friends" circle contains those people that I have a good working relationship with. (These are "good" but not "great" relationships—the latter being in the "confidant/companion" circle. Friendships are functional but not as intimate—the latter being in the "confidant/companion" circle.) These relationships have depth, but that depth is confined to the common project or the area of common interest or the recreational activity that the participants have in common. A more expansive depth (one deeper in the personal dimension of our life) is characteristic of the "confidant/companion" relationships.

How do you *enhance* relationships with friends? As with any living thing, if you want it to grow, you need to allow for or provide specific nutrients. In order for a friend to become a confidant/companion, the following is required:

- Since growth requires time and space, you will need to provide a friend with more access to your time and more access to you, across the roles that you are living out. (Such growth of access needs to be gradual and to be on your terms. Putting your life in the hands of another person is not usually healthy, but choosing to give more access is necessary.) So, you might invite the person to go for lunch; you might stay after the game for a drink; you might invite the person to your residence; you might involve yourself in something that he/she is involved in. (These are all active initiatives that you could take.) You could also plan to say "yes" to any relationship growth initiative that he/she may make toward you. (Freeing up of time and space is another kind of initiative you could take.)

- Such initiatives are not taken so that both of you can do more of the same together. They must move you toward more sharing on the personal dimension of your lives. For some people, this happens naturally; for some people, this happens by deliberate choice—but it needs to happen. For some people, this happens quickly; for some people, this happens slowly—but it needs to happen. So, talking about business can lead to personal opinions being expressed; talking about the game can lead to your personal history of the sport; talking of work dynamics can move to talk of the dynamics in your family of origin or family of construction; talking about spiritual growth can lead to talk about your spiritual growth.

- As that "personalization" of relationship grows, you begin to get access to information that is crucial to the ongoing decisions that you will need to make about this relationship. If the feedback you get within yourself is, "I sense his/her caring … He/she listens well and understands well … I feel safe sharing myself …My experience tells me that further sharing is a good risk to take …He/she looks interested in this relationship …," then further disclosure is warranted. (Conversely, if the feedback you are getting within yourself is, "I don't get a sense of genuine interest or caring … I'm not sure that he/she is hearing me or 'getting' me … I'm sensing that there might be a "hidden agenda" behind his/her wanting to talk with me …Something feels off, here," then further disclosure (or anything else that might deepen the relationship) may not be warranted. This feedback doesn't necessarily mean a "red light" (stop this relationship), but it does mean a "yellow light" (proceed with caution; be prepared to stop—at least temporarily). In addition to inside feedback, you also get feedback from outside yourself—from your friend. That feedback includes both verbal feedback and non-verbal feedback. Verbal feedback involves not only what is said but how it is said. When there is congruence between the "what" and the "how," an invitation to trust is given; when there is incongruence between the "what" and the "how," an invitation to distrust is given. Nonverbal feedback is everything that the body shows—from the subtle "tells" to repeated patterns of behavior. Even if we are not trained to read these behaviors, our exposure to them can give us an overall sense that this friend can be trusted in a more intimate way (or not). And what if you aren't sure? The standard operating procedure (if you aren't sure) is to gather more information—over more time and in a wider variety of situations—before deciding to admit this friend into the confidant/companion circle.

- Situations in which your relationship experiences "turbulence" are as crucial as situations in which you (both) experience smooth flying, for determining whether or not this friend can become a "fellow traveler." Only people who can find a constructive way to work through difficult times (as well as have good times together) qualify for the "inner circle" of relationships. So until your friendship has survived foul weather, you only have a "fair weather" friendship—one that is pleasant but untested. (War—which has generated some of the foulest weather on our planet—has forged many confidant/companion relationships; unrelated men have become a "band of brothers" in that storm.)

Maintaining friendships is a good investment but, because these relationships are less personal and more dependent upon circumstances (that can change), uprooting such a relationship can happen without the sense of betrayal that accompanies the loss of a confidant/companion. In my experience, friends that I have worked with were left behind (when I moved or they moved) with some sadness but with no attempt (on either my part or their part) to subsequently stay in touch (because our friendship was situation specific). Only as long as the situation remains intact, will these relationships remain intact. If you discover that you and your friend are trying to keep the relationship intact after a change of circumstances, then you have a key indicator that this relationship has confidant/companion level potential. (Confidant/companion level relationships transcend life circumstances.) Among the good reasons to maintain friendships is that all confidant/companions come from the friendship pool. (A definition of high risk behavior would be to admit a person into your confidant/companion circle without that person going through your friendship circle.) Friendships make the social world turn; they are valuable relationships in and of themselves.

How do you *lessen* friendships? In an ideal world, this question would never need to be answered; in this world, there will be (or are) people in our friendship circle who are toxic. You may not have discovered this until they got into that circle. (The change of relationship—as a person migrates from being an acquaintance to becoming a friend—may reveal some unpleasant realities about that person.) It is also possible that a functioning friendship can get toxified by the arrival of some issue that changes your status from "team mate" to "opposition." It is also possible that you begin to experience a growing discomfort with a long-standing friendship because both of you have been going in different directions. (This occurs, for instance, with family members or relatives that you have grown up with but, now, have grown apart from. I realize that distance is different than toxicity but distance, too, can—de facto—end a friendship.) Dysfunctional training may have taught you to accommodate or put up with toxic/distanced relationships. I suggest that you detoxify your life—whether it is a "rotten" relationship or a rotten tooth. Although I'd encourage you to do what you can to save the relationship (or the tooth), if that is not possible, an extraction is a life-renewing action to take. Once you have identified such a relationship and have given yourself permission to deal with it (which may include challenging and changing old training—like "Any relationship is better than no relationship" or "If something is going wrong in this relationship, it is my fault, so I need to fix it" or "If I just try harder/longer, it will work out"), the mechanics of lessening a friendship are simple. I stated earlier that a relationship is a living entity requiring nutrients, (so) if you want to stop its growth (or kill it), you simply reduce or eliminate those nutrients. (In the terms of the model I am using, this is how you move a friend to the "acquaintance" circle [of less involvement] or beyond that circle [where there is no further involvement].) The nutrients that I (previously) mentioned were time, space, and personal sharing. So toxic friends are moved to the acquaintance level by reducing the amount of time that you make available to them, by reducing your access to them (only leaving those roles in which you want to "do business" with them) and by reducing your personal sharing with them. Obviously, if you eliminate these nutrients, you move these people beyond the acquaintance circle. (In my experience, this is only infrequently necessary.)

To those readers whom (I imagine) are responding to this aspect of my model with, "What a cold and heartless way to do relationships! People are not pawns to be moved around on your chessboard!" I would say

- "You're right, people are not pawns, and they don't have to passively sit by and do nothing. In one instance where I was making myself less available to a toxic friend (after gathering good and sufficient data [for me] that I needed to do this, after praying about it, and after starting this process as kindly and gently as I could, [these steps, for me, are necessary to keep this process within the circle of biblical options]), he just 'walked away' from our relationship. (He was possibly reacting to the change that he was sensing in me.) (In my economy), he has every right to do that: I was working on changing what we had; he (I assume) preferred no relationship. I need to be prepared to accept his choices.
- What I have outlined here (with regard to this aspect of the model I am using) is what many people do in order to manage relationships. I have just made the tactics and dynamics involved in doing so explicit, without including the reasons/justifications/rationalizations that often mask these tactics and dynamics. If a person doesn't use these ways and means to manage relationships, he/she is left with the options of negotiating with the other person about what the relationship should look like. (And if the other person is a toxic friend, that could be a futile endeavor.)

One could also let the other person design what the relationship should look like. (And if the other person is a toxic friend, that could be a choice that leads to a destructive outcome). This whole book is about focusing on the tools that you can put in your hands to use—not tools that require the cooperation of others.

To those readers whom (I imagine) are responding to this aspect of my model with "Why don't you just talk to this friend and work it out? You don't have to go behind his/her back to get things to change!" I would say

- "Such a response indicates that you (like me) have received the (conventional wisdom) training that promotes the view that our relational goal is to enhance each and every relationship that we have and that there is always a way to do that (for example, if we are prepared to persevere in showing love to the person and inviting him/her to reciprocate). My experience, however, has convinced me that toxic friends are not always interested in working things out. Sometimes, their goal is to get me to do what they want and they are not above using power and manipulation tactics as means to reach that goal. If you have gathered enough data to be (reasonably) sure that they are going for control (not harmony), then "talking and a dollar will get you coffee." In fact, to such toxic friends ongoing talk (by me) may indicate (to them) that I am still available to be manipulated. Consequently, I have come to apply the principle of Ecclesiastes 3 to relationships: there is a time to talk (when, for instance, harmony is a goal of all the people involved) and a time to refrain from talking (when, for instance, harmony is not a goal of all the people involved). My response to a manipulative toxic friend should not be to out manipulate the manipulator (since I am instructed to not only be "as wise as a serpent" but also "as harmless as a dove"). Instead, my (action) response should involve the distancing of myself from this person—to whatever I consider to be a safe distance.

To those readers whom (I imagine) are responding to this aspect of my model with "I just couldn't manage relationships that way!" I would say

- "I am describing what works for me; I am not prescribing what will work for you. Take, leave, or modify what I am outlining here until it fits you and the circumstances you are in."

- "By saying what you have, you are implying that you have a different relationship management plan. If that plan is "working" for you (in other words, getting you the results you want, while staying within your system of values), then stay with (and develop) that plan. Only if that plan isn't working for you, should you consider something different (including some version of what I am doing)."

- "The plan I use is the result of one of the values that I have at the top of my value hierarchy: I manage relationships; I don't let them manage me. I am not trying to control other people; I am striving to control myself. I am taking responsibility for myself and what I do, no matter what other people do. People with different top values (and you may be one of those people, since the system that reflects my values is not a fit for you), may be doing relationships in ways that give others too much influence in their life. If that is true for you, then you may want to modify how you do relationships, since the implications of giving your power to others are pervasive (and usually not constructive).

The following questions will (hopefully) help you to specify your next steps in managing these friendships.

NEXT STEPS

(1a) Make a list of the friends that are presently in your life:

(i)_____

(ii) _____

(iii)_____

(iv) _____

(v) _____

(vi)_____

(vii) _____

(viii)_____

(ix)_____

(x) _____

(If you are a person with many friends, continue this list in the space at the end of this chapter—or elsewhere.)

(1b)

- Put an "E" beside the friend(s) that you want an *enhanced* relationship with (in other words, those friendships that you want to promote toward the confidant/ companion level). Do this only with the friendships where this can feasibly happen.

- What are your "next steps" for enhancing this/these relationship(s)? (Feel free to use the ideas that I have suggested, but don't be limited to those ideas.) Do this for each "E" friend.

_____
_____
_____
_____

(1c)

- Put an "M" beside the friend(s) that you want to *maintain* a friendship with. (This category will include friends with deeper relationship potential but limited feasibility—because of circumstances like time or proximity. Enjoy such relationships for what they can be, rather than struggling with the fact that some potentials here will never get actualized.)
- What are your "next steps" for maintaining these relationships? Do this for each "M" friend.

_____
_____
_____
_____

(1d)

- Put an "L" beside the friend(s) that you want to *lessen* a friendship with. (As I discussed in this appendix, this category includes friends that fit the label "toxic.") In the terms of the model I am using, you are moving such relationships to the acquaintance level.
- What are your "next steps" for lessening these relationships? Do this for each "L" friend.

_____
_____
_____
_____

Appendix E

INFORMATION AND EXERCISES FOR MANAGING MY RELATIONSHIPS WITH ACQUAINTANCES

If you would find it helpful to review what I have said about the "Secondary/Vital/ External" relationships that surround our lives, that information is found on pages 236–246 of this module. The pages that speak specifically to the "acquaintances" level of relationship are 236 and 241.

In the model I am using, the "acquaintance" circle contains those people that I interact with but don't have a significant relationship with. These interactions may be interesting and enjoyable but they are not sustained or ongoing. My wife and I—who are bird watchers—once met a couple from England on a trail south of Jasper. We had, as we walked, a pleasant conversation (about where they were from, why they were in Alberta and, of course, about birds). We shared some things we knew about local species and gave them a close-up view of some ducks (through our spotting scope)—then we went our own ways and never saw them again. The acquaintance circle may also contain people that we see more than once, but only in passing—like the cashier at the local grocery store. Characteristic of people in this category is transience.

How do you *enhance* such relationships? What I have said about enhancing a friendship (in appendix D) applies to enhancing an acquaintanceship. Because of the impermanence (fleetingness) of acquaintances, however, I would add another requirement: creating a context that allows for more sustained contact. If I had wanted to promote the meeting we had with the couple from England (mentioned above) toward a friendship, I would have had to find a way to connect with them in a more sustained way. To do that, I could have invited them for supper that evening or for coffee at our hotel (or, more indirectly, could have asked them, "Are you busy this evening?" or "We are hiking at Angel Glacier tomorrow—where we will no doubt see Clark's Nutcrackers and Golden Crowned Sparrows—would you like to hike with us?") If they were to have responded with interest and availability to any of these initiatives, the context for a more sustained conversation would have been established. For some people, the process of moving an acquaintance to a friend is quick; for others, more slow. (There is no right pace to do that, just the right pace for you.) For many people, there is an excitement in meeting new people, often because these acquaintances represent a world of new possibilities.

How do you *maintain* such relationships? The maintenance of acquaintances only requires that I be constructive during the time that I am in their presence. I love Tim Hortons coffee (or, to be more precise, "I enjoy Tim Horton's coffee very much"). As a result, I make daily pilgrimages to a coffee shop near my office. Since my office location has been the same for many years, I have become known to staff members at the coffee shop. When I arrive, there is usually a brief conversation, starting with "same as usual?" and moving on to the weather or something that is presently happening. If I smile, interact positively with them, and thank them for providing the coffee, that is all I need to do in order to set the stage for a pleasant interaction when I come again. These relationships are not squeaky wheels; they require very little grease.

How do you *lessen* such relationships? Often, these relationships lessen themselves. On the journey of life, we meet many people (on their journey); we interact but, if no initiatives are taken to bring about a more sustained contact, we are soon over the horizon from each other. If you intentionally stay on your course (thereby not allowing a change of course, which is what taking an initiative or receiving an initiative [from the other person] involves), that is all you need to do in order to end an acquaintanceship.

The following questions will (hopefully) help you to specify your next steps in managing these acquaintanceships.

NEXT STEPS

(1a) Make a list of (only) those acquaintances that are presently in your life and that you see having the potential to become friends.

(i) _____ ( )

(ii) _____ ( )

(iii) _____ ( )

(iv) _____ ( )

(v)_____ ( )

(vi) _____ ( )

(vii) _____ ( )

(viii) _____ ( )

(ix) _____ _____ ( )

(x)__ _____ ( )

(1b) Put a (1) beside the acquaintance that you most want to invest in (so as to move this relationship toward friendship), a (2) beside the next most, and so on. If there are some of these acquaintances that have potential to become friends but, for whatever reasons (time or energy or specific circumstances or …), you don't want to work toward actualizing that potential, leave the space behind that name blank.

(1c) For every acquaintance with a number after his/her name (and starting with "1"), develop your (action) plan for promoting that relationship toward a friendship:

- What will I do in order to create a context that allows for more sustained contact?

  _____
  _____
  _____

- What areas of common interest (or concern) could I emphasize (in my conversation) so that that interaction will be interesting and comfortable?

  _____
  _____
  _____

- What feedback (verbal or nonverbal)—from this acquaintance—will I see as crucial in helping me to decide what I should do next?

  _____
  _____
  _____

ENDNOTES

[1] Smedes, L., *The Art of Forgiving*, New York: Random House, Inc., 1996, p. 105–114.

[2] Silf, M., *One Hundred Wisdom Stories from Around the World*, Oxford: Lion Publishing, 2003, p. 121–122.

[3] Hugget, J., *The Joy of Listening to God*, Downers Grove, Illinois: Inter-Varsity Press, 1990.

[4] Foster, R., *Meditative Prayer*, Downers Grove, Illinois: Inter-Varsity Press, 1983.

[5] Powell, *He Touched Me*, Niles, Illinois: Argus Communications, 1974.

[6] Foster, R., *Celebration of Discipline*, New York: Harper Collins Pub., 1988.

[7] Foster, R., *Prayer: Finding the Heart's True Home*, New York: Harper Collins, 1992.

[8] Deere, J., *Surprised by the Voice of God*, Grand Rapids, Michigan: Zondervan Pub-House, 1996.

[9] Willard, D., *In Search of Guidance*, New York: Harper Collins, 1993.

[10] Wilson, E., *Does God Really Love Me*, Downers Grove, Illinois: Inter-Varsity Press, 1986.

[11] Chapman, G., *The Love Languages of God*, Chicago: Northfield Pub., 2002.

[12] Stott, I.R.W., *The Epistles of John*, Grand Rapids, Michigan: Eerdmans Pub. Co., 1983.

[13] Ward, W., *The Bible in Counseling*, Chicago: Moody Press, 1977.

[14] Ortberg, J., *Love Beyond Reason*, Grand Rapids, Michigan: Zondervan, 1988.

[15] Curtis, B. and Eldridge, J., *The Sacred Romance*, Nashville: Thomas Nelson, 1977.

[16] Goldsmith, J., *Knowing Me, Knowing God*, Nashville: Abingdon Press, 1997.

[17] Harbough, G., *God's Gifted People*, Minneapolis: Augsburg Fortress, 1990.

[18] Oswald, R.M., and Kroeger, O., *Personality Type and Religious Leadership*, New York: Alban Institute Pub., 1988.

[19] Kise, J.A.G., Stark, D., and Hirsh, S.K., *Life Keys*, Minneapolis: Bethany House Pub., 1996.

[20] Hirsh, S.K. and Kise, J.A.G., *Looking at Type and Spirituality*, Gainesville, Florida: CAPT, 1997.

[21] Johnson, R., *Your Personality and the Spiritual Life*, Wheaton, Illinois: Victor Books, 1988.

[22] Michael, C.P. and Norrisey, M.C., *Prayer and Temperament*, Charlottesville, Virginia: The Open Door Inc., 1984.

[23] Ackerman, J. *Finding Your Way*, Washington, D.C.: The Alban Institute Inc., 1992.

[24] Smedes, p. 96.

[25] Smedes, p. 45.

[26] Wangerin, W. *As for Me and My House*, Nashville: Thomas Nelson Pub., 1990, p. 94.

[27] Smedes, p. 56–57.

[28] Smedes, p. 7–8.

[29] Smedes, p. 154–155.

[30] Smedes, p. 17–18.

[31] Smedes, p. 6–7.

[32] Wilson, Sandra, *Released from Shame*, Downers Grove, Illinois: Inter-Varsity Press,1990, p. 171.

[33] Smedes, p. 26–27.

[34] O'Hanlon, B. and Hudson, P., *Love Is a Verb*, New York: W.W. Norton and Co. Inc., 1995, p. 84.

[35] Smedes, p. 165.

[36] Pascal, B., *Pensees*, translated by A.J. Krailsheimer, Baltimore: Penguin Books, 1966, series XXVI, No. 733, p. 252–253.

[37] Mollenkott, V.R., *In Search of Balance*, Waco, Texas: Word Books, p. 37–38.

[38] Mollenkott, p. 38–40.

[39] (In) Mollenkott, p. 75.

[40] Schiraldi, G.R. *The Self-Esteem Workbook*, Oakland California: New Harbinger Pub. Inc., 2001.

[41] Borysenko, J., *Inner Peace for Busy People*, Carlsbad, California: Hay House Inc., 2001.

[42] Emmons, R.A. and Hill, J., *Words of Gratitude*, Philadelphia: Templeton Foundation Press, 2001, p. 3.

[43] (In) Emmons and Hill, p. 14.

[44] Emmons and Hill, p. 15–19.

[45] Borysenko, p. 100–101.

[46] Borysenko, p. 45.

[47] Borysenko, p. 25.

[48] Borysenko, p. 31–32.

[49] Borysenko, p. 37–38.